HOW CHARTS WORK

Praise for *How Charts Work*

'This book is a chance to learn data visualisation from perhaps the best teacher there is. Alan Smith brings the secrets of his widely acclaimed Royal Statistical Society courses to the general public, helping you to present data and statistics clearly, honestly and insightfully. An essential read for anyone who wants to communicate with data!'

Stian Westlake, Chief Executive, Royal Statistical Society

'The quintessential activity of data visualisation is working out how to graphically show what it is you want to say. This invaluable addition to the library of texts in this subject gives readers the most comprehensive reference through the range of contemporary charting options, as well as their potential variations and smart innovations. Knowing what options are available is one thing, but knowing when and why - and when not and why not - you should use certain charts is the real art of this game and Alan expertly demonstrates the practical rationale for deploying each method. This is simply a fabulously useful book that will heighten the creative and critical thinking of novice and experienced data visualisation practitioners alike.'

Andy Kirk, Independent consultant, educator, and author; founder of visualisingdata.com

'With *How Charts Work,* Alan Smith has done us all a great favour. He has taken everything he knows about charts and put it all in a highly readable, hugely interesting and heavily illustrated book! Everything Alan knows - as the Head of Visual and Data Journalism at the *Financial Times* - is just about all there is to know, and the book is written in such a way that the reader is gripped from start to finish, with charts galore - and so much more. The book is meticulously researched and, in today's data saturated media world, essential reading for everyone from casual observers to experienced data journalists. As someone who works with data, charts and maps on a daily basis, I hadn't quite appreciated how much I would learn from this book, so if you already consider yourself a dataviz connoisseur, *How Charts Work* will definitely be a great new addition to your collection. This is a book interspersed with personal stories, and along the way you'll learn why charts matter, everything there is to know on chart types, why spatial is special (maps!), the importance of colour, layout and text - and who won the English First Division in 1950. You'll also learn about the science behind good charts, the importance of good writing, and the need to understand uncertainty. But I'm certain you'll love this book and that it will quickly become an essential reference for the global dataviz community.'

Alasdair Rae, founder of Automatic Knowledge; former Professor of Urban Studies and Planning at Sheffield University

HOW CHARTS WORK

Understand and explain data with confidence

Alan Smith

Harlow, England • London • New York • Boston • San Francisco • Toronto • Sydney • Dubai • Singapore • Hong Kong
Tokyo • Seoul • Taipei • New Delhi • Cape Town • São Paulo • Mexico City • Madrid • Amsterdam • Munich • Paris • Milan

PEARSON EDUCATION LIMITED
KAO Two
KAO Park
Harlow CM17 9NA
United Kingdom
Tel: +44 (0)1279 623623
Web: www.pearson.com/uk

First edition published 2022 (print and electronic)

ISBN: 978-1-292-34279-5 (print)
978-1-292-34280-1 (PDF)
978-1-292-34281-8 (ePub)

British Library Cataloguing-in-Publication Data
A catalogue record for the print edition is available from the British Library

Library of Congress Cataloging-in-Publication Data
Names: Smith, Alan, 1971- author.
Title: How charts work : understand and explain data with confidence / Alan Smith.
Description: First edition. | Harlow, England ; New York : Pearson, 2022. | Includes bibliographical references and index.
Identifiers: LCCN 2022027614 | ISBN 9781292342795 (paperback) | ISBN 9781292342818 (epub) | ISBN 9781292342801 (pdf)
Subjects: LCSH: Information visualization. | Charts, diagrams, etc.
Classification: LCC QA76.9.I52 S65 2022 | DDC 001.4/226--dc23/eng/20220906
LC record available at https://lccn.loc.gov/2022027614

10 9 8 7 6 5 4 3 2 1
26 25 24 23 22

Cover design by Kelly Miller
Print edition typeset in 10/12pt Open Sans by Straive

NOTE THAT ANY PAGE CROSS REFERENCES REFER TO THE PRINT EDITION

Contents

Pearson's Commitment to Diversity, Equity and Inclusion

Pearson is dedicated to creating bias-free content that reflects the diversity, depth and breadth of all learners' lived experiences. We embrace the many dimensions of diversity including, but not limited to, race, ethnicity, gender, sex, sexual orientation, socioeconomic status, ability, age and religious or political beliefs.

Education is a powerful force for equity and change in our world. It has the potential to deliver opportunities that improve lives and enable economic mobility. As we work with authors to create content for every product and service, we acknowledge our responsibility to demonstrate inclusivity and incorporate diverse scholarship so that everyone can achieve their potential through learning. As the world's leading learning company, we have a duty to help drive change and live up to our purpose to help more people create a better life for themselves and to create a better world.

Our ambition is to purposefully contribute to a world where:

- Everyone has an equitable and lifelong opportunity to succeed through learning.
- Our educational products and services are inclusive and represent the rich diversity of learners.
- Our educational content accurately reflects the histories and lived experiences of the learners we serve.
- Our educational content prompts deeper discussions with students and motivates them to expand their own learning and worldview.

We are also committed to providing products that are fully accessible to all learners. As per Pearson's guidelines for accessible educational Web media, we test and retest the capabilities of our products against the highest standards for every release, following the WCAG guidelines in developing new products for copyright year 2022 and beyond. You can learn more about Pearson's commitment to accessibility at:

https://www.pearson.com/us/accessibility.html

While we work hard to present unbiased, fully accessible content, we want to hear from you about any concerns or needs regarding this Pearson product so that we can investigate and address them.

- Please contact us with concerns about any potential bias at:

  https://www.pearson.com/report-bias.html

- For accessibility-related issues, such as using assistive technology with Pearson products, alternative text requests, or accessibility documentation, email the Pearson Disability Support team at:

  disability.support@pearson.com

"Figures and letters may express with accuracy, but they never can represent either number or space"

William Playfair

For a trio of people who inspired me along the way and are not here to see the result – Dad, Alan and Frank

About the author

Alan Smith is the head of Visual and Data journalism at the *Financial Times*. A data visualisation specialist, he regularly writes and lectures on using charts to convey insight. An experienced presenter, his TEDx talk "Why you should love statistics" was a TED.com featured talk.

Previously, he worked at the UK's Office for National Statistics where he founded its award-winning data visualisation team – he was appointed an OBE in the 2011 Queen's Birthday Honours List for services to official statistics.

Author's acknowledgements

The global news agenda has not been quiet since I joined the *Financial Times*. This may be a classic case of correlation without causation, but it has not stopped our newsroom from being a constant source of inspiration.

I'd like to thank my amazing colleagues in the Visual and Data journalism team without whom this book would have been genuinely impossible. I have been lucky enough to spend the past seven years working with a wonderfully talented group of journalists. You'll find their names underneath many of the graphics featured in this book but listing them collectively feels right. If there's one thing they've taught me, it's that teamwork makes for better graphics:

> Steven Bernard, Ian Bott, Chelsea Bruce-Lockhart, John Burn-Murdoch, Chris Campbell, Federica Cocco, Billy Ehrenberg-Shannon, Liz Faunce, Keith Fray, Max Harlow, Bob Haslett, Cleve Jones, Joanna S. Kao, Emma Lewis, Paul McCallum, Patrick Mathurin, Caroline Nevitt, Kripa Pancholi, Graham Parrish, Ændra Rininsland, Martin Stabe, Cale Tilford, Aleks Wisniewska, Christine Zhang.

A superb network of reporters and astute, diligent editors have provided a welcoming environment for creative collaboration. That we have managed to push on with our ambitious plans for data visualisation is also, in no small part, thanks to the support of the *FT*'s editors during this period — Lionel Barber and Roula Khalaf.

I also owe a debt of gratitude to Eloise Cook at Pearson for her encouragement and constructive feedback during the writing process.

Finally, I'd like to say a big thank you to my wife, Ellie. Her encouragement and support have been matched only by her patience and tolerance as long days making charts were followed by long evenings writing about them.

Alan Smith

February 2022

Foreword

"She may look at it because it has pictures." That was Florence Nightingale's withering comment, as she sent a report about public health reform to Queen Victoria. Nightingale was not much impressed with the Queen ("The least self-reliant person I have ever known"). But she clearly understood her audience: if you want to attract attention in a busy world, print a picture.

Newspaper editors have long appreciated this, but all too often the pictures of data that they have printed have tended to be purely decorative. In my own book, I compare them to "dazzle camouflage", which is designed to misdirect attention and bewilder the observer with incomprehensible shapes, lines and patterns.

But data visualisation can do so much more than attract attention by looking pretty. A well-chosen graph is worth far more than a thousand words, bringing understanding and clarity in a confusing world.

So, we can do better, and no journalist in the world understands this more fully than Alan Smith and his brilliant team at the *Financial Times*.

For an indication of the stakes, we could do worse than consider Florence Nightingale's own experience. Her message could hardly have been more important. After famously serving in an Istanbul hospital during the Crimean War in the 1850s, she returned from the place she called "the kingdom of hell" with a reforming mission.

The hospital had indeed been hellish. Men would arrive, bleeding from abdominal wounds, their bodies crawling with vermin; and leave, stitched up in their own blankets to be carried to a mass grave.

In January 1855 alone, the British army in Crimea lost one man in ten to the ravages of diseases such as dysentery and cholera. Nightingale was attempting – at first without success – to prevent a humanitarian catastrophe, as infectious disease tore the British Army to shreds.

But Nightingale found that the death toll in the hospitals was dramatically reduced after improvements to hygiene – whitewashing walls, for example, and pulling a dead horse out of the water supply.

She believed that similar efforts at public hygiene could dramatically improve public health back in Britain. What had worked in Istanbul could work elsewhere. "Nature is the same everywhere, and never permits her laws to be disregarded with impunity," she noted.

The insight was to drive her campaigning back in the UK. She was one of the only figures to emerge from the disaster of the Crimean War with reputation intact. But, despite her celebrity, she had an uphill struggle to convince the medical establishment.

With germ theory in its infancy, Nightingale's ideas were viewed as radical and, by many doctors, implausible. The chief medical officer, John Simon, opined in 1858 that, as a cause of premature death, contagious diseases were "practically speaking, unavoidable".

Nightingale was not only a nurse and a national icon, but a statistician, the first female fellow of the Royal Statistical Society. She had used her understanding of data to track the link between sanitary improvements and the falling death rate in the Istanbul hospitals.

To turn that understanding into action required statistical persuasion. With geek allies such as William Farr and John Sutherland, Nightingale began to campaign for better public health measures. But the crucial weapon in that campaign was Nightingale's data visualisation – most famously her "rose diagram". There had been brilliant data visualisers before – as this book will explain – but never had a diagram been so central to a high-stakes debate.

The diagram, which you can see in the Learning Point in Chapter 5, easily dismissed as mere decoration, was to change the world. As a piece of statistical rhetoric, it is breath-taking, telling a compelling story of disaster before the sanitary improvements, and redemption afterwards. Those two pale circles delivered a powerful two-part payload; John Simon and his allies felt the force of both barrels.

But as striking as the diagram itself was Nightingale's insight into the importance of data visualisation, at a time when British statisticians would invariably rely on tables of data.

On Christmas Day 1857, she sketched out a plan to use data visualisation for social change. She declared her plan to have her diagrams glazed, framed and hung on the wall at the Army Medical Board, Horse Guards and War Department: "This is what they do not know and ought to."

And she planned to distribute her diagrams to exactly the right people. "None but scientific men even look into the appendices of a Report, and this is for the vulgar public . . . Now, who is the vulgar public and who is to have it? . . . The queen . . . Prince Albert . . . all the crown heads in Europe, through the ambassadors or ministers of each . . . all the commanding officers in the army . . . all the regimental surgeons and medical officers . . . the chief sanitarians in both houses [of Parliament] . . . all the newspapers, reviews and magazines."

John Simon and his allies were helpless before this onslaught. Nightingale and her allies – and, particularly, her graphical rhetoric – proved irresistible. Public health practice evolved, new sanitary laws were passed, and John Simon quietly revised his views about the inevitability of death from contagion. Florence Nightingale had changed the world, armed with a souped-up pie chart.

Every modern data visualisation expert has an opinion on Nightingale's graphs. Some find them scintillating, others confusing or even misleading. But, to my mind, there is something shockingly, brilliantly modern about the battle she decided to fight, and the way she used persuasive data visualisations as her weapon.

More than ever, we need to understand how data visualisation works. We need to understand it as consumers – who may be enlightened or bamboozled, depending on our own "graphicacy" and the choices made by the producers of graphs.

And we need to understand data visualisation as producers. Graphs and diagrams are powerful tools, supercharged by the ready availability of data and versatile software. But like any tool, they can be used skilfully or clumsily. They may be used to build something wonderful or repurposed with sinister intent.

The book you have in your hands is the definitive answer to that need. I am proud to have Alan Smith as a colleague and you, dear reader, are in for a treat.

Tim Harford, *Financial Times* columnist and author of *How to Make the World Add Up*

Oxford, February 2022

1

Why you need this book

I've always loved charts: hand-drawn data in a cycling diary from my teenage years visualises my adventures on two wheels. Seasonal trends captured by a mechanical mileometer that (as I vividly recall to this day) noisily recorded every revolution of my bike's front wheel.

While a geography undergraduate, I always loved the visual challenges ("make a map!") more than the alternatives ("write an essay!"). Yet, it never occurred to me that visualising data would end up being a full-time career for me. And that's because, at the time, it was rarely a full-time career for *anyone*.

By contrast, there are now plenty of people faced with the visualisation challenge – to take data in their organisation and communicate it. Yet so many people faced with this responsibility have never received formal instruction on *how* to present data – a glaring oversight in academic curricula!

Hand-drawn data: my teenage cycling diary shows an early passion for charts

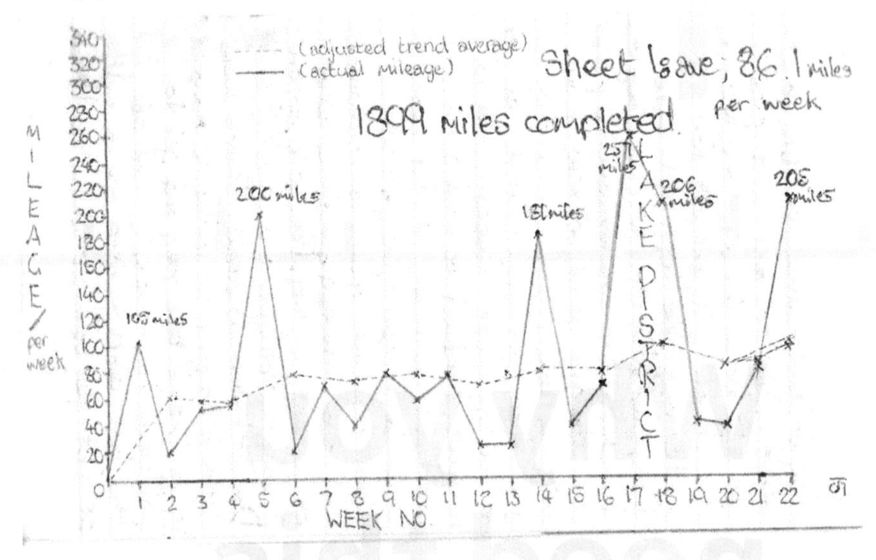

That's why I've written this book — to share my journey, or at least a specific part of it. Most of the charts featured in this book are either discarded drafts or published graphics from my seven years (and counting) with the *Financial Times*. And there's a very specific reason for this focus.

While it's been great to see so many wonderful books published recently on the topic of data visualisation, what makes this book (I hope) unique is its concentration on the work of one organisation and the effort that has gone into developing a coherent strategy for data visualisation that has served the *FT* well. I have documented some of this through the *FT*'s Chart Doctor series (ft.com/chart-doctor), but this book goes into far more detail.

Recent events, not least of which the Covid-19 pandemic, have accelerated the importance of data to the news agenda, and our data visualisations have been an essential part of that storytelling. So, I hope this book provides some practical insights on how to systematically use charts in the way that we aspire to at the *FT* – to convey insight that can help us understand and improve the world we live in.

I begin by looking at why charts are important, introducing the concept of graphicacy and our societal need to understand information.

Next, I introduce the *FT* Visual Vocabulary, a newsroom poster designed to promote chart literacy; greater awareness of different types of chart and the relationships in data that they emphasise.

The following nine chapters of the book take each of these relationships in turn, showcasing different chart types, their uses and applications. Subsequent chapters in the second part of the book help build out the toolkit, borrowing from topics as disparate as perceptual science, headline writing and colour theory.

Unlike my naïve hand-drawn charts of yesteryear, most people use computers to create charts these days. While software is obviously critical in this respect, I am keen that it shouldn't lead people unthinkingly to whizzy endpoints. So, while I mention tools that you could use to create charts from the Visual Vocabulary, this is not a book that focuses on software. Given the rate of change in data visualisation technology, I would like to think that decision will help keep this book relevant in the longer term.

More personal data – and an evolving literacy challenge

Like many people, I've spent a little time exploring my family tree. A 1911 Census return for Temple Street in the Irish city of Sligo lists my grandfather, John Gallagher, as a two-year-old child living with his parents and siblings.

CENSUS OF IRELAND, 1911.

Two Examples of the mode of filling up this Table are given on the other side.

FORM A.

No. on Form B.

RETURN of the MEMBERS of this FAMILY and their VISITORS, BOARDERS, SERVANTS, &c., who slept or abode in this House on the night of SUNDAY, the 2nd of APRIL, 1911.

Number	Christian Name	Surname	Relation to Head of Family	Religious Profession	Education	Age of Males	Age of Females	Rank, Profession, or Occupation	Whether Married, Widower, Widow, or Single	Completed years the present Marriage has lasted	Total Children born alive	Children still living	Where Born	Irish Language	If Deaf and Dumb; Dumb only; Blind; Imbecile or Idiot; or Lunatic
1	Patrick Joseph	Gallagher	Father	Roman Catholic	Read	40		Cattle Dealer	Married	[illegible]	[illegible]	6	Sligo Town		
2	Annie	Gallagher	Wife	"	Read & write	~~40~~	30		Married	13	7	6	"		
3	Thomas	Gallagher	Son	"	"	11		Scholar	Single		died		"		
4	Jannie	Gallagher	Daughter	"	"	~~7~~	9	"	"		at two		"		
5	Patrick	Gallagher	Son	"	"	8		"	"		months		"		
6	William	Gallagher	"	"	neither read nor write	5			"		of age		"		
7	Michael	Gallagher	"	"	"	4			"				"		
8	John	Gallagher	"	"	"	2			"						
9															
10															
11															
12															
13															
14															
15															

I hereby certify, as required by the Act 10 Edw. VII., and 1 Geo. V., cap. 11, that the foregoing Return is correct, according to the best of my knowledge and belief.

John Mallon[illegible] *Signature of Enumerator.*

I believe the foregoing to be a true Return.

Patrick Joseph Gallagher *Signature of Head of Family.*

Source: Data from Central Statistics Office/1911 Census

Census forms are remarkable time capsules of social history – they are also deeply personal. I was interested in the family's responses under the fourth heading – "Education". As you might expect, the pre-school children like John had no literacy, whereas the older children, along with their mother Annie, were able to read and write. But it is the patriarch, 40-year-old cattle dealer Patrick Joseph, whose entry really stands out: according to the document, he could "Read only".

Patrick was not alone in this respect. Official figures show that, in 1911, nearly 100,000 people across Ireland could read but not write. But just how big a proportion of the population was that? And was

Literacy in Ireland, 1911

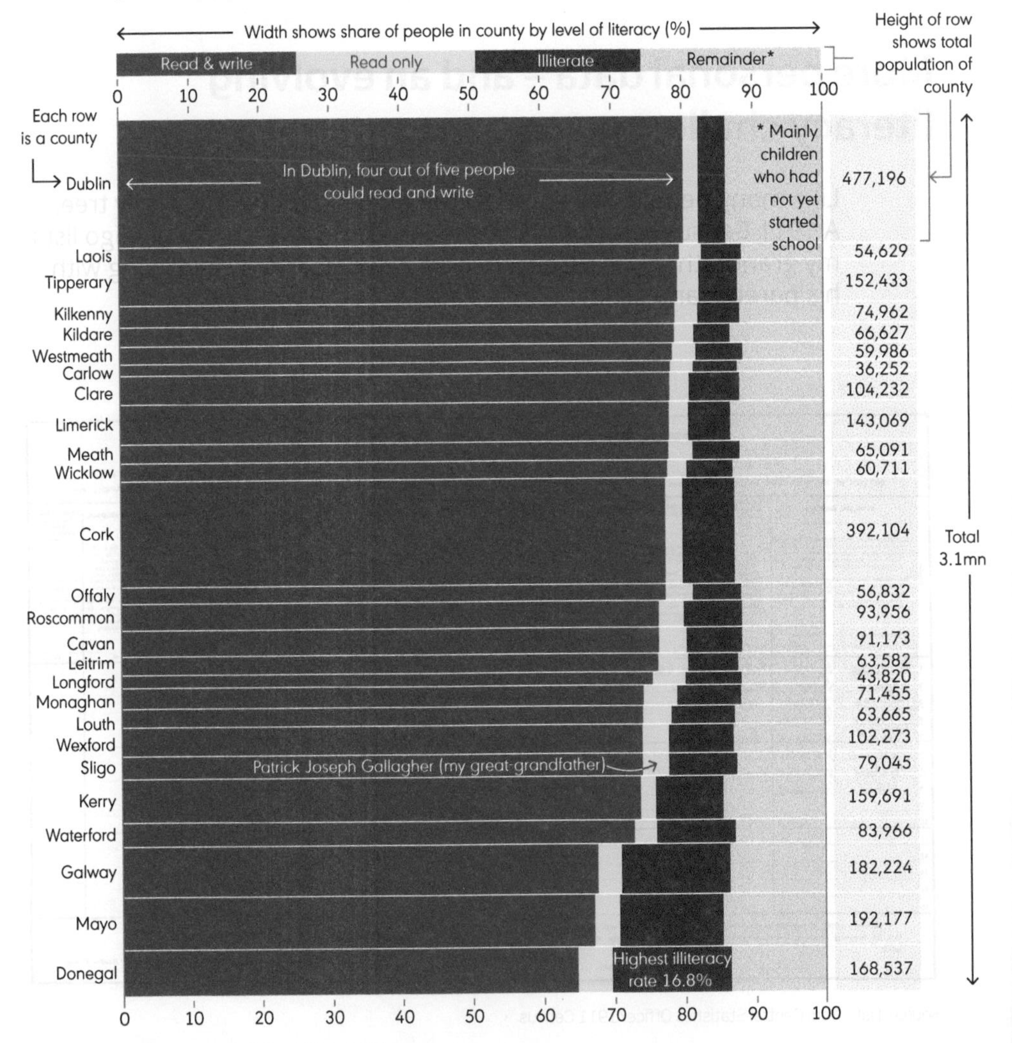

Source: Data from Central Statistics Office/1911 Census

illiteracy evenly distributed across Ireland or did specific counties like Sligo stand out? Let's look at a chart of census data from 1911 to find out the answers.

This chart shows two important pieces of information in a single view: the composition of Ireland's total population in 1911, county by county (represented by the *height* of each row), and sub-divisions of the population within each county based on responses to the education question (the *width* of each segment in a row). What can we understand by inspecting it?

First, look at the total area of the chart given to the first category (the darker blue) — despite widespread illiteracy, most people in Ireland could read and write. We can see that the most populous county Dublin (in the chart, the tallest row), also had the highest literacy rate (about 80 per cent, or four in five people).

Looking at the *illiteracy* rate (the width of the red segments), we can clearly see the highest levels were in Galway, Mayo and Donegal. In Donegal, the illiteracy rate of 16.8 per cent (about one in six people) was over double the national average.

Finally, being able to see yourself on a chart (or, in this case, a distant relative) is extremely powerful. By looking at the paler blue segments, we can see that the share of people who could "read only" was relatively small right across the country (a little over 3 per cent, nationally). So, Patrick Joseph Gallagher was atypical, both in Sligo and Ireland in general.

You might not have seen this type of chart before — or know that it is called a "*Marimekko chart*" — but once you've spent just a little time learning how to read it, it becomes a device of informational substance, rewarding the time spent reading it.

"Graphicacy"

This small slice of history from my family tree is from a time in Ireland's past when illiteracy was an acute societal problem. Thankfully, in most countries, literacy rates are higher than they were a century ago — but that doesn't mean all the barriers to participating in our fast-changing society have been removed.

In the 21st century our schools, homes and workplaces are increasingly saturated with *data*. It is our ability to handle and understand information that will increasingly determine our success in navigating the world around us.

In understanding the historical patterns of literacy in Ireland, our *chart* provides data — and enough context to turn it into *information* — that would be difficult to achieve using words alone. Our ability to interpret information visually, known as *graphicacy*, has long fallen between the gaps of academic curricula, but today it is more needed than ever.

It might seem extraordinary to us nowadays that, just one hundred years ago, official census forms were needed to differentiate between those that could just read and those that could write. But that's exactly where we are today with charts — far more people read them than make them.

2

Why charts matter

A firm grasp of the facts

There is a moment in *Double Indemnity*, the 1940s Hollywood noir classic, when you finally realise that anti-hero Walter Neff's attempt to get away with murder will end badly. His colleague, Barton Keyes, suspects foul play in a seemingly straightforward insurance case.

What makes it clear that Neff is up against a master logician? Keyes has outsized charts on his office walls that project a bold message: beware the intellectual power of an executive with a firm grasp of the facts.

Fast forward to the twenty-first century and the intervening decades have not necessarily been kind to the use of charts in business. A 2017 survey by Forbes Insights and Deloitte of over 300 senior executives sought to identify their preferred formats for receiving business insights. The least popular format — attracting zero per cent of responses — was "*infographics*".

The term is an interesting one. It was first used in the 1960s and 1970s to describe visually striking presentations of information. There is nothing wrong with that goal. And, indeed, they rapidly became popular, due in no small part to their mass adoption by newspapers and magazines across the world.

But over the decades, and as the Forbes/Deloitte survey shows, the word infographic has assumed pejorative connotations. It's likely that corporate designers, veering away from facts towards attention-grabbing aesthetics, played a supporting role. The prestigious newspaper I work for, the *Financial Times*, was not immune to this trend, which peaked at the turn of the century with regular doses of infographics that firmly prioritised "graphic" over "info".

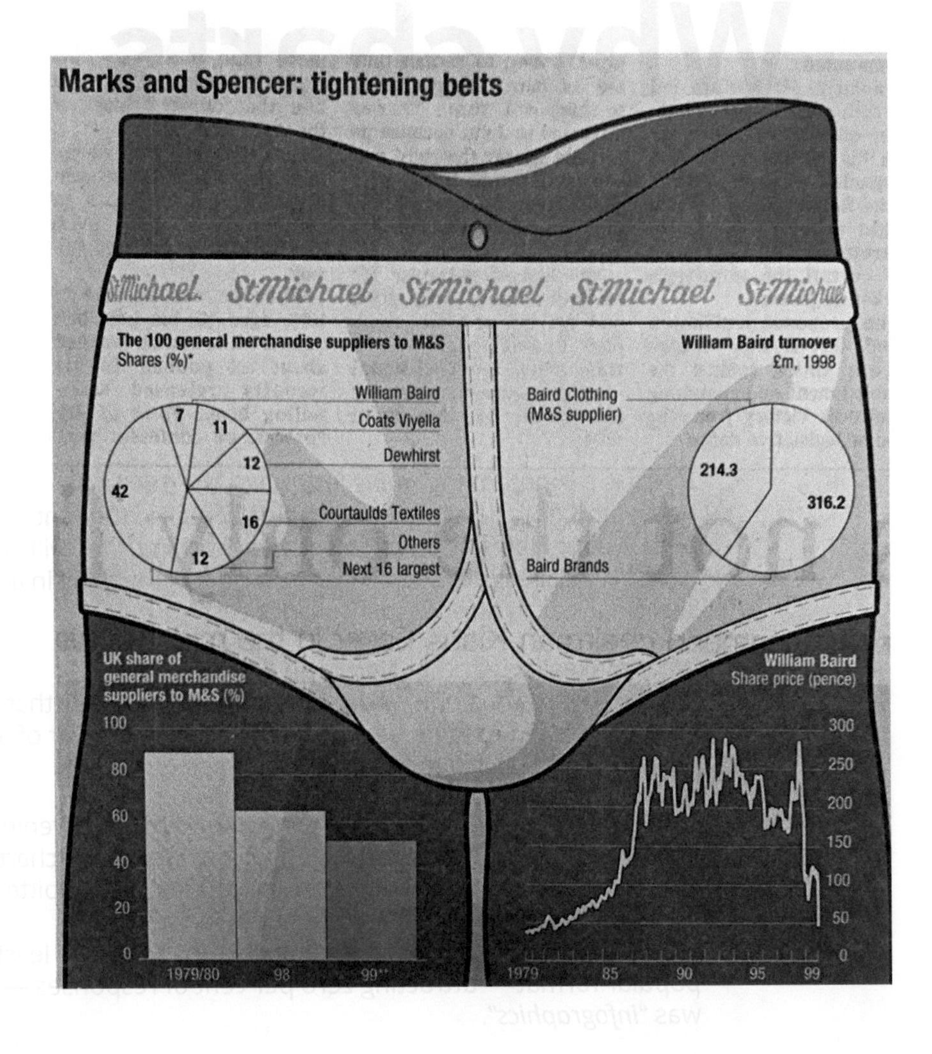

My personal favourites from the *FT* archives of this period are the "testicular pie charts" (my title, not the *FT*'s) packed into a pair of St. Michael underpants. Published in 1999, it is a classic of the genre. Memorable, certainly, but not necessarily for the right reasons. I doubt that Barton Keyes would have put this up on his office wall — if he had, I suspect Walter Neff might have got away with it after all.

The charts, unlike the overall graphic, are very modest: two pie charts, a column chart and a line chart. In terms of grabbing attention, the underpants are going to win every time.

The pioneer of modern information design, Edward Tufte, would describe this graphic as an example of "chartjunk". He does not hold back on his feelings for this approach to presenting information:

> *"Lurking behind chartjunk is contempt both for the information and for the audience. Chartjunk promoters imagine that numbers and details are boring, dull and tedious, requiring ornament to enliven . . . Chartjunk can turn bores into disasters, but it can never rescue a thin dataset . . . credibility vanishes"*

Edward Tufte, *Envisioning Information* (1990)

While subsequent academic research[1] has called into question some of the minimalist approaches to chart design favoured by Professor Tufte, when it comes to chartjunk, he has my sympathy.

When I first arrived in the *FT* newsroom in 2015, I spent some time studying how our editors and reporters interacted with the graphics desk to commission charts.

Many staff had a limited knowledge of different chart types. A limited chart vocabulary meant that many charts ended up looking alike, often leading to criticism that they were boring and repetitive. Subsequently, the graphics desk would be asked to provide adornments to make them "interesting".

[1] See Bateman, *et al.* (2010), Borkin, *et al.* (2015).

It is not a crime for a graphic to draw attention to itself – indeed, it should shout as loud as it can to the intended audience. But not at the expense of credibility – and there should be a reward of substance for the reader whose attention you've hijacked.

The graphics language gap

The chart that follows is known as a *scatterplot*. This example was produced by my colleague at the *FT*, John Burn-Murdoch, immediately after the UK referendum on EU membership in June 2016.

Leave vote was strongest in regions most economically dependent on the EU

The regions with the highest share of votes for Leave also tend to be the most economically intertwined with the EU. A higher percentage of East Yorkshire & Northern Lincolnshire's economic output is sold to other EU countries than is the case for any other UK region, yet 65 per cent of its electorate voted to Leave

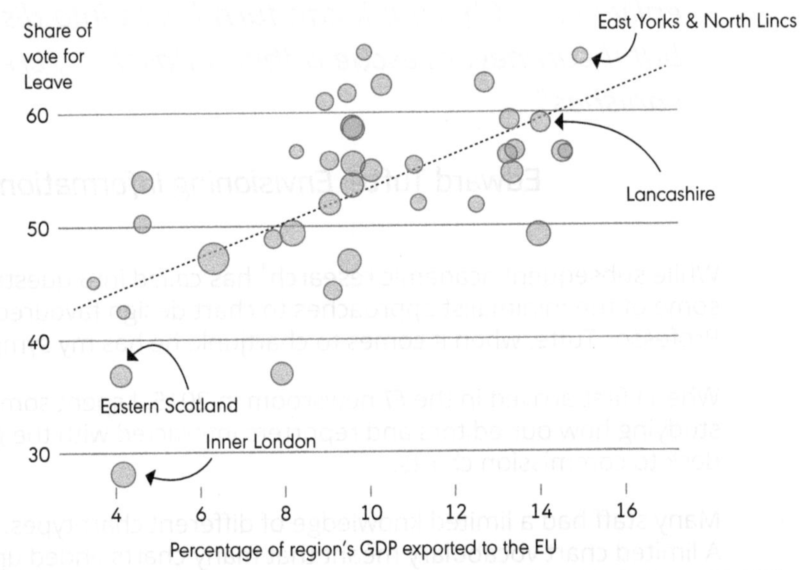

Source: Referendum results: Press Association EU trade research: John Springford, Philip McCann, Bart Los and Mark Thissen Graphic by John Burn-Murdoch/@jburnmurdoch appeared in https://twitter.com/ft/status/746275255354818561. Used by permission from The Financial Times Limited

Scatterplots show the relationship between two pieces of information, one plotted on the horizontal axis (known as the x axis), the other on the vertical (y axis). A single dot on the chart therefore represents two pieces of information based on its location relative to the two dimensions of the plot: in this example, Lancashire had both a high share of votes to leave and exported a relatively high proportion of its GDP to the EU, whereas the reverse is true of Inner London.

Scientists have used this type of chart for decades to visualise "*correlations*" – the extent to which two things are linked. In this example, John's research suggested, perhaps somewhat paradoxically, that areas in the UK with the highest vote to leave the EU were generally those areas that also traded more with the EU.

The chart reveals this as a clear trend because the dots on the chart are laid out in a pattern that sweeps from bottom left (low score on both axes) to top right (high score on both axes). If the dots were laid out randomly across the chart space, there would be no relationship between the two variables.

Scatterplots are valuable because, without having to inspect each individual point, we can see overall aggregate patterns in potentially thousands of data points. But does this density of information come at a price — just how easy are they to read?

Analysis from the Pew Research Center in 2015 suggested that, overall, about 63 per cent of American adults can correctly interpret scatterplots. The figure was higher (79 per cent) for college graduates, but only half of those with a high school education or less could read the chart correctly.

With these figures, it may be tempting to exclude charts like scatterplots from common usage in newspapers, business reports and presentations — after all, would we regularly use a word that only two in three people understand?

The truth is such charts can shed light on complex stories in a way words alone — or simpler charts you might be more familiar with — cannot. The EU referendum scatterplot was the top-performing tweet of all 24,000 published on Twitter by the *FT* in 2016.

As the Pew research suggests, education is important. In most countries, while students of subjects — for example, economics, mathematics or physics — may spend time developing more advanced chart-making and chart-reading skills as part of their analytical training, there is no educational strategy for ensuring everyone does.

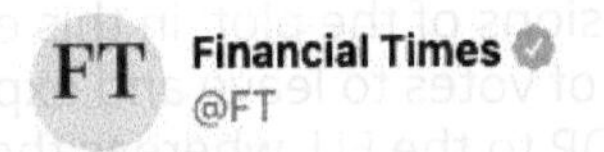
FT
Financial Times
@FT

Regions with the biggest votes for Leave are also the most economically dependent on the EU
on.ft.com/28V7FO6

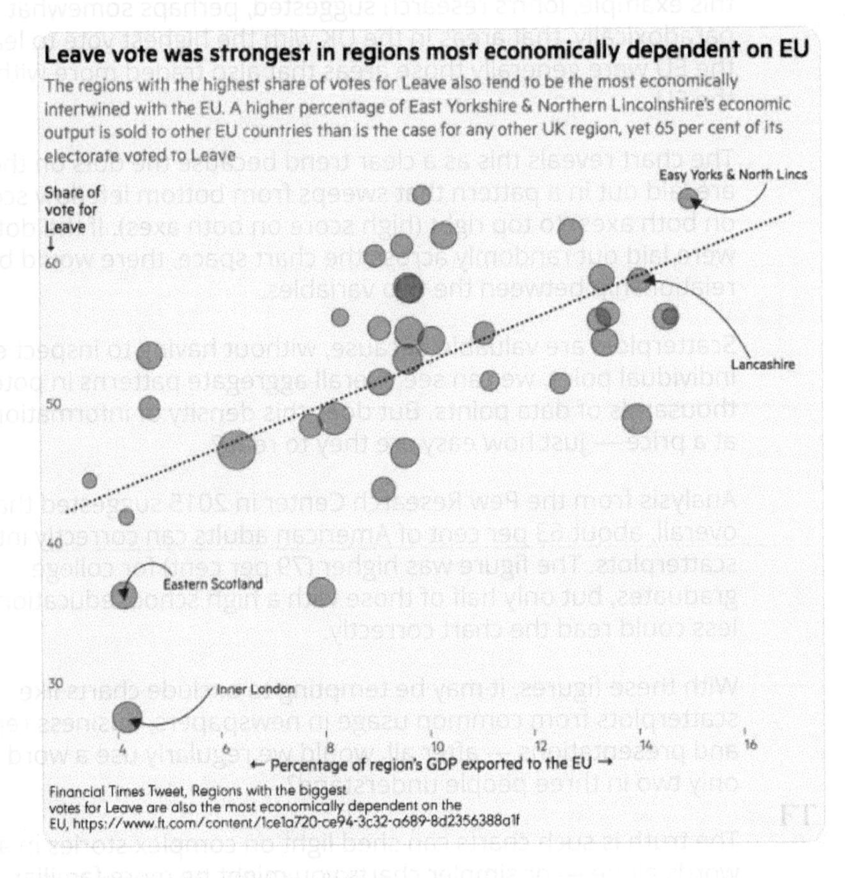
Leave vote was strongest in regions most economically dependent on EU
The regions with the highest share of votes for Leave also tend to be the most economically intertwined with the EU. A higher percentage of East Yorkshire & Northern Lincolnshire's economic output is sold to other EU countries than is the case for any other UK region, yet 65 per cent of its electorate voted to Leave
Share of vote for Leave
60
50
40
30
Easy Yorks & North Lincs
Lancashire
Eastern Scotland
Inner London
4
6
8
10
12
14
16
← Percentage of region's GDP exported to the EU →

Financial Times Tweet, Regions with the biggest votes for Leave are also the most economically dependent on the EU, https://www.ft.com/content/1ce1a720-ce94-3c32-a689-8d2356388a1f

11:40 AM · Jun 24, 2016 · SocialFlow

8.4K Retweets **5.8K** Likes

Conversely, most of the professional statisticians and economists I have worked with have never received any formal academic training on how to present complex information to *non-expert* audiences. Entire organisations can suffer from this two-way skills gap: researchers and policy analysts often find it difficult to communicate effectively with leaders, even if they are in acute need of support.

Learning to read charts

When I teach introductory classes on chart design, I often begin by asking students to name the charts that they already know. Without fail, three charts dominate the answers:

- line charts
- pie charts
- bar/column charts.

Note that this is the same combination of charts featured in the "testicular pie charts" graphic we saw earlier. Why those three? Are they more intuitive than other forms of chart? In fact, there is no such thing as an innately intuitive chart – even the inventor of these, the first three statistical chart types, understood that they needed to be learned first before they could be read:

> *"It remains only for me to request that those who do not, at the first sight, understand the manner of inspecting the Charts, will read with attention the few lines of directions facing the first Chart, after which they will find all the difficulty entirely vanish, and as much information may be obtained in five minutes as would require whole days to imprint on the memory, in a lasting manner, by a table of figures."*
>
> **William Playfair, *Introduction to the Commercial and Political Atlas*, 1801**

Playfair's invention of modern statistical charts in the late eighteenth century was a landmark in scientific communication — in fact, so ubiquitous have charts become, it's quite hard to imagine a time when they *didn't* exist. But invented they were — and the first readers of Playfair's charts had to teach themselves how to read them.

Of course, once you learned to read them, they became straightforward. Nobody needs to re-learn how to read a pie chart — rather like riding a bike, it's something you never forget once you've overcome the initial challenge.

Playfair's three fundamental chart types continue to dominate the public subconscious largely because they remain the only charts that are the subject of universal education: most children learn to make and read them when they are at primary school. And then, for many, their chart education stops, before serious academic study has even begun.

Our challenge, therefore, is not to hold people back and "play it safe" by sticking to just the charts people learned when they were six years old. Instead, we need to fill in the gaps and extend the common vocabulary of charts in a way that allows us to present and socialise information more fluently and eloquently.

No one should find interesting and relevant data, well-charted, so boring that it needs to be dressed in a pair of underpants.

Charts don't show numbers; they show relationships

"Just show me the numbers!" is a business cliché born of some tacit acknowledgement of the value of figures. But in fact, if there's something good charts generally don't do, it is show you *all* the numbers. Charts are more efficient than that — they concentrate on showing patterns or *relationships* in the numbers that matter.

What do we mean by a "relationship"? It's all to do with the *context* in the numbers that's important to us.

For example, using our earlier data from the 1911 Irish Census, we might be interested simply in the number of people living in each county and how they compare to each other.

A simple bar chart allows us to see the size – or *magnitude* – of each county population. Visually comparing the length of the bars allows us to see that the population of Dublin was over four times that of Wexford (notice how the tick marks, in 100,000 subdivisions along the x axis, make that job easier).

What this chart doesn't show us clearly is *other* contexts. For example, it's much harder to identify the fifth biggest county, or the second smallest county. That's because the bars are organised in alphabetical order (Carlow at the top, Wicklow at the bottom). If we re-sort the data into order of the population totals, we can see that information more clearly. This adds another context, or relationship between the numbers — *ranking*.

Population of Ireland, by county, 1911

(000s)

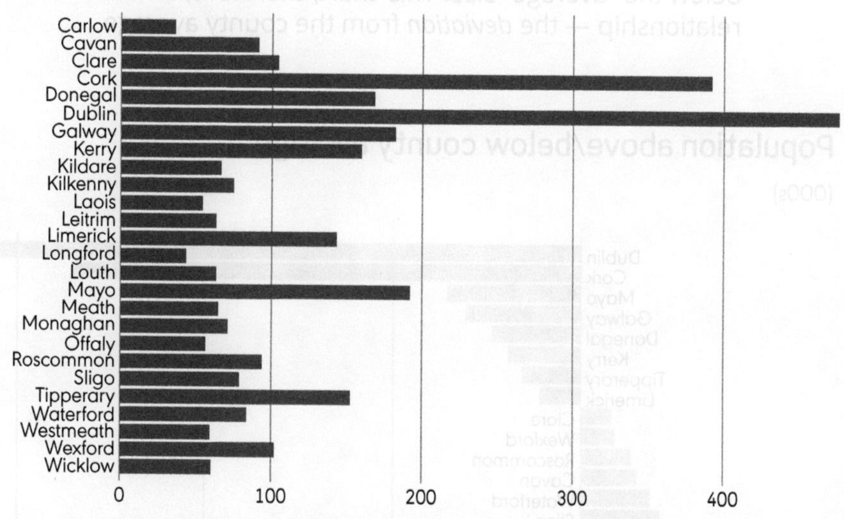

Source: Data from Central Statistics Office/1911 Census

Population of Ireland, by county, 1911

(000s)

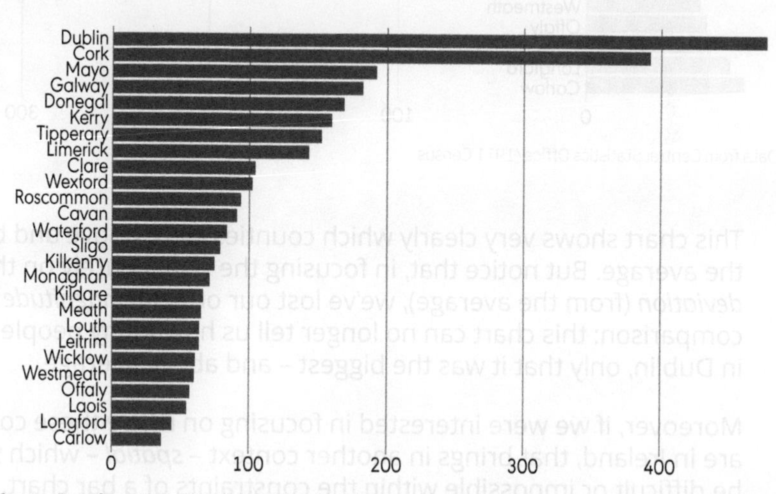

Source: Data from Central Statistics Office/1911 Census

But we might also be interested in seeing whether a county's population was bigger or smaller than the average county size in 1911. One simple way of achieving this is to plot each county's population relative to the average for all 26 counties.

Because the total population of Ireland included a few highly populated counties, we can see that most of the counties were below the "average" size. This chart, therefore, shows us another relationship — the *deviation* from the county average.

Population above/below county average

(000s)

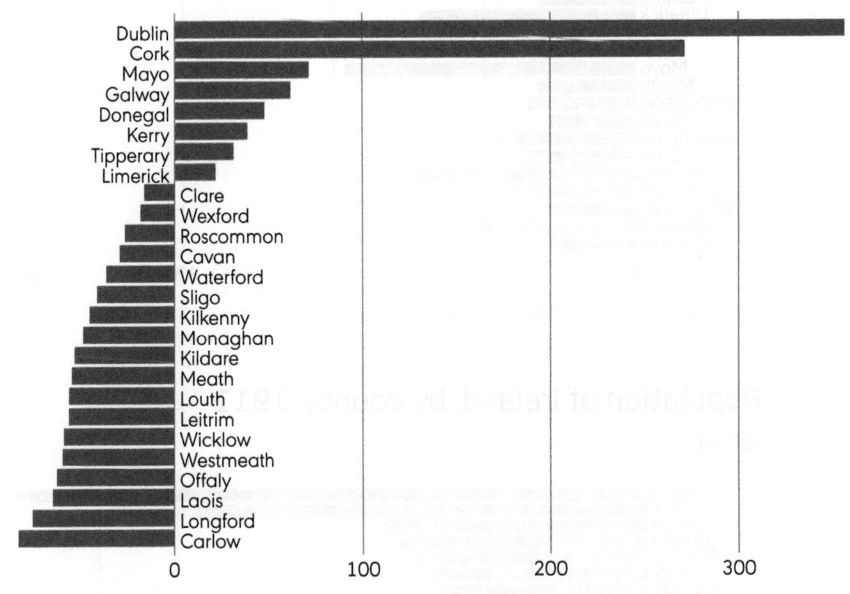

Source: Data from Central Statistics Office/1911 Census

This chart shows very clearly which counties were above and below the average. But notice that, in focusing the visual purely on the *deviation* (from the average), we've lost our original *magnitude* comparison: this chart can no longer tell us how many people lived in Dublin, only that it was the biggest - and above average.

Moreover, if we were interested in focusing on *where* these counties are in Ireland, that brings in another context - *spatial* - which would be difficult or impossible within the constraints of a bar chart.

This very simple example shows us that there is no such thing as a *perfect* chart. Every chart is a design compromise, aiming to emphasise the most important relationships in a set of numbers at the expense of the less important.

In this book, we're going to focus on nine key relationships in data that charts are often intended to communicate:

- magnitude
- change over time
- deviation
- correlation
- distribution
- part-to-whole
- ranking
- spatial
- flow.

This list is not meant to be exhaustive – but it represents a good starting point from which to finally extend our vocabulary of charts beyond William Playfair's 200-year-old starting point.

Part 1

Know your charts

3

The *Financial Times* visual vocabulary

A chart thesaurus

In 2016, I set about the task of expanding the range of charts in regular use at the *Financial Times*. Doing so would involve introducing unfamiliar chart forms to everyone across the newsroom, not just my colleagues in the Visual journalism team. But how to do it? An email newsletter? A website? An app? I considered and discarded various approaches. None seemed to hit the spot I was aiming for.

What I really wanted was something physical – that would make it much harder to ignore in the newsroom. It needed to be both attractive and informative. Above all, it needed to be in a format that would make it easy to use in

Deviation

Emphasise variations (+/-) from a fixed reference point. Typically the reference point is zero but it can also be a target or a long-term average. Can also be used to show sentiment (positive/neutral/negative).

Example FT uses
Trade surplus/deficit, climate change

Diverging bar

Diverging stacked bar

Spine

Surplus/deficit filled line

Correlation

Show the relationship between two or more variables. Be mindful that, unless you tell them otherwise, many readers will assume the relationships you show them to be casual (i.e. one causes the other).

Example FT uses
Inflation and unemployment, income and life expectancy

Scatterplot

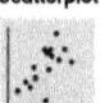

Column + line timeline

Connected scatterplot

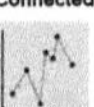

Bubble

XY heatmap

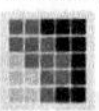

Ranking

Use where an item's position in an ordered list is more important than its absolute or relative value. Don't be afraid to highlight the points of interest.

Example FT uses
Wealth, deprivation, league tables, constituency election results

Ordered bar

Ordered column

Ordered proportional symbol

Dot strip plot

Slope

Lollipop

Bump

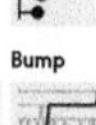

Distribution

Show values in a dataset and how often they occur. The shape (or 'skew') of a distribution can be a memorable way of highlighting the lack of uniformity or equality in the date.

Example FT uses
Income distribution, population (age/sex) distribution, revealing inequality

Histogram

Dot plot

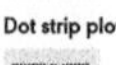

Dot strip plot

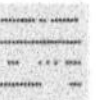

Barcode plot

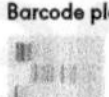
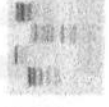

Boxplot

Violin plot

Population pyramid

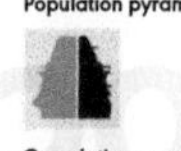

Cumulative curve

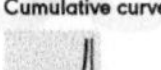

Frequency polygons

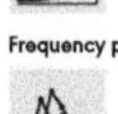

Beeswarm

Visual vocabulary

Designing with data

There are so many ways to visualise data - how do we know which one to pick? use the categories across the top to decide which data relationship is most important in your story, then look at the different types of chart within the category to form some initial ideas about what might work best. This list is not meant to be exhaustive, nor a wizard, but is a useful starting point for making informative and meaningful data visualisations.

Chris Campbell, Ian Bott, Liz Faunce, Graham Parrish, Billy Ehrenberg-Shannon, Paul McCallum and Martin Stabe. Inspired by the Graphic Continumm by Jon Schwabish and Severino Ribecca appeared in Charts that work: FT visual vocabulary guide, Financial Times, March 8, 2021. Available at: https://www.ft.com/content/c7bb24c9-964d-479f-ba24-03a2b2df6e85. Used by permission from The Financial Times Limited

Full printable version available online at ft.com/vocabulary.

ft.com/vocabulary

Change over Time

Give emphasis to changing trends. These can be short (intra-day) movements or extended series traversing decades or centuries: Choosing the correct time period is important to provide suitable context for the reader.

Example FT uses
Share price movements, economic time series, sectoral changes in a market

Line
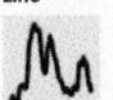

Column

Column + line timeline

Slope
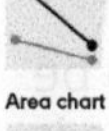

Area chart

Candlestick
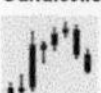

Fan chart (projections)
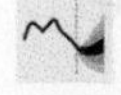

Connected scatterplot

Calendar heatmap

Priestley timeline

Circle timeline
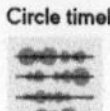

Vertical timeline

Seismogram

Streamgraph

Magnitude

Show size comparisons. These can be relative (just being able to see larger/bigger) or absolute (need to see fine differences). Usually these show a 'counted' number (for example, barrels, dollars or people) rather than a calculated rate or per cent.

Example FT uses
Commodity production, market capitalisation, volumes in general

Column

Bar

Paired column

Paired bar

Marimekko

Proportional symbol

Isotype (pictogram)
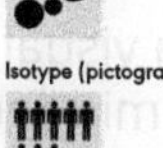

Lollipop

Radar
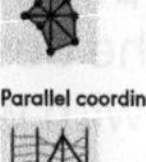

Parallel coordinates

Bullet

Grouped symbol

Part-to-whole

Show how a single entity can be broken down into its component elements. If the reader's interest is solely in the size of the components, consider a magnitude-type chart instead.

Example FT uses
Fiscal budgets, company structures, national election results

Stacked column/bar

Marimekko

Pie

Donut

Treemap
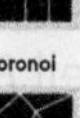

Voronoi

Arc

Gridplot
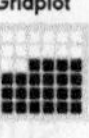

Venn

Waterfall

Spatial

Aside from locator maps only used when precise locations or geographical patterns in data are more important to the reader than anything else.

Example FT uses
Population density, natural resource locations, natural disaster risk/impact, catchment areas, variation in election results

Basic choropleth (rate/ratio)
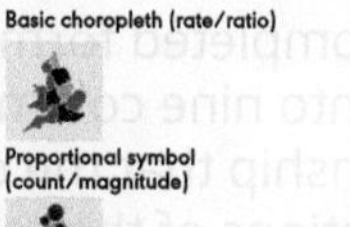

Proportional symbol (count/magnitude)

Flow map

Contour map

Equalised cartogram

Scaled cartogram (value)

Dot density
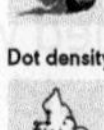

Heat map

Flow

Show the reader volumes or intensity of movement between two or more states or conditions. These might be logical sequences or geographical locations.

Example FT uses
Movement of funds, trade, migrants, lawsuits, information; relationship graphs.

Sankey

Waterfall

Chord

Network
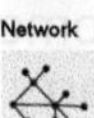

collaborative groups in an open-plan newsroom environment. For a progressive digital newsroom, it seemed slightly anachronistic – but we needed a poster.

Working with my colleague Chris Campbell, with contributions from others in the Visual journalism team, the early drafts of a new resource quickly emerged.

In its completed form, the poster arranges more than 70 chart types into nine columns, each headed by a particular statistical relationship that the charts below are intended to emphasise. Brief descriptions of the relationships are supplemented by concise notes against each chart type, detailing potential advantages and disadvantages.

Some charts feature in more than one category – because they carry the ability to show more than one relationship. Some chart types don't feature at all – because the poster is not designed to be a complete list of every possible chart type. Instead, the resource is designed to be a dictionary, or perhaps more properly, a *thesaurus* of the charts that could help us tell *Financial Times* stories.

It was also designed with *FT* readers in mind: a visual index of the charts they could expect to see, at least semi-regularly, in the *Financial Times*.

We agonised for some time on the name of this new resource until Martin Stabe, the *FT*'s data editor, suggested "Visual Vocabulary". This grammatical hint made *a lot* of sense: the power of the poster lies in the concept that there is a grammar to the design and use of charts that everyone can learn, just as there is with words, or indeed music: composers know that, to produce good music, you'll need to break musical scales. But you still start by learning those scales.

Impact in the *FT* newsroom

From the moment it first appeared on the newsroom wall in the *FT*'s former head office in Southwark, the Visual Vocabulary sparked interest.

At a basic level, the poster served as a walk-up meeting point to discuss chart design. Conversations between other *FT* journalists and the graphics desk subtly shifted from the transactional, kiosk-style "What do you want?" to the more collaborative "What do you want *to show?*", focusing discussions on the columns on the poster – and the relationships in the numbers at the heart of our stories.

We used the poster as the heart of editorial training sessions outlining our new approach to visual journalism, resulting in other small, but important, changes. Journalists learning the names of new chart types transformed editorial discussions: at morning news conference, an editor from the World Desk talked about the possibility of "a *Sankey* of the latest German election results".

Translating the poster into other languages also made us realise that the names of charts are not universal – in France, a pie chart is called a "*Camembert*".

A resource for everyone

The Visual Vocabulary was designed primarily as a resource for the *Financial Times* newsroom, to improve the use of charts in our journalism. But there was a clear sense that this was a resource that would be of interest to a much wider audience, so we made the decision to make the Visual Vocabulary freely available via a Creative Commons Attribution-ShareAlike licence, allowing unlimited use and reuse.

The Visual Vocabulary is freely available to download[2]. Printable versions of the poster, in high resolution pdf format, are available in English, Spanish, French, Japanese and Chinese.

Before the Visual Vocabulary – the Graphic Continuum

The *FT* Visual Vocabulary was inspired by an earlier project conceived by a frustrated economist in Washington DC.

Jon Schwabish was working at the Congressional Budget Office (CBO) in 2010 when he attended a session on information design by Edward Tufte. Inspired by the workshop, Schwabish says he saw an opportunity to extend his role at CBO as the technical reviewer

[2] ft.com/vocabulary.

THE GRAPHIC CONTINUUM

The Graphic Continuum shows several ways that data can be illustrated individually or combined to show relationships.

Use of various shapes, chart types, and colors can help identify patterns, tell stories, and reveal relationships between different sets and types of data. Bar charts, or histograms, for example, can illustrate a distribution of data over time, but they also can show categorical or geographic differences. Scatterplots can illustrate data from a single instance or for a period, but they also can be used to identify a distribution around a mean.

This set of charts does not constitute an exhaustive list, nor do the connections represent every possible pathway for linking data and ideas. Instead, the Graphic Continuum identifies some presentation methods, and it illustrates some of the connections that can bind different representations together. The six groups do not define all possibilities: Many other useful, overlapping data types and visualization techniques are possible.

This chart can guide graphic choices, but your imagination can lead the way to other effective ways to present data.

DISTRIBUT

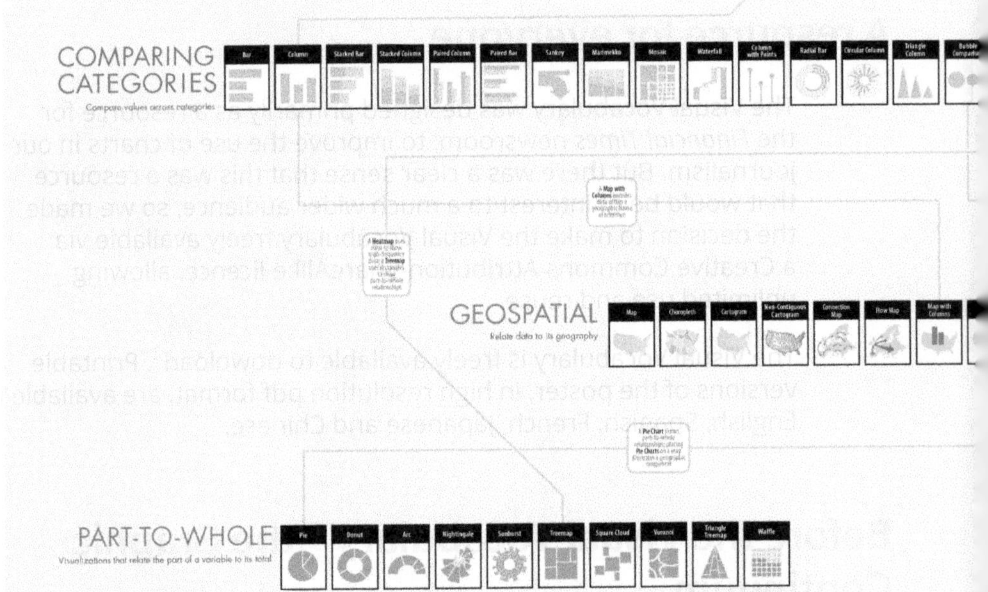

RELATIONSH

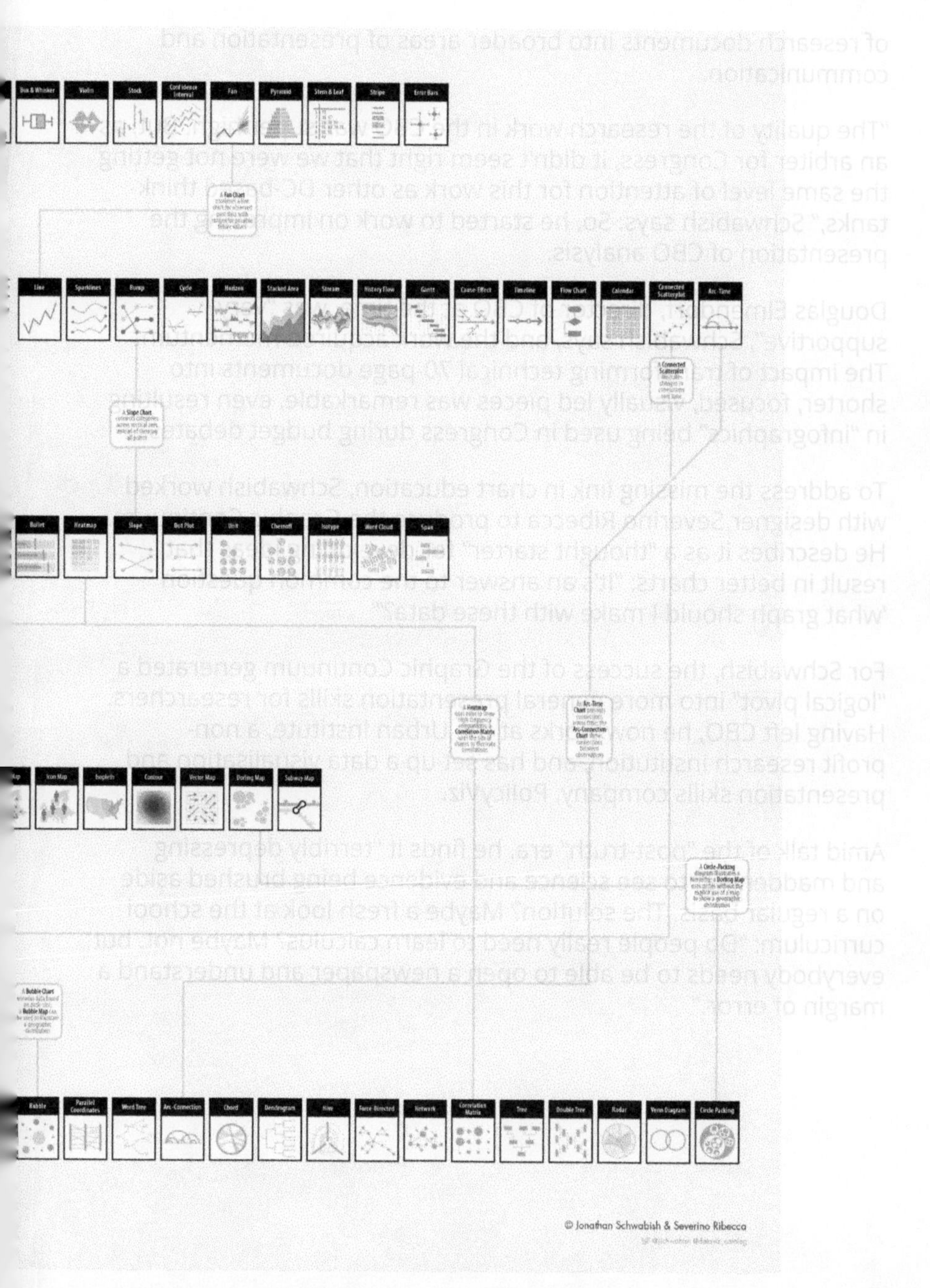

Source: Used by permissions from Jonathan Schwabish, PolicyViz.

of research documents into broader areas of presentation and communication.

"The quality of the research work in the CBO was super high. But, as an arbiter for Congress, it didn't seem right that we were not getting the same level of attention for this work as other DC-based think-tanks," Schwabish says. So, he started to work on improving the presentation of CBO analysis.

Douglas Elmendorf, director of CBO at the time, was "very supportive", Schwabish says, and the work acquired momentum. The impact of transforming technical 70-page documents into shorter, focused, visually led pieces was remarkable, even resulting in "infographics" being used in Congress during budget debates.

To address the missing link in chart education, Schwabish worked with designer Severino Ribecca to produce the Graphic Continuum. He describes it as a "thought starter" for developing ideas that result in better charts: "It's an answer to the common question 'what graph should I make with these data?'"

For Schwabish, the success of the Graphic Continuum generated a "logical pivot" into more general presentation skills for researchers. Having left CBO, he now works at the Urban Institute, a non-profit research institution, and has set up a data visualisation and presentation skills company, PolicyViz.

Amid talk of the "post-truth" era, he finds it "terribly depressing and maddening" to see science and evidence being brushed aside on a regular basis. The solution? Maybe a fresh look at the school curriculum: "Do people really need to learn calculus? Maybe not, but everybody needs to be able to open a newspaper and understand a margin of error."

4

Charts of magnitude

These charts emphasise simple size comparisons. These can be relative comparisons (just being able to see larger/bigger) or absolute (the need to be able to see fine differences). These types of charts very often show a "counted" number of things (for example, barrels, dollars or people) – but can also be used with a wide range of data.

There's a strong possibility that the first chart you ever saw was a bar chart. And with good reason – they offer an excellent solution to perhaps the simplest visual comparison of all – size.

Disparities in US wealth

Median net worth of a family, by race, 2019 ($000s)

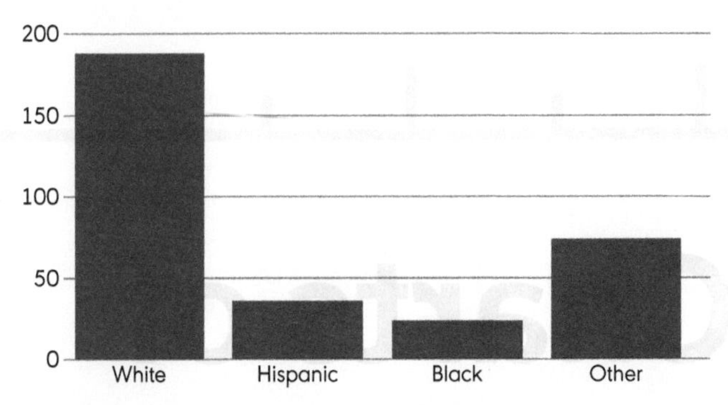

Source: Data from US Federal Reserve Survey of Consumer Finances

This chart visualises long-standing disparities in US wealth. A typical White family has around eight times the wealth of an average Black family – and five times the wealth of a Hispanic family. When there are notable differences in an important set of numbers like this, there is nothing more likely to succinctly answer the question of scale than a bar chart.

Learning point – Missing data

It always pays to question what a simple chart like this *doesn't* show. It's impossible for us to know the median net worth of an *Asian American* family – because that data is not published as a separate category in the survey, instead forming part of the vague catch-all category "Other".

For the sake of brevity, in this chapter, I am going to use the term "bar chart" to refer interchangeably to two chart types from the Visual Vocabulary. They are identical, apart from their geometric orientation.

- *Column chart:* vertical bars projecting from a *horizontal baseline*. This orientation exploits a sense of visual gravity: low numbers stay near the bottom; higher numbers grow towards the top.

- *Bar chart*: a *vertical baseline* with horizontal bars. If all the numbers being plotted are positive, the baseline will be on the left, with horizontal rectangles extending to the right. This method does have one big practical advantage over column charts – the ability to deal with longer labels without having to rotate text to unwieldy angles.

Bar charts: good for long labels

Top ten longest single word placenames in the world

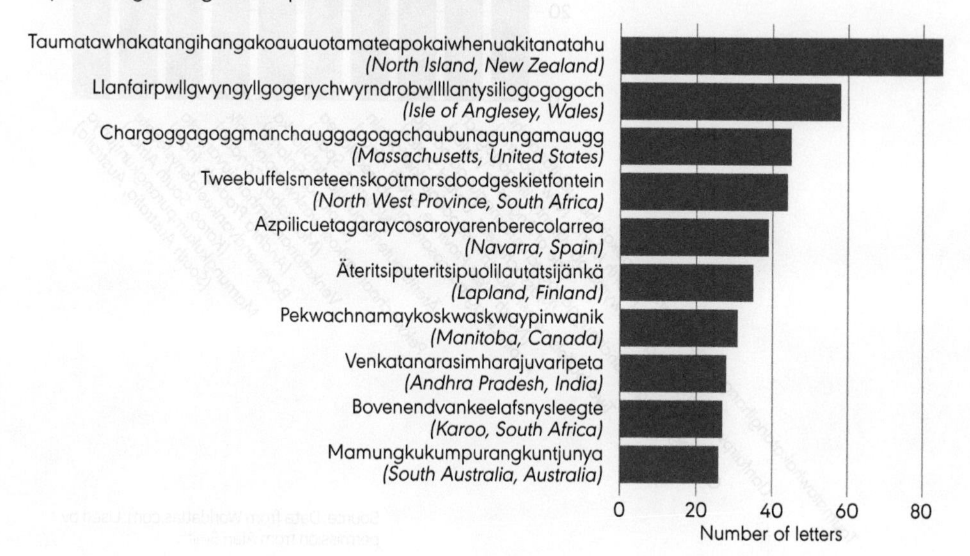

Source: Data from Worldatlas.com. Used by permission from Alan Smith

Bar charts can be used with a wide range of data. Although their canonical use is in showing physical quantities, they can also be used to show virtually any kind of numerical comparison including rates, ratios and percentages.

A bar chart of death rates of the world's highest mountains is confident enough in its data to highlight a star attraction – the deadly K2 – and provide a valuable insight (don't even think about climbing it).

Column charts: more likely to involve chiropractic adjustment

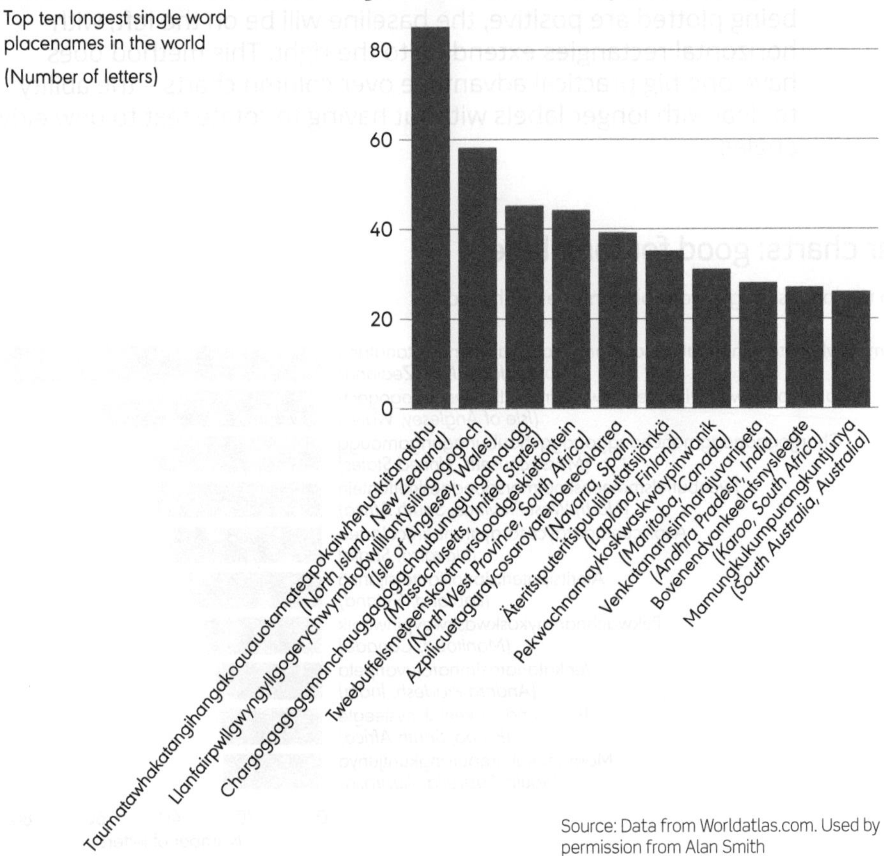

Source: Data from Worldatlas.com. Used by permission from Alan Smith

High risk: fatality rates on the world's highest peaks

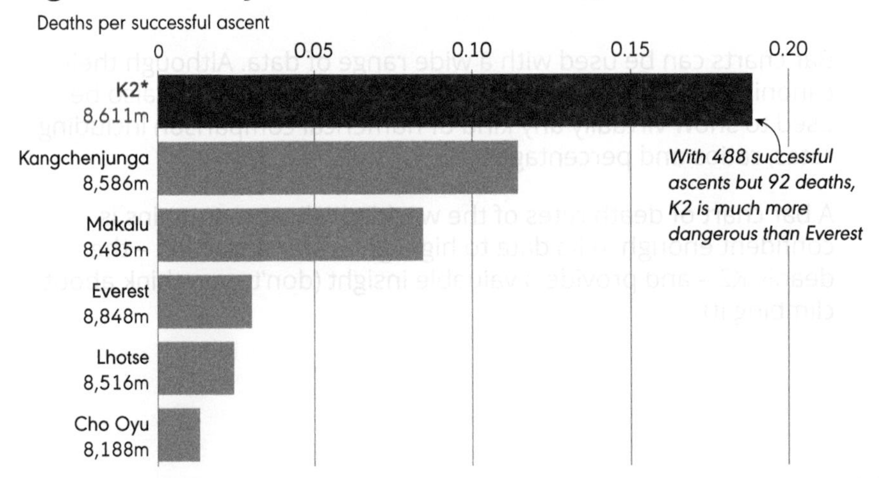

Source: No authoritative central database of K2 statistics exists, these figures have been compiled from Eberhard Jurgalski/8000ers.com, Alan Arnette and expedition reports. Graphic: Chris Campbell; Source: Data from Himalayandatabase.com appeared in Triumph and tragedy on K2. Available at: https://www.ft.com/content/b6340707-25c4-4b01-9747-ad44f0bef50b. Used by permission from The Financial Times Limited

Stacked bar chart

Bar charts usually show aggregated information – a total amount of some measure. But sometimes we're also keen to see further detail on how those totals are comprised. Stacked bar charts offer one way of doing this, allowing us to subdivide totals into a secondary "*part-to-whole*" composition.

Potential US tax increases a double blow for Wall Street stocks

Expected impact on earnings per share (%)

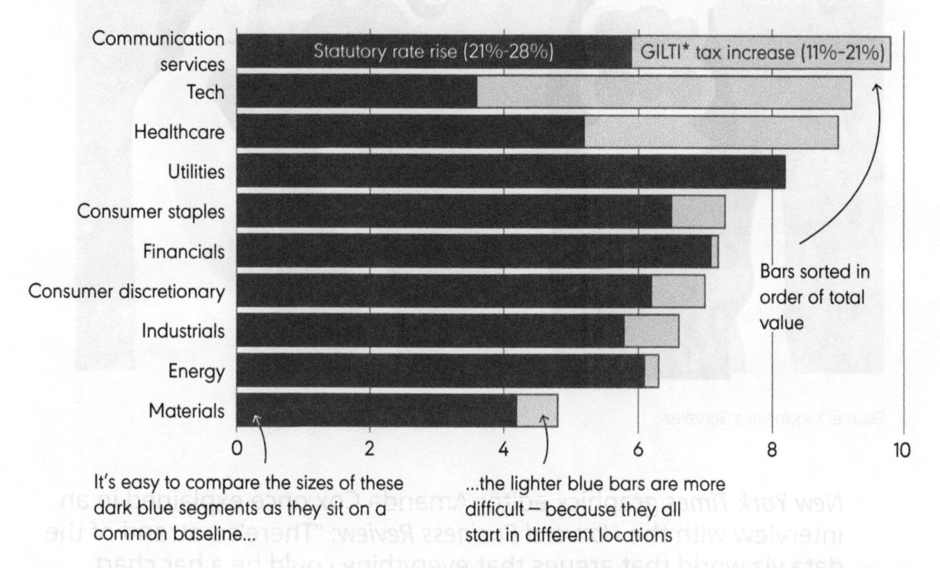

* Category of income that is earned abroad by US-controlled foreign corporations

Source: Goldman Sachs appeared in Aziza Kasumov, Wall Street braces itself for tax rises from Biden's new stimulus plan, Financial Times, 2021. Available at: https://www.ft.com/stream/2abbd410-644b-4073-a5ab-dbf9b2ab2c43

The emphasis in the chart is still very much on the total *magnitude* (the size of the combined stack). Only one layer of the stack can really be compared very precisely across the chart – the first layer of bars that touch the baseline. Other layers in a stack are displaced (i.e., they don't line up from a common starting point) making size comparisons of these elements a little more difficult. So, there are limits with stacked bars – but not enough to prevent them contributing to the overall utility of bar charts.

"Boring" bar charts?

Despite their undoubted flexibility, the sad truth is that bar charts are often seen as – how can I politely put this? – a little dull. They have, consequently, acquired a reputation as the worthy-but-boring member of the chart world, nicely captured by this playful take on the "distracted boyfriend" meme from Xaquín Veira González.

Source: Xaquín Veira González

New York Times graphics editor Amanda Cox once explained in an interview with the *Harvard Business Review*: "There's a strand of the data viz world that argues that everything could be a bar chart. That's possibly true but also possibly a world without joy."

No one wants a world without joy, but we shouldn't be so hard on ourselves – or bar charts. We simply need to understand the two primary reasons that lead to their overuse.

Reason 1: Some magnitude comparisons simply don't need to be visualised

> *"China produced more steel in two years than the total cumulative output of the UK since the industrial revolution"*

This great fact, calculated by Ed Conway of *The Times*, is both memorable and insightful – but does it need a chart? Let's produce one to find out.

China produced more steel in two years than the entire output of the UK since the industrial revolution

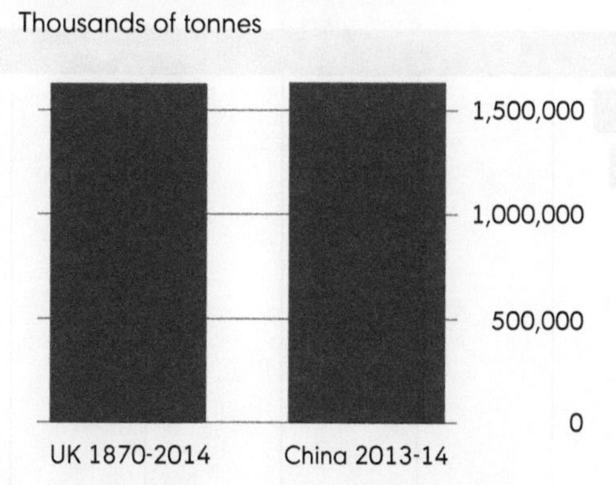

Source: Ed Conway analysis of data from World Steel Association and Stevenson & Cook

What do you learn from the geometry of this chart that you cannot glean from the title alone? Very little, if anything at all. The units themselves are almost impossibly big to wrestle with mentally. And it's very difficult to see that the column for China is bigger than the column for the UK, because the numbers are very similar.

Just because an interesting fact is made of numbers, it doesn't mean we have to show it on a chart. Much time and effort spent worrying about how to dress up a dull chart could be saved by realising that some data comparisons should be explained succinctly using words alone.

Reason 2: Bar charts sometimes aren't the best option for magnitude comparisons that *do* need to be visualised

Bar charts are effective at displaying magnitude comparisons because they require readers to make visual interpretations in one dimension only – the length (or height) of its constituent rectangles. This is *usually* a good thing – it's simple to interpret and, combined with full-length tick marks, makes comparing values quick and easy.

However, condensing all differences between the data being compared into a one-dimensional axis can present chart readers with problems of interpretation when there are very big differences – of many orders of magnitude – in the data being presented.

In the *Financial Times* newsroom, I've sometimes referred to this issue of extreme magnitudes as the *"Jupiter/Pluto problem"* – but perhaps the *"Sun/Pluto problem"* might be a better label for it.

This bar chart compares the mean radius of objects in the solar system – I have recalled Pluto from its controversial exile as a dwarf planet to re-join the eight official planets, along with their parent star.

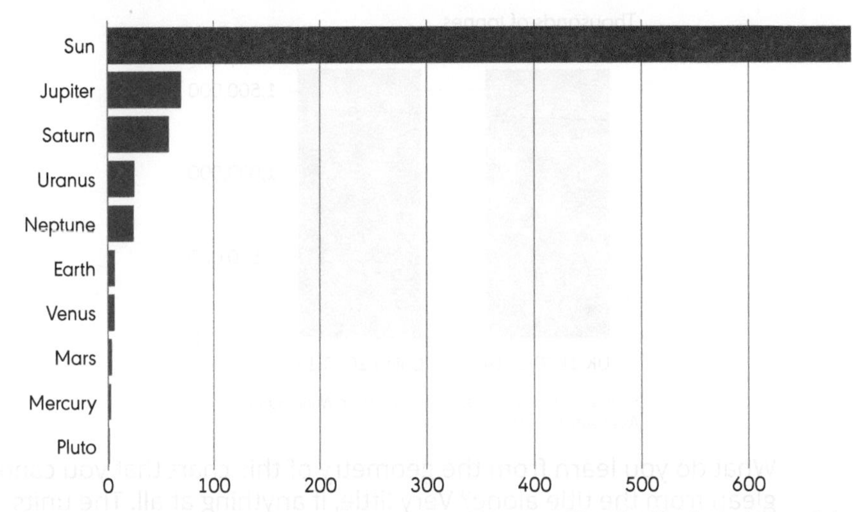

Sources: Data from Nimmo et al (2017); Emilio et al (2012); Seidelmann et al (2007); Wikipedia. Used by permission from Alan Smith

As you can see from the bar chart, the Sun is extremely big. So big, it makes Jupiter look small. Which it isn't, because it's much bigger than Earth, which in turn is much bigger than Pluto.

The visual problem is that our axis is so massively stretched to accommodate the Sun, it is incredibly difficult to see and compare the size differences of the far smaller planets. So, this chart is fine if your only interest is in understanding how enormous the Sun's radius is, but not if you're interested in size comparisons across the full range of objects.

Dot plot with log scale

One method for dealing with extreme values in a dataset is to chart it using a log scale.

Note that log scales can't start from zero. (If you've never seen log scales before, don't worry, we'll discuss them in more detail later in the book – see Chapter 14 "Scales of justice; axes of evil"). So, instead of a conventional bar chart and zero baseline, we'll use dots to plot the data.

The chart certainly allows us to make comparisons across all the objects on the chart from the Sun, right down to Pluto – once you notice that each main axis tick is the previous value multiplied by 10.

The use of a log scale means we need to think about the audience for our chart. For a general readership, the chart might require a

Solar system objects arranged in order of size

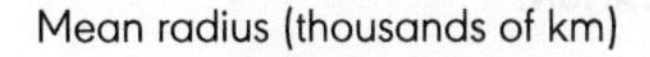

Mean radius (thousands of km)

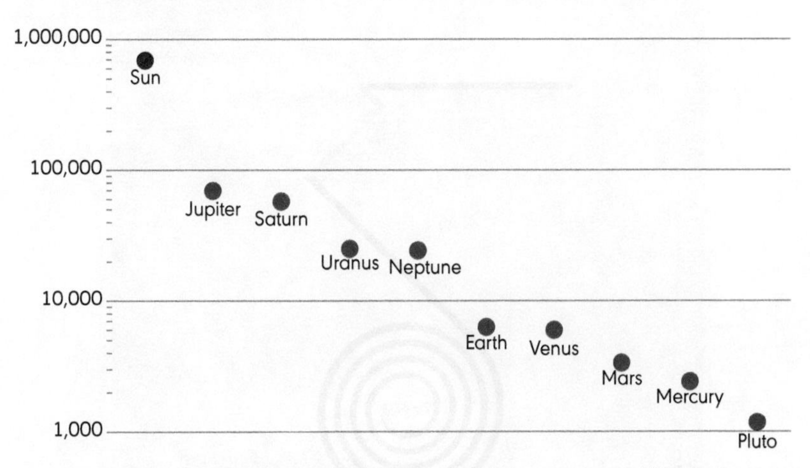

Sources: Data from Nimmo et al (2017); Emilio et al (2012); Seidelmann et al (2007); Wikipedia. Used by permission from Alan Smith

little extra effort to decode; in the scientific community, log scales are used frequently without causing a stir. At the *Financial Times*, we certainly use log scales – but rarely for pure *magnitude* comparisons. So, it's one solution, but not necessarily one we should always use without considering other options.

Taking inspiration from the past

The problem of handling extreme scale differences in a chart is not a new problem and has led to some remarkably creative solutions throughout the history of data visualisation.

The US sociologist W.E.B. Du Bois produced a series of outstanding charts as part of his ground-breaking contribution to the 1900 Paris Exposition. Among the many visualisations Du Bois created to draw attention to, and highlight the progress of, African Americans in the USA, plate 11 is worth particular attention.

The chart shows the number of Black Americans living in urban and rural settings. Depicting just four data points, the chances are you won't have seen another chart like it. In fact, it seems less a chart and more like a work of modern art.

The dominant red spiral representing those living in "the country and villages" likely catches your attention first. But it probably doesn't lead you to make an instant *size* comparison with the smaller, linear segments that reflect those living in cities; that comparison is secondary to the primary challenge of decoding the beautiful graphic's visual form.

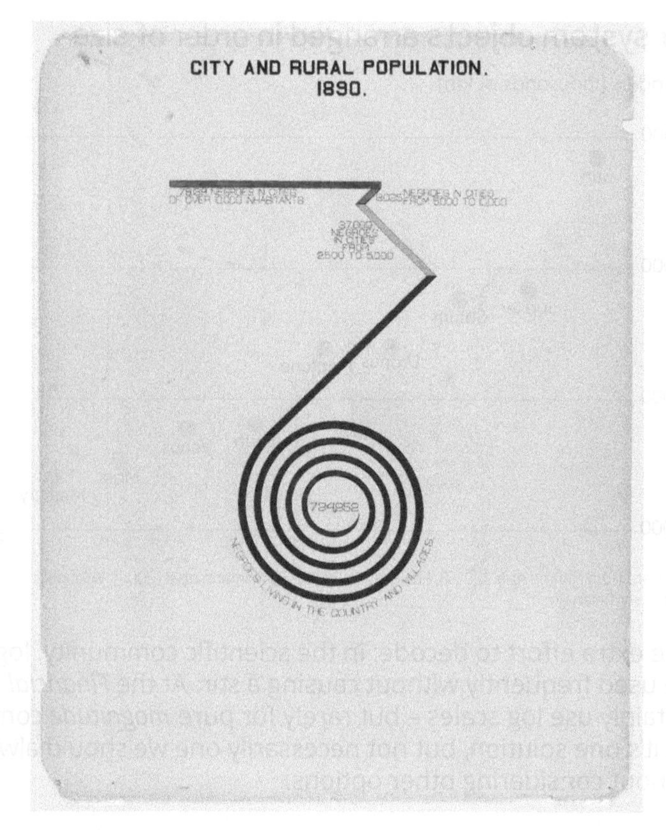

Source: Library of Congress, see: https://www.loc.gov/item/2013650430

Here's a bar chart version of the same numbers Du Bois charted.

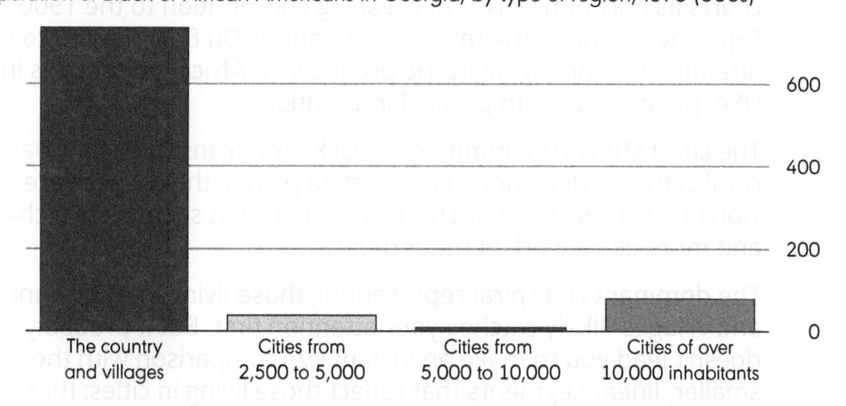

Geometrically precise and easier to understand than the original – but would it make you linger as long studying it, or consider framing in a gallery? I suspect not. The uniqueness of Plate 11 is part of its appeal; it wasn't designed to be a replacement for every over-stretched, over-used bar chart.

Snakeplot

A more routinely practical solution is shown in an English dictionary from 1912. A series of charts depict global trade and production figures for different countries of the world. Values that are too big to fit on the axis start again and build over into multiple rows. Under "coffee production", notice how Brazil needs six rows, yet Hawaii is hardly out of the starting blocks on its only row.

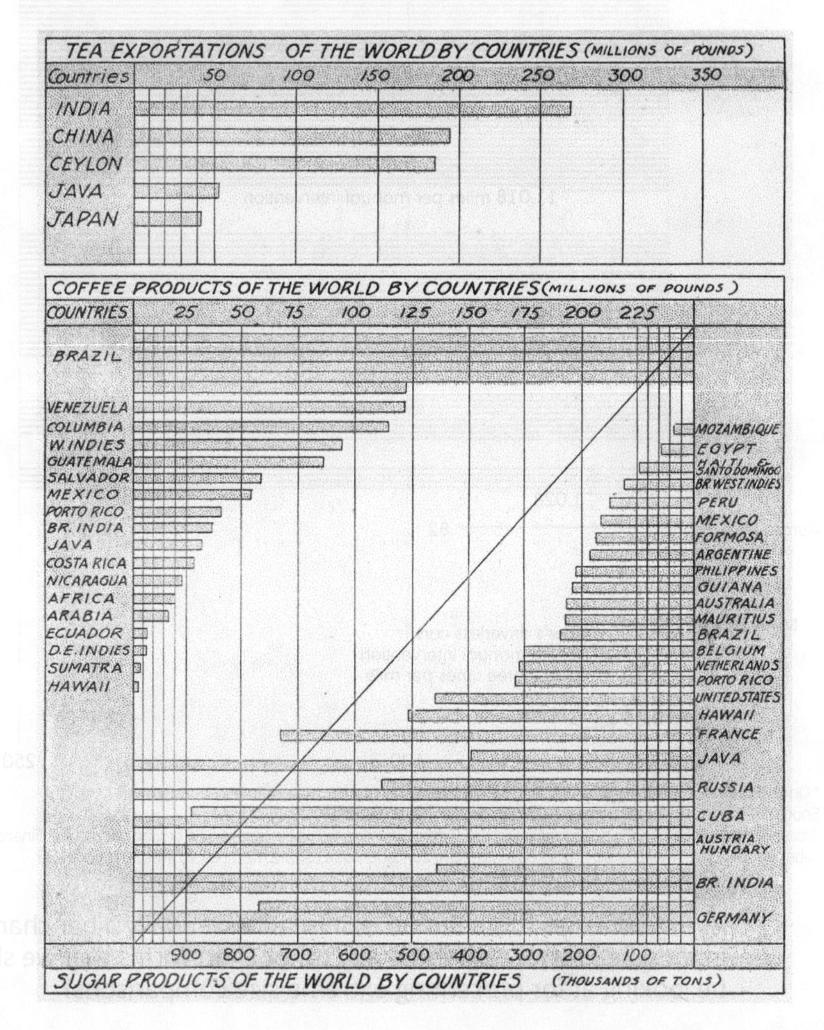

It's a simple and clever solution, and one that we've used at the *Financial Times* very recently. In this example, which visualises the distance that self-driving vehicles can travel without human intervention, the linear form of the bars is a perfect visual analogy to the data being portrayed – journeys along a road.

Waymo's autonomous vehicles require fewer manual interventions than any other driverless car manufacturer. Uber's self-driving cars need the most help

Number of miles travelled* per driver intervention, December 2017 - November 2018

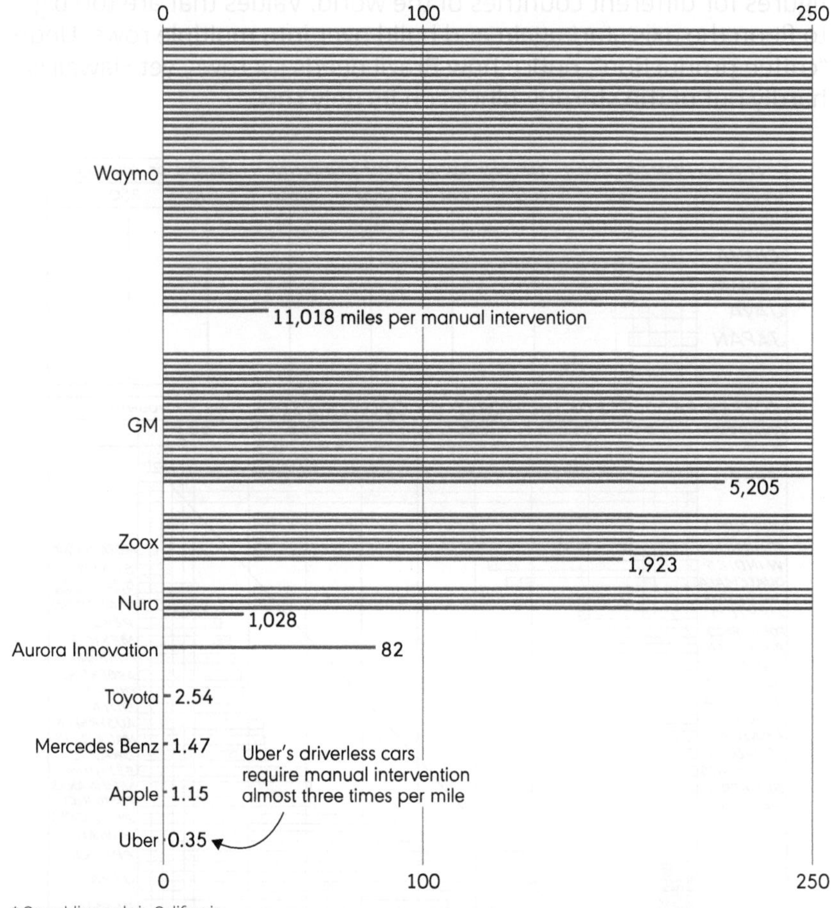

* On public roads in California
Source: Data from State of California Department of Motor Vehicles
Graphic: John Burn-Murdoch appeared in Richard Waters, Waymo builds big lead in self-driving car testing, Financial Times, February 24,2019. Available at: https://www.ft.com/content/7c8e1d02-2ff2-11e9-8744-e7016697f225

As ingenious as this solution is, it is still essentially a bar chart, albeit in modified form – are there any other chart forms that we should be looking at for presenting extreme size comparisons?

Proportional symbol chart

Here's another look at our celestial neighbours, this time using *proportional symbols* to represent magnitude.

Planets arranged in order of size

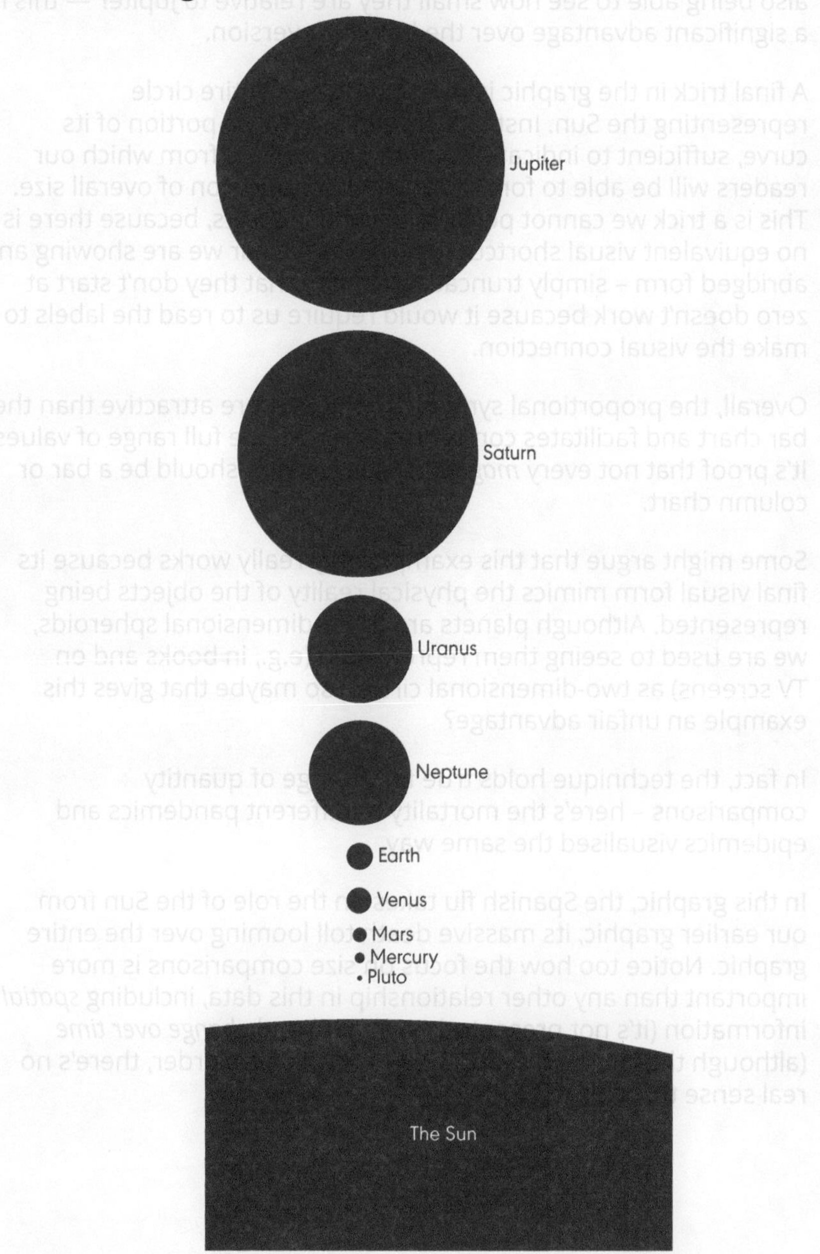

Sources: Nimmo et al (2017); Emilio et al (2012); Seidelmann et al (2007); Wikipedia. Used by permission from Alan Smith

Proportional symbol charts use area (a two-dimensional property) to show quantity. Although it is more difficult to see fine differences in data in two dimensions, it brings the considerable advantage of being space efficient, while still allowing us to see *relative* differences. Importantly, in our solar system example, we can make comparisons between the sizes of Pluto, Mars and Mercury, while also being able to see how small they are relative to Jupiter — this is a significant advantage over the bar chart version.

A final trick in the graphic is to not show the entire circle representing the Sun. Instead, we can use only a portion of its curve, sufficient to indicate its looming presence from which our readers will be able to form a projected impression of overall size. This is a trick we cannot perform using bar charts, because there is no equivalent visual shortcut that makes it clear we are showing an abridged form – simply truncating axes so that they don't start at zero doesn't work because it would require us to read the labels to make the visual connection.

Overall, the proportional symbol graphic is more attractive than the bar chart and facilitates comparisons across the full range of values. It's proof that not every *magnitude* comparison should be a bar or column chart.

Some might argue that this example only really works because its final visual form mimics the physical reality of the objects being represented. Although planets are three-dimensional spheroids, we are used to seeing them represented (e.g., in books and on TV screens) as two-dimensional circles, so maybe that gives this example an unfair advantage?

In fact, the technique holds true for a range of quantity comparisons – here's the mortality of different pandemics and epidemics visualised the same way.

In this graphic, the Spanish flu takes on the role of the Sun from our earlier graphic, its massive death toll looming over the entire graphic. Notice too how the focus on size comparisons is more important than any other relationship in this data, including *spatial* information (it's not presented on a map) and *change over time* (although the circles are loosely in chronological order, there's no real sense that this is a timeline).

Putting coronavirus in context

Death toll worldwide (total number of deaths represents multiple years)

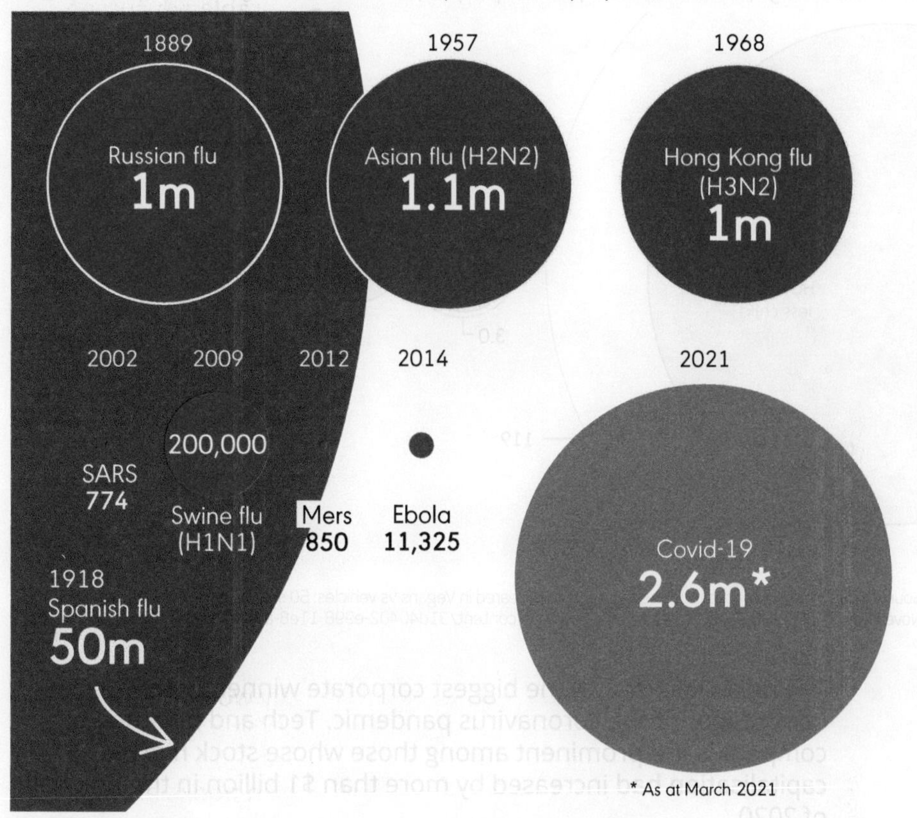

Sources: Graphic: Liz Faunce Sources: Data from University of Maryland; CDC; WHO; Johns Hopkins appeared in From plague to polio: how do pandemics end?
Available at: https://www.ft.com/content/4eabdc7a-f8e1-48d5-9592-05441493f652

Here's another example, this time comparing the emissions savings that would result from making different personal lifestyle adjustments. A bar chart would make it very difficult for us to make visual comparisons between 119 tonnes of CO2 and 0.1 tonne as this graphic does.

All these proportional symbol chart examples have essentially laid our information out sequentially (in size or date order) – but the organisation of our circles can also be more sophisticated, bringing with it the possibility of introducing more data relationships from the Visual Vocabulary.

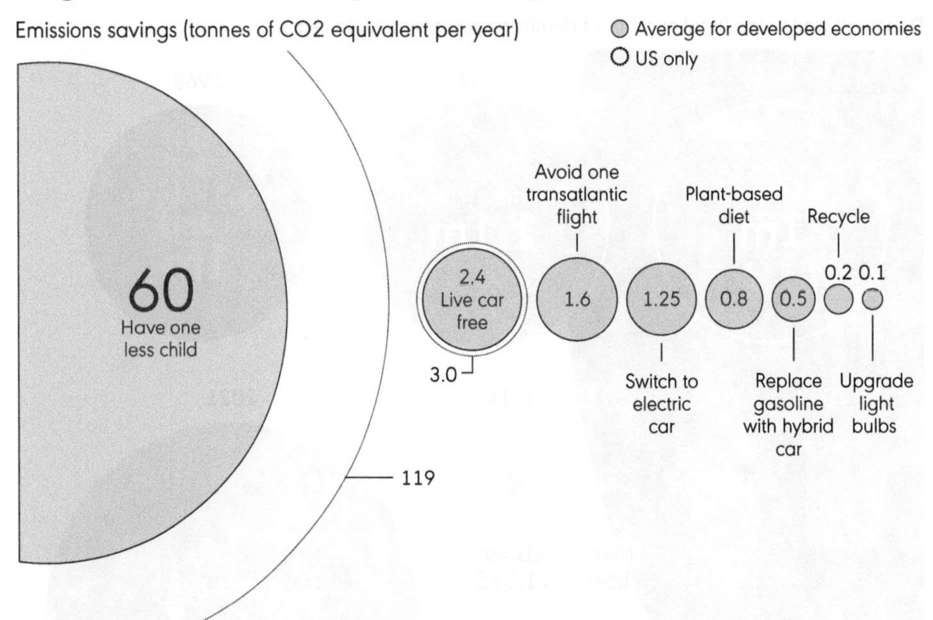

Source: Data from Environmental Research Letters appeared in Vegans vs vehicles: 50 shades of green, Financial Times, November 16, 2018. Available at: https://www.ft.com/content/31d40402-e998-11e8-a34c-663b3f553b35

The next chart shows the biggest corporate winners from the early stages of the coronavirus pandemic. Tech and healthcare companies are prominent among those whose stock market capitalisation had increased by more than $1 billion in the first half of 2020.

The graphic uses what's known as a "circle packing" layout, with each group of circles organised into its market sector. This hierarchical arrangement means we can see a "*part-to-whole*" relationship, with the number and size of companies in each sector allowing us to make magnitude comparisons across and within the sectors.

To help with these comparisons, note that the companies within each sector circle are laid out in size order, as are the sectors themselves (biggest sectors in the centre, smallest to the outside), aiding understanding with a gentle *ranking* treatment.

This graphic also carries another advantage over a bar or column chart. There are over 800 companies shown, with 25 labelled – the space efficiency of our circle packing layout allows us to include far more information than a traditional bar or column chart would in the same space.

Big tech companies lead stock market winners

Companies with net market cap gain of more than $1bn in 2020, by sector.
Circle size shows market cap added YTD*, top 100 highlighted, top 25 labelled

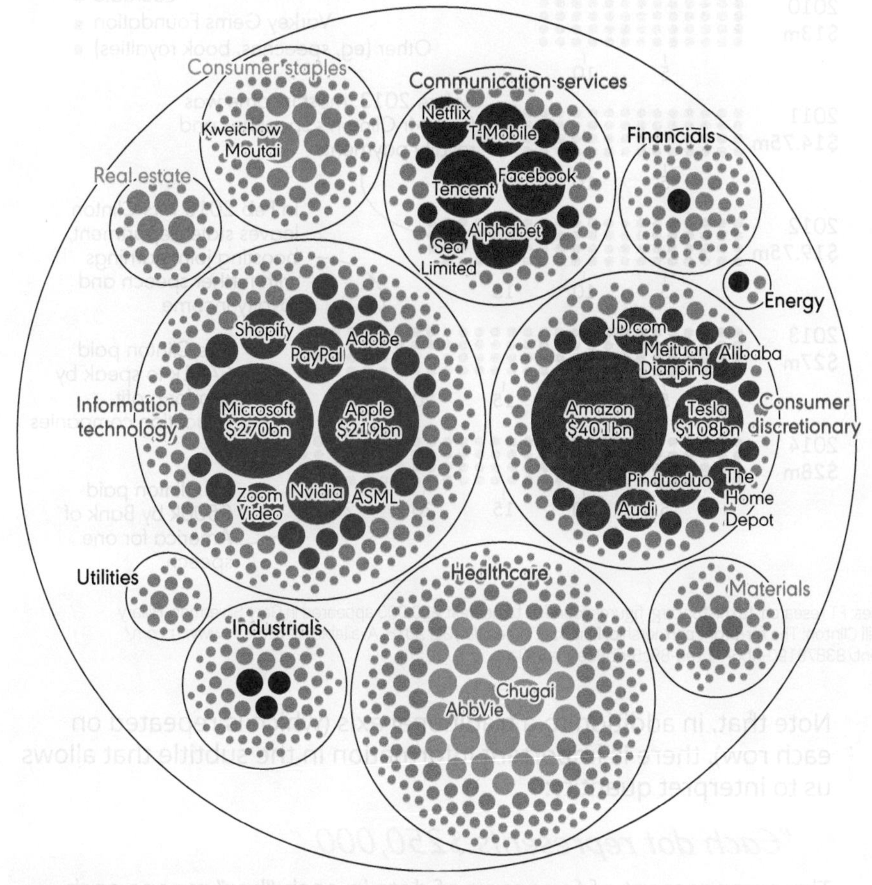

* As at Jun 17
Source: Capital IQ appeared in Chris Nuttall, Tech prospers in the pandemic, Financial Times, June19, 2020. Available at: https://www.ft.com/content/a157d303-01ac-4a9b-af2d-d6ffbc3593c2

Grouped symbol chart

Another example of using circles – or, more precisely, dots – to represent quantity comes from a story looking at how Bill and Hillary Clinton's income rose considerably once they were out of public office.

While compiling information on their incomes, interesting information emerged on fees for individual speeches that the Clintons had made. A *grouped symbol chart* works much like a regular bar chart but allows us to highlight and annotate some of these individual speeches as part of the Clintons' income.

Better off out of office: the Clintons' rising income

Adjusted gross income ($m), each dot represents $250,000

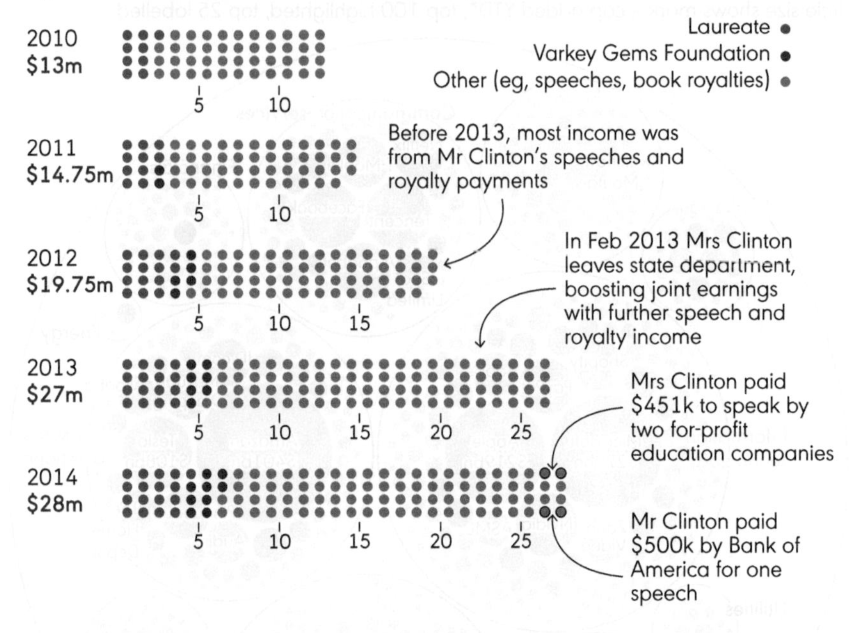

Sources: FT research, taxhistory.org, figures rounded to nearest 250,000 appeared in Gary Silverman, Hillary and Bill Clinton: The for-profit partnership, Financial Times, July21, 2016. Available at: https://www.ft.com/content/83878190-4b64-11e6-88c5-db83e98a590a

Note that, in addition to a traditional axis (which is repeated on each row), there is important information in the subtitle that allows us to interpret quantity:

> *"Each dot represents $250,000."*

The arrangement of four rows of dots in each "bar" means each individual column of dots represents $1 million. The regular year-on-year increases in the columns of dots play an effective part in showing the Clintons' income as it *changes over time*.

Isotype (pictogram)

Our *grouped symbol chart* is a form of *pictogram*, a type of graphic that uses repeating icons to show quantity. These were integral to the Isotype (International system of typographic picture education) method of statistical communication conceived in 1920s Vienna by Otto Neurath, Gerd Arntz and Marie Reidemeister (later Marie Neurath).

The pictograms were hugely influential — and deceptively sophisticated. Take the following graphic on Home and Factory Weaving in England from 1820 to 1880.

Home and Factory Weaving in England

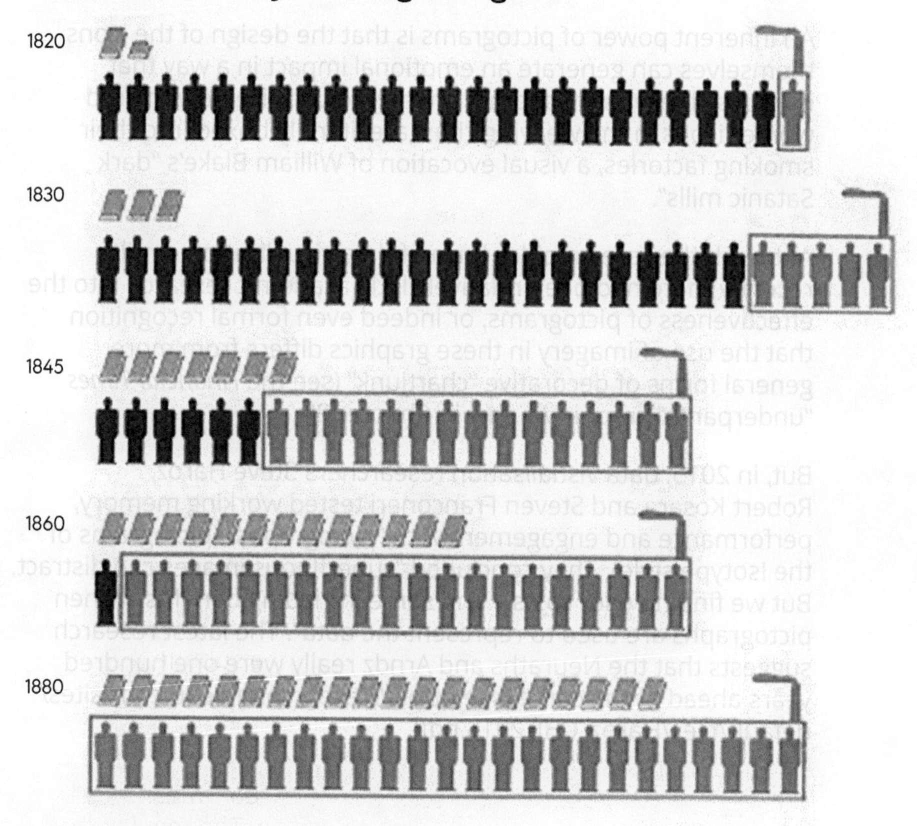

Each blue symbol represents 50 million pounds total production
Each black man symbol represents 10,000 home weavers
Each red man symbol represents 10,000 factory weavers

The graphic shows multiple *magnitude* comparisons – the key tells us that each blue symbol represents 50 million pounds total production, while differently-coloured human forms denote 10,000 home and factory weavers respectively. But study the picture for a short while and other relationships from the Visual Vocabulary soon emerge.

In addition to *magnitude*, the graphic depicts a *part-to-whole* relationship by contrasting differing proportions of home and factory weaving. It also shows how this proportion *changed over time*, along with the progression in output from less than 100 million pounds of total production in 1820 to 1,000 million pounds by 1880.

An inherent power of pictograms is that the design of the icons themselves can generate an emotional impact in a way that is impossible with most other chart types. Notice how the red worker icons in the weaving chart are literally boxed into their smoking factories, a visual evocation of William Blake's "dark Satanic mills".

Although they are an older form of data visualisation, until recently there had been relatively little academic research into the effectiveness of pictograms, or indeed even formal recognition that the use of imagery in these graphics differs from more general forms of decorative "chartjunk" (see the *Financial Times* "underpants" graphic we saw in Chapter 2).

But, in 2015, data visualisation researchers Steve Haroz, Robert Kosara and Steven Franconeri tested working memory, performance and engagement with "pictographs" (pictograms of the Isotype style). They concluded "superfluous images can distract. But we find no user costs – and some intriguing benefits – when pictographs are used to represent the data". The latest research suggests that the Neuraths and Arndz really were one hundred years ahead of the curve (see https://research.tableau.com/sites/default/files/Haroz_CHI_2015.pdf).

Paired bar chart

When a bar chart is extended to accommodate two or more series, the result is known as a *paired bar chart*. For each category, there are multiple bars, usually distinguished by colour. Here's an example that shows the proportion of people in 14 countries who believe that global climate change and the spread of infectious diseases are a major threat.

Global majority see climate change as major threat

% of people who consider the following a major threat to their country

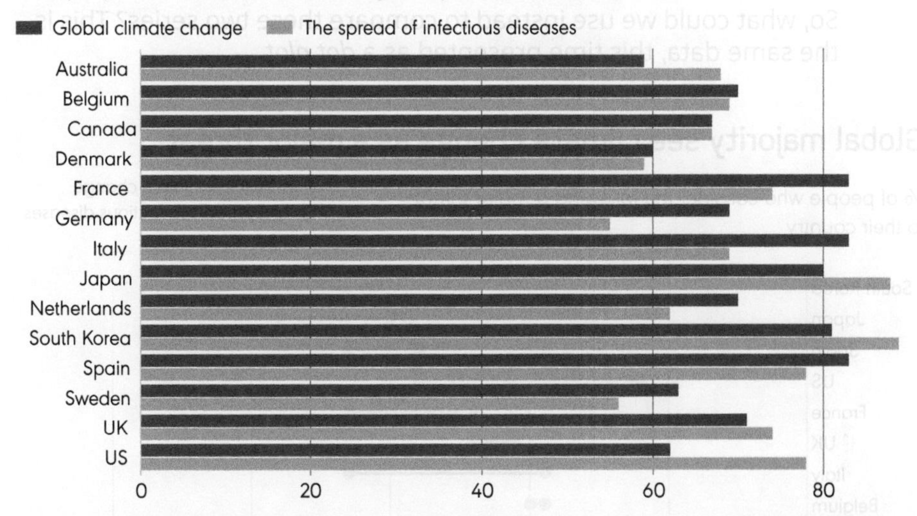

Source: Pew Research Center, Summer 2020 Global Attitudes Survey appeared in Climate change and disease at forefront of global anxieties by Alan Smith APRIL 2 2021. Available at: https://www.ft.com/content/f19afda4-d848-45ae-aebf-6c3e30737c8e

We know how to read basic bar charts, so surely adding one extra series shouldn't really create many problems? In fact, as part of a broader category of charts that are already overused, the paired variety is in a league of its own – it's frequently not the right type of chart to use. Let's examine why.

Of course, it doesn't help that this chart is sorted in alphabetical rather than numerical order, creating a range of jagged peaks that make it difficult to see patterns in the data. But it goes beyond that.

Try and concentrate just on the darker bars (climate change) and read up and down the chart to compare values. It's quite difficult, because our visual focus keeps being interrupted by the paler bars lying in between.

Similarly, comparing the values for an individual country is tricky. Our eyes must navigate a densely packed forest of rectangles to pick out the values we're interested in. And with the labels for the bars on the far left and the ends of the bars that we want to compare on the far right, it's hard to confirm that our eyes have settled on the right pair of bars.

Finally, looking at the graphic overall, notice how the parallel stripes created by the tightly packed bars on the left of the chart catch your eye more than the ends of the bars (the part of the chart we're most interested in). Most of this chart's real estate is dominated by what's not different in the numbers.

Dot plot revisited

So, what could we use instead to compare these two series? This is the same data, this time presented as a *dot plot*.

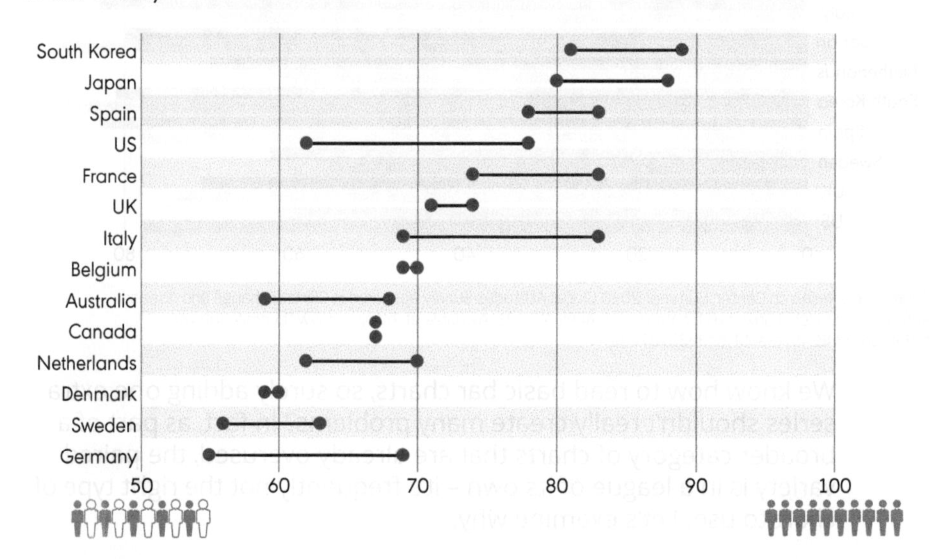

Source: Pew Research Center, Summer 2020 Global Attitudes Survey appeared in Climate change and disease at forefront of global anxieties. Available at: https://www.ft.com/content/f19afda4-d848-45ae-aebf-6c3e30737c8e

This chart instantly seems easier on the eye than our paired bar chart. Let's take a moment to understand why.

First, look at how the symbology has changed. Dot plots use small shapes – in this case, circles – to denote a value on an axis. For our two series, we use two different colours, and connect them with a line, which helps with readability. Where two values are identical, as is the case with Canada, they would be obscured, so we can just nudge the circles outwards in opposite directions so they can both be seen. Subtle alternating background shading helps us read across the chart.

The data is no longer arranged alphabetically, but clearly sorted in order of the pink dots (those who believe the spread of infectious diseases is a major threat). Combined with clearer symbology, comparisons are now easier to make.

Notice how the US now stands out – concern there for climate change is much lower than infectious disease. At some 16 percentage points, it's the biggest "concern gap" on the chart. We could hardly see that on the paired bar chart. Similarly, Italy catches our attention – but for the opposite reason. Far more people there believe climate change is a major threat compared to infectious disease.

Making comparisons *across* the countries is also better now. Following the pattern of pink or blue dots up and down the chart is far easier than scanning the spiky rectangles of our paired bar chart.

Finally, notice that the chart's axis doesn't start at zero – we've zoomed in to the range of the data. Trusty pictograms help us to understand the ratios involved in the comparison. The chart begins at 50 per cent – half of all people – while the far right of the chart is where a country would be, if everyone agreed that something posed a threat.

Picturing quantity

The power of illustrative elements to add both aesthetic appeal and functional purpose to size comparisons isn't restricted to just pictograms. We can fuse them with our overused, unloved bar chart to breathe new life into it.

Graphic: Paul McCallum, Sources: FT research; Dreamstime appeared in Hugh Carnegy, Wish I were there: the glory of California's redwoods, Financial Times, October 21, 2020. Available at: https://www.ft.com/content/0cd7146c-374a-4240-8a02-a5b3fabd98d0

In this chart of comparative heights, the use of illustration not only makes the graphic more attractive, but it also brings a practical benefit – not many readers will need to read the labels to understand which objects are being compared. This is in part due to the iconic nature of the selected landmarks, this technique always benefiting from being used with the most easily recognisable shapes.

This use of illustration, as with pictograms, does not constitute chartjunk because it helps us understand the data, rather than distract. A simple bar chart of the same data strips away the aesthetic joy – and means the resulting chart is instantly forgettable.

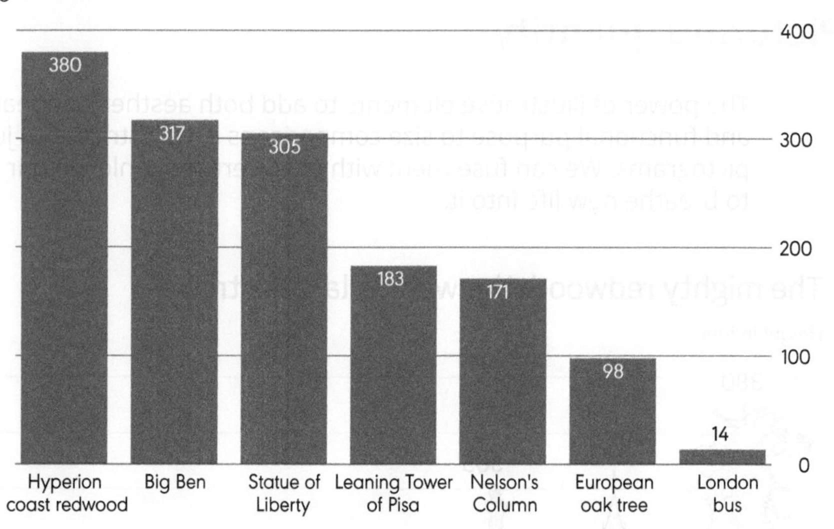

Sources: FT research, Dreamstime appeared in Hugh Carnegy, Wish I were there: the glory of California's redwoods, Financial Times, October 21, 2020. Available at: https://www.ft.com/content/0cd7146c-374a-4240-8a02-a5b3fabd98d0

Last, another graphic reveals itself to be a *magnitude* comparison just by its title alone – *How far droplets travel*. Once again, illustration provides a powerful vehicle for what could have been a simple bar chart of just three numbers.

A human silhouette, combined with oversized projected droplets, convincingly explains why sneezing is more likely than coughing to bring you pariah status.

How far droplets travel

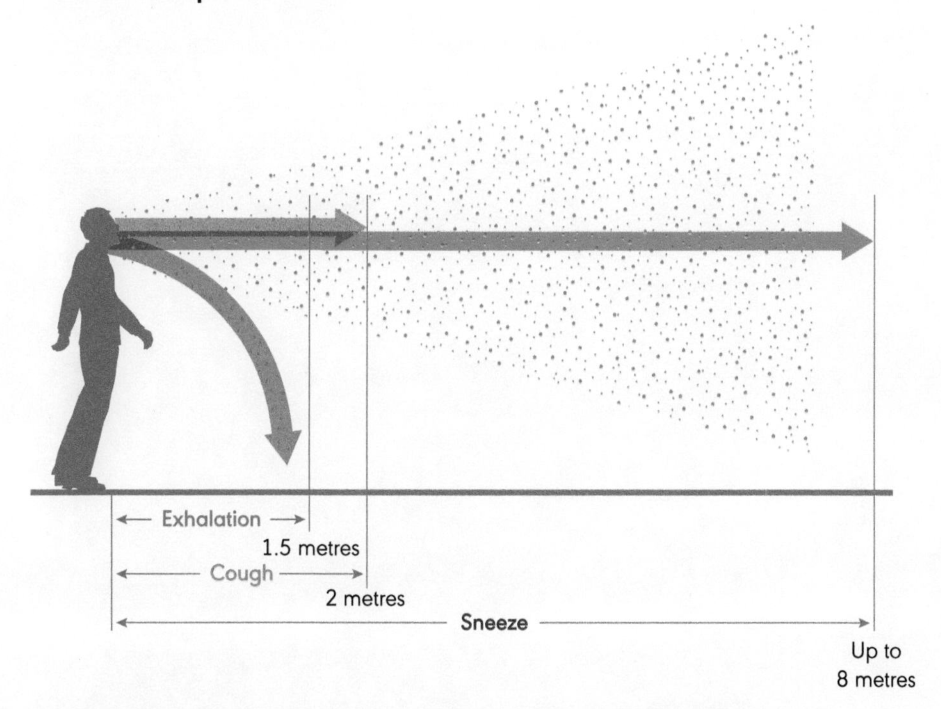

Graphic: Graham Parrish, Sources: MIT; FT research appeared in Michael Peel, Lifesaver or false protection: do face masks stop coronavirus?, Financial Times, April 3, 2020. Available at: https://www.ft.com/content/64ac8848-a005-466a-bc93-fb1e38b19182

5

Charts of change over time

Charts that give emphasis to changing trends. These can be short (intra-day) movements or extended series traversing decades or centuries: choosing the correct time period is important to provide suitable context for the reader.

By any measure, William Playfair's life was remarkable. Largely forgotten following his death in 1823, a recent revival of interest in the Scotsman has been capped by a fine biography from Bruce Berkowitz that paints details of a life less ordinary: a famous engineer's draftsman who stormed the Bastille; a political economist and secret agent who masterminded a counterfeiting operation; an inmate of a debtor's prison who also invented line, bar and pie charts.

Playfair introduced line charts to the world in *The Commercial and Political Atlas* (1786), a work that marks the beginning of what we would today recognise as modern data visualisation.

Describing the benefit of his new charts, Playfair wrote that they united "proportion, progression, and quantity, all under one simple impression of vision, and consequently one act of memory". Looking at this example from the Atlas, which clearly – and beautifully – shows England's changing trade patterns with Denmark and Norway across the eighteenth century, it's difficult not to agree.

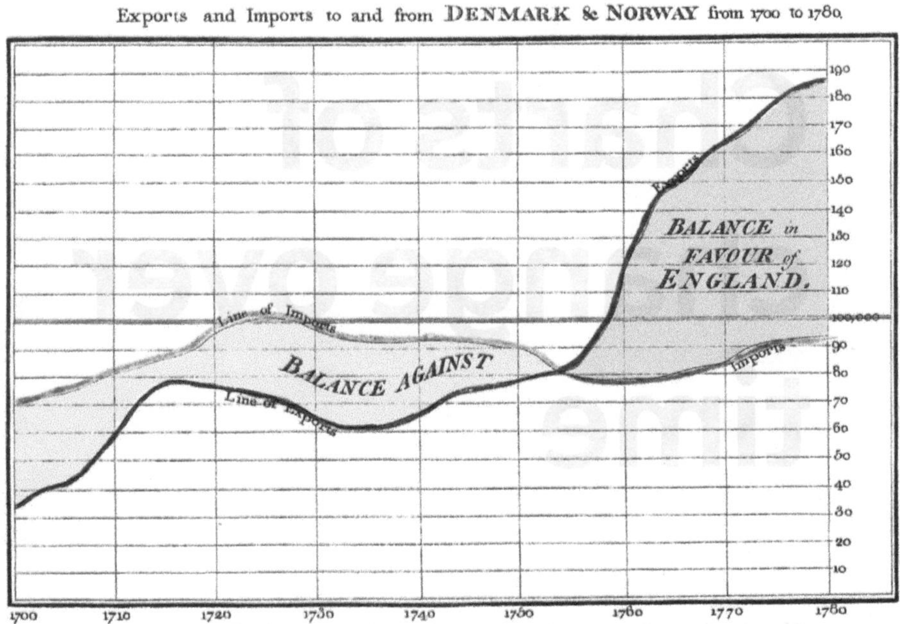

The Bottom line is divided into Years, the Right hand line into L10,000 each.

The brilliance of Playfair's work is reflected in its longevity – modern audiences will be familiar with how to read his line charts because their basic design remains in daily use, essentially unchanged, more than two centuries after their first appearance.

A horizontal (x) axis shows the progression of time from left to right, while a vertical (y) axis denotes a measurable quantity. One or more lines are plotted across the chart, each representing a data "series" (data that tracks a measured value changing over time).

Playfair may not have been the most talented draftsman (as a youthful assistant to James Watt, he received less than glowing reviews from his esteemed employer), but outstanding design details mean his line charts remain arguably more elegant and readable than most of its descendants produced today. Let's examine why.

First, there's no legend on Playfair's chart. Instead, the lines are labelled directly, with text that closely tracks the undulations of the unfolding data. As a result, there is no ambiguity in what the numbers represent – and less of a burden on the reader's working memory.

Next, notice that while the graphic appears to show only two variables (imports and exports), Playfair's use of text and shading between the two lines reveals an important third variable: the balance of trade, and whether it was in favour of England or Denmark/Norway.

Both techniques remain incredibly useful in the *Financial Times* newsroom. In the following example, shading means we can readily spot surpluses and deficits in UK Government finances (much like Playfair's trade chart). Meanwhile, the addition of coloured lines and shading to show election manifesto pledges at the time of the 2017 general election allows us to understand contrasting plans for the years ahead; the Conservatives aimed to reduce the deficit through a reduction in expenditure, while Labour proposed both higher spending and receipts, with a larger overall deficit.

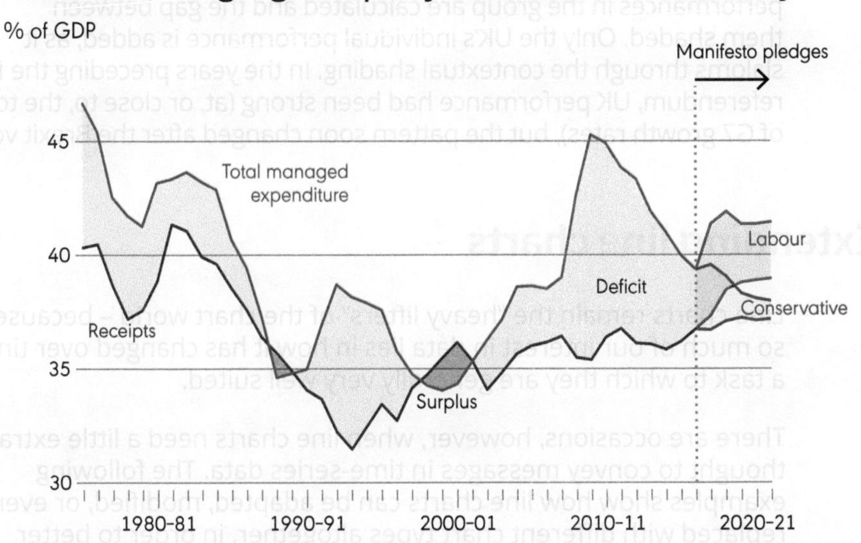

Source: IFS appeared in Tories seek wriggle room on spending as Hammond sticks to austerity by Gemma Tetlow, Jim Pickard and George Parker, June 21, 2017. Available at: https://www.ft.com/content/5d94202c-55c9-11e7-80b6-9bfa4c1f83d2

You might expect a line chart comparing the UK's economic performance with its G7 peers to feature seven lines. But Playfair-inspired treatments can allow us to reduce complexity.

Reversal of fortune: since the EU referendum, strong growth relative to other G7 economies has tailed off

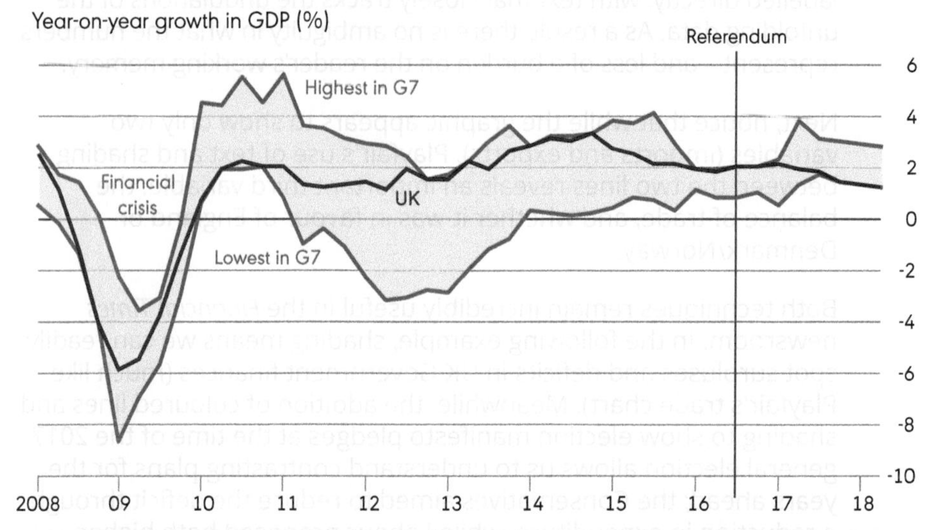

Graphic Alan Smith, Chris Giles; Source: IMF appeared in Chris Giles, The UK economy since the Brexit vote — in 6 charts, Financial Times, October 11, 2018. Available at: https://www.ft.com/content/cf51e840-7147-11e7-93ff-99f383b09ff9

Rather than show all the data for all countries, highest and lowest performances in the group are calculated and the gap between them shaded. Only the UK's individual performance is added, as it slaloms through the contextual shading. In the years preceding the EU referendum, UK performance had been strong (at, or close to, the top of G7 growth rates), but the pattern soon changed after the Brexit vote.

Extending line charts

Line charts remain the "heavy lifters" of the chart world – because so much of our interest in data lies in how it has changed over time, a task to which they are generally very well suited.

There are occasions, however, when line charts need a little extra thought to convey messages in time-series data. The following examples show how line charts can be adapted, modified, or even replaced with different chart types altogether, in order to better understand how the world is changing.

Zoom for detail

Sometimes, the part of a chart that we most want to focus on occupies only a small part of a graphic's overall display area. Yet cropping the chart to show just the area of interest would lose valuable context. In this case, a good solution is to use an inset chart for the full-time series, while using the main chart area for the detail.

The main portion of this chart shows a surge in UK Government debt since the financial crisis, compounded by the Covid-19 pandemic. With debt more than 100 per cent of GDP, the level seems unprecedented – and it is in recent decades. But the inset – known to some in the *FT* newsroom as a "Cocco loupe" – reveals that it still has some way to rise until it matches figures seen during, and immediately after, the two world wars.

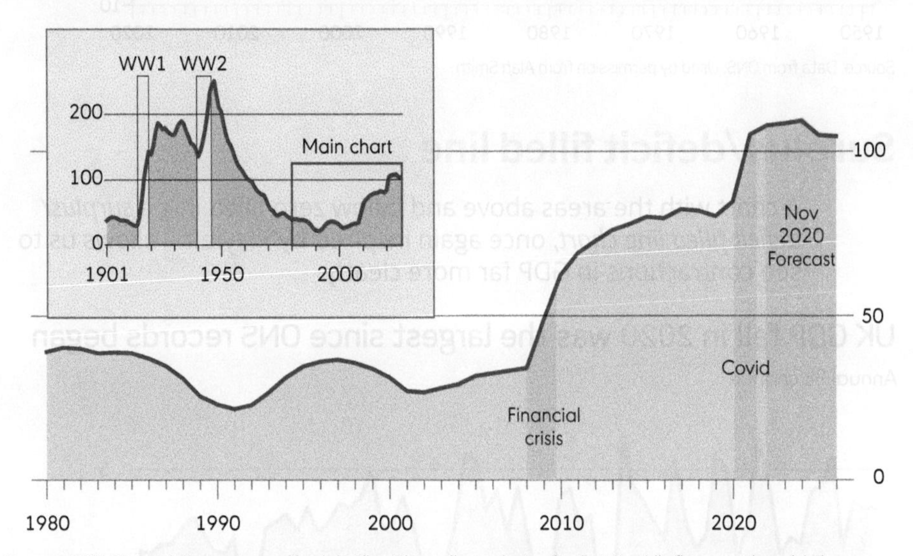

Sources: OBR; FT calculations appeared in Chris Giles, Chancellor navigates fragile UK public finances, Financial Times, March2, 2021. Available at: https://www.ft.com/content/0e48c8ab-e3b4-404f-8776-d9a42df27ce1

Handling negativity

Line charts can be problematic when the data being plotted falls either side of zero. Often, as with this chart of the UK's economic performance over the past 70 years, we are just as interested in whether something grew or contracted – as we are the numeric difference between one figure and the next.

This chart of UK GDP is not wrong, but it doesn't make important economic contractions shout as loudly as we would like, despite the zero line being more pronounced than the other axis lines.

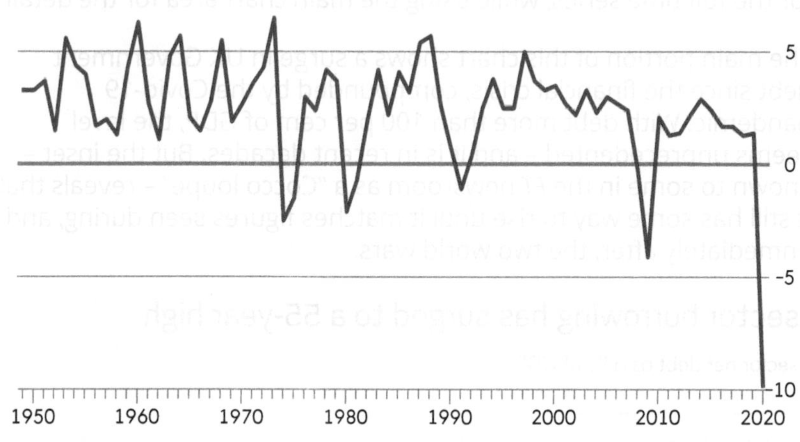

Source: Data from ONS. Used by permission from Alan Smith

Surplus/deficit filled line

A chart with the areas above and below zero filled in – a *surplus/deficit filled line chart*, once again inspired by Playfair – allows us to see contractions in GDP far more clearly.

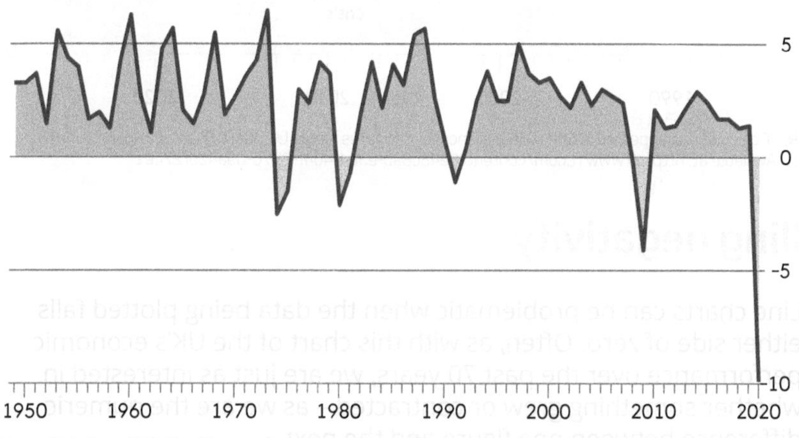

Source: Data from ONS. Used by permission from Alan Smith

Diverging column chart

In this example, an even better solution is to use columns to show the data. They draw readers' eyes to the contractions, especially with a highlight colour applied. And notice how much easier it is to read and compare values for individual years compared with the surplus-deficit filled line chart.

UK GDP fall in 2020 was the largest since ONS records began

Annual % change

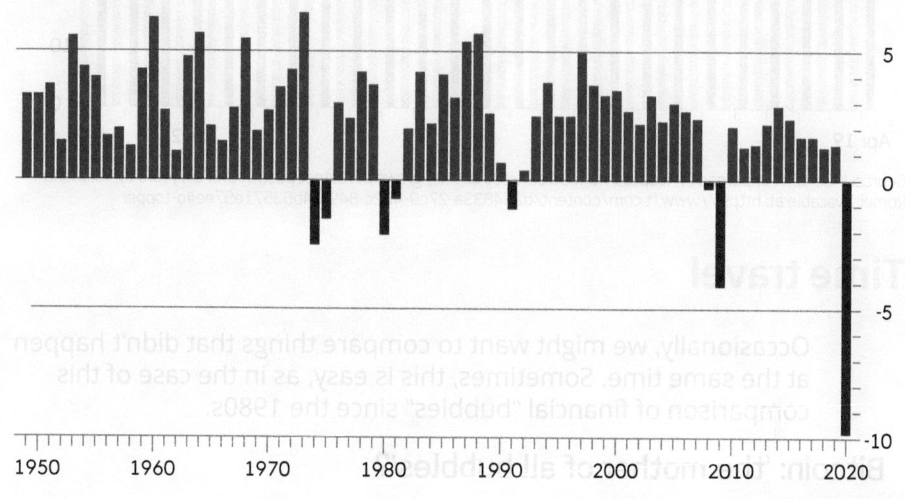

Source: Data from ONS. Used by permission from Alan Smith

However, using columns for time series data is a technique to be used sparingly. Data should be relatively sparse (if the above chart showed quarterly rather than annual data over the same period, the columns would simply be too thin) and the fewer data series the better (ideally just one).

As an example of what not to do, most readers would find this chart of European manufacturing and services activity a tough read. With multiple series of columns competing for attention, focusing on any one series to understand how it changes over time is extremely difficult.

Eurozone expansion gathers pace as manufacturing enjoys record boom

Purchasing managers' index (above 50 = a majority of businesses reported expansion in activity)

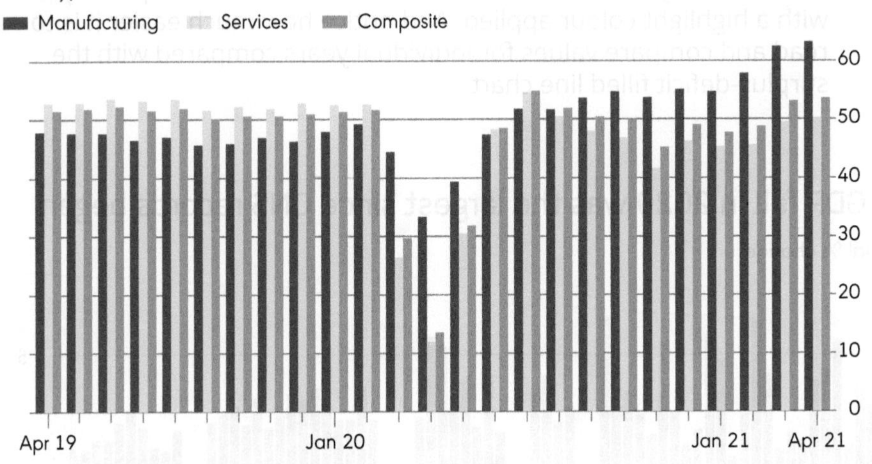

Source: IHS Markit apperead in Adapted from UK services activity grows at fastest pace in over six years by Valentina Romei. Available at: https://www.ft.com/content/b254833a-27c9-482c-8492-4b63571e57ee#o-topper

Time travel

Occasionally, we might want to compare things that didn't happen at the same time. Sometimes, this is easy, as in the case of this comparison of financial "bubbles" since the 1980s.

Bitcoin: 'the mother of all bubbles'?

% change from trough

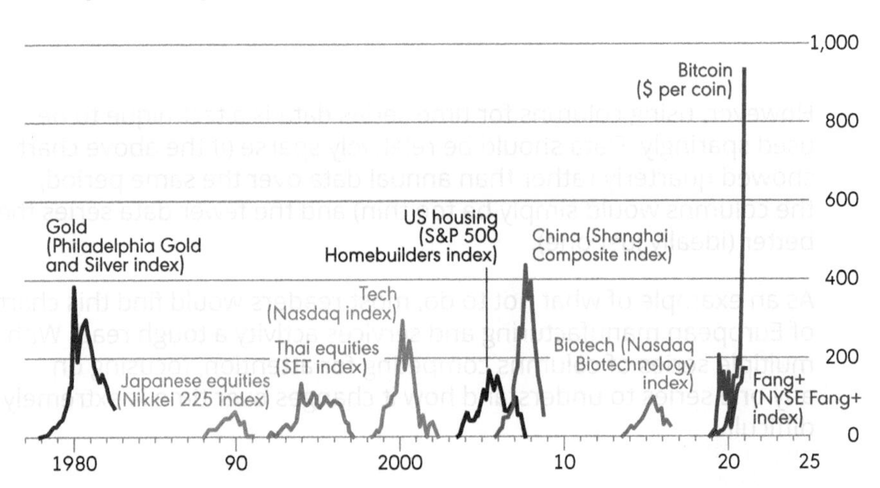

Sources: BofA Global Investment Strategy; Bloomberg appearead in Eva Szalay, Bitcoin's wild ride leaves traditional money managers queasy, Financial Times, January13, 2021.Available at: https://www.ft.com/content/0746e3c6-9177-4fcd-91bb-e427aa9f9267

With most financial "bubbles" (lines) sitting neatly in their own space on the timeline, direct labels and a splash of colour are all we need to produce a readable chart. However, what if the events we want to compare happened so far apart that it would be impossible to compare them directly on the same timeline?

Small multiple timelines

The answer, as in this comparison of energy sources from different eras, is to split the chart into multiple timelines, which eliminates the gaps in between the events we want to compare.

Rather than splitting the data into different charts entirely, keeping a single y (vertical) axis unifies the comparison, allowing us to see how peak natural gas was proportionally lower than peak oil, which was proportionally lower than peak coal. The low, single dot for modern renewables allows us to see how much progress is required for a greener energy future.

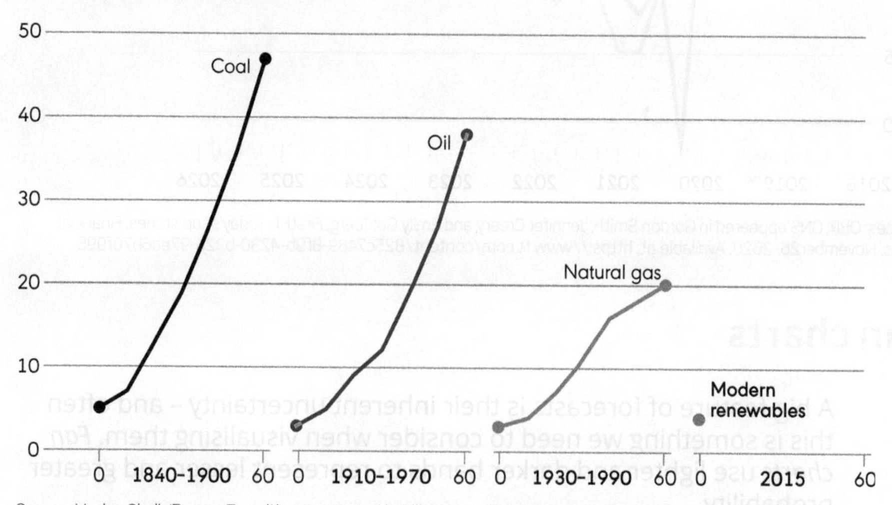

Source: Vaclav Simil, 'Energy Transitions appeared in Bill Gates, Bill Gates: My green manifesto, Financial Times, Febraury19, 2021. Available at: https://www.ft.com/content/c11bb885-1274-4677-ba05-fcbac67dc808
Graphic: Steven Bernard

Projections

In fact, understanding data that is yet to happen is a unique challenge of its own. Forecasts allow us to see different pathways into the future – and it's yet another occasion where Playfair-style shading can help. In this chart of possible economic recoveries from the impact of Covid-19, the gap between optimistic and pessimistic scenarios from the UK's Office for Budget Responsibility (OBR) is shaded, with a central forecast denoted in lipstick-bright pink. The pre-pandemic March 2020 forecast and actual figures recorded in 2020 are also shown, providing valuable context about the possible long-term economic impact of the coronavirus.

Covid-19's economic impact in the UK will last far into this decade

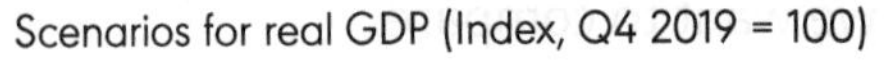

Scenarios for real GDP (Index, Q4 2019 = 100)

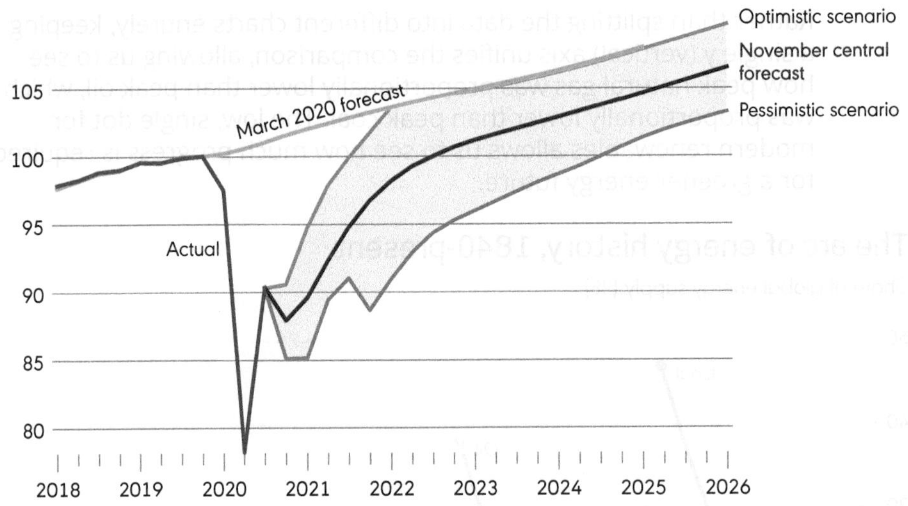

Sources: OBR; ONS appeared in Gordon Smith, Jennifer Creery and Emily Goldberg, FirstFT: Today's top stories, Financial Times, November26, 2020. Available at: https://www.ft.com/content/825c7489-8f9b-4230-b326-97eb6b70f995

Fan charts

A big feature of forecasts is their inherent uncertainty – and often this is something we need to consider when visualising them. *Fan charts* use lighter and darker bands to represent lesser and greater probability.

The bands in this inflation forecast chart cover 90 per cent probability between them. It's a useful way of understanding the nuances of what might happen – particularly because human perception of risk and probability is demonstrably problematic and in need of all the help it can get.

Measurement problems may make it harder to forecast inflation

Consumer price index and February 2021 projections (% change on a year earlier)

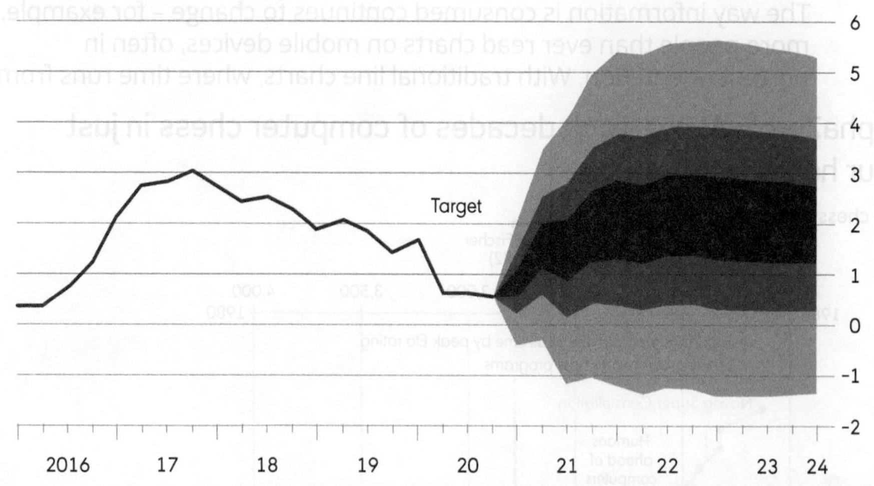

Central darker band and pairs of lighter bands each account for 30% of probability

Source: Bank of England appeared in Delphine Strauss, Why the UK inflation risk after lockdown is hard to assess, Financial Times, March15, 2021. Available at: https://www.ft.com/content/6925a0bb-f233-4a86-8556-6d03dee23dc0

Hedgehog chart

As a chart reader, it's also worth remembering that, in many cases, central forecasts will miss their mark. This hedgehog chart pokes just a little fun at historically over-optimistic forecasts for UK productivity produced by the OBR.

In November the OBR radically changed its productivity outlook

Output per hour (non-oil), outturn and successive OBR forecasts (Q1 2009 = 100)

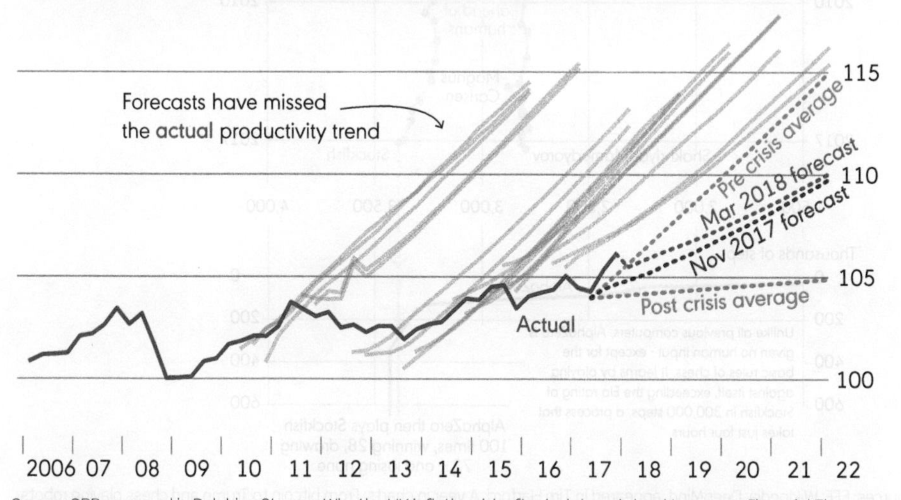

Source: OBR appeared in Delphine Strauss, Why the UK inflation risk after lockdown is hard to assess, Financial Times, March15, 2021. Available at: https://www.ft.com/content/6925a0bb-f233-4a86-8556-6d03dee23dc0

Vertical timeline

The way information is consumed continues to change – for example, more people than ever read charts on mobile devices, often in portrait orientation. With traditional line charts, where time runs from

AlphaZero's AI overtook decades of computer chess in just four hours

Elo chess skill rating

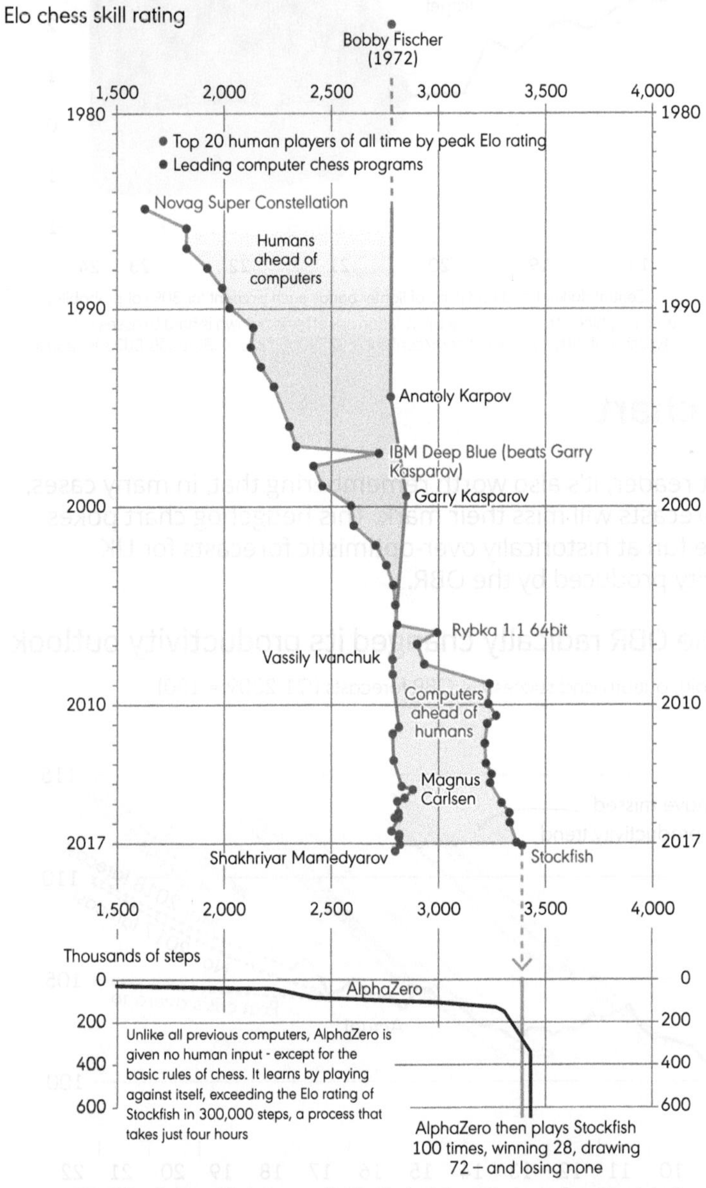

Sources: EFF; Wikipedia; DeepMind appeared in Tim Harford, A year in charts: From bitcoin to Trump and chess playing robots, Financial Times, December18, 2017. Available at: https://www.ft.com/content/7020a6e4-e4e3-11e7-8b99-0191e45377ec

left to right, this means that the narrowest part of a small screen is often used for displaying an entire time series. This creates problems when we wish to highlight and describe data points on a chart.

But there is a good solution to this – by reorienting a line chart through 90 degrees, we can create a *vertical timeline*.

The example above, taken from an article by my *FT* colleague Tim Harford in 2017, shows two data series – the Elo chess skill ratings of the world's all-time best chess players and their increasingly sophisticated software rivals. It's a fascinating story of humans vs computers that merits extensive commentary, concluding with the remarkable story of DeepMind's AlphaZero program, which took just four hours to overtake the entire history of chess.

Creating a taller, vertical timeline gives data space to breathe, making it a chart type perfectly suited to the infinite vertical scroll of modern smartphones.

Animating time

Another technique for displaying time series on digital screens is animation – after all, it seems logical to use time to represent time. It's a very good technique to use with charts that can't spare an entire axis to time, such as the iconic yield curve, a chart that shows the yields of government bonds of varying maturities. Analysts use the shape of its eponymous curve to gauge market expectations, and some have suggested it might even help predict recessions.

How to read a yield curve

The curve shows the yields of different government bonds, ordered by their date of maturity

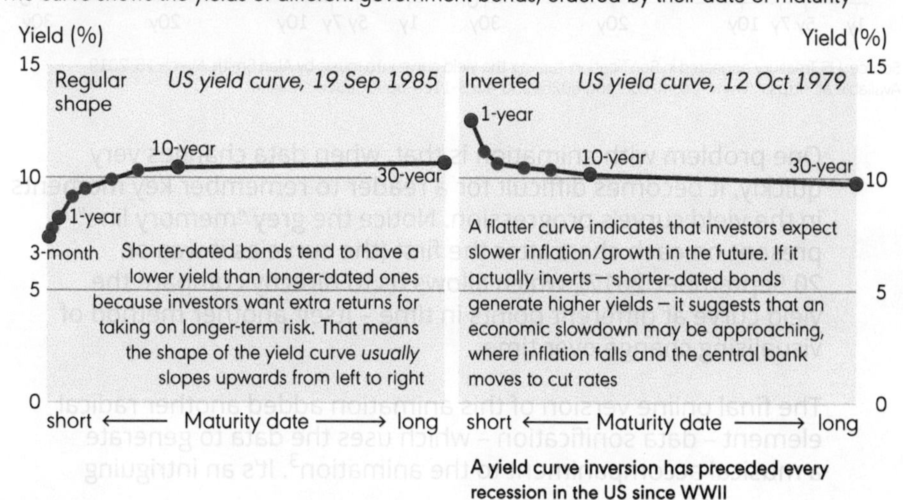

Source: US Treasury appeared in Alan Smith, Sonification: turning the yield curve into music, Financial Times, March 15, 2019. Available at: https://www.ft.com/content/80269930-40c3-11e9-b896-fe36ec32aece

The following "filmstrip" shows excerpts from a three-minute animation that displays daily movements of the US yield curve over a 40-year period.

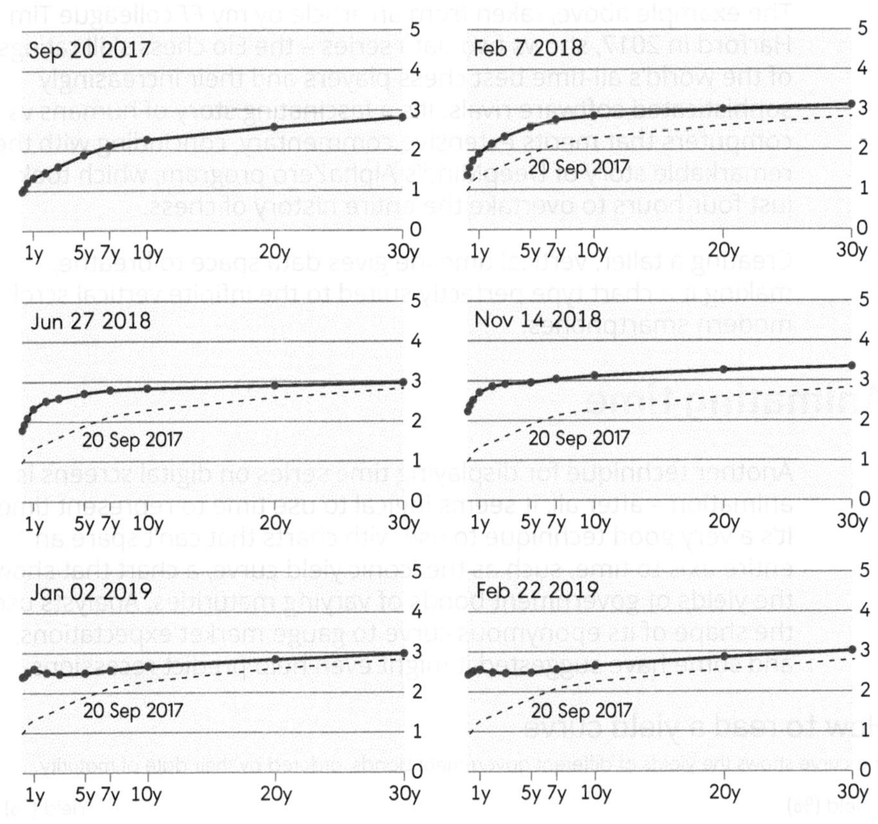

Source: US Treasury appeared in Sonification: turning the yield curve into music by Alan Smith, March 15, 2019. Available at: https://www.ft.com/content/80269930-40c3-11e9-b896-fe36ec32aece

One problem with animation is that, when data changes very quickly, it becomes difficult for a reader to remember key moments in the yield curve's progression. Notice the grey "memory line" present on each chart after the first (the curve as it was on 20 September 2017), which allows us to directly compare the yield curve at different points in time – itself another method of visualising change over time.

The final online version of this animation added another radical element – data sonification – which uses the data to generate a musical accompaniment to the animation[3]. It's an intriguing

[3] https://www.youtube.com/watch?v=NbiX2SSes40.

emerging technique that might make data presentation available to wider audiences – for example, the visually impaired, and/or users of the increasing number of screenless devices (e.g., smart speakers) and products (podcasts).

How to avoid spaghetti

A common issue with line charts is the “spaghetti problem” created by the overlapping display of too many lines. For an example, look at this draft, unpublished chart on changing patterns of English Premier League shirt sponsorship. Nine jagged lines create huge problems, with awkward use of both colour and texture doing little to rescue the situation. While we MIGHT ask readers to study a graphic like this, they would probably deserve a medal for doing so.

Premier league clubs turn to gambling for shirt sponsorship

Shirt sponsors 1992–2020, by sector

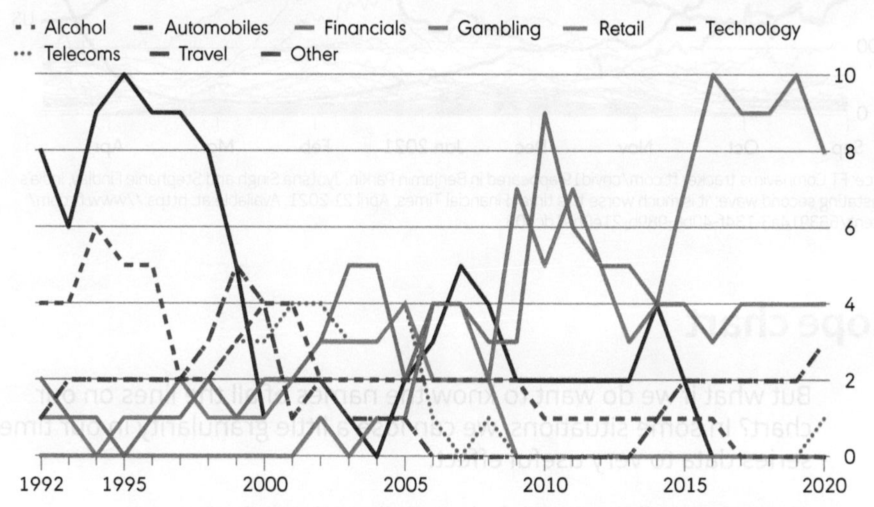

Source: FT research appeared in Patrick Mathurin, Premier League shirt sponsorship shifts with the times, Financial Times, August 11 2018. Available at: https://www.ft.com/content/61f3c8fc-9c86-11e8-9702-5946bae86e6d

A simple and effective solution can be to introduce some visual hierarchy. In this chart looking at a deadly Covid-19 surge in India in April 2021, selected comparator countries have been promoted into the foreground, labelled and highlighted.

Meanwhile, most of the lines on the chart are relegated into the background, anonymous and grey. You may well question why they are even there at all? The answer lies in the value of having all global data on the chart, as opposed to just a few countries. The grey lines generally represent countries with much lower fatalities, putting India's rising death toll – and indeed the US peak from earlier in the year – into stark context.

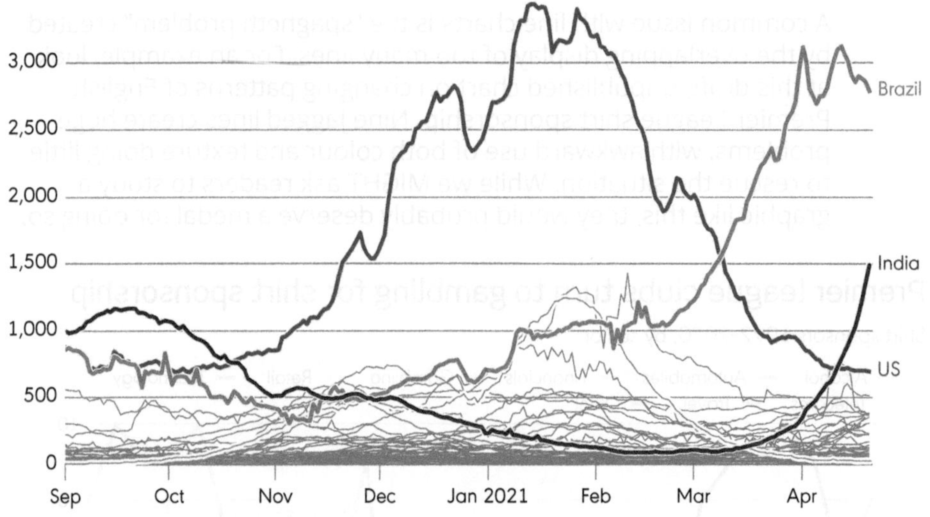

Source: FT Coronavirus tracker ft.com/covid19 appeared in Benjamin Parkin, Jyotsna Singh and Stephanie Findlay, India's devastating second wave: 'It is much worse this time', Financial Times, April 21 2021. Available at: https://www.ft.com/content/683914a3-134f-40b6-989b-21e0ba1dc403

Slope chart

But what if we do want to know the names of all the lines on our chart? In some situations, we can lose a little granularity in our time series data to very useful effect.

Slope charts allow us to label every line – by reducing our presentation of time to just two reference points – "before" and "after". They can be tremendously effective at highlighting contrasting fortunes, as this end-of-decade summary of changes in participation in primary education shows.

Notice how colour is used to highlight the risers and fallers, allowing us to spot how South and West Asia managed to bridge the gap to the top tier of global regions by increasing its participation rate by over 10 percentage points, overtaking the world average in the process.

How participation in primary education changed in a decade

Adjusted net enrolment rate (%)

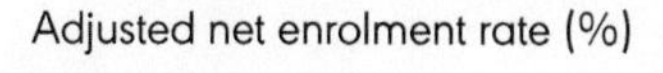
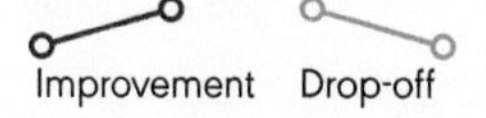

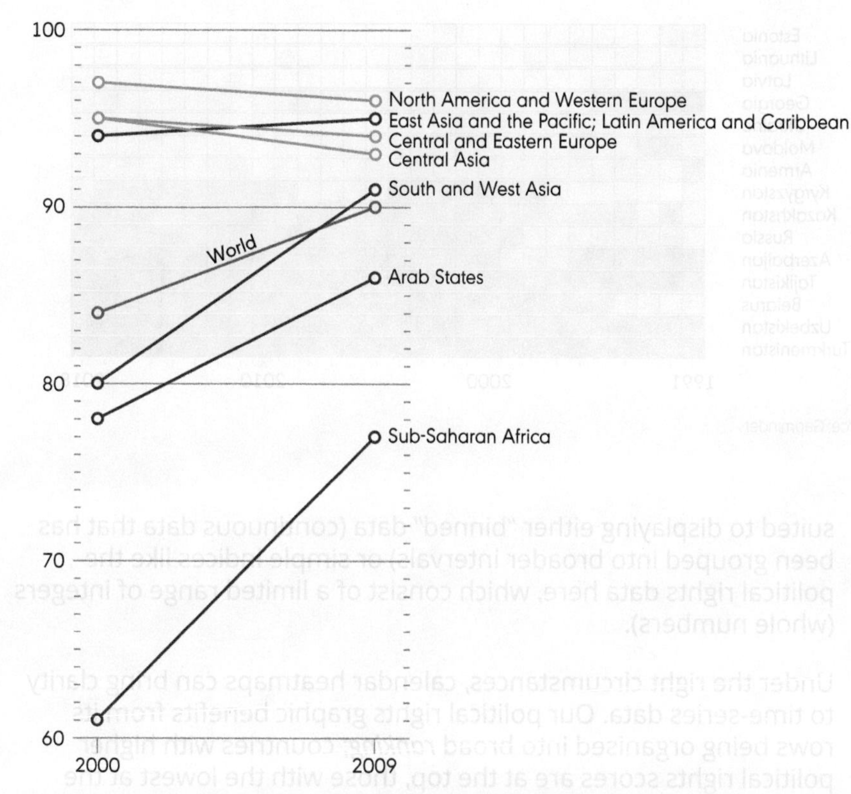

Source: Data from Statistical Annex, UIS, 2011. Used by permission from Alan Smith

Calendar heatmap

Another way of dealing with the "spaghetti problem" is to avoid using lines altogether. This *calendar heatmap* of the political rights index uses contiguous rectangles with different tints to convey trends in the scores of post-Soviet states. It's certainly easier to read than a line chart with 15 lines.

However, it's important to realise the trade-off being made here. Compared with a line chart, heatmaps make it more difficult for readers to quantify the individual scores in the data. They are best

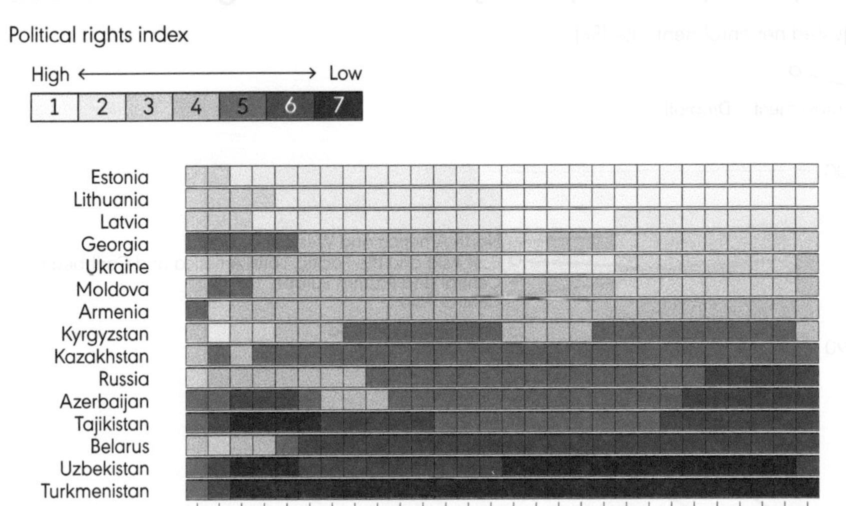

suited to displaying either "binned" data (continuous data that has been grouped into broader intervals) or simple indices like the political rights data here, which consist of a limited range of integers (whole numbers).

Under the right circumstances, calendar heatmaps can bring clarity to time-series data. Our political rights graphic benefits from its rows being organised into broad *ranking*; countries with higher political rights scores are at the top, those with the lowest at the bottom. This allows us to see common patterns – for example, many states saw increasing political rights in the 1990s and early 2000s (colours getting lighter), only for many to reverse course in later years (colours getting darker).

Calendar heatmaps can also be used to present categorical differences changing over time. This graphic shows an important trend in the movie industry – the rise of film franchises – by plotting all 1,950 top 50 movies of the past 39 years and simply marking whether it was an original release or some sort of sequel/prequel/remake or reboot. A clear pattern emerges – original movies are in decline when it comes to topping the rankings.

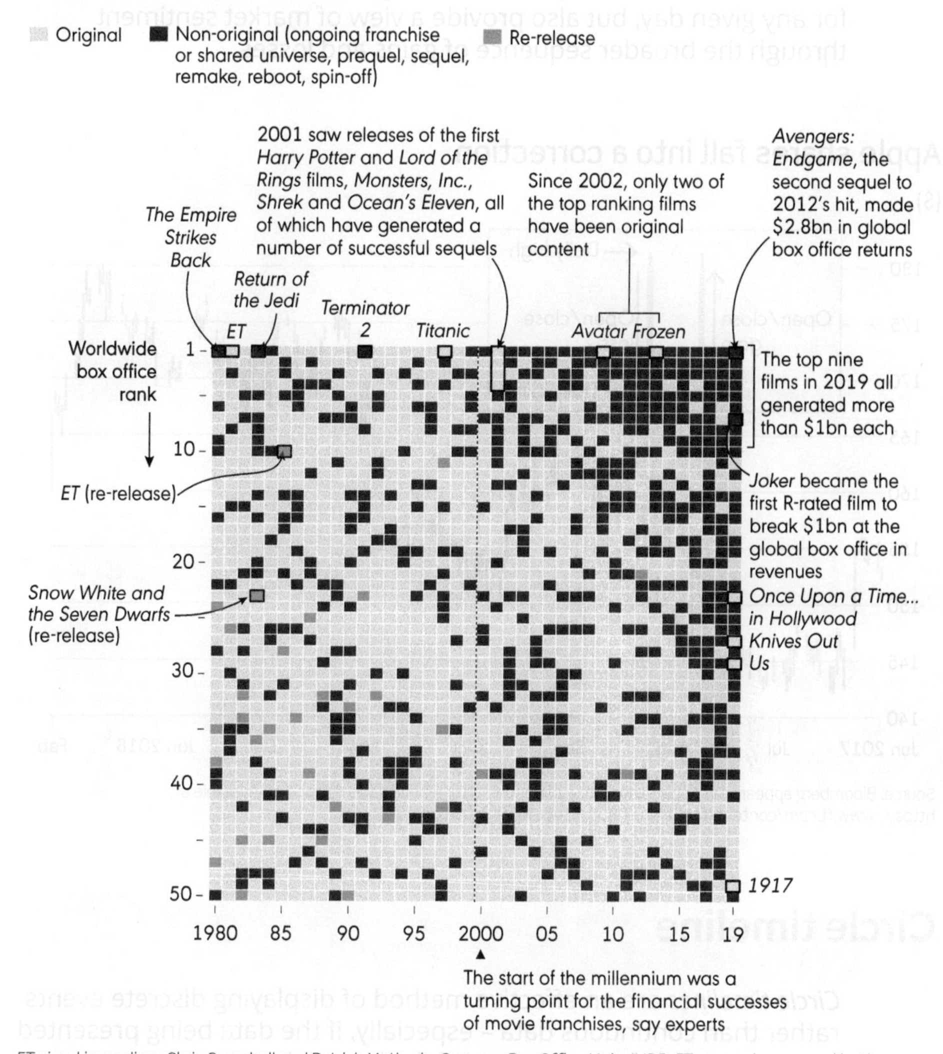
Less risky franchise films are more likely to appeal to financiers post-coronavirus
Top 50 cinema releases per year
Original
Non-original (ongoing franchise or shared universe, prequel, sequel, remake, reboot, spin-off)
Re-release
2001 saw releases of the first Harry Potter and Lord of the Rings films, Monsters, Inc., Shrek and Ocean's Eleven, all of which have generated a number of successful sequels
Since 2002, only two of the top ranking films have been original content
Avengers: Endgame, the second sequel to 2012's hit, made $2.8bn in global box office returns
The Empire Strikes Back
Return of the Jedi
Terminator 2
ET
Titanic
Avatar
Frozen
Worldwide box office rank
The top nine films in 2019 all generated more than $1bn each
ET (re-release)
Joker became the first R-rated film to break $1bn at the global box office in revenues
Snow White and the Seven Dwarfs (re-release)
Once Upon a Time... in Hollywood
Knives Out
Us
1917
1
10
20
30
40
50
1980
85
90
95
2000
05
10
15
19
The start of the millennium was a turning point for the financial successes of movie franchises, say experts

FT visual journalism: Chris Campbell and Patrick Mathurin, Sources: Box Office Mojo; IMDB; FT research appeared in Alex Barker, The Unhinged bet to jump-start the movie business, Financial Times, June 16, 2020. Available at: https://www.ft.com/content/e68ec86c-cfe8-4d54-996d-da876b4a285c

Candlestick chart

Candlestick charts are a very specific type of change over time chart. Surprisingly antique,[4] they are used to denote sequential changes

[4] Research by Steve Nison, who has helped popularise candlestick charts in the modern era, suggests the chart's origins lie in nineteenth-century Japan.

in the values of equities, currencies and other financial market data. Most commonly, each "candlestick" depicts a day's trading, but they can be used for longer time periods. What makes them particularly useful for financial analysts is that they are both a source of details for any given day, but also provide a view of market sentiment through the broader sequence of gains and losses.

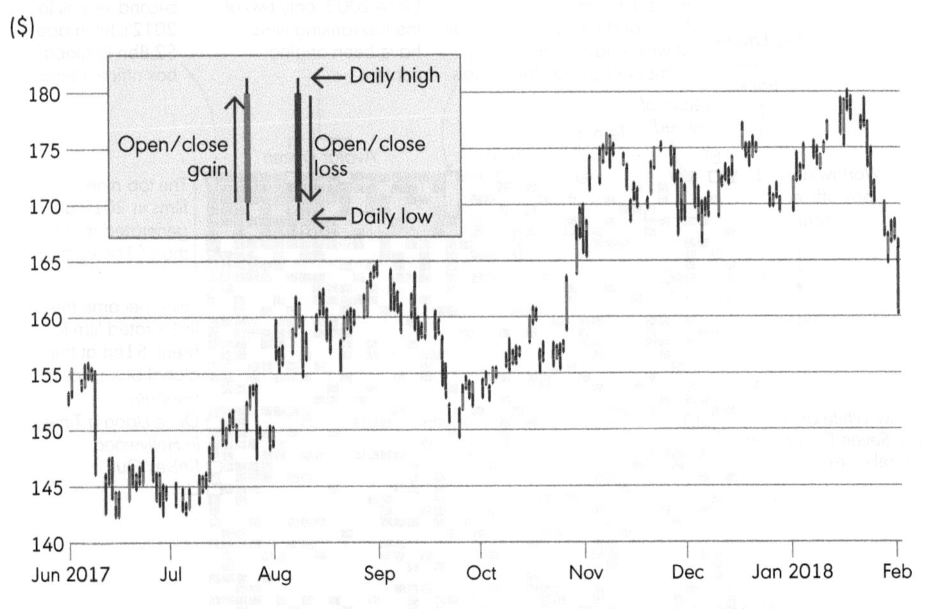

Source: Bloomberg appeared in Apple slides into a correction after iPhone sales disappoint. Available at: https://www.ft.com/content/f1c3e2e0-0853-11e8-9650-9c0ad2d7c5b5

Circle timeline

Circle timelines are an effective method of displaying discrete events rather than continuous data – especially, if the data being presented covers a range of magnitudes. While that might naturally suggest that they are best suited to displaying environmental data such as earthquakes and hurricanes, they are equally useful for displaying important financial and business events, like major acquisitions and mergers.

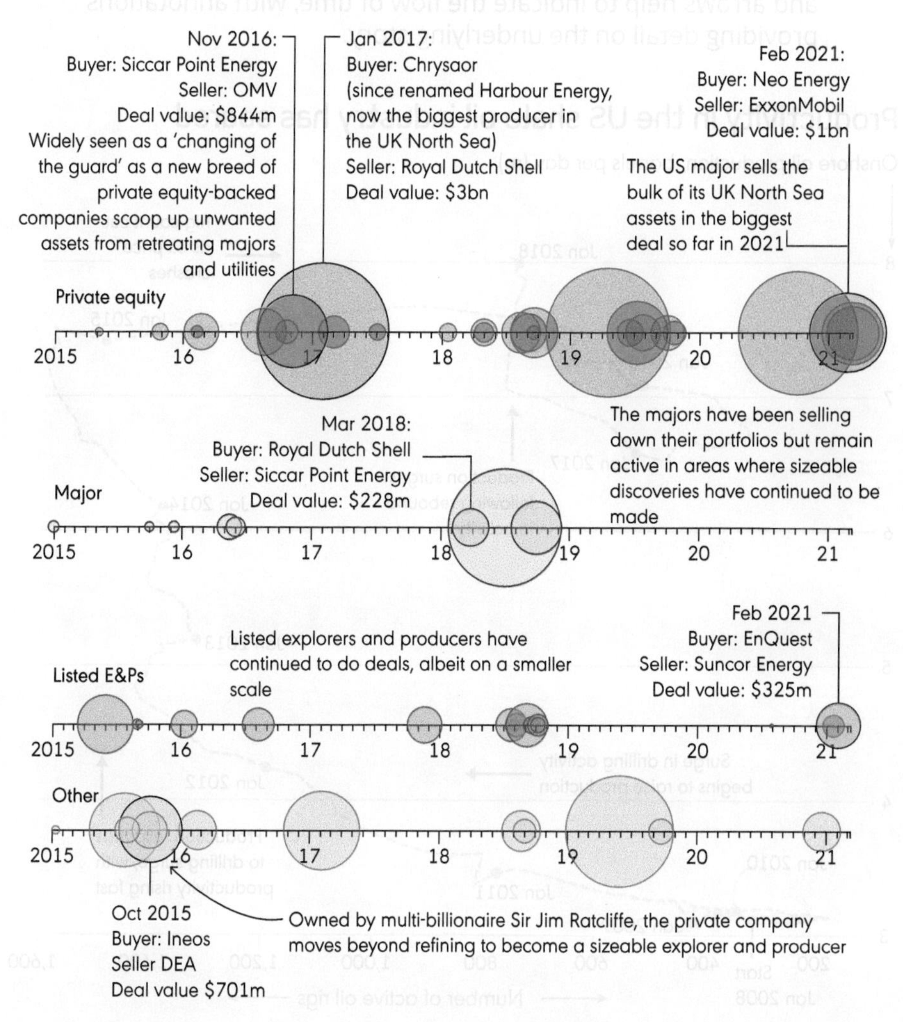
Private players replacing the oil majors in the UK's North Sea
UK North Sea deals, by category of buyer. Circle size denotes deal value
Nov 2016:
Buyer: Siccar Point Energy
Seller: OMV
Deal value: $844m
Widely seen as a 'changing of the guard' as a new breed of private equity-backed companies scoop up unwanted assets from retreating majors and utilities
Jan 2017:
Buyer: Chrysaor
(since renamed Harbour Energy, now the biggest producer in the UK North Sea)
Seller: Royal Dutch Shell
Deal value: $3bn
Feb 2021:
Buyer: Neo Energy
Seller: ExxonMobil
Deal value: $1bn
The US major sells the bulk of its UK North Sea assets in the biggest deal so far in 2021
Private equity
2015
16
17
18
19
20
21
Mar 2018:
Buyer: Royal Dutch Shell
Seller: Siccar Point Energy
Deal value: $228m
The majors have been selling down their portfolios but remain active in areas where sizeable discoveries have continued to be made
Major
Listed explorers and producers have continued to do deals, albeit on a smaller scale
Feb 2021
Buyer: EnQuest
Seller: Suncor Energy
Deal value: $325m
Listed E&Ps
Other
Oct 2015
Buyer: Ineos
Seller DEA
Deal value $701m
Owned by multi-billionaire Sir Jim Ratcliffe, the private company moves beyond refining to become a sizeable explorer and producer

Source: Wood Mackenzie appeared in The new North Sea players riding the wake of the retreating majors. Available at: https://www.ft.com/content/93d5f778-833c-4553-ae29-785e3aa3d4d3

Connected scatterplot

These allow us to bring a time-series treatment to a *correlation* plot. Also known as "snail trail charts", due to their winding form, they offer a way of visualising the change over time of two variables with different measurement units.

The following plot shows how onshore US oil production has changed relative to the active number of rigs. Annual date markers and arrows help to indicate the flow of time, with annotations providing detail on the underlying story.

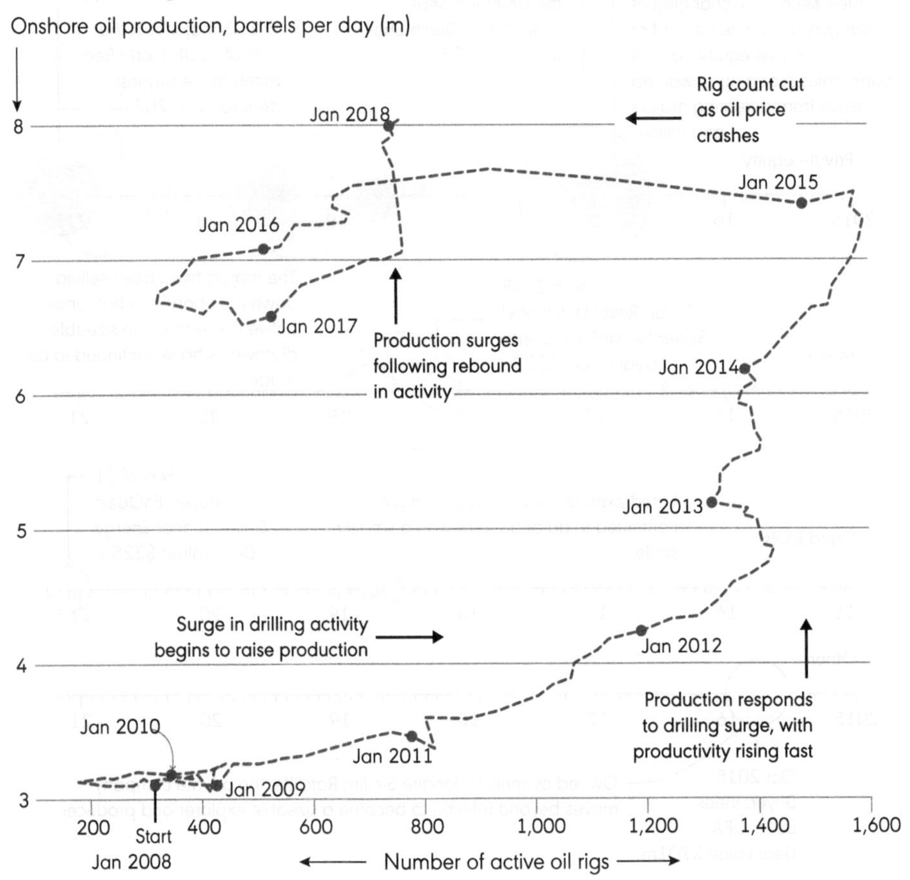

Graphic: Billy Ehrenberg-Shannon Source: Energy Information Administration, Baker Hughes, a GE Company appeared in Boom times for US shale oil producers. Available at: https://www.ft.com/content/2c7f6a38-1d37-11e8-956a-43db76e69936

Connected scatterplots are another chart type that can benefit from digital animation, with the trail decaying over time, reinforcing the notion of passing time.

Nevertheless, they should be used with caution, as they are prone to generate the sort of chart spaghetti that can make charts difficult to decipher. But, used sparingly, they are a useful addition to our chart vocabulary.

Priestley timeline

To conclude this chapter, let us return to the history of data visualisation and consider the work of Joseph Priestley. Famous in his own lifetime (1733–1804) for the invention of soda water, and with at least a partial claim to the discovery of oxygen (or "dephlogisticated air", as he preferred to call it), Priestley's popular writings covered theology, politics, science and history.

He was also a passionate teacher and, as well as writing essays on approaches to education, he prepared materials to aid students. Among these were highly popular timelines including *A Chart of Biography* (1765), of which a "specimen" (teaser) is shown below.

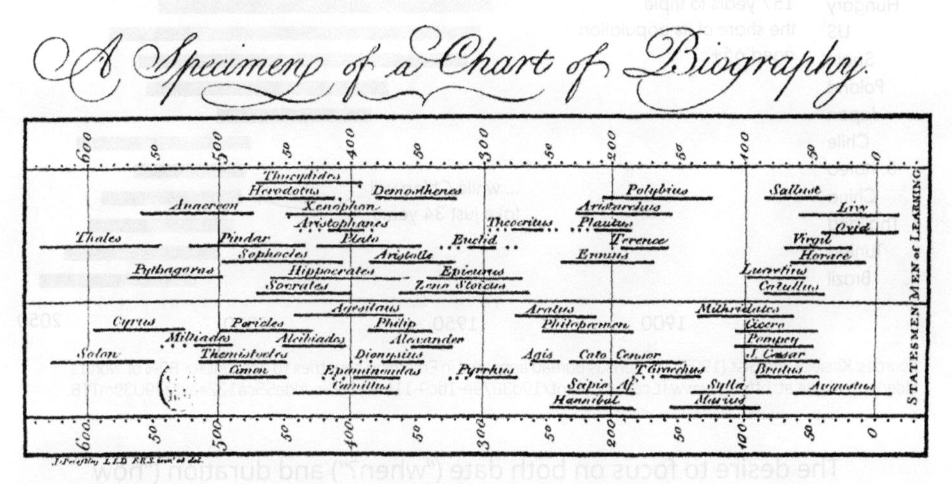

Source: J. Priestley L.L.D A Chart of Biography (1765), of which a 'specimen' (teaser)

A particular innovation of Priestley's was the use of a horizontal axis to represent time running from left to right, with tick marks dividing the space into regular subdivisions. In the central section of the chart, markers of various length depict the lifespans of famous names from antiquity. In the full version, over 2,000 names are organised into six categories.

William Playfair acknowledged Priestley's work as an important influence on his own financial time series charts – and, like Playfair, Priestley's method continues to find uses to this day.

The following chart depicts the time taken for different countries' older populations to double and triple in size. In general, developed countries that started "ageing" earlier will take longer than emerging economies starting the process later.

Emerging markets are ageing at a rapid rate

Time taken for population aged 65+ to **double** and **triple** from 7% of total population

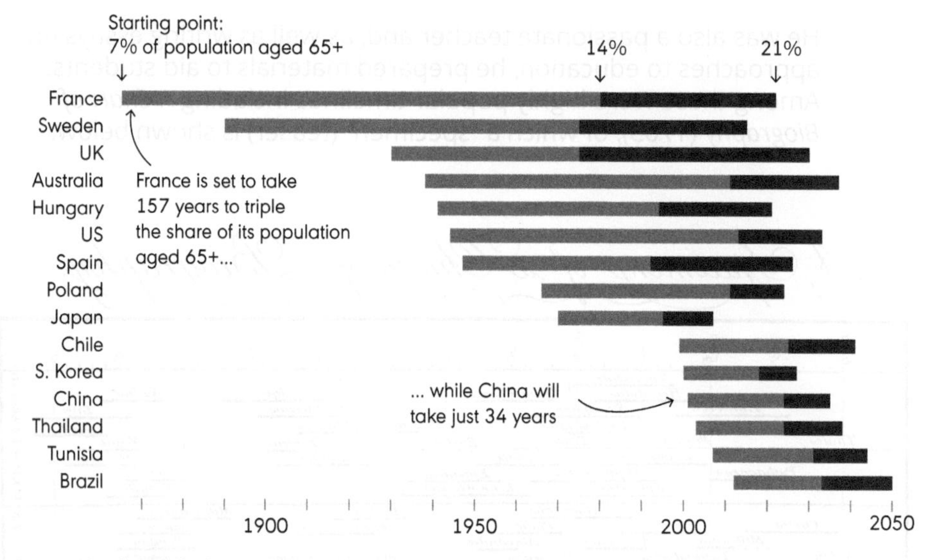

Sources: Kinsella and Gist (1995), US Census Bureau appeared in Emerging countries to account for 80% of world's elderly. Available at: https://www.ft.com/content/19d3879e-1dc9-11e6-b286-cddde55ca122#axzz49U39mTT8.

The desire to focus on both date ("when?") and duration ("how long?") makes this data a perfect candidate for a *Priestley timeline* treatment. There is a clear visual pattern: the bars that start earlier are longer, those that start later, shorter.

It is certainly easier to see the story compared with a stacked bar chart, the visual treatment I noticed one research agency had chosen to visualise this data. As you can see, with date ranges relegated to mere labels, it's very difficult to make a visual connection between both date and duration. The bars are arranged in date order, but the actual progression of time is difficult to see immediately.

Emerging markets are ageing at a rapid rate

Years taken for population aged 65+ to double and triple from 7% of total population

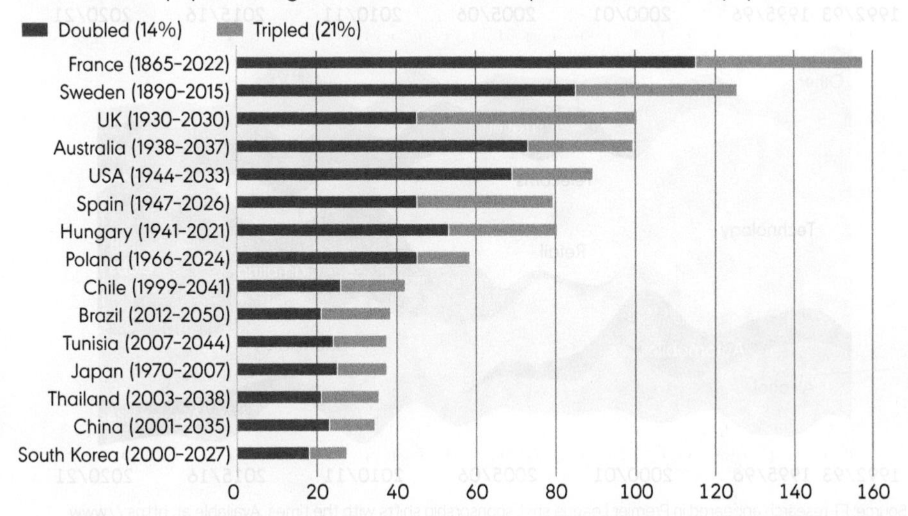

Sources: Kinsella and Gist (1995), US Census Bureau appeared in Communicating with data – timelines. Available at: https://www.ft.com/content/6f777c84-322b-11e6-ad39-3fee5ffe5b5b. Used by permission from The Financial Times Limited.

Streamgraph

Priestley wrote somewhat philosophically about his biographical timeline:

> *"Time is continually suggested to us, by the view of this chart, under the idea of a river, flowing uniformly on, without beginning or end . . ."*

As such, a *streamgraph* is a type of chart that would, perhaps, have gained the polymath's approval. A form of stacked area chart that can be used to present part-to-whole relationships as they change over time, streamgraphs lack an orthodox y axis and instead present data around a displaced central spine, producing a fluid, organic feel to the presentation.

This streamgraph shows the same English Premier League shirt sponsor data we saw previously in "spaghetti" line chart form. Notice that the emphasis here is less on numbers and more on shifting trends – which makes the lack of a y axis unimportant. So clear is the central pattern now – increasing dependence on gambling companies – that it's difficult to accept that we're looking at the same data.

How Premier League clubs turned to gambling

Shirt sponsors 1992-2020, by sector

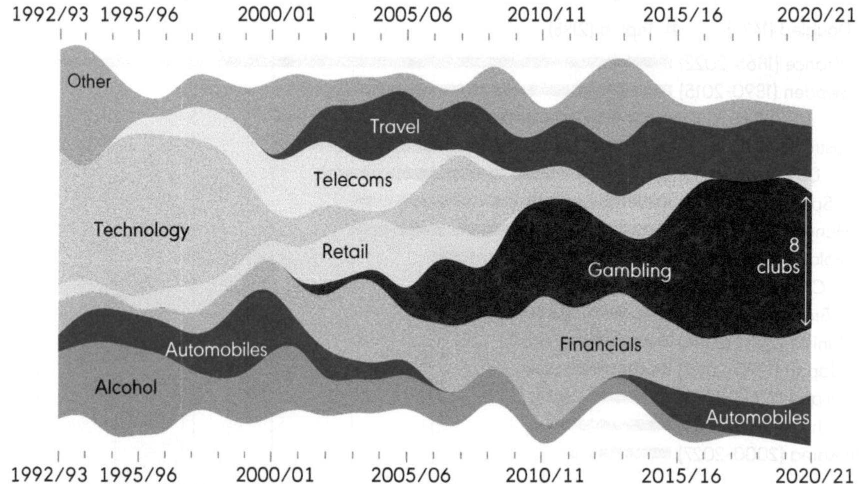

Source: FT research appeared in Premier League shirt sponsorship shifts with the times. Available at: https://www.ft.com/content/61f3c8fc-9c86-11e8-9702-5946bae86e6d

Stacked area chart

More conventional stacked area charts with regular y axes are also effective for considering purely compositional changes, as in the case of the remarkable decline in coal usage by the UK national grid. The *part-to-whole* relationship of fuel usage at any time in the past 50 years is crystal clear, as is the declining role of coal.

Coal's importance to the UK's national grid has declined rapidly

Fuels used for electricity generation (%)

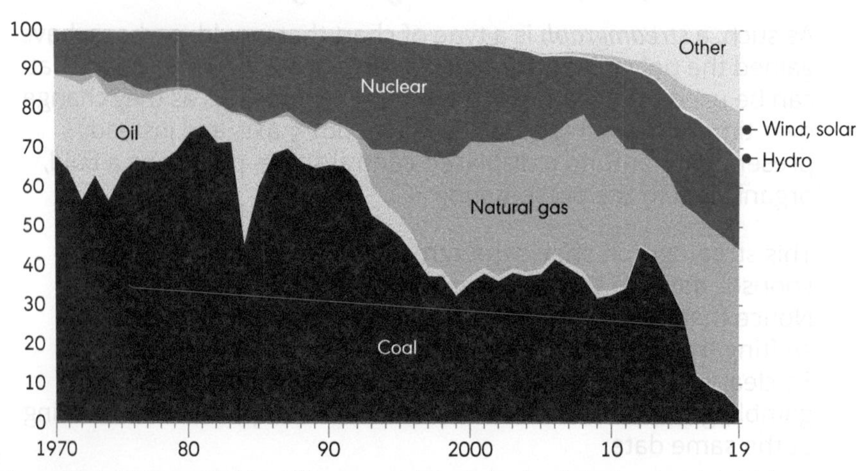

Source: Digest of UK Energy Statistics, 2020 appeared in UK coal mine plan pits local needs against global green ambitions. Available at: https://www.ft.com/content/0e731ce2-1f45-4f50-bcb2-729467156d75

Area charts can also be used to show compositional changes as parts of moving totals that include *magnitude*. In this visualisation of British alcohol consumption, the ordering of the chart's layers makes it easy to see that an increase in wine consumption has largely offset a long-term decline in beer since the 1980s.

Since the 1970s an increasing share of Britons have swapped beer for wine

Volume consumption per capita (Litres of alcohol)

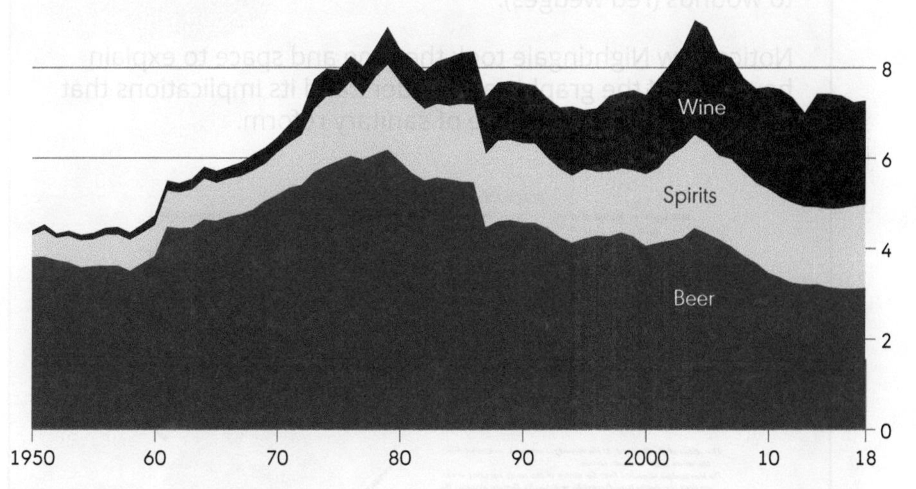

Source: University of Adelaide Wine Economics Research Centre appeared in UK wine drinkers face higher prices as Brexit hangover kicks in. Available at: https://www.ft.com/content/2747ddf8-7f6c-4b34-9e40-36d6c4178203

In all these area charts, notice the lingering influence of William Playfair, with directly labelled segments helping to ensure each chart unites proportion, progression and quantity in "one act of memory".

Learning point – Florence Nightingale's polar area diagrams

It's impossible to talk about visualising *change over time* and *part to whole* without mentioning the work of Florence Nightingale. Her work is a pioneering example of how well-presented data can make all the difference.

Nightingale meticulously collected figures on causes of death in the British army during the Crimean War. In 1858, she produced diagrams based on this data as part of an extensive report submitted to Queen Victoria – and an official commission investigating sanitary conditions in the army.

Her charts were designed to draw attention to the proportion of deaths in the calendar year due to "Preventable or Mitigable Zymotic disease" (the blue wedges, each representing a calendar month), far higher than deaths due to wounds (red wedges).

Notice how Nightingale took the time and space to explain how to read the graphic and understand its implications that underlined the importance of sanitary reform.

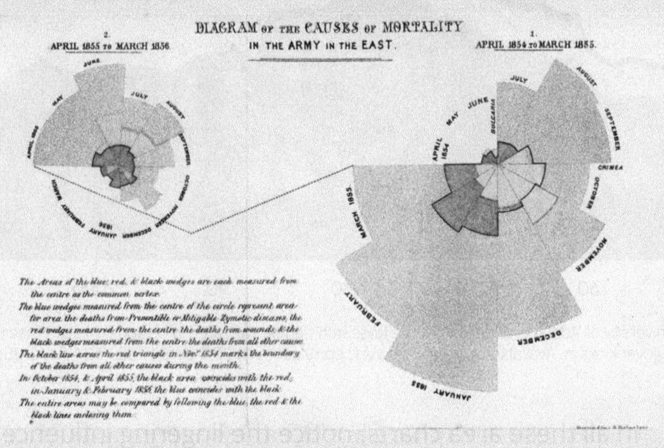

Source: Florence Nightingale's polar area diagrams 1858

6

Charts of correlation

Show the relationship between two or more variables. Be mindful that, unless you tell them otherwise, many readers will assume the relationships you show them to be causal (i.e., one causes the other).

The word "correlation" is, perhaps, second only to "significance" in the pecking order of statistical terms most likely to generate a fist fight (OK, statisticians are a mostly civilised bunch, let's just leave it at "a heated debate").

Correlation allows us to see the extent to which two things are *related*. This is useful. For example, if we know something is usually high in value when another thing is low (a "*negative correlation*"), it's possible to start making predictions.

Learning point - Correlation and causation

Before we go any further, it's time to flag one of the perennial banana skins in the world of statistics.

A correlation might be *causal* (cold weather *causes* higher heating bills), or the link might be associated with an unseen third variable (sales of ice cream and violent crimes are correlated - but only because both are associated with warmer weather). It might also be that a correlation is completely spurious . . .

At www.tylervigen.com[5], we can see that per capita cheese consumption is strongly correlated with the number of people who died by becoming tangled in their bedsheets, while the marriage rate of Wyoming correlates with the number of domestically produced passenger cars sold in the USA.

Statistics are not necessarily a good determinant of underlying causes, but they can help you spot patterns - just make sure they're helpful ones.

Visualising *correlations* is important because it helps us see the extent to which things are connected.

As with the chart relationships we've already looked at - *change over time* (line chart) and *magnitude* (bar chart) - there is a single chart type that dominates our visual thinking in this relationship. Welcome to the scatterplot.

Scatterplot

Data visualisation historians Michael Friendly and Daniel Denis have credited the astronomer John Herschel with the publication of the very first scatterplot in 1833, but it would be a further 50 years before Francis Galton's use of it helped make them a staple of the scientific community.

[5] https://www.tylervigen.com/spurious-correlations.

Anatomy of a scatterplot

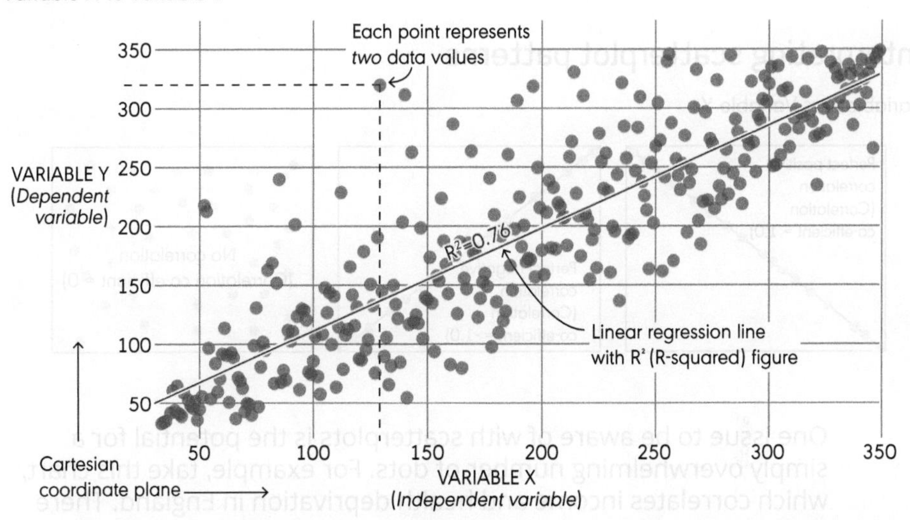

The bedrock of a scatterplot is a two-dimensional Cartesian coordinate plane, whose two perpendicular axes (x and y) mean each data point represents two values corresponding to its position relative to each axis.

Conventionally, the horizontal (x) axis is used for the so-called "independent" variable, while the vertical (y) axis is used for the "dependent" variable. These terms are linked to the contentious notion of cause and effect: you can think of the independent variable as "cause" and the dependent variable as "effect".

For example, in a plot of data studying hair loss in men, we would put age on the x axis (independent) and the extent of hair loss on the y axis (dependent).

In practice, many scatterplots don't portray a "causal" relationship, but it's useful to be aware of the convention.

Finally, when you see scatterplots in the wild (particularly in academic papers), you'll often see them overlaid with "regression lines", which are intended to summarise the trend between the two variables. This will be accompanied by a correlation co-efficient value, which describes the strength of that trend. The possible values run between –1 and 1 as follows:

Interpreting scatterplot patterns

Variable X vs Variable Y

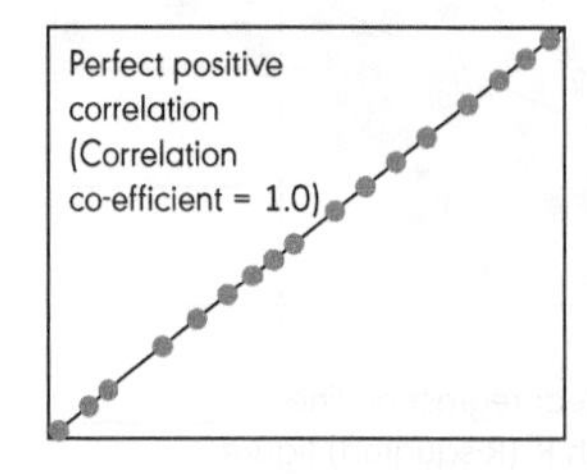

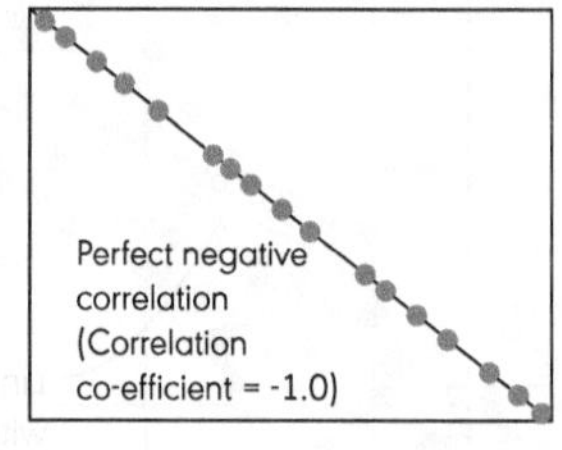

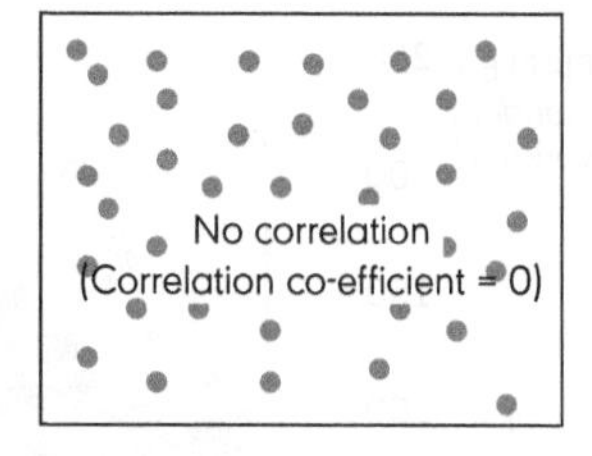

One issue to be aware of with scatterplots is the potential for a simply overwhelming number of dots. For example, take this chart, which correlates income and health deprivation in England. There are 32,844 dots on this chart (don't worry, I won't ask you to count them), each representing data for a small neighbourhood.

Scatterplots: sometimes there are just too many dots...

Income deprivation and health deprivation, England, 2019, by neighbourhood*

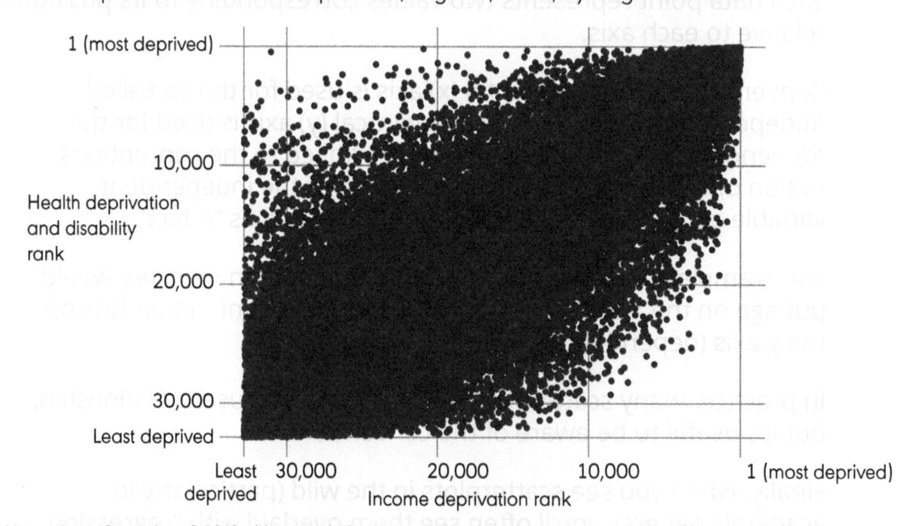

* Lower Layer Super Area (LSOA) with a population between 1,000 and 3,000

Source: Ministry of Housing, Local Communities & Local Government

Adding a regression line helps us see the strength and direction of the underlying relationship – but it also reinforces how visually impenetrable the rest of the chart is.

Scatterplots: sometimes there are just too many dots...

Income deprivation and health deprivation, England, 2019, by neighbourhood*

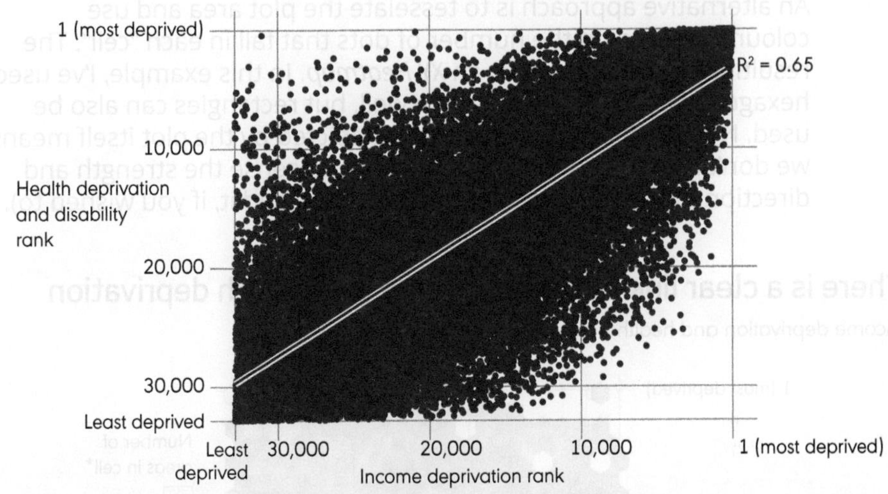

* Lower Layer Super Area (LSOA) with a population between 1,000 and 3,000

Source: Ministry of Housing, Local Communities & Local Government

One option is to reduce the amount of "ink" used for each dot, either by applying just an outline to it, or applying some transparency, so that we can see through them. Applying transparency to our deprivation chart yields a *little* improvement, but the tremendous data density remains a problem.

Scatterplots: sometimes there are just too many dots...

Income deprivation and health deprivation, England, 2019, by neighbourhood*

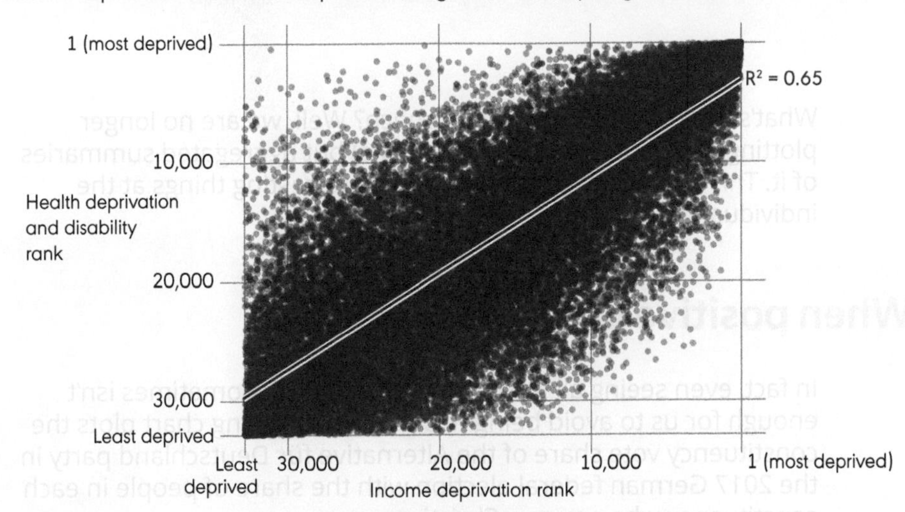

* Lower Layer Super Area (LSOA) with a population between 1,000 and 3,000

Source: Ministry of Housing, Local Communities & Local Government

XY Heatmap

An alternative approach is to tesselate the plot area and use colour to represent the number of dots that fall in each "cell". The resulting chart is known as an *XY Heatmap*. In this example, I've used hexagons because they tesselate well, but rectangles can also be used. Notice that the visual pattern depicted by the plot itself means we don't really need the regression line to sense the strength and direction of the relationship (but you could add it, if you wished to).

There is a clear link between income and health deprivation

Income deprivation and health deprivation, England, 2019

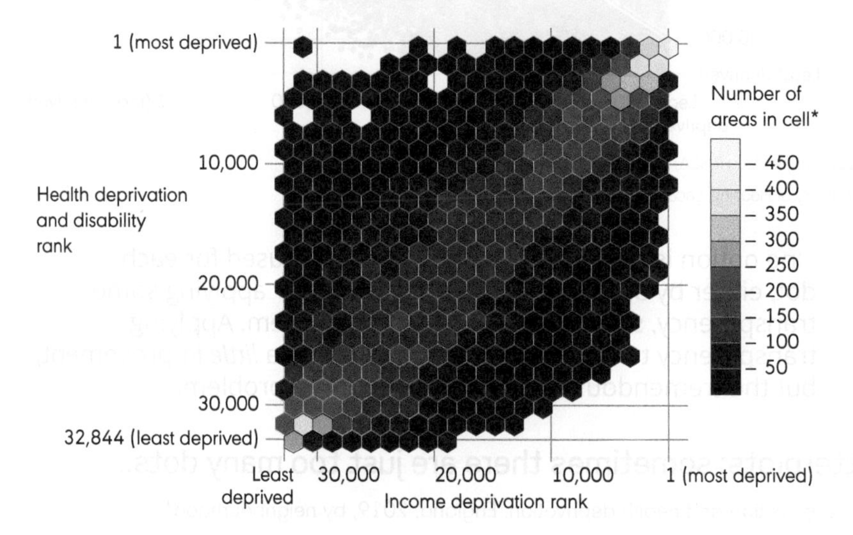

What's the drawback to this approach? Well, we are no longer plotting all the data (our 32,844 points) but aggregated summaries of it. This might mean we miss seeing interesting things at the individual level.

When positive is negative

In fact, even seeing all the data in a scatterplot sometimes isn't enough for us to avoid being misled. The following chart plots the constituency vote share of the Alternative für Deutschland party in the 2017 German federal election with the share of people in each constituency who are non-Christian.

AfD votes: a positive correlation with less Christian constituencies

Each point represents a German constituency

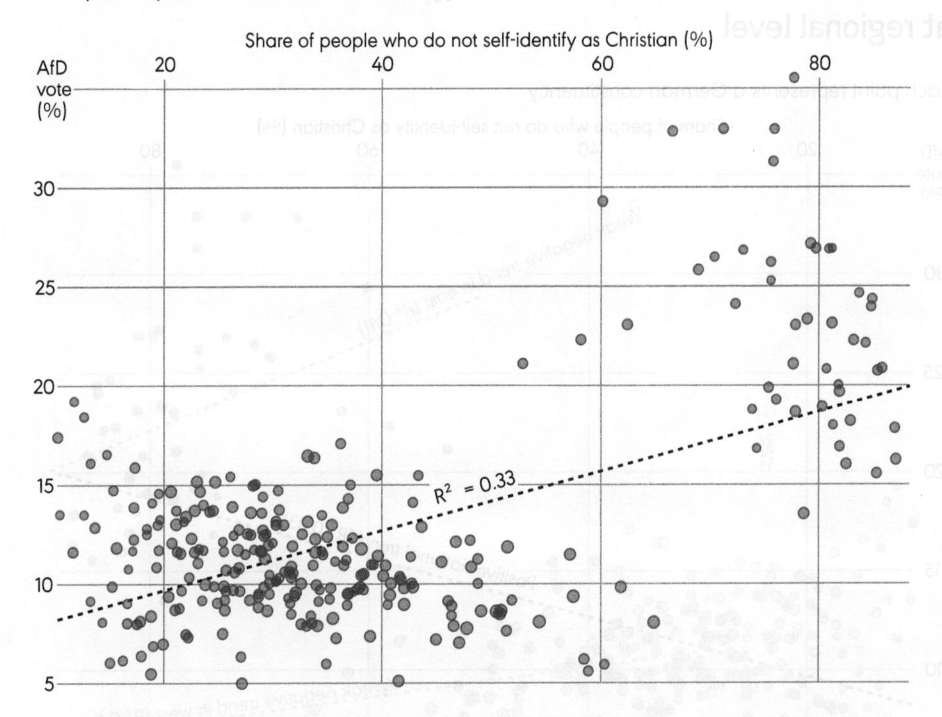

Source: Federal Returning Officer Graphic: John Burn-Murdoch / @jburnmurdoch appeared in Germany's election and the trouble with correlation. Available at: https://www.ft.com/content/94e3acec-a767-11e7-ab55-27219df83c97

It seems an open and shut case: a positive correlation with an R^2 value of 0.33. It suggests that the smaller proportion of Christians there are in an area, the higher the likely vote for AfD (remember our dependent and non-dependent variables).

But let's look at the same data, this time with each point coloured according to whether the constituency is in the east or the west of the country. Suddenly, the trends on the chart look very different – in fact, they are reversed!

This chart from my *FT* colleague John Burn-Murdoch, is an example of a paradox named after Edward Simpson, the Bletchley Park codebreaker who first fully described it. The slightly alarming top line of the paradox is that trends that appear when different groups of data are plotted can reverse when those groups are combined.

Simpson's paradox: the national trend is driven entirely by differences between east and west, and the trend is reversed at regional level

Each point represents a German constituency

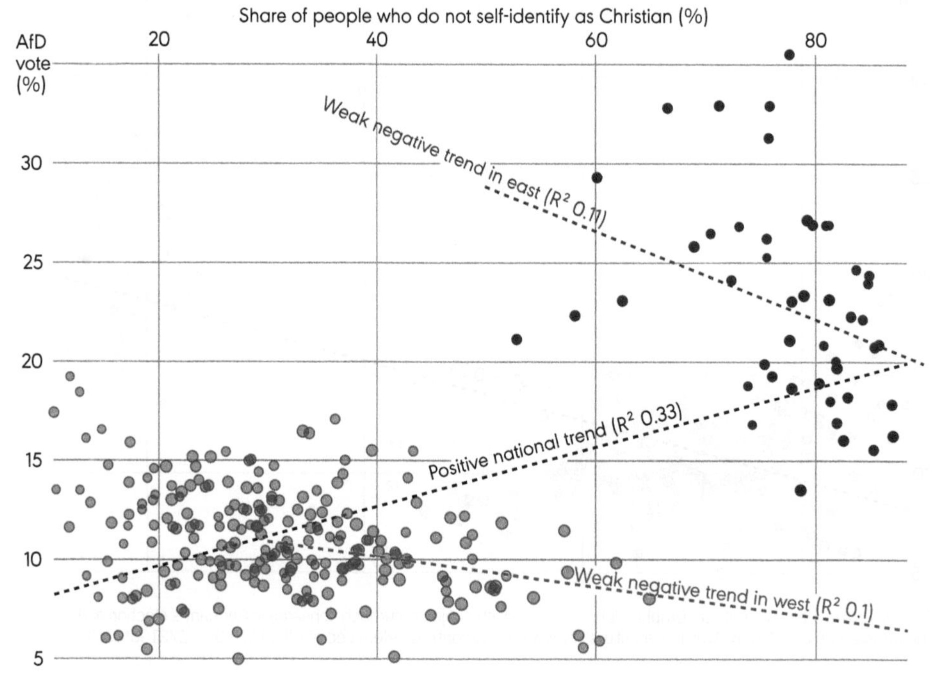

Source: Federal Returning Officer Graphic: John Burn-Murdoch / @jburnmurdoch appeared in Germany's election and the trouble with correlation. Available at: https://www.ft.com/content/94e3acec-a767-11e7-ab55-27219df83c97

> **Learning point** – Missing variables
>
> Simpson's Paradox is a good reminder that, as well as considering the variables being presented in a graphic, greater chart literacy comes from considering the variables that *aren't* being shown. And as our Simpson's paradox example shows, it is possible to add further information to scatterplots.

Bubble chart

One of the most notable chart makers of the early twenty-first century was the late Hans Rosling, a gifted science communicator. Rosling used scatterplots extensively, but for him they were only the beginning of his data visualisation designs. Let's take a closer look at one of the iconic charts behind his famous 2006 TED talk "The best stats you've ever seen".

A positive correlation between income and life expectancy

Income per capita and life expectancy at birth, 2019

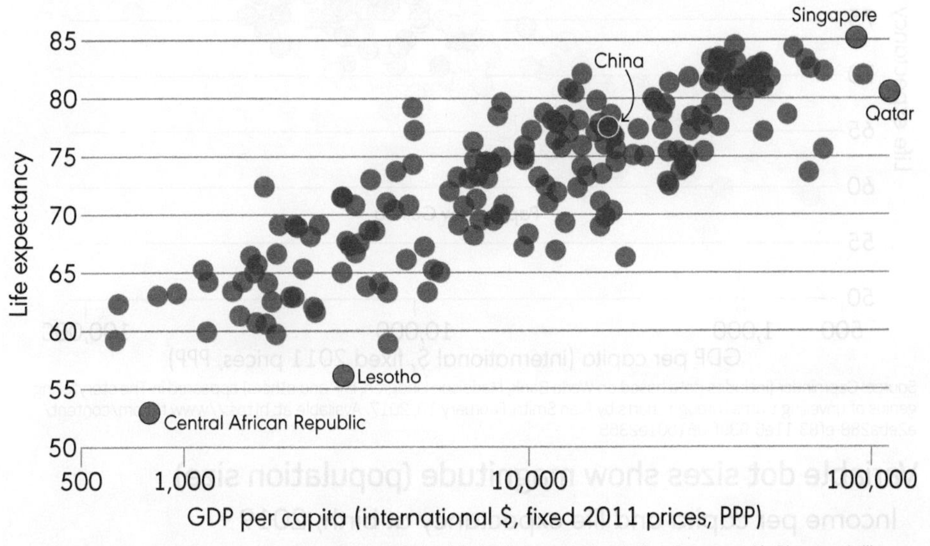

Source: Gapminder (includes data based on World Bank, Maddison Lindgren, IMF and others) appeared in The storytelling genius of unveiling truths through charts by Alan Smith, February 10, 2017. Available at: https://www.ft.com/content/e2eba288-ef83-11e6-930f-061b01e23655

The chart starts life as a conventional scatterplot (notice the log scale on the x axis – we'll look in more detail at this design decision later in Chapter 14 "Scales of justice; axes of evil").

It's easy to spot a positive correlation: countries with a higher income tend to experience longer life expectancy (notice that there are no countries in the bottom right-hand corner of the chart, which is the space that would be occupied by rich countries with poor life expectancy).

Things get even more interesting as Rosling adds colour to show regional groupings. This introduces a *spatial* relationship to the chart – without having to resort to a map. For example, differences can now be seen between countries in Africa (poorer, shorter lives) and the Americas (richer, longer lives), although there is some visible overlap.

The next stage of evolution in Rosling's chart is to modify the size of each dot on the chart according to the population of each country. This allows us to see both the relative *magnitude* of each country's population and the overall *distribution* of income and life expectancy population across the world.

Colour reveals a spatial relationship

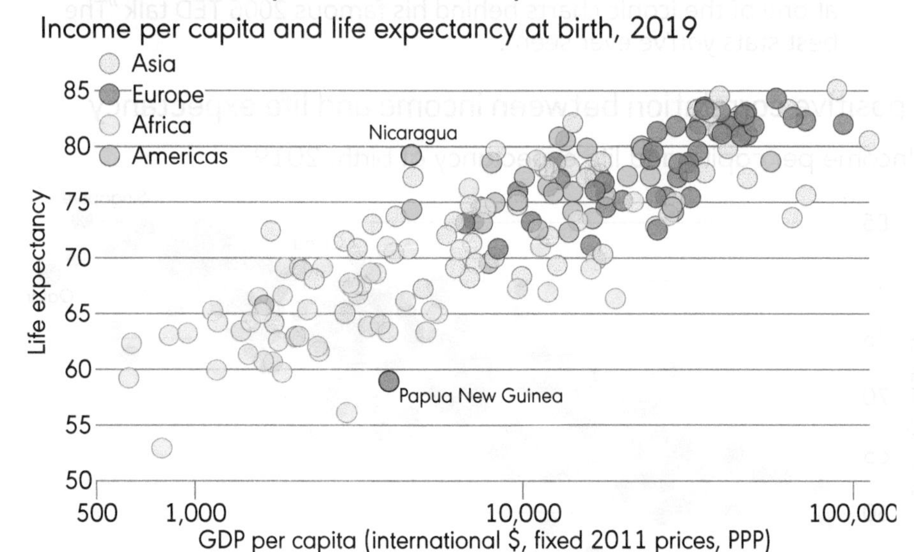

Source: Gapminder (includes data based on World Bank, Maddison Lindgren, IMF and others) appeared in The storytelling genius of unveiling truths through charts by Alan Smith, February 10, 2017. Available at: https://www.ft.com/content/e2eba288-ef83-11e6-930f-061b01e2365

Variable dot sizes show magnitude (population size)

Income per capita and life expectancy at birth, 2019

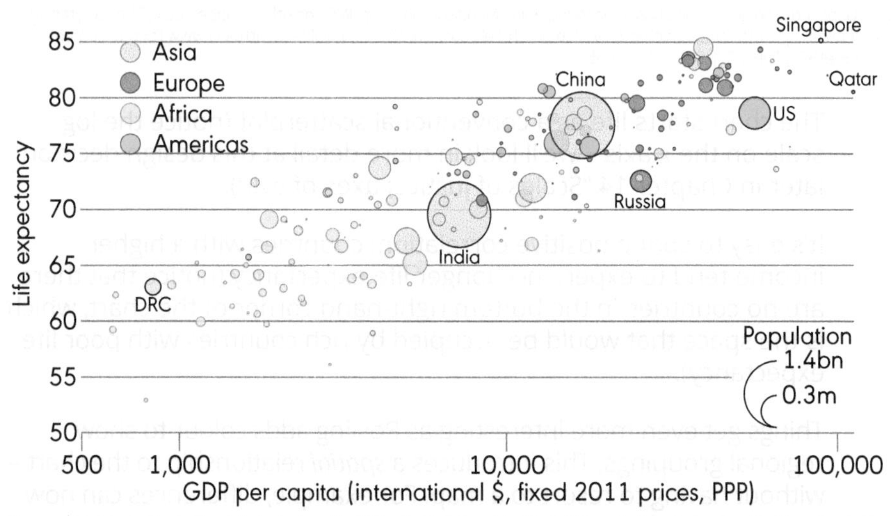

Source: Gapminder (includes data based on World Bank, Maddison Lindgren, IMF and others) appeared in The storytelling genius of unveiling truths through charts by Alan Smith, February 10, 2017. Available at: https://www.ft.com/content/e2eba288-ef83-11e6-930f-061b01e23655

The final stroke of genius in Rosling's charts is his recognition that how countries have *changed over time* is such an important part of the story. For this, he turned to animation.

Rosling was passionate in his belief that the world was getting better – people getting wealthier and living longer – and the final, complete moving bubble chart allows us to see just that. Notice how China's bubble surges from 1989, seeing major improvements in income and life expectancy relative to other countries.

Animation reveals change over time

Income per capita and life expectancy at birth, 2019

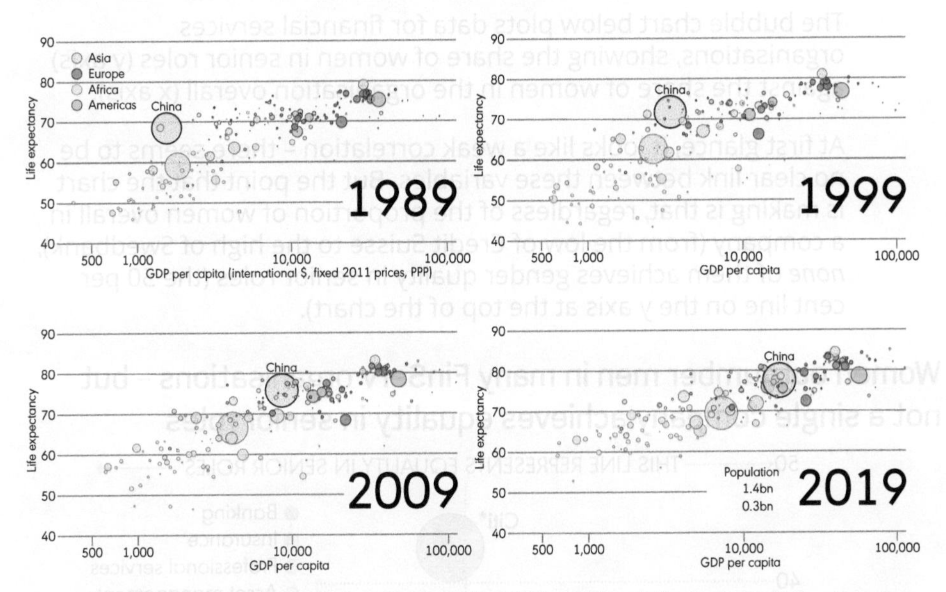

Source: Gapminder (includes data based on World Bank, Maddison Lindgren, IMF and others) appeared in The storytelling genius of unveiling truths through charts by Alan Smith, February 10, 2017. Available at: https://www.ft.com/content/e2eba288-ef83-11e6-930f-061b01e23655

Of course, in print, we are restricted to just seeing a "film strip", but the onscreen fluid movement of Rosling's visuals are no doubt part of the appeal that has seen his TED talk tally up over 15 million views since its publication.

So, although it began life just as a standard scatterplot, Rosling's animated bubble charts show no fewer than *five* of the nine statistical relationships on the *FT* Visual Vocabulary:

- *Correlation* – the x/y axes on the scatterplot.
- *Magnitude* – the proportional circles showing the size of the population in each country.
- *Spatial* – each circle is coloured according to its world region.
- *Distribution* – the combination of the axes and the proportional circles do a passable job of showing the overall distribution of global GDP and life expectancy.
- *Change over time* – the animated element allows us to see the evolution of the chart data.

A key takeaway here is that Rosling generated broad public interest by *adding* information to his charts, not stripping it away or dumbing it down – a remarkable achievement in the field of data communication. As a direct result of Rosling's efforts, bubble chart usage has increased in recent years. And their capabilities go beyond depicting simple correlations.

The bubble chart below plots data for financial services organisations, showing the share of women in senior roles (y axis) against the share of women in the organisation overall (x axis).

At first glance, it looks like a weak correlation – there seems to be no clear link between these variables. But the point that the chart is making is that, regardless of the proportion of women overall in a company (from the low of Credit Suisse to the high of Swedbank), *none* of them achieves gender quality in senior roles (the 50 per cent line on the y axis at the top of the chart).

Women outnumber men in many FinServ organisations – but not a single company achieves equality in senior roles

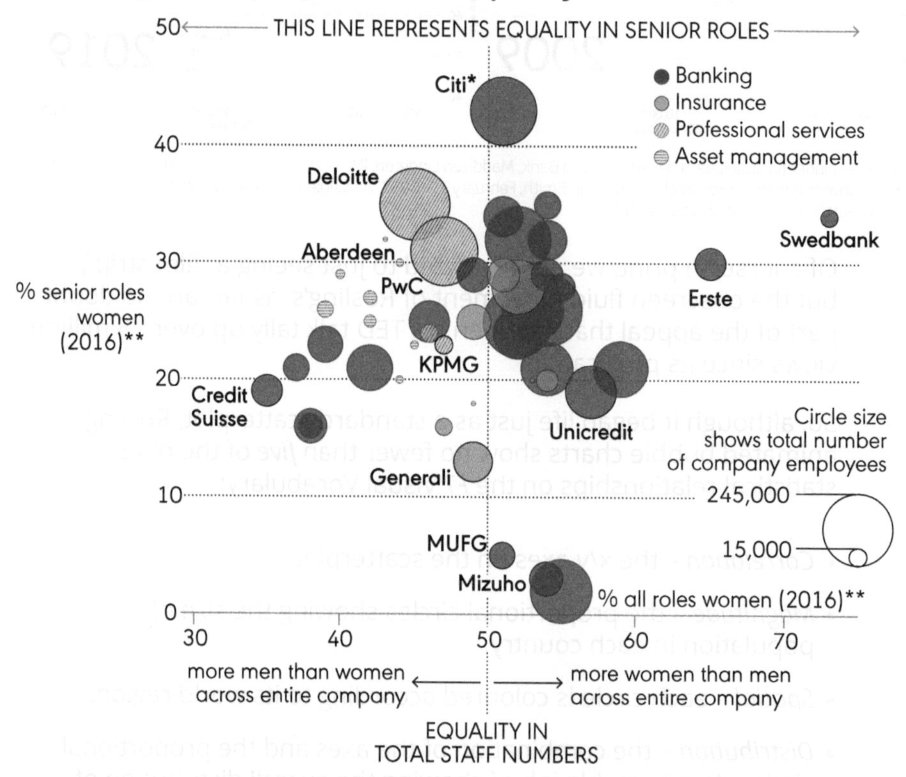

* Citi's 'senior' figures also include mid-level managers ** Certain organisation's figures are for home regions only
FT graphic Alan Smith/Laura Noonan
Sources: Companies, FT research appeared in Women still miss out on management in finance. Available at: https://ig.ft.com/managements-missing-women-data. Used by permission from The Financial Times Limited.

In fact, extending the axes to reveal the full extent of the chart's possible values (0 to 100 in both directions) allows the story to be told not by the bubbles, but by the white space on the chart. This is one of the bravest, but often most effective, chart design decisions: to deliberately put the data into just a small portion of the plot area. The labelled quadrants in each corner of the chart help draw attention to the real story – the areas where there are no data.

Women outnumber men in many FinServ organisations – but not a single company achieves equality in senior roles

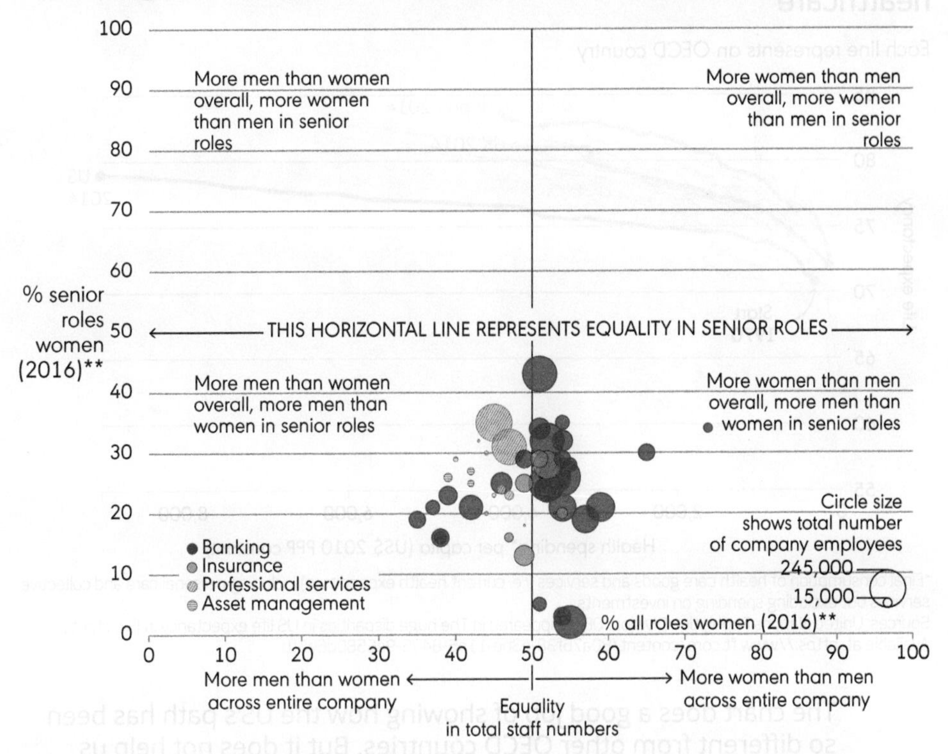

* Citi's 'senior' figures also include mid-level managers ** Certain organisation's figures are for home regions only
Source: FT graphic Alan Smith/Laura Noonan Sources: Companies, FT research appeared in Women still miss out on management in finance by Laura Noonan, Alan Smith, David Blood and Martin Stabe, April 4, 2017. Available at: https://ig.ft.com/managements-missing-women-data/

We saw in the previous chapter that *connected scatterplots* are a good way of showing how correlations have *changed over time*. The chart below contrasts spending on healthcare with life expectancy in OECD countries. As you might expect, life expectancy has risen as spending on healthcare has increased. But there is one important outlier on the chart.

Plotting correlation trails

In the US, spending on health care, per capita, has not yielded life expectancy improvements that one might expect, considering the experience of other countries. Notice that the line of the US is longer than other lines – this means spending has been increasing at a faster rate than elsewhere because every line, regardless of length, represents the same *duration*.

US life expectancy has not risen in line with spending on healthcare

Each line represents an OECD country

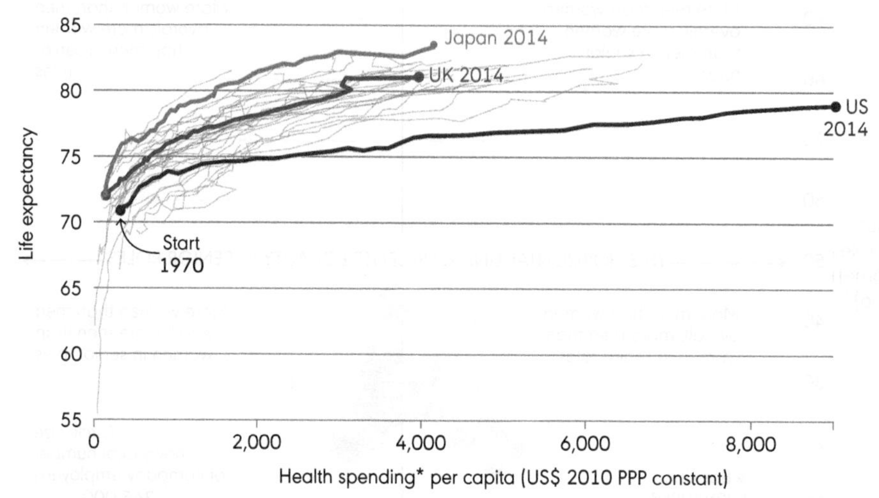

*Final consumption of health care goods and services (i.e. current health expenditure) including personal care and collective services but excluding spending on investments

Sources: United Nations Population Division, OECD appeared in The huge disparities in US life expectancy in five charts. Available at: https://www.ft.com/content/80a76f38-e3be-11e6-8405-9e5580d6e5fb

The chart does a good job of showing how the US's path has been so different from other OECD countries. But it does not help us understand *why* its trajectory is so different. To do that, we need to look at another statistical relationship in the data. We'll revisit this story in the next chapter.

Connected scatterplots are also very effective for generational comparisons, as with this chart comparing how wealth has progressed in the US across different cohorts. With median age on the x axis, rather than time itself, it allows us to compare the wealth progression of different generations at equivalent periods. Although the positive correlation between age and wealth is clear in every line, the generational comparison does not make pleasant reading for millennials.

In 2020, the millennials' share of household wealth remains stubbornly low

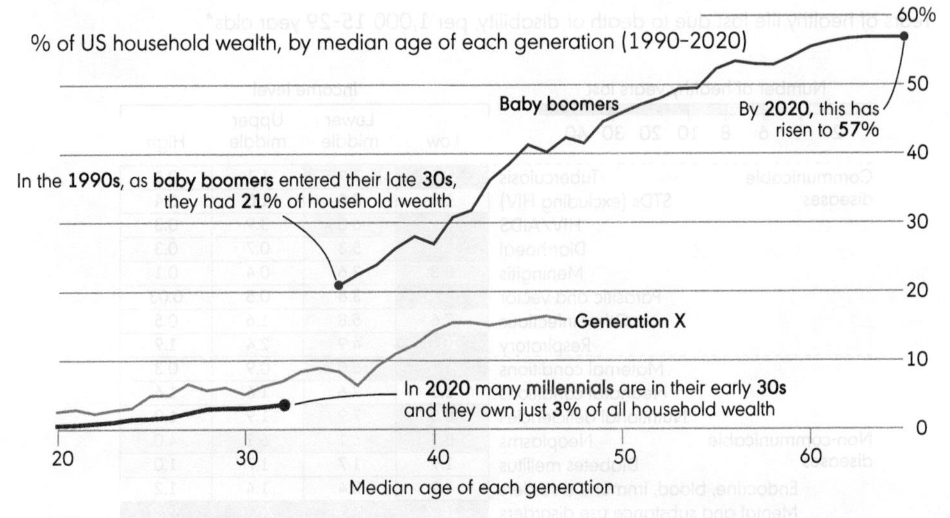
% of US household wealth, by median age of each generation (1990–2020)
60%
50
40
30
20
10
0
Baby boomers
By 2020, this has risen to 57%
In the 1990s, as baby boomers entered their late 30s, they had 21% of household wealth
Generation X
In 2020 many millennials are in their early 30s and they own just 3% of all household wealth
20
30
40
50
60
Median age of each generation

Source: Federal Reserve distributional financial accounts FT graphic: Aleksandra Wisniewska appeared in The Recessionals: why coronavirus is another cruel setback for millennials I Free to read. Available at: https://www.ft.com/content/241f0fe4-08f8-4d42-a268-4f0a399a0063

A different take on the XY Heatmap

Sometimes, we're not interested in comparing the correlation between two continuous variables, but rather deconstructing a single metric into two sub-categories. In these cases, we can revisit the *XY Heatmap* approach we saw earlier in the chapter. The following graphic shows how many healthy years are typically lost due to death or disability – at different income levels. It's a graphic that rewards a second glance.

The general pattern is of more years lost among lower income groups – but a big exception to that lies in mental and substance use disorders, where more years are lost at higher income levels.

Notice how both the x and y axes are categorical, with the tint of each cell in the heatmap representing the measured value. This is a big departure from the scatterplot, which typically uses two continuous axes.

One weakness of heatmaps is the way that, with the values just classed into different categories, it is difficult to compare the actual *magnitude* of the values. For example, at lower income levels, maternal conditions and mental/substance abuse are both

The 'dual burden' of disease for young people in low income countries

Years of healthy life lost due to death or disability, per 1,000 15–29 year olds*

Number of healthy years lost: 2 4 6 8 10 20 30 40

		Income level			
		Low	Lower middle	Upper middle	High
Communicable diseases	Tuberculosis	15.5	7.9	1.1	0.1
	STDs (excluding HIV)	1.8	0.8	1.0	0.4
	HIV/AIDS	17.9	6.0	3.9	0.3
	Diarrhoeal	14.6	5.3	0.7	0.3
	Meningitis	8.8	2.6	0.4	0.1
	Parasitic and vector	15.4	3.8	0.5	0.03
	Other infectious	7.6	5.8	1.6	0.5
	Respiratory	10.0	4.9	2.4	1.9
	Maternal conditions	21.2	8.0	0.9	0.3
	Neonatal conditions	1.5	2.6	1.6	1.6
	Nutritional deficiencies	8.5	7.9	1.9	1.0
Non-communicable diseases	Neoplasms	8.9	6.1	6.1	4.0
	Diabetes mellitus	1.9	1.7	1.7	1.0
	Endocrine, blood, immune disorders	4.9	3.4	1.4	1.2
	Mental and substance use disorders	26.7	24.4	26.8	39.2
	Neurological conditions	10.0	10.1	7.6	9.1
	Sense organ	6.3	5.9	4.7	3.4
	Cardiovascular	11.7	9.4	5.4	3.4
	Respiratory	4.8	3.3	2.4	3.0
	Digestive	8.5	7.8	1.8	1.4
	Genitourinary	5.9	5.5	3.6	2.3
	Skin	3.7	3.5	3.4	3.5
	Musculoskeletal	5.8	7.6	7.2	10.5
	Congenital anomalies	3.1	2.7	2.3	2.4
	Oral conditions	1.2	1.2	1.1	1.2
Injuries	Unintentional	42.4	31.4	23.6	15.2
	Intentional	25.1	21.2	17.7	12.1

*Based on a measure of Disability-Adjusted Life Years
FT graphic: Chelsea Bruce-Lockhart; Chris Campbell
Source: World Health Organization appeared in In charts: Healthcare apps target tech-savvy youth. Available at: https://www.ft.com/content/7aba9066-dffe-4829-a1cd-1d557b963a82

shaded the same tint, despite the latter being over five percentage points higher. Sometimes, it's worth seeing the actual values in the cells they describe, making the whole graphic work more like an enhanced table; the figures provide the exact value, the shading behind them illustrates the pattern.

We'll finish this section by looking at some charts that move away from the x/y format of the scatterplot entirely.

Visualising risk

The Winton Centre for Risk and Evidence Communication used a *spine chart* to show the potential harms and benefits of the AstraZeneca covid vaccine. Following several highly publicised incidents involving blood clots among people who had been vaccinated, the Winton Centre's timely research suggested that the potential benefits outweighed the harms in all but one scenario – younger adults in a low exposure risk setting.

The chart provides good quantification of the benefits and harms at low exposure risk but makes it just a little difficult to compare the *ratio* of harm to benefit across age groups – and we would need three versions of this necessarily wide chart to see all the scenarios.

Understanding risk: the AstraZeneca vaccine

For 100,000 people with low exposure risk*

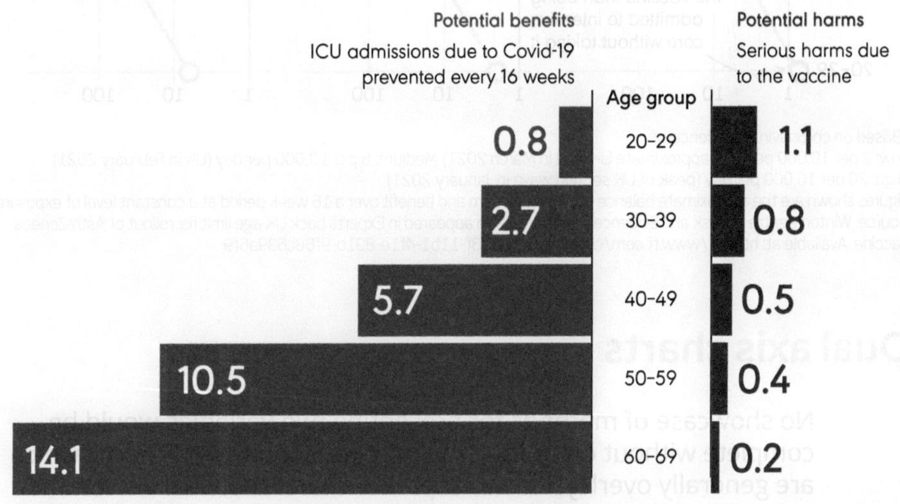

* based on coronavirus infection rate of 20 cases per 100,000
Source: Winton Centre for Risk and Evidence Communication appeared in Why we shouldn't worry about Covid vaccine blood clots. Available at: https://www.ft.com/content/090f1b3c-95d9-4b10-9a7c-ba3a7f290fee

Another view of the data converts the harms and benefits into a ratio, generating a single value – ICU admissions prevented per blood clot caused. This new metric allows us to bring all three risk exposure scenarios together in a compact form, highlighting the one combination of age and risk where the risk outweighs the benefit (i.e., the ratio is below one) – adults in their twenties in a low-risk environment. Note the gently helpful role of the log scale on the x axis.

The potential benefits of the AstraZeneca vaccine outweigh the harm in all but one scenario

ICU admissions prevented per blood clot caused, by age and exposure risk*

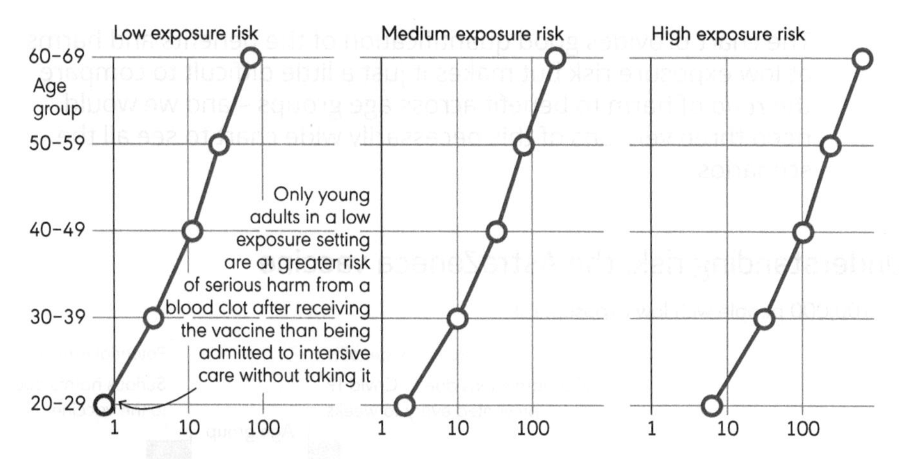

*Based on coronavirus incidence of:
Low: 2 per 10,000 per day (approximate UK rate in March 2021) Medium: 6 per 10,000 per day (UK in February 2021)
High: 20 per 10,000 per day (peak of UK second wave in January 2021)
Figures shown are the approximate balance of potential harm and benefit over a 16 week period at a constant level of exposure
Source: Winton Centre for Risk and Evidence Communication appeared in Experts back UK age limit for rollout of AstraZeneca vaccine. Available at: https://www.ft.com/content/5db4a13f-11b1-4f1e-891b-9f68c639a6f9

Dual axis charts

No showcase of methods for presenting two variables would be complete without discussing the infamous "dual axis" charts, which are generally overlays of two separate charts that share a common x axis to denote *change over time*.

I say "infamous" because many data visualisation practitioners advise against their use.

First, there is an argument that using two separate vertical axes makes this chart type difficult to read.

Second, some argue that dual axes charts are open to manipulation, with arbitrary scaling being used on one or both axes to create visual relationships that don't exist. Both arguments are grounds for healthy scepticism – but not necessarily a reason to outlaw them altogether.

Effective design techniques that use colour and shape can help readers tune in to the two separate series and my experience at the *Financial Times* suggests that certain audiences (such as markets analysts, who see them daily) are very literate when it comes to reading them.

They are perhaps at their most effective when showing a "mirroring" pattern between two series – as in this chart of changes in both the number and value of bitcoin futures over a three-year period.

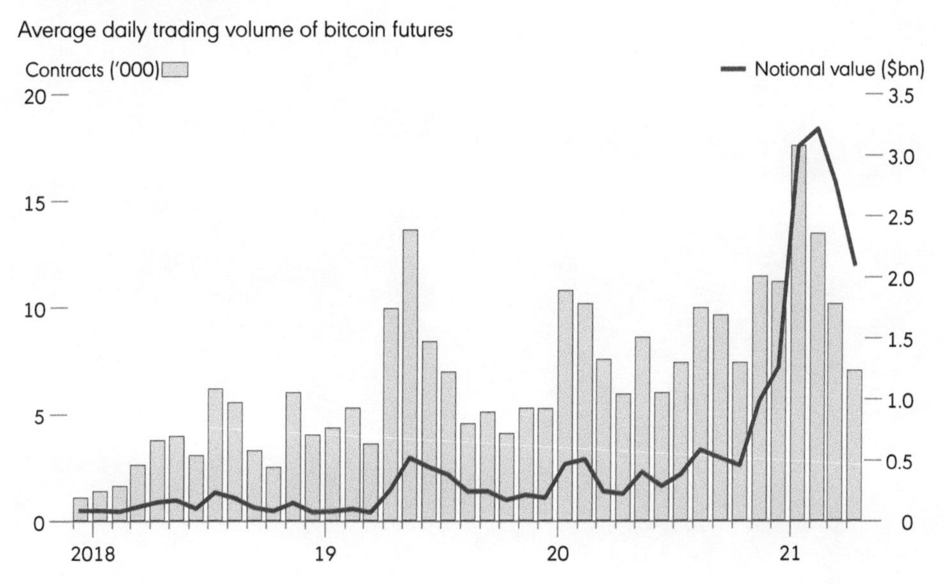

Source: CME Group appeared in Netscape 2.0: Coinbase stock debut rekindles memories of web breakthrough. Available at: https://www.ft.com/content/cbd46d95-6866-4c32-b7af-51b1772e388d

Let's conclude this section on correlation by giving the final word to Hans Rosling.

In 2010, I had the pleasure of being on a panel with him at a United Nations conference in New York. A statistician in the audience asked my esteemed fellow panellist, with just a hint of disdain, why he thought all policymakers' decisions could be informed by being provided with just two variables (from the *correlations* shown on his bubble charts). Rosling paused, smiled politely and then replied with a twinkle in his eye: "If I could get policymakers to make decisions using just *one* variable, well then that would be significant progress."

Effective design techniques that use colour and shape can help readers tune in to the two separate series and my experience at the *Financial Times* suggests that certain audiences (such as markets analysts, who see them daily) are very literate when it comes to reading them.

They are perhaps at their most effective when showing a "mirroring" pattern between two series – as in this chart of changes in both the number and value of bitcoin futures over a three-year period.

Hedge funds and big money managers are actively trading bitcoin futures

Average daily trading volume of bitcoin futures

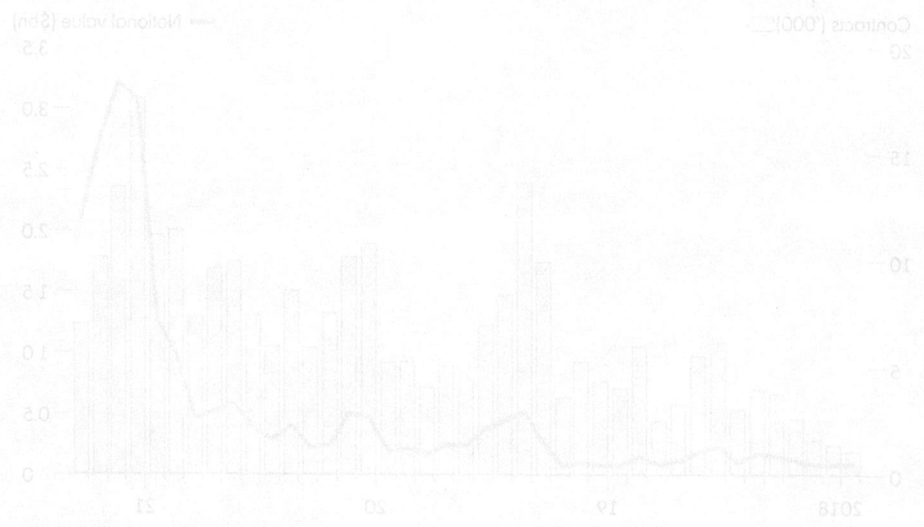

Source: CME Group appeared in Netscape 2.0: Coinbase stock debut rekindles memories of web breakthrough. Available at: https://www.ft.com/content/cbe1d085-c665-4c22-b7af-51b177ae38bd

Let's conclude this section on correlation by giving the final word to Hans Rosling.

In 2010, I had the pleasure of being on a panel with him at a United Nations conference in New York. A statistician in the audience asked my esteemed fellow panelist, with just a hint of disdain, why he thought all policymakers' decisions could be informed by being provided with just two variables (from the correlations shown on his bubble charts). Rosling paused, smiled politely and then replied with a twinkle in his eye: "If I could get policymakers to make decisions using just one variable, well then that would be significant progress."

7

Charts of distribution

Show values in a dataset and how often they occur. The shape (or "skew") of a distribution can be a memorable way of highlighting the lack of uniformity or equality in the data.

In early April 2016, the race for the Democratic presidential nomination was entering its final phase. Early primaries had seen the race whittled down to a head-to-head between establishment favourite Hillary Clinton and maverick Vermont Senator Bernie Sanders.

Prominent in the Sanders campaign was a pledge to address income and wealth inequality in the US, a topic he frequently wrote about in momentum-generating social media posts.

On 11 April, Sanders wrote on Facebook, "The reality is that for the last 40 years there's been an enormous transfer of wealth from the middle class to the wealthiest people in this country." The post included a small preview of a chart and a link to an article by Michael Hiltzik, a Pulitzer Prize-winning journalist at the *Los Angeles Times*.

The article's headline – "America's explosion of income inequality, in one amazing, animated chart" – caught my attention because (pre-Covid) it was still relatively rare to see a chart given top billing in news headlines. This was swiftly followed by a sense of familiarity. I knew the chart in question very well – because I had made it.

The animation was produced about six months before it appeared on Senator Sanders' Facebook page, using new analysis from Pew Research Center, as part of a *Financial Times* story on the US middle class. It showed how the *distribution* of household income in the US, adjusted for inflation, had changed between 1971 and 2015. Let's look at the animation step-by-step.

The shape-shifting US income distribution

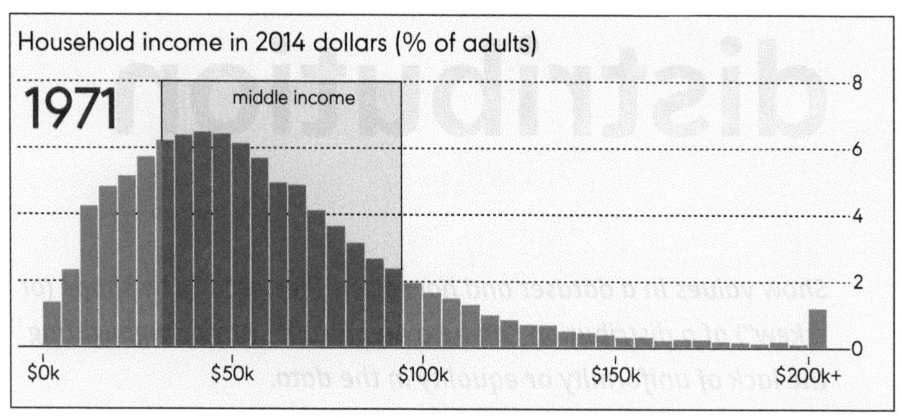

Source: Data from Pew Research Center appeared in Sam Fleming and Shawn Donnan, America's Middle-class Meltdown: Core shrinks to half of US homes, Financial Times, December 10 2015. Available at: https://www.ft.com/content/98ce14ee-99a6-11e5-95c7-d47aa298f769

Initially, a view of US household income for 1971 is shown. Most Americans are located on the left-hand side of the chart (as part of households with incomes well under $100,000) – with a much shallower "long tail" extending to the right, terminating in a notch that represents people living in households with incomes of $200,000 and above.

Pew's definition of "middle income" – two-thirds to double median household income – is shown by a shaded area.

A firm blue line sweeps over the top of the chart to provide a permanently visible reminder of the starting point before the animation begins in earnest. The chart's shape then transforms as we follow changes in US income distribution through the decades before finally coming to a rest in 2015.

The shape-shifting US income distribution

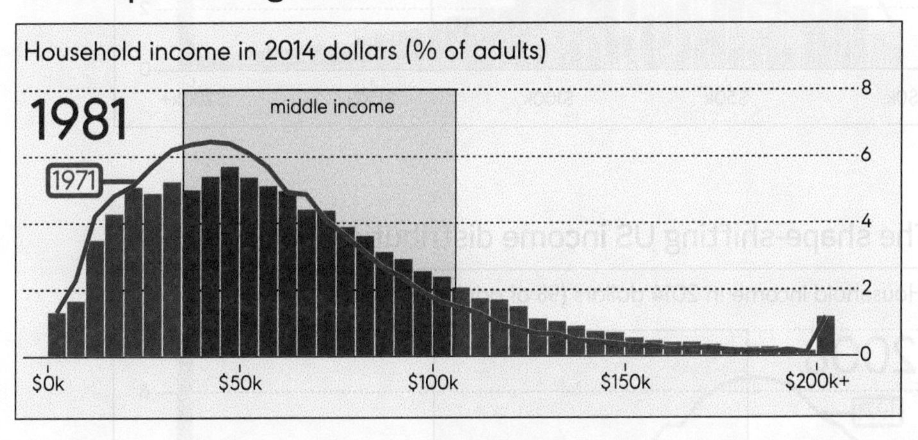

The shape-shifting US income distribution

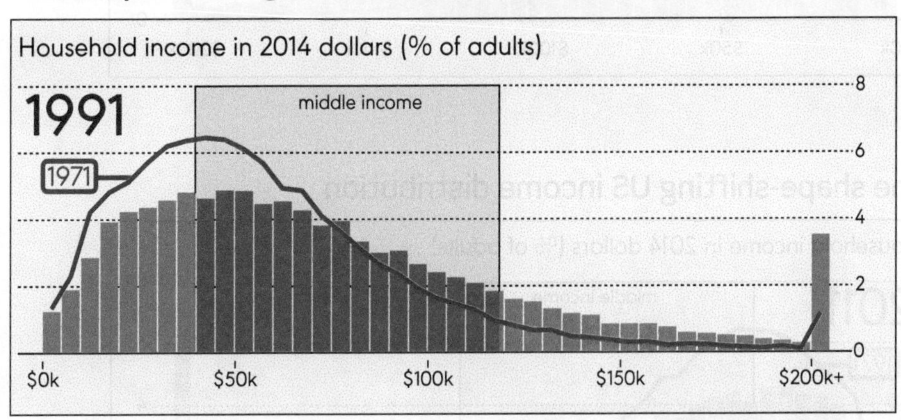

The shape-shifting US income distribution

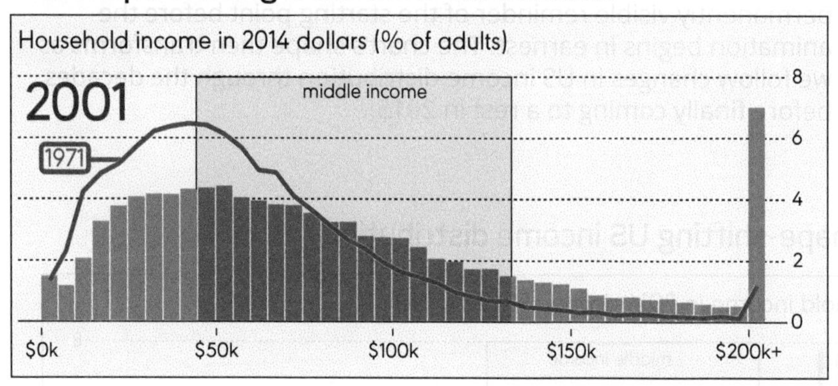

The shape-shifting US income distribution

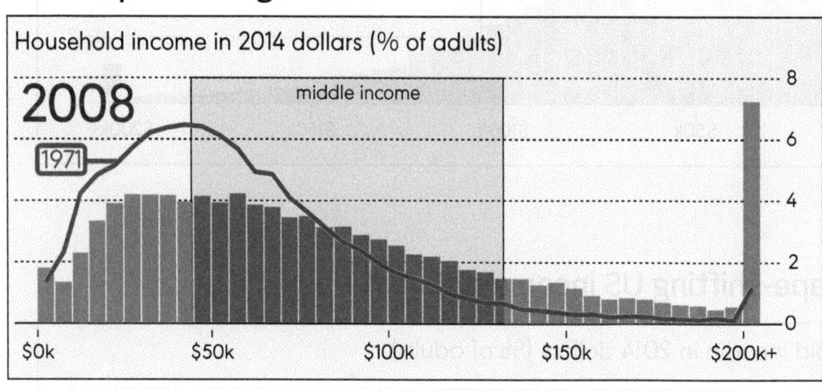

The shape-shifting US income distribution

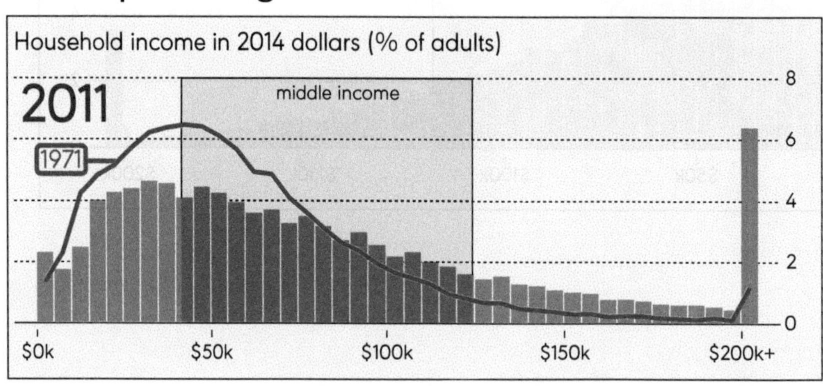

The shape-shifting US income distribution

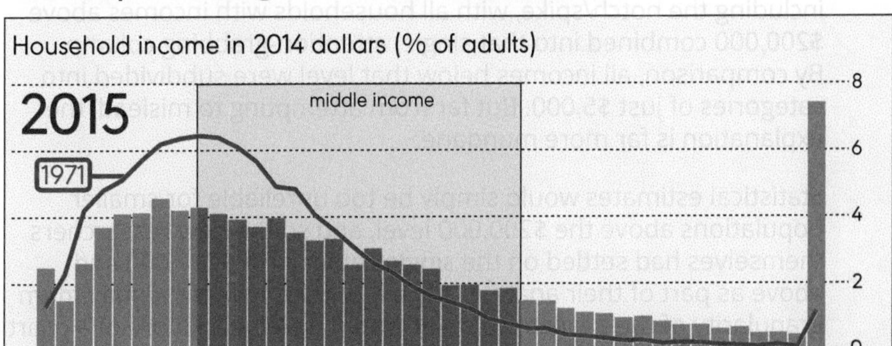

Source: Data from Pew Research Center appeared in Sam Fleming and Shawn Donnan, America's Middle-class Meltdown: Core shrinks to half of US homes, Financial Times, December 10, 2015. Available at: https://www.ft.com/content/98ce14ee-99a6-11e5-95c7-d47aa298f769

Visually, the most striking element of the chart's transformation is undoubtedly the way the 1971 "notch" of people at $200,000+ (just over 1 per cent) had become a towering spike (nearly 8 per cent) by 2015. But there are plenty of other stories on the chart.

For example, the difference between the blue "memory line" of 1971 and our final finishing position in 2015, shows that the US middle class had been "hollowed out" – the pronounced hump from 1971 on the left of the chart has been eroded. This is because many of those on the distribution shifted to the right (a sign of growing incomes).

But notice also that the share of people in the very poorest area of the chart (the first column on the chart, with household incomes of $0–$5k) is higher in 2015 than it was in 1971. You can see that pattern emerge in the 2011 panel, which followed the financial crisis of 2008. Clearly, what had been a time of progress for many was not a time of progress for all.

The stark impression given by the chart was enough for it to make the front page of the *Financial Times* print edition in December 2015.

Thanks, in no small part, to Senator Sanders, the animated version of the chart continued to be widely shared and debated online for months afterwards, particularly on social media. It says a lot about the power of charts as objects of mass communication that most people who saw the animation saw it in places other than the article in which it was originally published.

Some commenters accused me of biasing the presentation by including the notch/spike, with all households with incomes above $200,000 combined into that single, attention-grabbing column. By comparison, all incomes below that level were subdivided into categories of just $5,000. But far from attempting to mislead, the explanation is far more mundane.

Statistical estimates would simply be too unreliable for smaller populations above the $200,000 level, and so the Pew researchers themselves had settled on the single category of $200,000 and above as part of their analysis. My chart just showed the maximum granularity of the available data. It would have been more of a chart crime to hide the $200,000+ category, because it no longer would have been a summary of the entire dataset.

In any case, I was certainly not disappointed that the spike created such a stir – it's a better way of drawing attention to a chart than encasing the graphic in a pair of underpants (see "A firm grasp of the facts" in Chapter 2 for a grim reminder!).

Ultimately, the chart informed an enormous amount of (often partisan) debate, itself revealing a lot about the electorate that would head to the polls later in 2016 to choose its new president. As the *FT* front page headline foresaw, the splintered society depicted by the chart ultimately fuelled the successful campaign of Donald Trump.

Histogram

For a brief period, my animated chart was probably the most famous – and widely discussed – histogram in the world. Which leads us to an interesting question. What exactly *is* a histogram? And how is it different from a column chart?

The shape of a histogram tells us a lot about whether the data (in our first example, income) are evenly distributed – and, consequently, how much we can trust simple summary figures like averages.

In a symmetric distribution, all three averages – the mean, the median and the mode – will be near identical (i.e., in the centre of the chart) because the data are evenly distributed. However, with skewed distributions, both positive and negative, the data are not evenly distributed, and we therefore need to take great care when summarising the data with averages.

How to read a histogram

Histograms summarise a dataset into 'bins' (containers for similar values). This allows us to see how the data are distributed across the full range of values

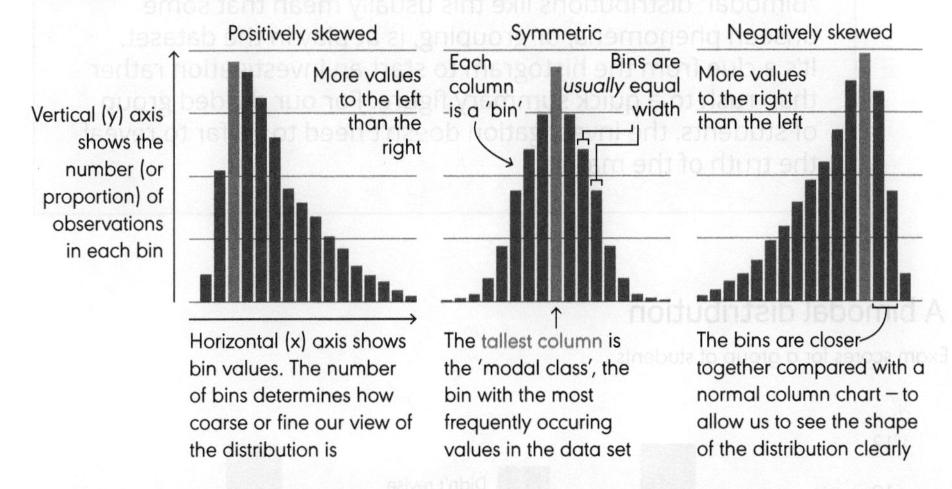
Positively skewed
Symmetric
Negatively skewed
Vertical (y) axis shows the number (or proportion) of observations in each bin
More values to the left than the right
Each column is a 'bin'
Bins are usually equal width
More values to the right than the left
Horizontal (x) axis shows bin values. The number of bins determines how coarse or fine our view of the distribution is
The tallest column is the 'modal class', the bin with the most frequently occuring values in the data set
The bins are closer together compared with a normal column chart – to allow us to see the shape of the distribution clearly

The median (the middle point if the data were sorted in order) is generally the most used summary figure because it is not influenced by extreme values (known as "outliers"). It is for this reason that statisticians refer to the median as a "resistant" measure.

But even the median is an unhelpful summary figure in some cases, as this histogram of fictional exam scores helps show. In this data, there are *two* modal classes, meaning it's just not appropriate to describe this dataset with a single summary figure.

A bimodal distribution

Exam scores for a group of students

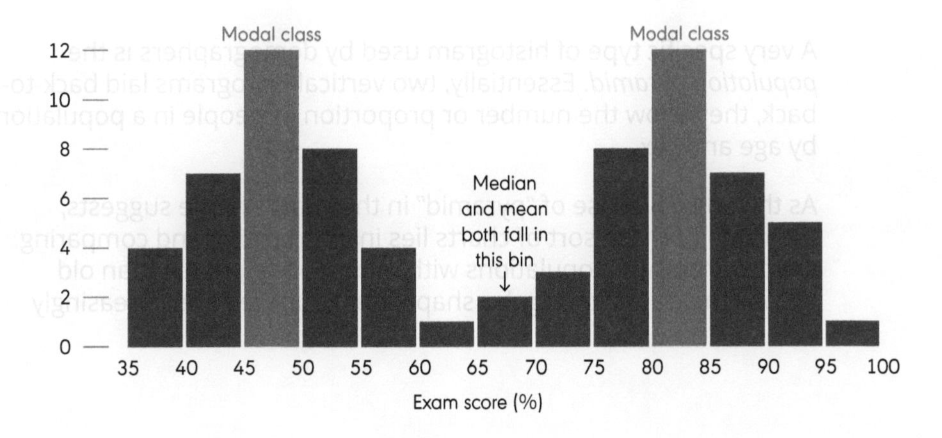
Modal class
Modal class
Median and mean both fall in this bin
12
10
8
6
4
2
0
35
40
45
50
55
60
65
70
75
80
85
90
95
100
Exam score (%)

> ## **Learning point** – Bimodal distributions
>
> "Bimodal" distributions like this usually mean that some unseen phenomena, or grouping, is at play in the dataset. It's a clue from the histogram to start an investigation rather than rush to a quick summary figure. For our divided group of students, the investigation doesn't need to go far to reveal the truth of the matter.

A bimodal distribution

Exam scores for a group of students

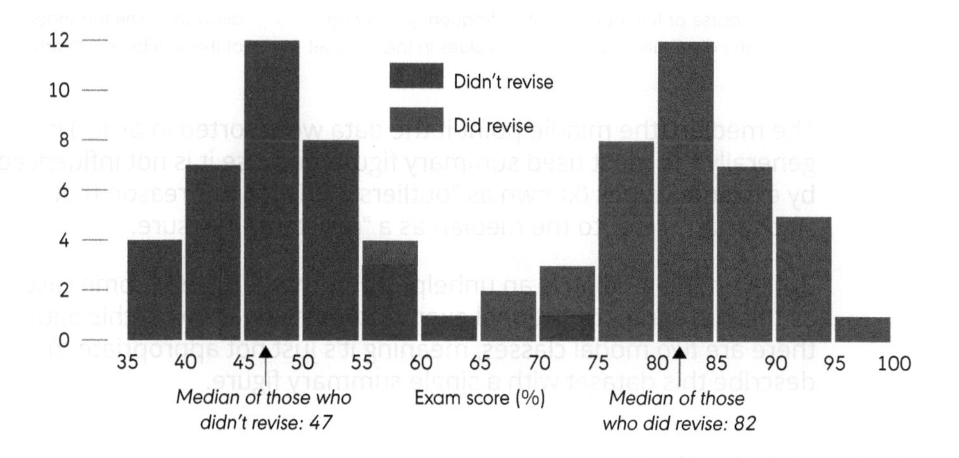

Population pyramid

A very specific type of histogram used by demographers is the *population pyramid*. Essentially, two vertical histograms laid back-to-back, they show the number or proportion of people in a population by age and sex.

As the adjectival use of "pyramid" in the chart's name suggests, the value of these sort of charts lies in interpreting and comparing shapes. Youthful populations with more young people than old deliver the classic triangular shape, but countries are increasingly concerned about the prospect of inverted pyramids that reflect ageing populations resulting from falling birth rates and longer life expectancy.

Because of the interest in how population pyramids change over time, they can benefit from the same use of animation and "memory lines" to compare past/future/present, as we saw with our US income distribution.

This set of population pyramids for half a dozen countries contrasts their population structures of 1960 with current UN projections for 2050 and provides additional information on generational cohorts. Note the supporting information on how to interpret the various shapes, a useful guide for readers unfamiliar with this chart type.

The rise of Generation Z

Projected share of population in 2050, by age and sex (%)

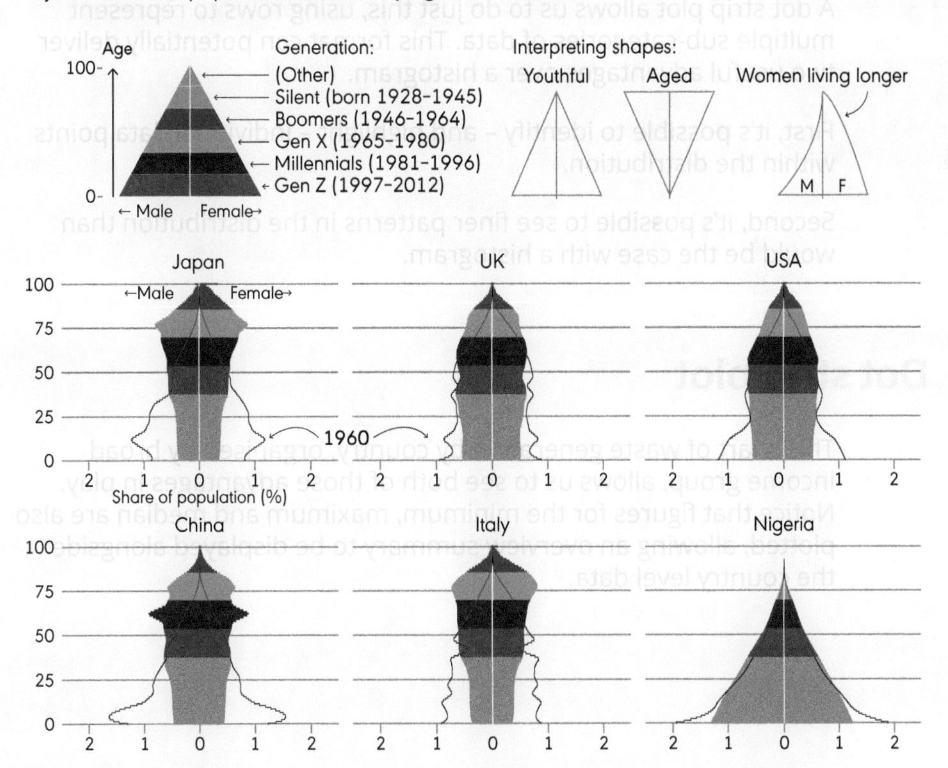

Source: UN appeared in Alan Smith, Tomorrow's world in charts: Gen Z, climate change, China, Brexit and global trade, Financial Times, December 16, 2020. Available at: https://www.ft.com/content/af4631f3-fed3-476c-b9c0-bd460a930a48

Population pyramids like these were my first foray into the world of modern data visualisation and its potential as a communication and policy tool.

In 2003, I created a series of interactive, animated population pyramids of local area data while working at the UK Office for National Statistics. As experimental graphics, I wondered what uses people might find for them. Soon after they were published, I was delighted to receive a letter from an educational analyst who described how she had been able to use the animations in the middle of a school governors meeting to explain falling admission rates in their catchment area: "We've never used data in a meeting like that before!" she exclaimed – I've loved a good population pyramid ever since.

Although I'm a big fan of histograms, we need to remind ourselves that what we're looking at is a *summary* of all the values in a dataset. Sometimes, it pays to plot *all* the data.

A dot strip plot allows us to do just this, using rows to represent multiple sub-categories of data. This format can potentially deliver two useful advantages over a histogram.

First, it's possible to identify – and highlight – individual data points within the distribution.

Second, it's possible to see finer patterns in the distribution than would be the case with a histogram.

Dot strip plot

This chart of waste generation by country, organised by broad income group, allows us to see both of those advantages in play. Notice that figures for the minimum, maximum and median are also plotted, allowing an overview summary to be displayed alongside the country level data.

How waste generation rates vary by income level

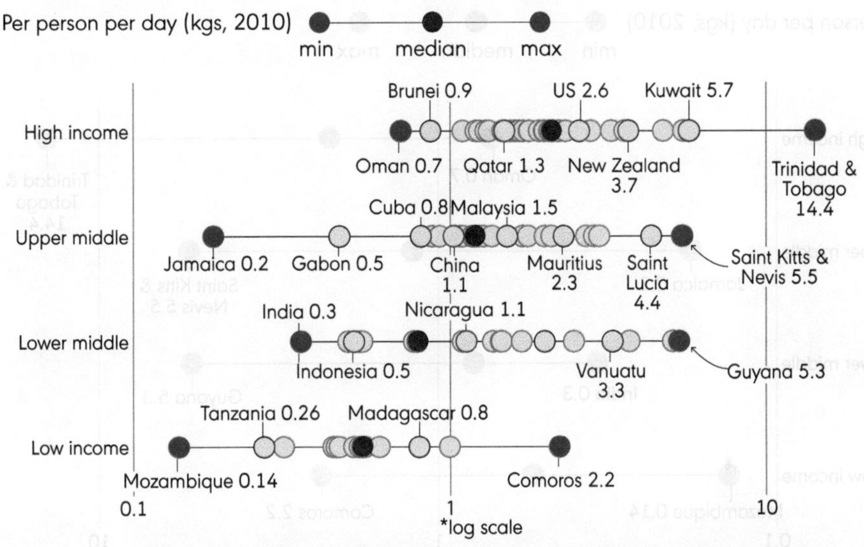

Source: Jambeck Research Group: Report 'Plastic waste inputs from land into the ocean, (2015)' appeared in Consumer goods groups join war on plastic by John Aglionby in Nairobi, Anna Nicolaou in New York and Scheherazade Daneshkhu in London, January 22, 2018. Available at: https://www.ft.com/content/61629224-fc9f-11e7-9b32-d7d59aace167

Dot plot

In fact, the summary points alone could be the focus of a chart, resulting in a much simpler *dot plot*. Notice the important trade-off – the summary dot plot is clearer in terms of showing how waste generation varies by income level, but it's at the expense of details that allow us to compare country performance. In fact, we now have even less summary information than we would have from using a histogram – it's impossible to see characteristics like skew.

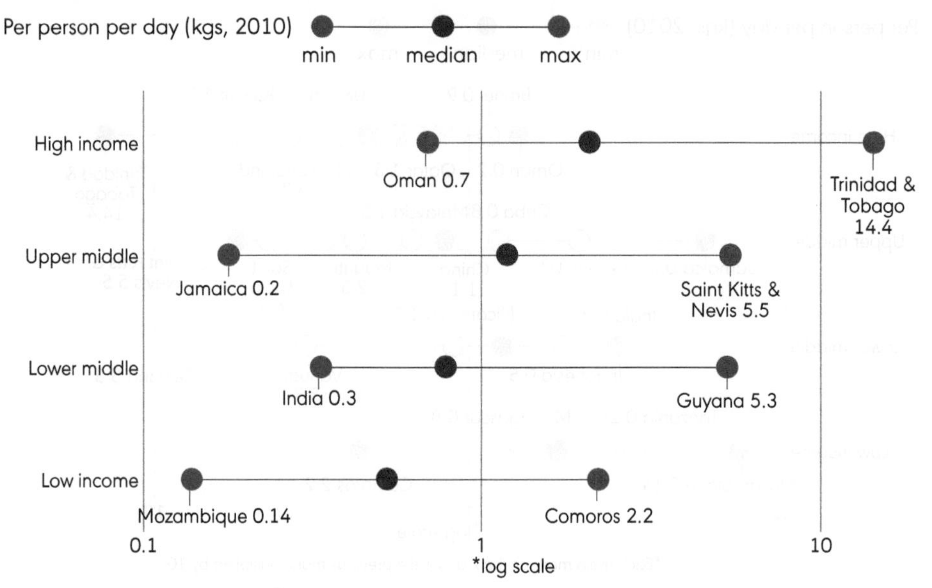

Barcode plot

A related chart type to the dot strip plot is the barcode plot. These work in a similar way but use a different type of marker – thin vertical stripes – instead of dots. The advantage of this approach? They are effective when values are clustered close together, where overlapping dots might create problems of occlusion.

This chart of how Tony Award-winning plays receive a box office boost after award season is a good example – if this were a dot strip plot, the circles would simply be too close to each other.

Armed with dot strip plots and barcode plots, it might be tempting to think that we should dispense with distribution summaries altogether and just stick to looking at the entire dataset. But messy real-world data means that this is not always possible, or even desirable.

Best Play winners always see a bump in takings after the Tonys

Original plays from 2002–2017

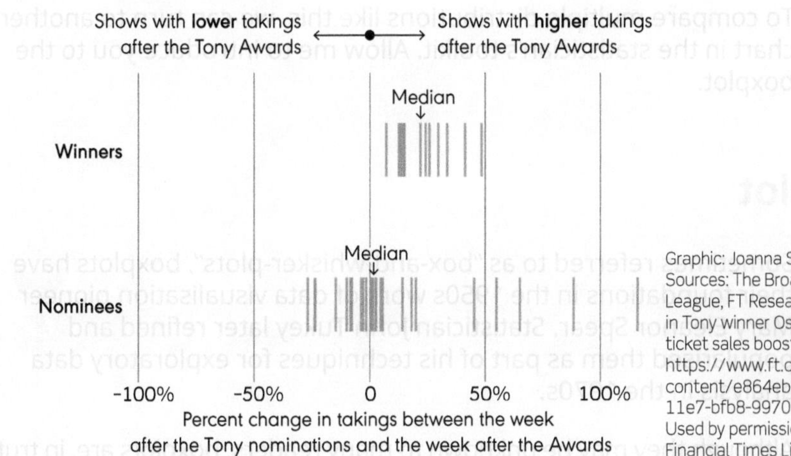

Graphic: Joanna S Kao
Sources: The Broadway League, FT Research appeared in Tony winner Oslo set for ticket sales boost. Available at: https://www.ft.com/content/e864eb26-4e00-11e7-bfb8-997009366969. Used by permission from The Financial Times Limited.

To illustrate this point, our next chart plots the change in vote at the local (ward) level for the Labour Party at the 2021 local elections in England.

The move away from Labour

Change in vote, by region (percentage points, each point represents a ward)

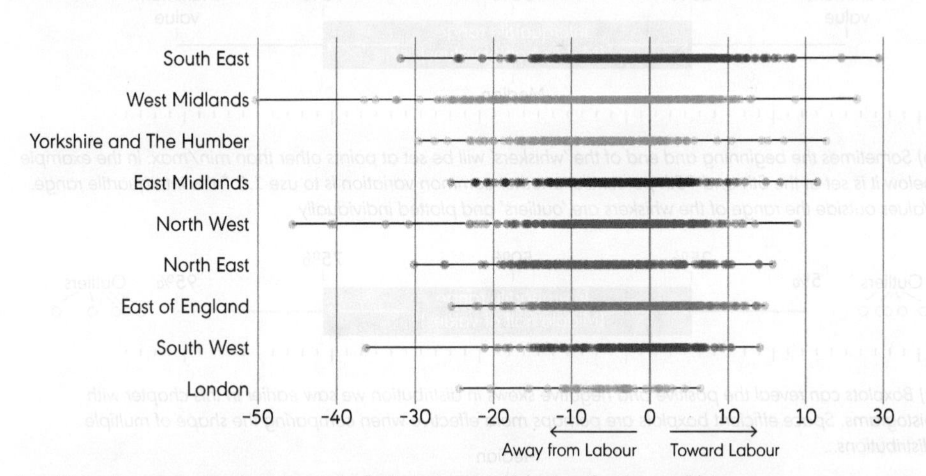

In multi-member wards, the vote share used reflects each party's highest-performing candidate
Source: Britain Elects appeared in Based on Boris Johnson's levelling-up agenda takes toll on southern Tories by George Parker. Available at: https://www.ft.com/content/273c58af-6d3e-4c36-b4a5-4f4e7d941875

Although the data are divided into regions, it's difficult to see the distribution of data, even on just one row of data, let alone make comparisons between the distributions. There are over 8,000 wards in England – not even a barcode plot would be able to rescue our eyes from the density of displaying so much raw data in such a small space.

To compare multiple distributions like this, we can turn to another chart in the statistician's toolkit. Allow me to introduce you to the boxplot.

Boxplot

Sometimes referred to as "box-and-whisker-plots", boxplots have their foundations in the 1950s work of data visualisation pioneer Mary Eleanor Spear. Statistician John Tukey later refined and popularised them as part of his techniques for exploratory data analysis in the 1970s.

Although they may be unknown to many readers, boxplots are, in truth, simple data visualisations to read, once you are familiar with them.

Anatomy of a boxplot

Box plots summarise how the values in a dataset are distributed

a) At their most basic, boxplots show the location of the minimum and maximum, together with the 25th, 50th (median) and 75th percentiles. 50% of the dataset's values lie the middle box - this is the 'interquartile range'

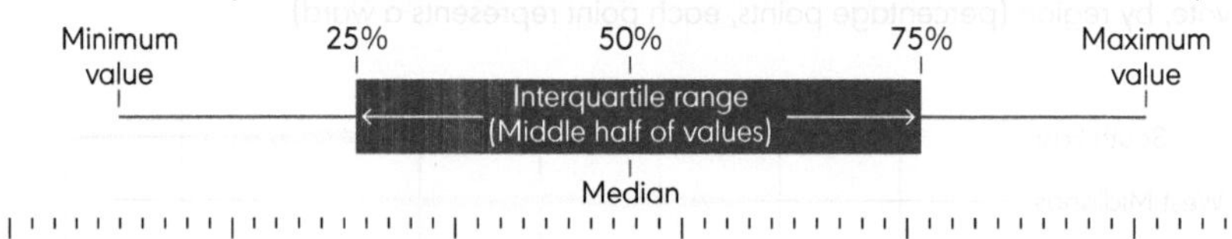

*b) Sometimes the beginning and end of the 'whiskers' will be set at points other than min/max: in the example below it is set at the 5th and 95th percentile; another common variation is to use 1.5 * the interquartile range. Values outside the range of the whiskers are 'outliers' and plotted individually*

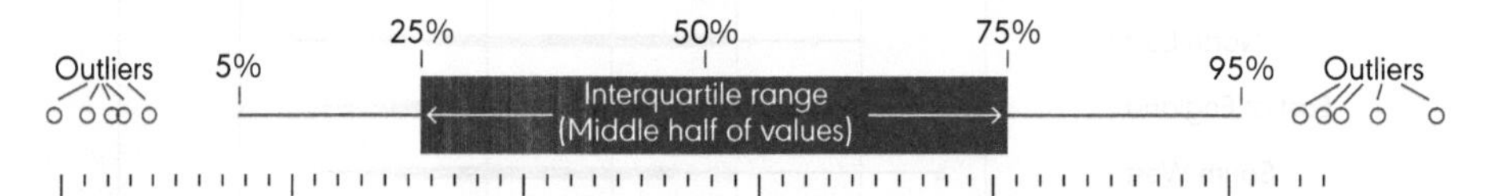

c) Boxplots can reveal the positive and negative skews in distribution we saw earlier in this chapter with histograms. Space efficient boxplots are perhaps more effective when comparing the shape of multiple distributions...

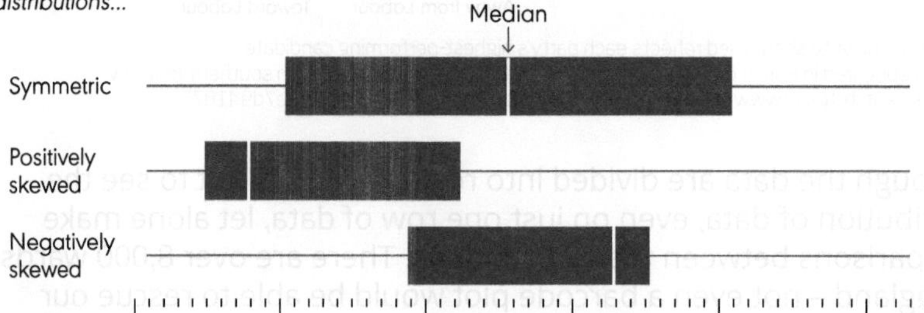

Boxplots can be oriented vertically or horizontally. For visualising multiple distributions (the best use of boxplots), like horizontal boxplots, as they stack more efficiently and are easier to label.

What are the benefits of learning to read this exotic new chart type? Well, let's look at the same ward level election data from our dot strip plots in boxplot form.

Labour's gains in the South East bucked their overall poor performance

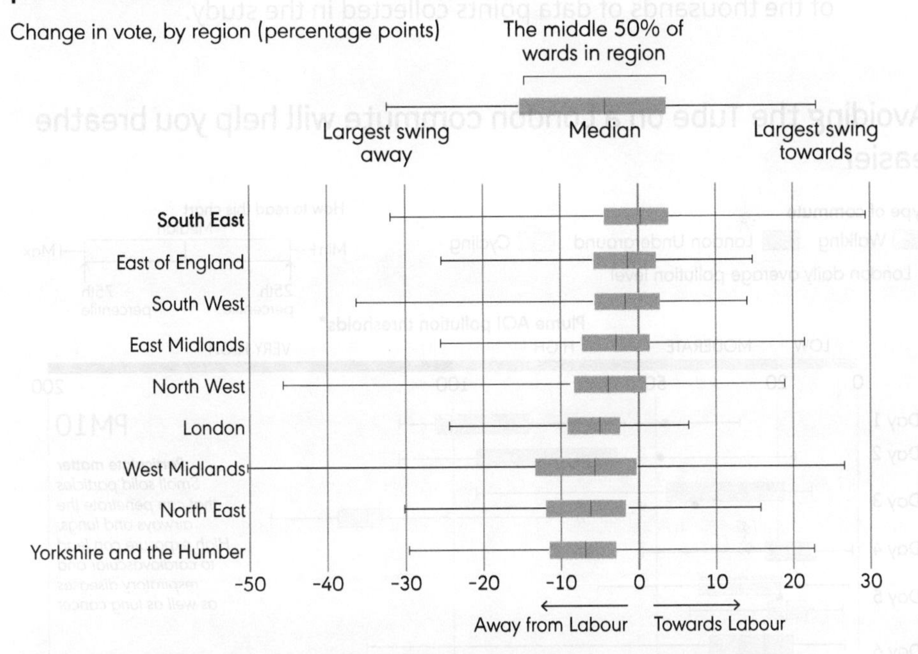

In multi-member wards, the vote share used reflects each party's highest-performing candidate
Source: Britain Elects appeared in George Parker, Boris Johnson's levelling-up agenda takes toll on southern Tories, Financial Times, May 14 2021. Available at: https://www.ft.com/content/273c58af-6d3e-4c36-b4a5-4f4e7d941875

This view provides real clarity on the regional performance of the Labour Party. We can see that the South East was the only region where the median value of its constituent wards was above zero (i.e., a very faint swing towards Labour).

In all the other regions, you'll see the distributions edging more into the "Away from Labour" side of the chart. Because the rows are sorted by median value, we can see a *ranking* relationship in the data too (South East = best performance, Yorkshire and the Humber = the worst).

As with all chart types, boxplots have their strengths and weaknesses. As visualisations of distributions, they don't allow us to spot multimodal or bimodal distributions as we did with the histogram. But they are a very space-efficient way of showing multiple distributions, as in our local election example.

Once you know how to read a boxplot, their value to creating sophisticated yet educational graphics becomes apparent. The following chart of particulate pollution faced by London commuters from my colleague Steve Bernard is a good example.

Steve has cleverly used each row of boxplots to represent different days of data, making this a view of *distributions* and *change over time*. His use of colour to denote category of transport means we can see a very clear message in the data (if you want to avoid the highest levels of pollution, avoid the Tube) without having to plot all of the thousands of data points collected in the study.

Avoiding the Tube on a London commute will help you breathe easier

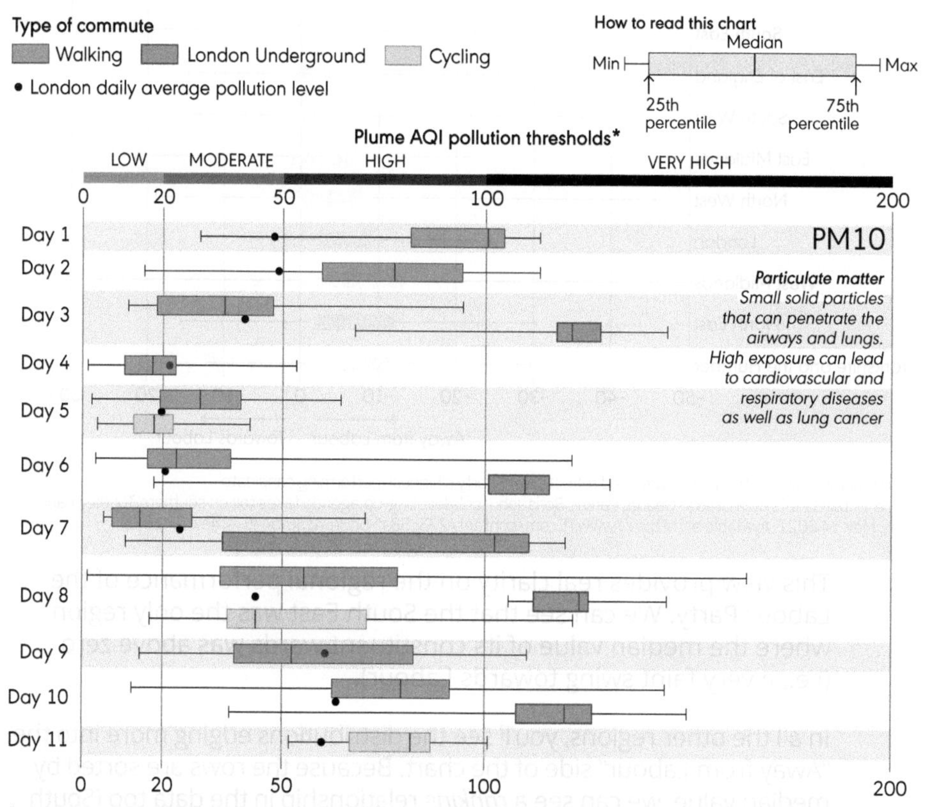

* Plume Labs Air Quality Index pollution thresholds based on World Health Organization guidelines

Low: Below the threshold for **one year** of exposure
Moderate: Over the threshold for **one year** of exposure
High: Over the threshold for **24 hours** of exposure
Very high: Over the threshold for **one hour** of exposure

Source: Graphic: Steven Bernard Sources: Plume Labs; Defra; FT research appeared in Leslie Hook, Neil Munshi, How safe is the air we breathe?, Financial Times, September 5, 2019. Available at: https://www.ft.com/content/7d54cfb8-cea5-11e9-b018-ca4456540ea6

The field of data visualisation is constantly innovating and finding new ways of addressing the limitations of traditional chart types. For visualising distributions, there's been a surge in popularity recently for the evocatively named beeswarm chart.

Beeswarm plot

Here, all the points are plotted as per a dot strip plot, but, to avoid overlapping points, each point is randomly displaced, or "jittered" so that we can see all the data – and the shape of the distribution. It can be a remarkably effective technique.

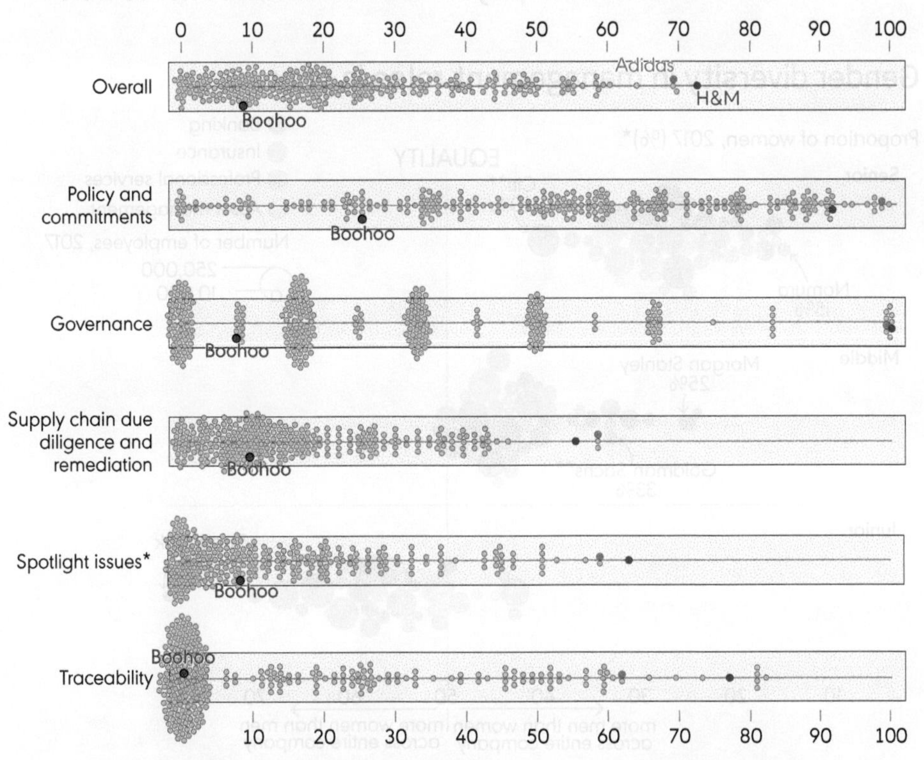

* Measures what brands are doing to address forced labour, gender equality, living wages, freedom of association, waste, circularity, overproduction, use of more sustainable materials, microplastics, deforestation, climate change and water use
Source: Fashion Transparency Index appeared in How Boohoo came to rule the roost in Leicester's underground textile trade by Robert Wright in Leicester and Patricia Nilsson in London, July 11, 2020. Available at: https://www.ft.com/content/bbe5dfc5-3b5c-41d2-9637-50e91c58b26b

If you look closely, you'll spot that in many cases the "jittering" process moves the dots away from the precise location of its transparency index score. For example, if you look at the thick cluster of dots at the start of the "Traceability" row, those all score zero – the displacement algorithm behind the chart keeps them as close to zero as possible without forcing dots to overlap each other.

This is an effective technique but reveals a slight compromise in precision. I would use a beeswarm chart to highlight individual points in terms of their broad position in a distribution (just as we have with Boohoo here), but I wouldn't use it if I wanted readers to quantity individual scores by reading off values against the axis.

As with the scatterplot, we can inject colour and size variation into beeswarm plots to add categorical and *magnitude* elements. This beeswarm plot shows the distribution of women at junior, middle and senior positions in financial companies – but also allows us to see broad number of employees and its financial sector as well.

Gender diversity in management roles is poor

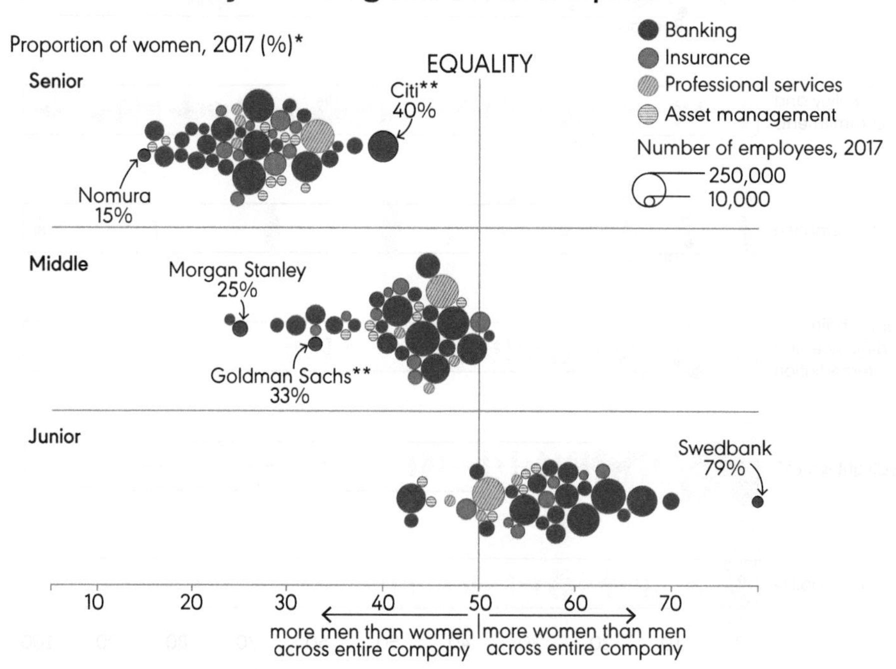

*Certain organisations figures are for home regions only
**Includes FT estimates; Citi's 'senior' figures also include mid-level managers
Source: Graphic: Liz Faunce, Helena Robertson Sources: Companies, FT research appeared in Executives optimistic on improving gender diversity by Laura Noonan, Oliver Ralph and Jennifer Thompson, September 10, 2018. Available at: https://www.ft.com/content/80200a46-b27c-11e8-8d14-6f049d06439c

Lorenz curve

We started this chapter by looking at income inequality, a topic that frequently involves a visual analysis of distributions. In fact, one type of chart was specifically conceived for just this purpose.

The American economist Max Otto Lorenz was still an undergraduate in 1905 when he created a deceptively simple plot: the cumulative share of people against the corresponding cumulative share of income earned.

Today, the convention is for the share of people to be plotted on the horizontal (x) axis, and the share of income on the vertical (y) – although, curiously, Lorenz's original had the reverse layout.

On the *Lorenz curve*, important context is provided by a diagonal line from bottom left to top right – it represents a perfectly equal distribution (income evenly shared across an entire population). Measured data are then plotted ready for interpretation. As Lorenz put it himself:

> *"With an unequal distribution, the curves will always begin and end in the same points as with an equal distribution [0 and 100], but they will be bent in the middle; and the rule of interpretation will be, as the bow is bent, concentration increases."*

A Lorenz curve

After Max Otto Lorenz (1905)

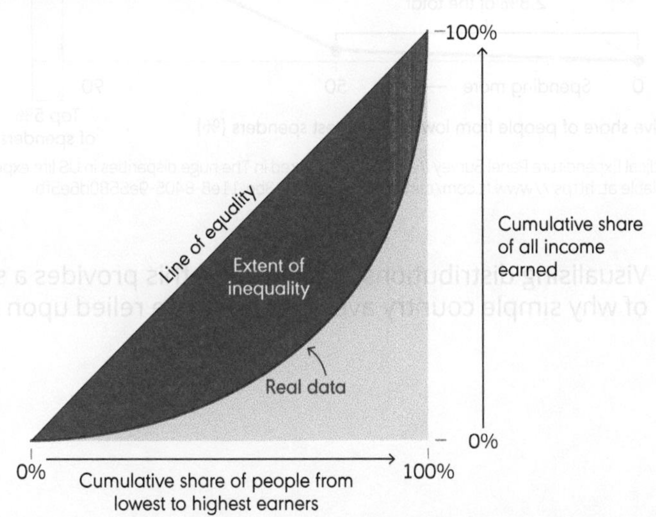

In other words, the further the bent line (representing the real data) diverges from the diagonal, the greater the level of inequality.

With the image of Lorenz's "bent bow" fresh in our minds, let us return to the US healthcare paradox we encountered in the last chapter on *correlation*. How can it be that Americans spend so much on healthcare yet see very little return in life expectancy improvements?

A big part of the answer is that spending on healthcare is not evenly distributed in the US. In fact, the inequality in terms of spending is truly astounding with the top 5 per cent of spenders contributing half of all healthcare spending in the country.

It's a perfect opportunity to use the Lorenz curve – the resulting "bent bow" looks set to snap.

Spending on healthcare in the US is not evenly distributed

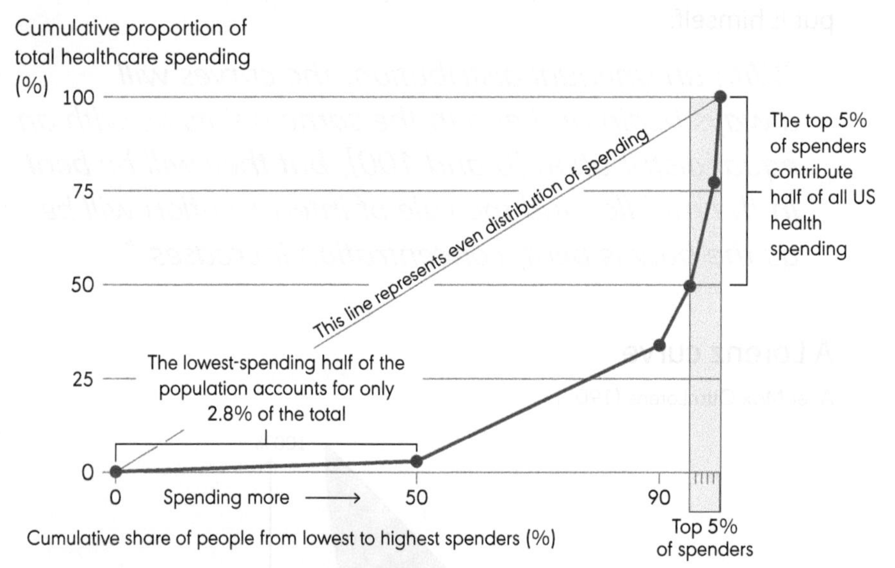
Cumulative proportion of total healthcare spending (%)
100
75
50
25
0
This line represents even distribution of spending
The top 5% of spenders contribute half of all US health spending
The lowest-spending half of the population accounts for only 2.8% of the total
0
Spending more
50
90
Cumulative share of people from lowest to highest spenders (%)
Top 5% of spenders

Source: Medical Expenditure Panel Survey (Nov 2016) appeared in The huge disparities in US life expectancy in five charts. Available at: https://www.ft.com/content/80a76f38-e3be-11e6-8405-9e5580d6e5fb

Visualising distributions as skewed as this provides a stark reminder of why simple country averages are to be relied upon at your peril.

8

Charts of flow

Show the reader volumes or intensity of movement between two or more states or conditions. These might be logical sequences or geographical locations.

Many people think that the only charts that the world needs are the ones we've had for centuries: line charts, bar charts and pie charts. Anything else is just "too complicated". And after all, surely every chart needs to be instantly understood within five seconds of first viewing?

Sometimes, we need to minimise the time between glancing at a visual display and making a related decision. The display on a car dashboard is a good example – I think every driver would rank the speed with which it can be read as a top priority.

Another advantage of simple charts is that you generally don't need to explain to people how to read them. That doesn't necessarily mean they are more "intuitive" than any other type of chart, but most people are likely to have developed expertise in reading them very early on in their education, perhaps even at primary school.

But the biggest advantage of simple charts – their simplicity – is also their biggest constraint. Nowhere is that more apparent than when we come to look at data involving flows.

Flows are a natural result of the innate human desire for interaction. People (migration), goods (trade), money (finance), even company ownership – they are all subject to transactions, connections or movements that are often complex in nature.

Take the following table of figures which, on the face of it, doesn't seem too terrifying. In total, there are only 64 numbers here – just how difficult could it be to turn this data into a chart that tells us something?

Global mergers and acquisitions (M&A)

By region, 2017 ($bn)

Origin ↓ / Destination →	China	N America	LatAm	Europe	Asia*	Japan	Other	
China	431.1	3.6	1.2	0.9	28.6	5.8	0.1	471.4
N America	15.4	1,297.7	11.3	122.3	23.5	31.4	6.4	1,508.2
LatAm	7.8	19.8	48.0	24.9	6.6	0.1	0.2	107.4
Europe	41.4	167.6	7.2	576.7	38.7	6.8	9.4	847.9
Asia*	69.7	33.8	6.6	53.8	252.5	12.2	5.5	434.2
Japan	2.0	23.9	0.0	1.3	2.8	40.0	0.0	70.0
Other	4.1	26.0	1.9	11.1	1.4	2.0	18.0	64.6
	571.6	1,572.5	76.3	791.1	354.1	98.3	39.8	3,503.7

Source: Data from Refinitiv

The table shows the value of all worldwide company mergers and acquisitions (known as M&A) for 2017, grouped into seven regions. You'll notice that each region is named twice, once in the column headings and once in the row headings. That's because this type of dataset, known as an *origin-destination matrix*, shows two-way flows – the *origin* region of the company being acquired and the *destination* of the acquiring company or merged entity.

Before even thinking about charts, it should be recognised that the table on its own is extremely useful. Its clear structure, with destination regions organised in columns and origins in rows, allows the reader to quickly look up any value – including totals – quickly and precisely. That's what tables are good for.

The deficiency of the table, however, is in identifying *patterns* within the data. Trying to understand the relationships between the numbers is difficult because, to compare the numbers with each other, the reader needs to store a lot of information in working memory, creating what psychologists refer to as a high "cognitive load".

So, it's time to get visual – first up, let's see what we can do with our traditional charts.

Of our three canonically "simple" charts, it's perhaps the pie chart that we should turn to. After all, it is designed to show *part-to-whole* relationships, and we clearly have that here with our total global M&A activity subdivided into its constituent parts.

We quickly run into a problem, though – our pie chart can only sensibly tackle one column or row of this data at a time. For example, we can show the composition of M&A activity where China was the destination – but nothing else.

A solitary pie chart is not suited to displaying flow data

Chinese inward M&A, 2017 ($bn)

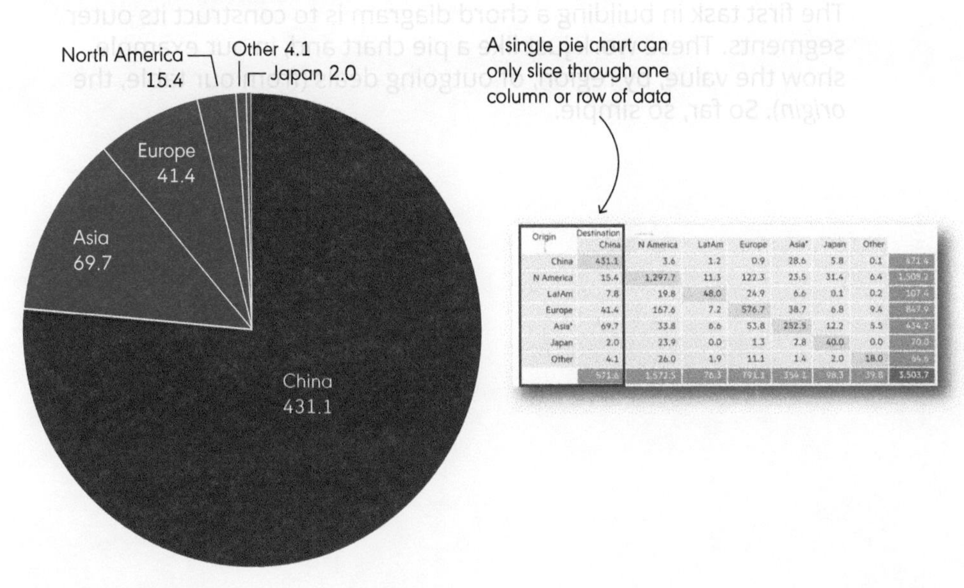

Source: Data from Refinitiv

Of course, we could generate seven separate pie charts (one for each region), but, even then, we would only see the *inward* M&A activity. Another seven charts would be needed to show the *outward* regional activity and two more for the totals (one inward, one outward).

Trying to understand patterns by comparing segments across 16 different pie charts would be considerably harder than even the table. So, we should put a stop to such madness – using an array of pie charts will bring us back to the memory issues we're trying to get away from when reading the table.

Let's try a graphical form designed to work with this sort of data – it's time to introduce you to the "chord diagram".

Chord diagram

This type of chart was first conceived as part of the Circos tool, an initiative to support visualisations in comparative genomics developed by scientists at Vancouver's Michael Smith Genome Sciences Centre.

You can probably tell by this description that it's a sophisticated visualisation, designed by scientists to show complex data. Like all unfamiliar charts, we need to learn how to read it. Let's work through it in a series of steps.

The first task in building a chord diagram is to construct its outer segments. These work just like a pie chart and, in our example, show the value, by region, of outgoing deals (from our table, the *origin*). So far, so simple.

Understanding a 'chord diagram'

Global M&A flows, 2017
($bn)

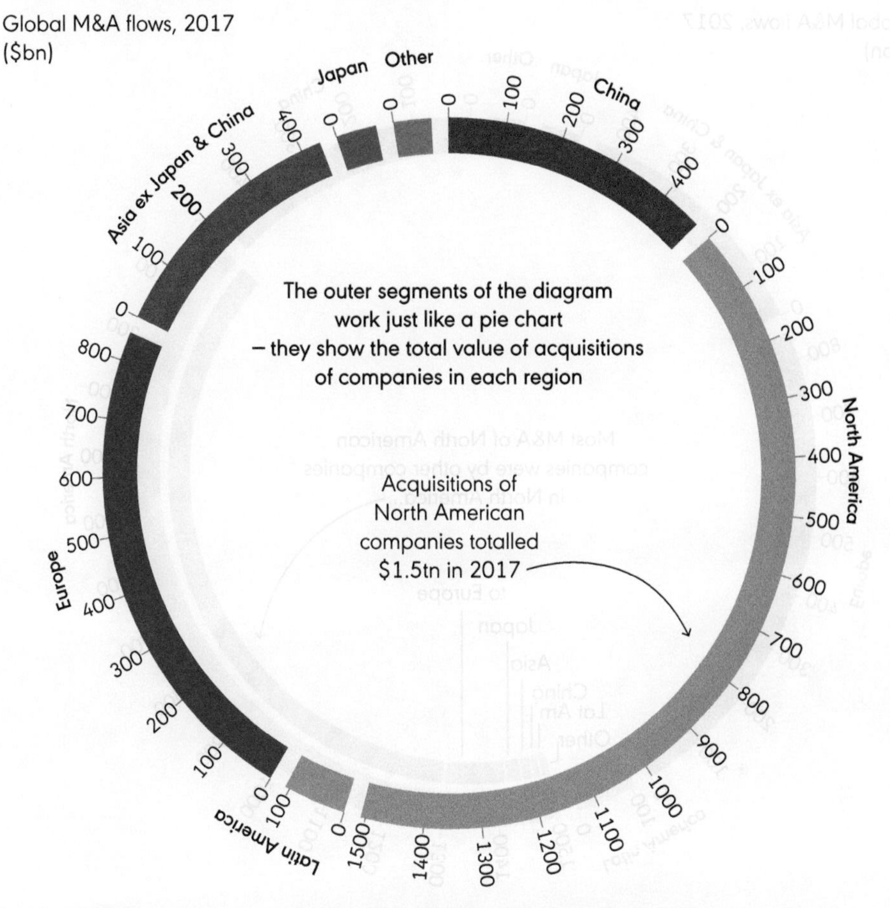

Japan
Other
China
Asia ex Japan & China
North America
Europe
Latin America
The outer segments of the diagram work just like a pie chart – they show the total value of acquisitions of companies in each region
Acquisitions of North American companies totalled $1.5tn in 2017

Source: Refinitiv appeared in Arash Massoudi, M&A boom set to continue in 2017, Financial Times, December 30, 2016. Available at: https://www.ft.com/content/0e9afdce-cdb6-11e6-b8ce-b9c03770f8b1

Next, we need to embrace a little more complexity by understanding that each region segment in the circle can be subdivided into the *destination* regions for our M&A deals. Below, we break down North America's outgoing deals to show those regional destinations.

The outer segments in more detail

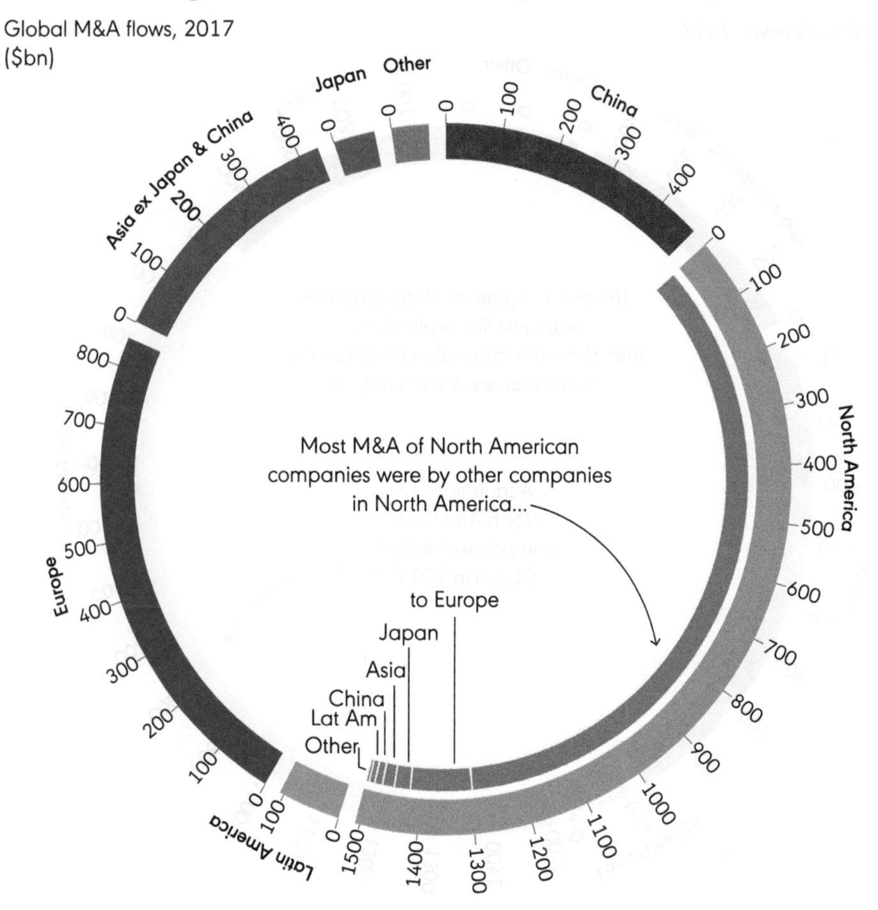

Source: Refinitiv appeared in Arash Massoudi, M&A boom set to continue in 2017, Financial Times, December 30, 2016. Available at: https://www.ft.com/content/0e9afdce-cdb6-11e6-b8ce-b9c03770f8b1

At this stage, we need to think about the two-way flows that are central to our data: North American companies acquire European companies and vice versa. If we draw a "chord" that links these two data points, the mutual relationship between North America and Europe is visualised: the width of the chord at each end reflects the size of the outgoing deals from that region.

Note that a major part of the dataset is the deals that never leave the region – for example, acquisitions of North American companies by other North American companies. We can represent these by drawing a chord that simply connects with itself.

Creating 'chords'

Global M&A flows, 2017
($bn)

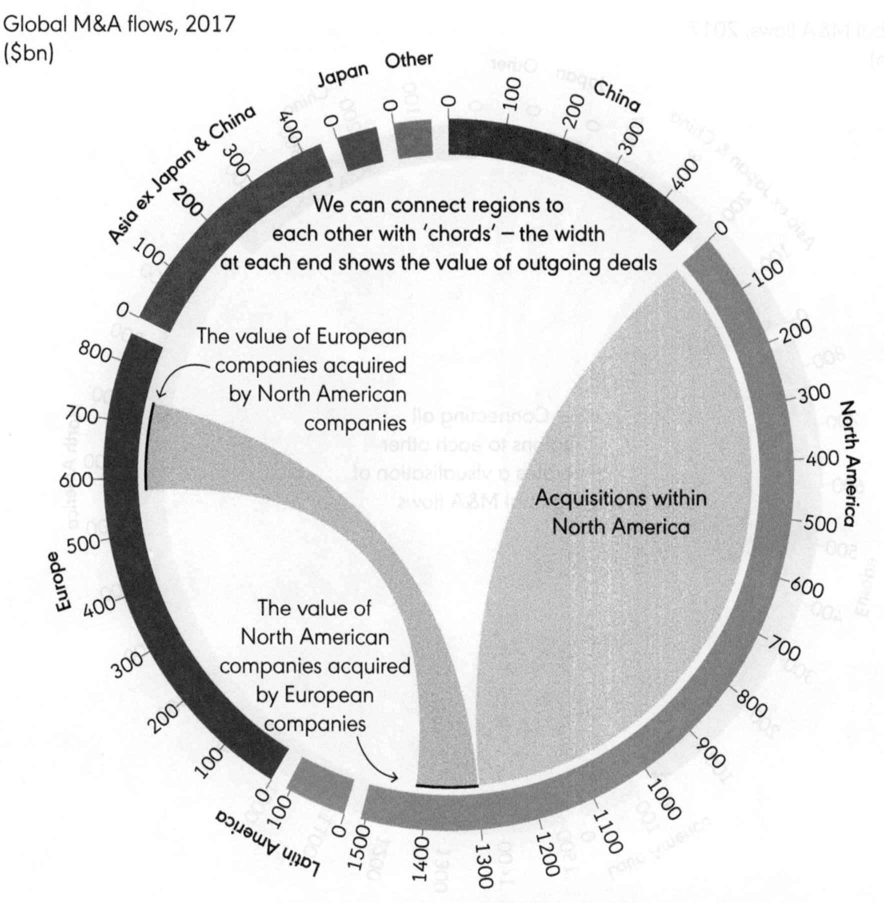
Japan
Other
China
Asia ex Japan & China
North America
Europe
Latin America
We can connect regions to each other with 'chords' – the width at each end shows the value of outgoing deals
The value of European companies acquired by North American companies
Acquisitions within North America
The value of North American companies acquired by European companies

Source: Refinitiv appeared in Arash Massoudi, M&A boom set to continue in 2017, Financial Times, December 30 2016. Available at: https://www.ft.com/content/0e9afdce-cdb6-11e6-b8ce-b9c03770f8b1

Drawing chords between all the outgoing segments and their destination segments means that all 64 numbers from the origin and destination data are now visible in one single diagram. But we need to add some clarity to bring out the patterns in the data.

Squaring the circle

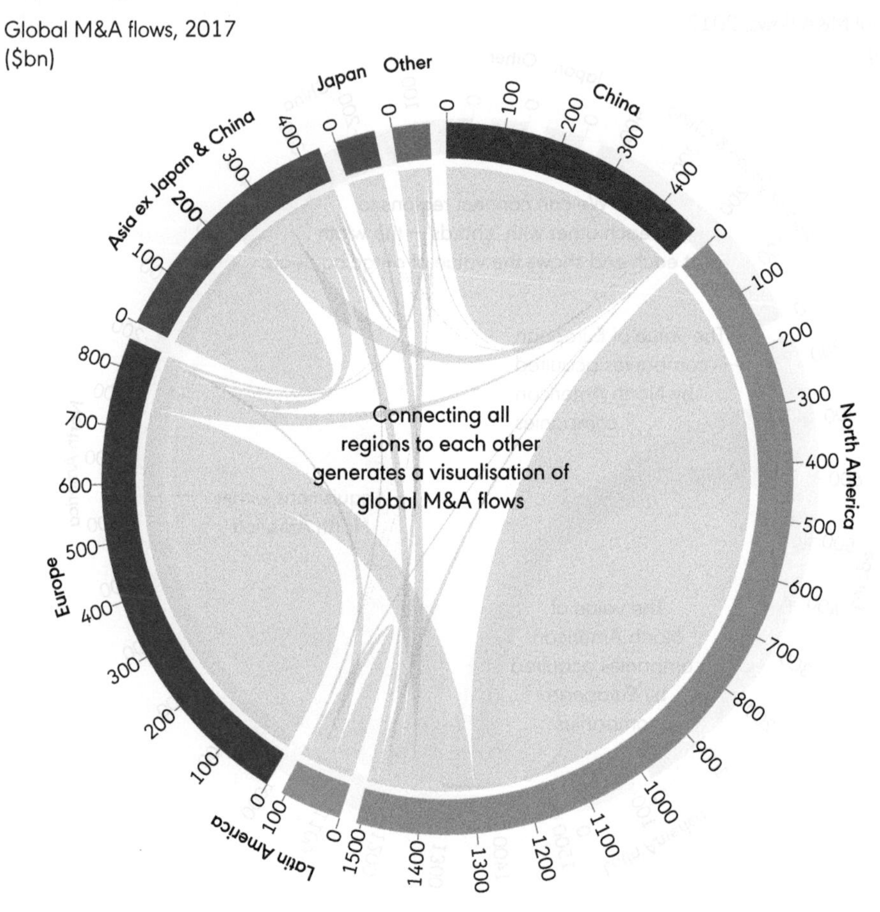

Source: Refinitiv appeared in Arash Massoudi, M&A boom set to continue in 2017, Financial Times, December 30, 2016. Available at: https://www.ft.com/content/0e9afdce-cdb6-11e6-b8ce-b9c03770f8b1

We can use colour to tell us something about the chords and what they represent. In this example, it makes sense to use colour to show the dominant partner in the M&A relationship.

For example, if we take the first chord we drew between North America and Europe, which becomes light blue, the same colour as North America in the outer segment. That's because North America acquires European companies of greater value than go in the opposite direction.

A global view of M&A activity

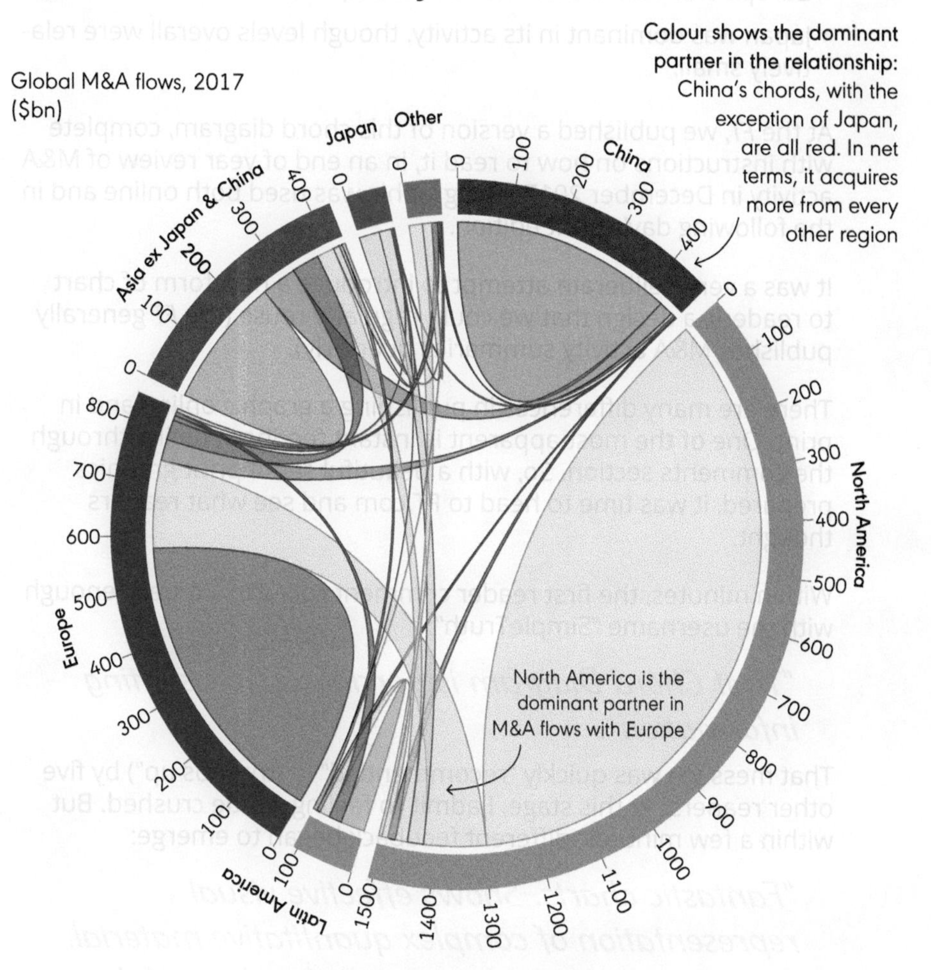
Global M&A flows, 2017
($bn)
Colour shows the dominant partner in the relationship: China's chords, with the exception of Japan, are all red. In net terms, it acquires more from every other region
Asia ex Japan & China
Japan
Other
China
North America
Latin America
Europe
North America is the dominant partner in M&A flows with Europe

Source: Refinitiv appeared in Arash Massoudi, M&A boom set to continue in 2017, Financial Times, December 30, 2016. Available at: https://www.ft.com/content/0e9afdce-cdb6-11e6-b8ce-b9c03770f8b1

Look at China's chords. They may be relatively thin, but except for the chord that connects to Japan, they are all red, meaning that it is the dominant partner in virtually all its M&A dealings.

Armed with a firm grasp of how the chart works, other patterns begin to emerge – among other things, we can now see:

- North America was the biggest region in terms of the value of outgoing M&A activity – and most of its activity was internal to North America.

- Europe was dominant in its relationship with Asia.
- Japan was dominant in its activity, though levels overall were relatively small.

At the *FT*, we published a version of this chord diagram, complete with instructions on how to read it, in an end of year review of M&A activity in December 2017. The graphic was used both online and in the following day's print edition.

It was a very deliberate attempt to introduce a new form of chart to readers, a design that we could regularly reuse (the *FT* generally publishes M&A activity summaries quarterly).

There are many differences in publishing a graphic online and in print. One of the most apparent is instant feedback online through the comments section. So, with a beautiful set of print graphics prepared, it was time to head to FT.com and see what readers thought.

Within minutes, the first reader comment rolled in – cruelly enough with the username "SimpleTruth".

> *"That Chord Diagram is horrible for presenting information".*

That message was quickly "recommended" (a "thumbs up") by five other readers. At this stage, I admit to feeling a little crushed. But within a few minutes, different feedback began to emerge:

> *"Fantastic charts. Shows effective visual representation of complex quantitative material. The 'chord' chart gets my vote for chart of the year." [24 thumbs up]*

In reviewing the success, or otherwise, of the chart, for me the most important element of the reader comments is the ratio between those thumb icons. With five effective "dislikes" and 24 "likes", it was evidence that, although we were pushing readers to understand a new and complex chart type, most of them felt rewarded by the information rewards it brought.

As for the dislikes, there will always be some people who feel that all charts can and should only be pies, lines or bars. As this example shows, that rigid stance means they could be potentially missing out on vital insight.

One final reflection on the chord diagram is on the use of colour, which might be overwhelming for some readers, especially those with colour vision deficiencies. One solution to this problem is to simply focus on specific parts of the dataset, in this instance China.

China is the dominant partner in most of its M&A dealings

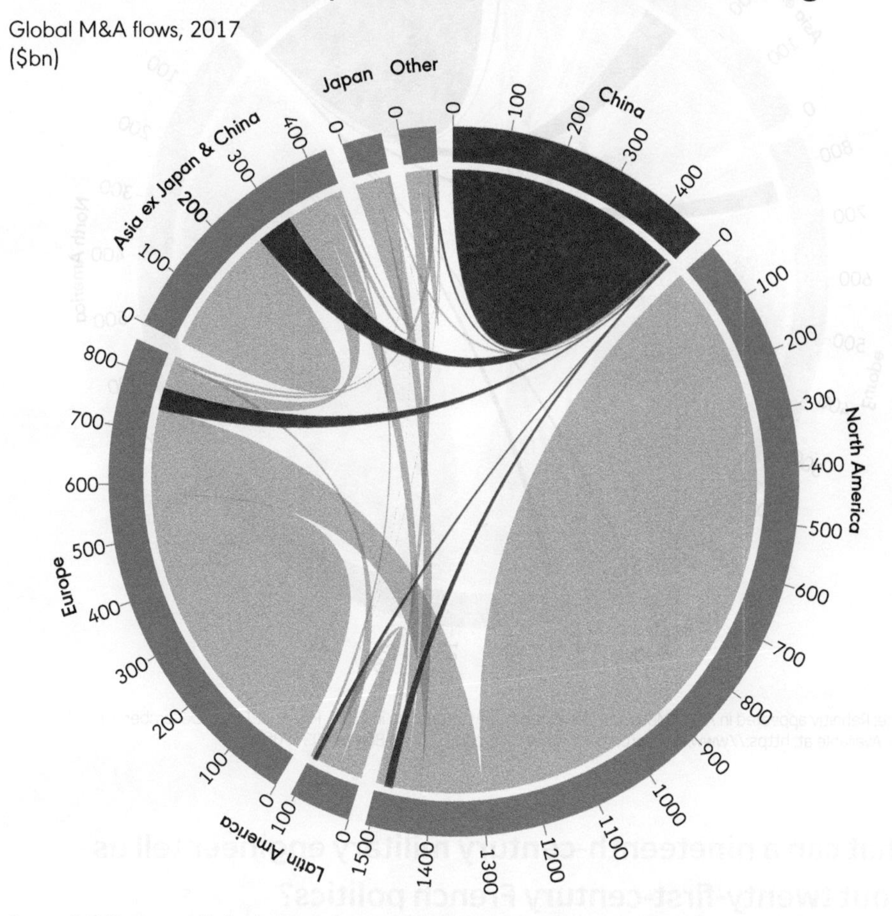

Source: Refinitiv appeared in Arash Massoudi, M&A boom set to continue in 2017, Financial Times, December 30, 2016. Available at: https://www.ft.com/content/0e9afdce-cdb6-11e6-b8ce-b9c03770f8b1

Restricting the use of colour allows you to create sufficient contrast between China and all other chords, even in greyscale. Online, complex graphics like this can benefit from interactivity to allow the reader to explore and investigate the data iteratively rather than in one single view.

China is the dominant partner in most of its M&A dealings

Global M&A flows, 2017
($bn)

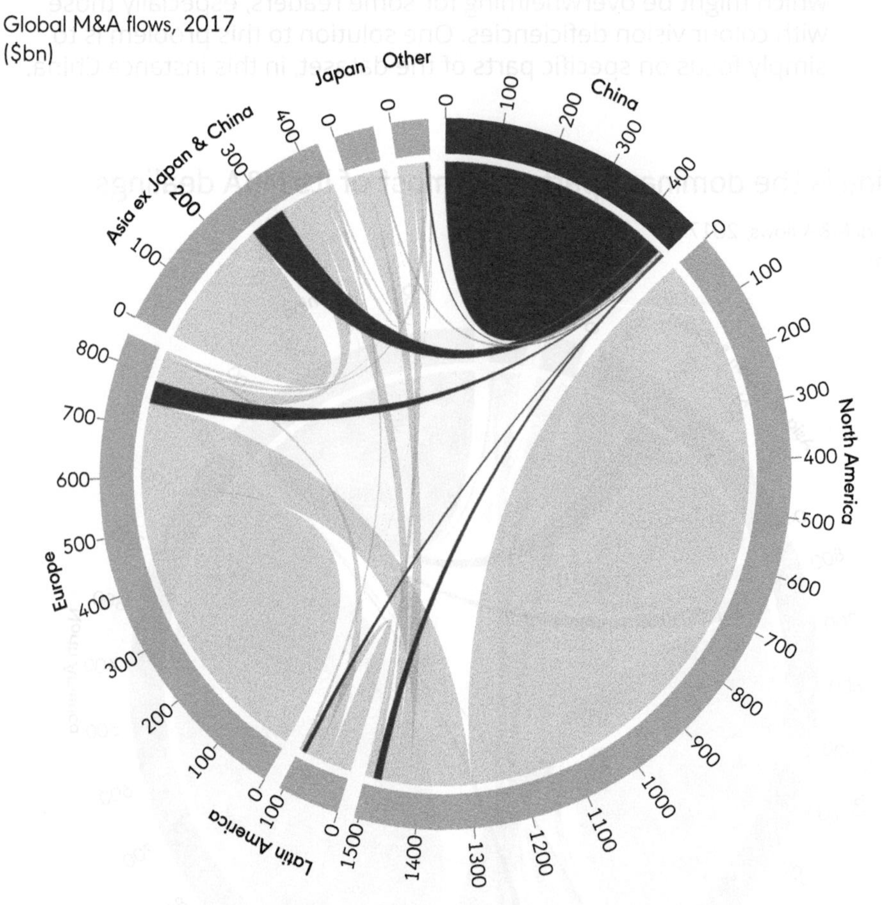

Source: Refinitiv appeared in Arash Massoudi, M&A boom set to continue in 2017, Financial Times, December 30, 2016. Available at: https://www.ft.com/content/0e9afdce-cdb6-11e6-b8ce-b9c03770f8b1

What can a nineteenth-century military engineer tell us about twenty-first-century French politics?

Pandemics aside, elections are, perhaps, the most public of data visualisation events. Endless polling in the run-up, with on-the-night results followed by retrospective analyses of what happened: all are underpinned by the judicious use of charts.

And yet, for the most part, to "keep it simple", we often see incredibly straightforward charts of election data. How about this for a pain-free visualisation of exit poll data from the French election of 2017?

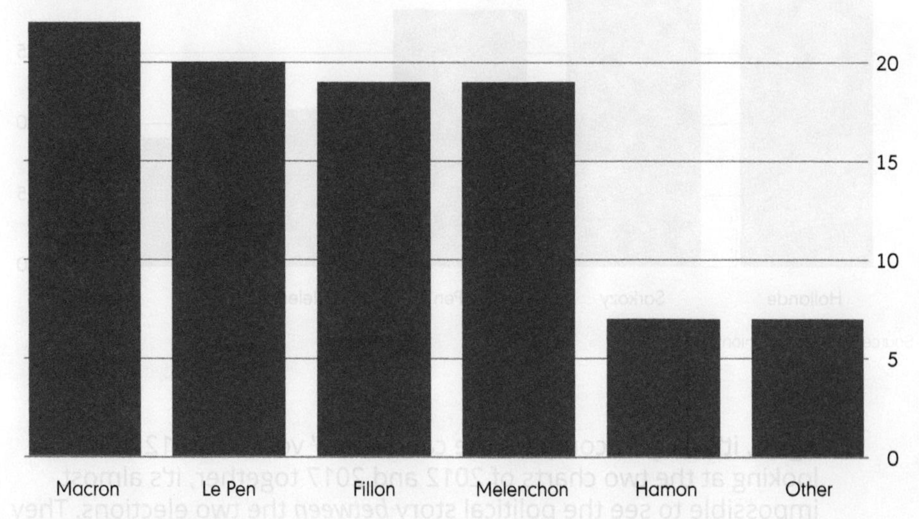

It's clean, it's clear and it's easy to see both the *magnitude* of each candidate's votes (Emmanuel Macron won around three times the vote of Benoît Hamon) and *ranking* (Marine Le Pen was second, while Jean-Luc Mélenchon and François Fillon tied for third). It's a useful, if limited, chart.

One of the things that make elections so interesting is that they reflect the ebb and flow of political fortunes. Here's how the same exit poll audience voted in the previous election five years earlier.

Hollande wins the first round

First round votes in the French presidential election, 2012 (%)

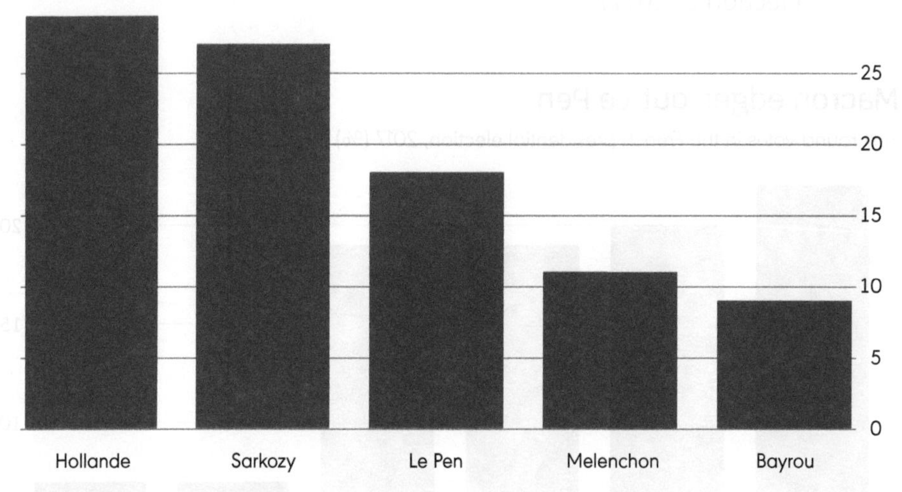

Source: Data from OpinionWay

Again, it's easy to compare the candidates' votes in 2012. But, looking at the two charts of 2012 and 2017 together, it's almost impossible to see the political story *between* the two elections. They are both snapshots at a single point of time, so comparisons and interpretations are difficult. Even the candidate lists are largely different, so how can we possibly produce anything meaningful from looking at them together?

Sankey diagram

It's time to use another type of flow diagram, this time named after the nineteenth-century army engineer Captain Matthew Henry Phineas Riall Sankey. Thankfully, as a concession to brevity, the chart takes just his surname – this is a Sankey diagram.

Source: OpinionWay, based on exit polls of 9,010 people conducted in 2017 appeared in Eir Nolsoe and Ella Hollowood, Emmanuel Macron's election victory over Marine Le Pen in charts, Financial Times, April 25, 2022. Available at: https://www.ft.com/content/f9f5009b-9f67-4d16-920e-22e91449a031

This chart shows the same data as our previous column charts, but it also incorporates extra information from the exit poll. Rather like our chord diagram of M&A deals, the extra information creates a matrix of data allowing us to understand voter flows between 2012 and 2017.

So, we can still see exactly the same information from the column charts – the left-hand and right-hand sides show us our candidate totals in 2012 and 2017. But, crucially, it now shows incredibly useful insight about *where* the votes for our 2017 candidates came from by showing the *flows* of votes between different candidates, with the width of each flow segment being proportionally sized.

Looking at Macron, we can see that many of his votes came from voters who had previously supported François Hollande, with smaller contributions from voters of Nicolas Sarkozy and François Bayrou. Contrast this with the voting flows heading towards Marine Le Pen in 2017 – almost all her votes came from people who had also voted for her five years earlier. This reveals that she had a very loyal following, but generally failed to build significant gains from elsewhere.

It's a beautiful and fascinating chart which, rather like our chord diagram, requires the reader to study it for a longer period, perhaps even a few minutes. It might not be as immediately readable as the preceding column charts, but it will tell you more.

The French election diagram is one of the simpler Sankey diagrams you'll see. Like other data visualisation pioneers, such as William Playfair and Charles Minard, Captain Sankey was an engineer – his eponymous charts are commonly used to represent flows through more complex systems, often with many more "stages" than just the two elections represented in our example.

Here's a Sankey diagram by my *FT* colleague Ian Bott showing the UK's priority groups for its 2021 Covid-19 vaccination program. The nine priority groups in the middle are preceded by 13 individual inputs. Notice how group 2 is actual formed of 3 separate subgroups. The priority groups then unite with all other groups to form the UK's adult population on the far right. You simply can't communicate information like this with pie charts.

Breakdown of the priority groups

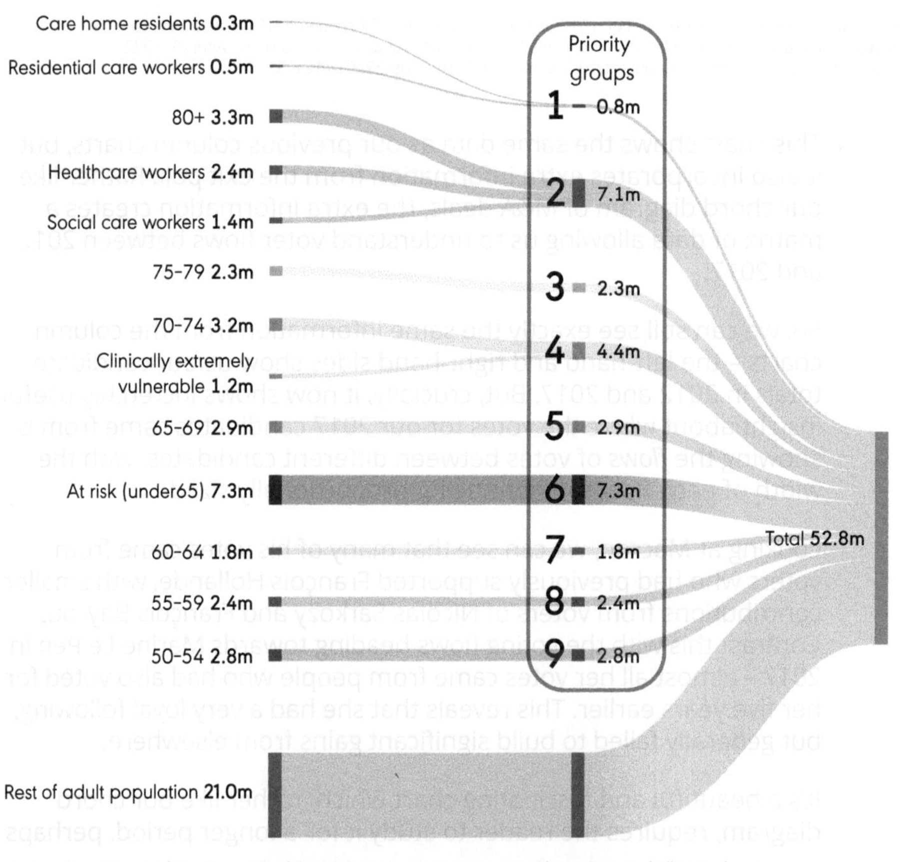

Source: Department of Health and Social Care Graphic: Ian Bott appeared in Ian Bott and Clive Cookson, In graphics: the UK vaccine supply chain, Financial Times, January 30 2021. Available at: https://www.ft.com/content/8b48a853-5b14-4378-91d4-17026fa15472

In another example, Christine Zhang shows how 12 rounds of the new ranked-choice voting system in New York's mayoral race could play out. Inspired by a graphic from RCVis.com, each individual round of voting could, no doubt, have been represented clearly on a bar chart. But the single composite view of successive rounds of voting is most elegantly handled by a Sankey.

In a recent survey of the NYC mayoral primary, Eric Adams comes out as winner after 12 rounds of ranked-choice votes are tallied

Based on the WNBC/Telemundo 47/POLITICO/Marist Poll conducted June 3 to 9

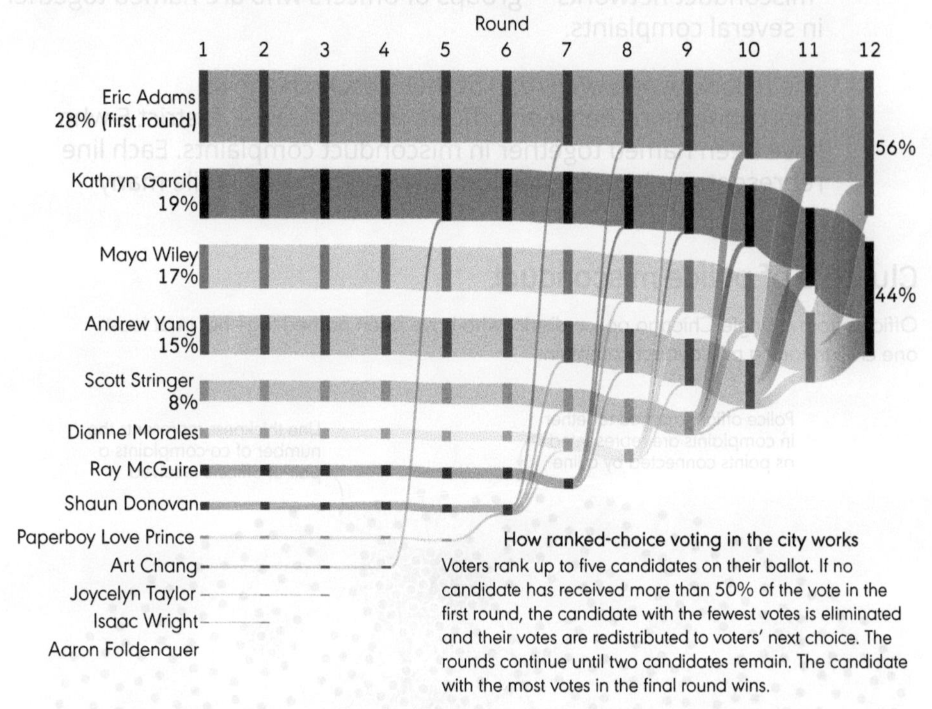
Round
1
2
3
4
5
6
7
8
9
10
11
12
Eric Adams
28% (first round)
Kathryn Garcia
19%
Maya Wiley
17%
Andrew Yang
15%
Scott Stringer
8%
Dianne Morales
Ray McGuire
Shaun Donovan
Paperboy Love Prince
Art Chang
Joycelyn Taylor
Isaac Wright
Aaron Foldenauer
56%
44%
How ranked-choice voting in the city works
Voters rank up to five candidates on their ballot. If no candidate has received more than 50% of the vote in the first round, the candidate with the fewest votes is eliminated and their votes are redistributed to voters' next choice. The rounds continue until two candidates remain. The candidate with the most votes in the final round wins.

Inspired by a graphic on RCVis.com. Excludes undecided voters
Source: Inspired by a graphic on RCVis.com. Excludes undecided voters Source: FairVote calculations using WNBC/Telemundo 47/POLITICO/Marist Poll of 876 likely Democratic primary voters FT Graphic: Christine Zhang / @christinezhang appeared in Gordon Smith, Jennifer Creery and Emily Goldberg, FirstFT: Today's top stories, Financial Times, June 22, 2021. Available at: https://www.ft.com/content/ebc5fc9d-fa13-4649-bb57-85baf18715c3

Finally, to conclude our section on the challenges and rewards of visualising flows and interactions, let's turn to another powerful example of interaction visualisation from Christine.

Network graph

Scrutiny of police misconduct intensified in the period following the 2020 murder of George Floyd by a Minneapolis police officer. The officer in question, Derek Chauvin, had at least 17 complaints made against him during his 19-year police career, of which just 1 led to disciplinary action. But how typical is such a litany of complaints? And was Chauvin's behaviour representative of his peers?

Analysis by sociologist Andrew Papachristos and colleagues at Northwestern University, suggested that, while relatively rare, officers with high levels of complaints could draw colleagues into "misconduct networks" – groups of officers who are named together in several complaints.

The following *network graph* of their research shows interconnections between officers from Chicago's District 5 who have been named together in misconduct complaints. Each line represents an interconnection between officers. While many

Clusters of police misconduct

Officers from a single Chicago police district who have been named together in at least one civilian-facing misconduct complaint

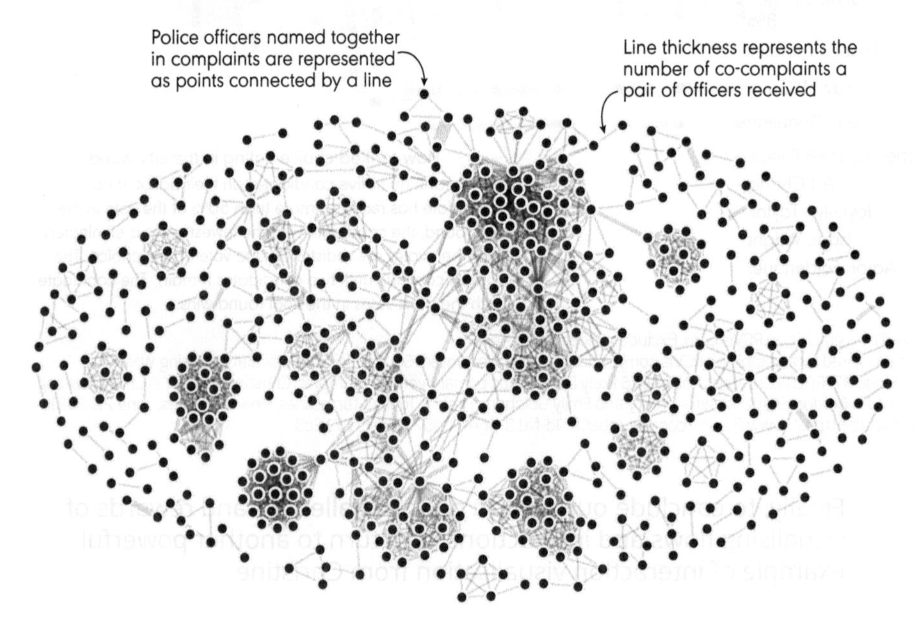
Police officers named together in complaints are represented as points connected by a line
Line thickness represents the number of co-complaints a pair of officers received

Source: Invisible Institute, George Wood, Daria Roithmayr, Andrew Papachristos appeared in Claire Bushey, Small share of US police draw third of complaints in big cities, Financial Times, May 28 2021. Available at: https://www.ft.com/content/141182fc-7727-4af8-a555-5418fa46d09e

officers are connected to just one other officer, the striking pattern revealed by the chart is that there are several clusters of interconnected officers.

The power of this chart is not in its quantification – counting the dots on this chart would be a thankless task – but showing that the agglomerations exist at all. In common with many data visualisations, it's the *pattern* that matters, not the number. Or, as Andrew Papachristos puts it, "Deviance is a group behaviour . . . the idea that it's just 'bad apples' always forgets the rest of the analogy. Bad apples spoil the bunch."

9

Charts of ranking

Use where an item's position in an ordered list is more important than its absolute or relative value. Don't be afraid to highlight the points of interest.

For a chart to be truly insightful, *context* is crucial because it provides us with the visual answer to an important question – 'compared with what'? No number on its own is inherently big or small – we need context to make that judgement.

Common contextual comparisons in charts are provided by *time* ("compared with last year . . . ") and *place* ("compared with the north . . . "). With *ranking*, context is provided by relative performance ("compared with our rivals . . . ").

In charts that emphasise rank, being able to see ordinal position in the data – first, second, third, etc. – is often just as important as being able to see the figures those rankings are derived from. It's the relationship in the Visual Vocabulary that allows us to focus on winners and losers.

In fact, in focusing on rank, some chart types sacrifice our ability to see the underlying measured values altogether.

Bump chart

This *bump chart* of Manchester City's surge up football's rich list doesn't allow us to see how much revenue the club has generated. Instead, it shows how the club's *rank* in the revenue list has *changed over time*, a job it does very clearly.

Notice that it uses a technique borrowed from the more orthodox line charts we saw in Chapter 5 "Charts of Change over time" – most lines are in the background, with the series of interest (in this case, Manchester City) in the foreground. Without the clarity provided by this technique, it would be a tangle of spaghetti.

Manchester City's surge up football's money league

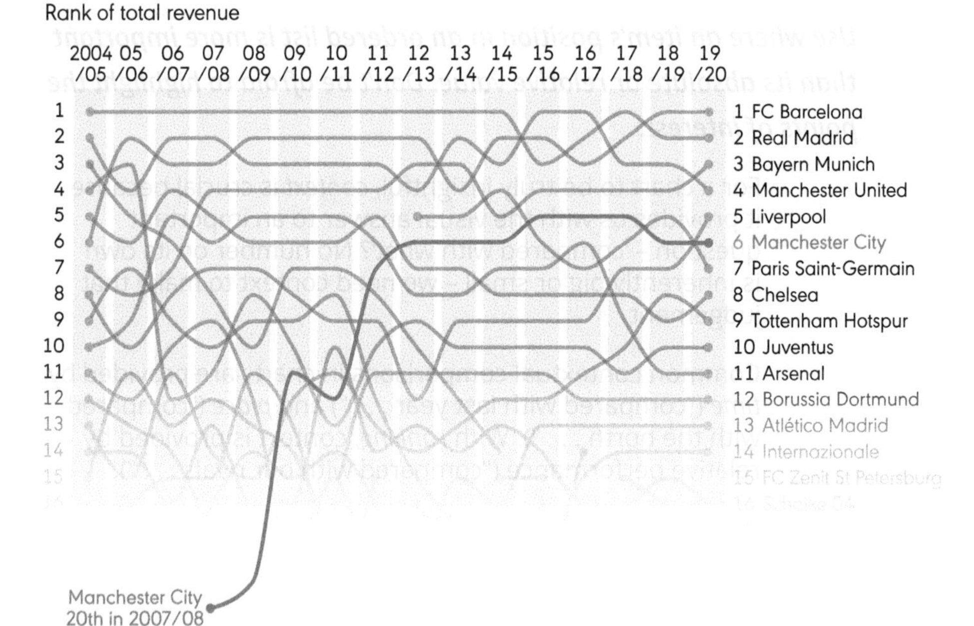

Source: Deloitte appeared in Adapted from Man Utd's financial success belies its on-pitch performance by Murad Ahmed and Patrick Mathurin, January 25, 2019. Available at: https://www.ft.com/content/9d1e5e68-208b-11e9-b126-46fc3ad87c65

Bump charts are useful when *position* in a constant changing list is all you need to see key trends, as in this chart of the rise of the mining company BHP to the top of the FTSE 100 in terms of market capitalisation. Just as with the football money league chart, we can't see the market cap data itself, but we can see some simple trends in relative performance. Sometimes, this might be all you need.

BHP rises to the top of the FTSE 100

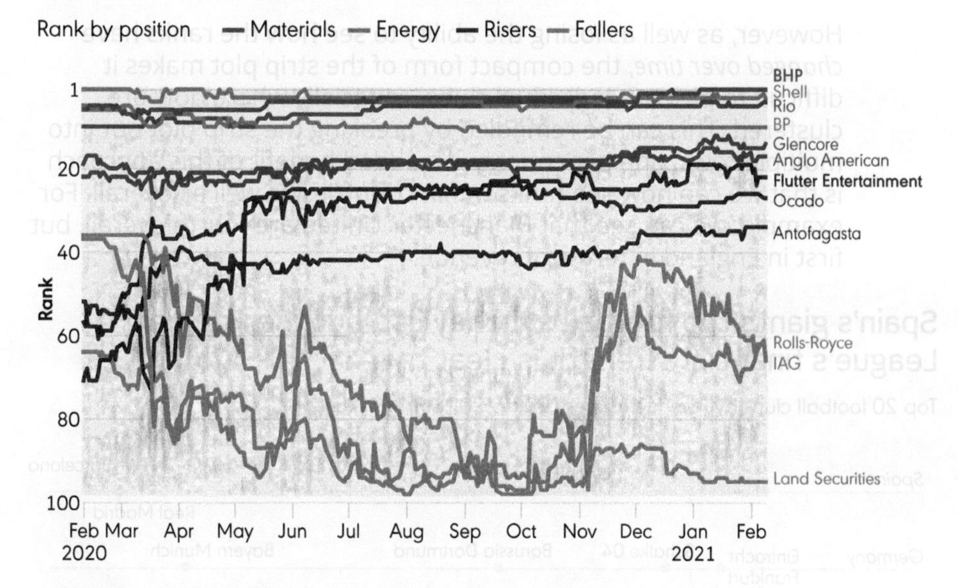

Graphic: Bob Haslett, Patrick Mathurin, Source: Bloomberg appeared in Neil Hume, How BHP became the UK's biggest listed company, Financial Times, February 13, 2021. Available at: https://www.ft.com/content/2da09da5-3034-4418-9eef-029dbef7fcfe

But what if we want to see rank *and* the underlying values from which they have been derived?

Dot strip plot

Returning to the data we saw in our first bump chart, a *strip plot* provides an effective yet compact visualisation of the *distribution* of revenue values for the world's top clubs. With all the dots arranged in order of value along the same line, it is also easy to see the order (rank) of the dots.

It reveals much about the data that the bump chart hides, most notably the gaps and clusters in the revenue data that are absent when looking at just ordinal ranking. Despite the recent progress revealed by the bump chart, you can see that Manchester City are still some way – over €150m – off top spot.

Barcelona top football's money league

Top 20 football clubs by revenue earned, 2019/20 (€m)

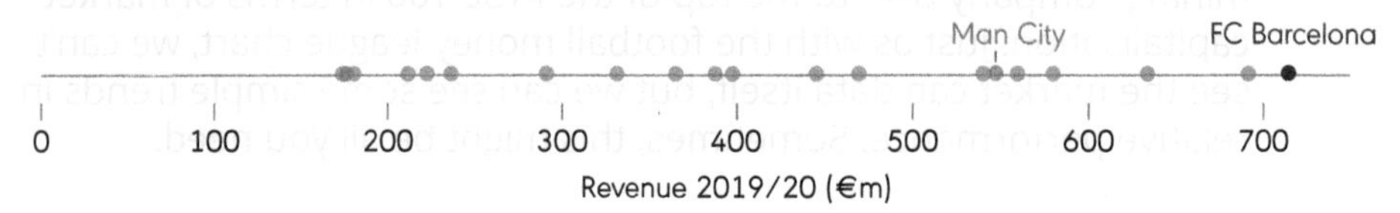

Source: Data from Deloitte

However, as well as losing the ability to see how the ranks have *changed over time*, the compact form of the strip plot makes it difficult to pick out individual clubs, especially where dots are clustered. This can be remedied by breaking the strip plot out into multiple rows, one per country. An added benefit of this approach is that we can now see ranks *within* countries as well as overall. For example, we can see that Manchester United are fourth overall, but first in England in terms of revenue.

Spain's giants top football's money list, but the Premier League's financial strength is clear

Top 20 football clubs by revenue earned, 2019/20 (€m)

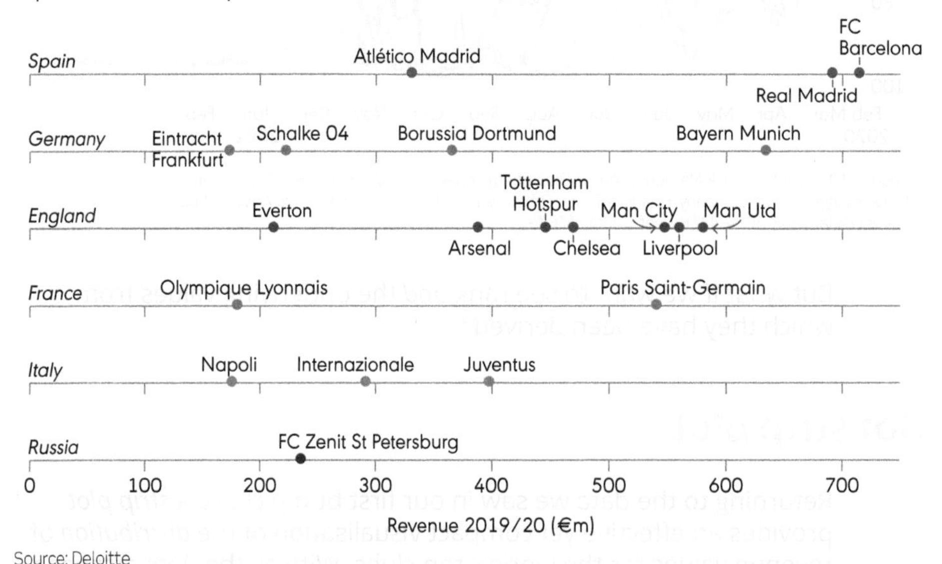

Source: Deloitte

The importance of sorting data

Of course, we could just use a bar chart and sort the bars according to value. This chart shows how ranking is often used as a complementary relationship that can be visualised alongside others (in this case, the *magnitude* of club income) to add real clarity.

Barcelona top football's money league

Top 20 clubs by revenue earned, 2019/20 (€m)

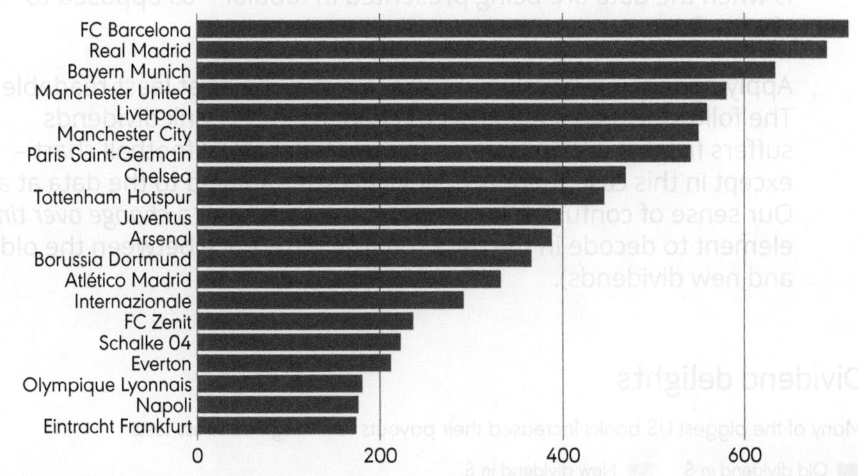

Source: Deloitte

Notice how, if the data are sorted by *alphabetical* order, rather than income value, we get a spiky chart that makes it much more difficult to read and compare values as well as identify rank. To test this out, use the chart below to try and identify the club with the seventh highest income. While possible, it is more difficult than it should be . . . (I bet it involved counting in your head).

Arsenal lead football's money league — at least in alphabetical order

Top 20 clubs by revenue earned, 2019/20 (€m)

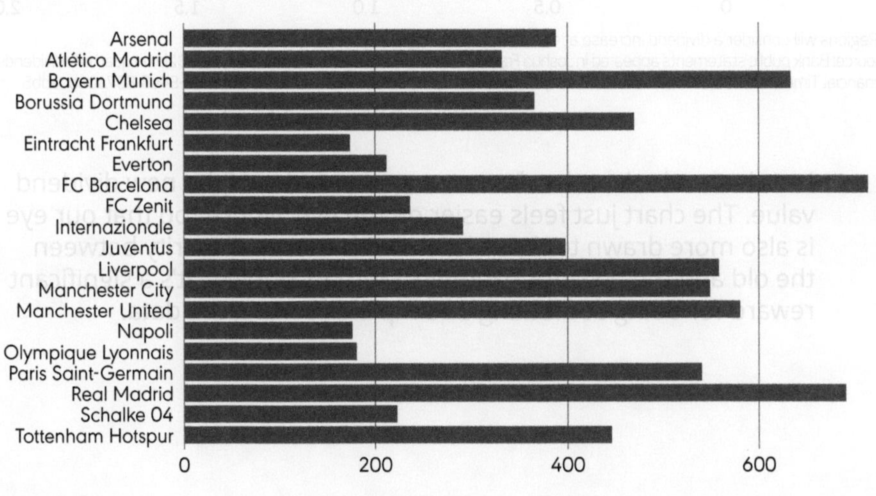

Source: Data from Deloitte

Being able to see data in alphabetical order is sometimes useful, particularly where we might expect readers to scan through data looking for a particular element. But often the best time to do this is when the data are being presented in tabular – as opposed to chart – form.

Applying ranking by value can make awful charts at least readable. The following *paired bar chart* of changes in US bank dividends suffers from similar problems to our alphabetical football chart – except in this case there is no logical order applied to the data at all. Our sense of confusion is compounded by having a *change over time* element to decode in the data too (the difference between the old and new dividends).

Dividend delights

Many of the biggest US banks increased their payouts following Fed stress tests

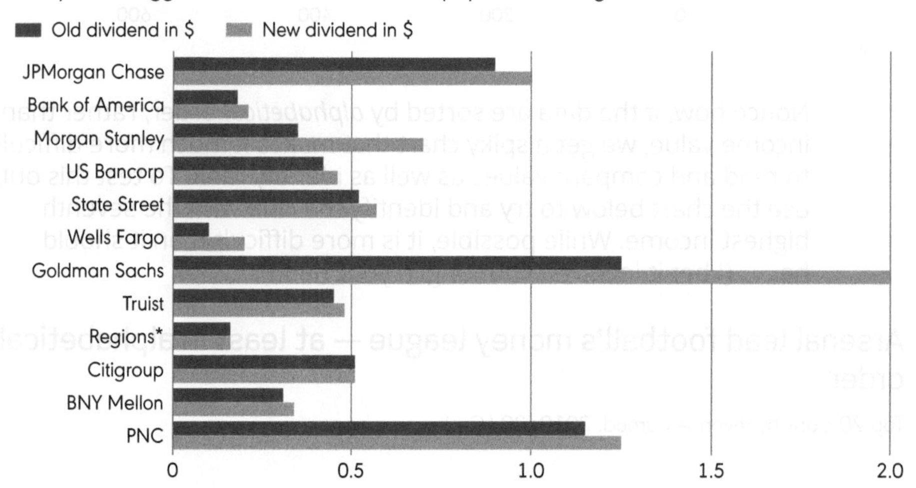

*Regions will consider a dividend increase at the board's meeting in July 2021
Source: Bank public statements appeared in Joshua Franklin and Imani Moise, US banks to pay extra $2bn in quarterly dividends, Financial Times, June 29, 2021. Available at: https://www.ft.com/content/1c904432-479c-45b3-84e5-857a06bdadb5

Let's have a look at the data arranged in order of the new dividend value. The chart just feels easier on the eye. Notice too that our eye is also more drawn to those banks with a large disparity between the old and the new (for example, Morgan Stanley). It's a significant reward for doing something as simple as sorting the data.

Dividend delights

Many of the biggest US banks increased their payouts following Fed stress tests

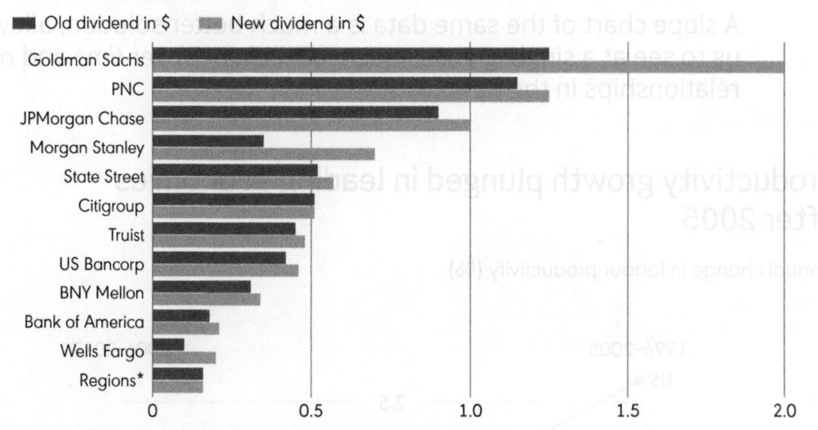

*Regions will consider a dividend increase at the board's meeting in July 2021
Source: Bank public statements appeared in Joshua Franklin and Imani Moise, US banks to pay extra $2bn in quarterly dividends, Financial Times, June 29, 2021. Available at: https://www.ft.com/content/1c904432-479c-45b3-84e5-857a06bdadb5

However, we should be mindful of falling into the trap of thinking this is the only way of presenting changing ranks. A big drawback of sorting paired bar charts is that you can only sort them on *one* element (before or after).

Using a paired bar chart, it's impossible to clearly present ranks for *both* time periods. For example, in this chart of productivity growth, the data are sorted according to growth during the period 1996–2005. It's easy to identify rank for the earlier period, but we are back to "counting and remembering" to piece together the rank of the most recent time period.

Productivity growth plunged in leading economies after 2005

Annual change in labour productivity (%)

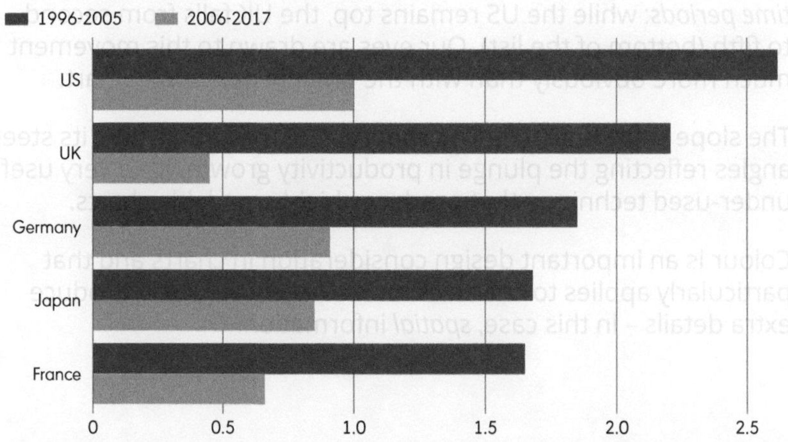

Source: University of Oxford appeared in How to create a durable economic recovery. Available at: https://www.ft.com/content/cfb2bd91-6a77-4b5a-8423-b922f6754179

Slope chart

A slope chart of the same data is a much better solution, allowing us to see at a single glance, *magnitude*, *change over time* and *ranking* relationships in the data.

Productivity growth plunged in leading economies after 2005

Annual change in labour productivity (%)

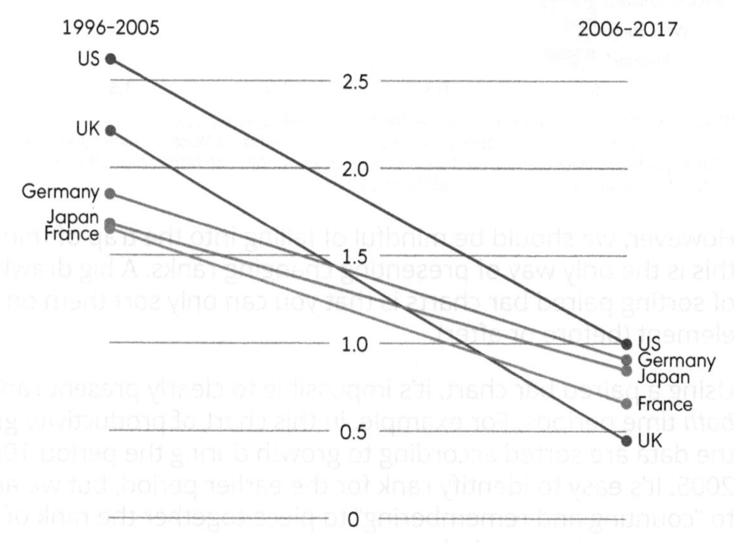

Source: University of Oxford appeared in How to create a durable economic recovery from Covid by Chris Giles, May 27, 2021. Available at: https://www.ft.com/content/cfb2bd91-6a77-4b5a-8423-b922f6754179

Notice that we can now clearly see the rank of each country for *both time periods*: while the US remains top, the UK falls from second to fifth (bottom of the list). Our eyes are drawn to this movement much more obviously than with the original paired bar chart.

The slope chart is also more supportive of the chart's title, its steep angles reflecting the plunge in productivity growth. It's a very useful, under-used technique that produces highly readable charts.

Colour is an important design consideration in charts and that particularly applies to charts of rank. We can use it to introduce extra details – in this case, *spatial* information.

Spanish giants dominate football's money league

Top 20 clubs by revenue earned, 2019/20 (€m)

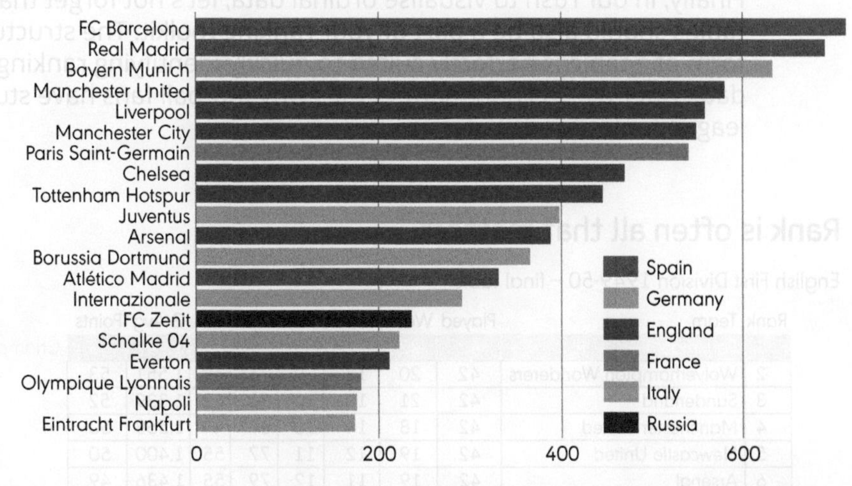

Source: Data from Deloitte

But with ranking, our interest is often just in the extremes – those at the top or those at the bottom. So, sometimes, it pays just to use colour only to highlight the rankings of interest. In doing this, notice how the title of the chart and the chart content reinforce each other. There is no ambiguity about what this chart aims to show.

Spanish giants dominate football's money league

Top 20 clubs by revenue earned, 2019/20 (€m)

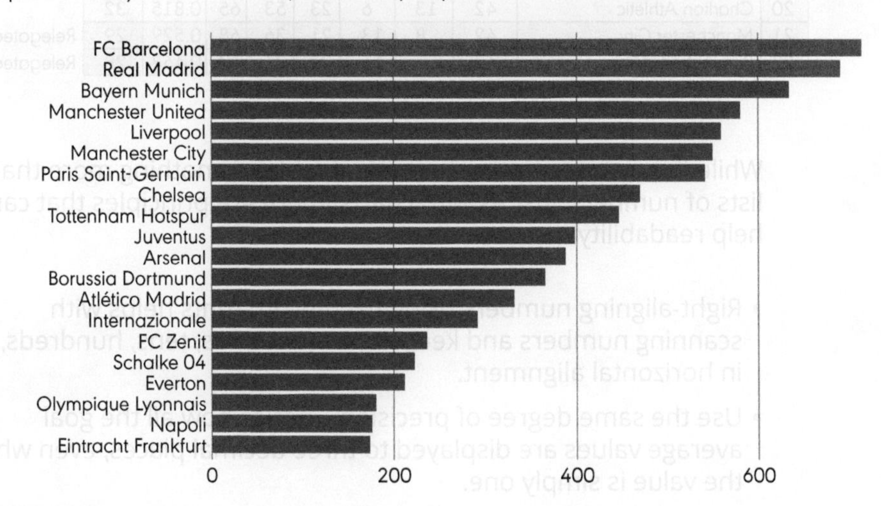

Source: Data from Deloitte

Tables

Finally, in our rush to visualise ordinal data, let's not forget that tables should also be a part of your ranking toolkit. The structured form of a table is perfectly suited to quickly identifying rankings in data. After all, position matters – it's why football fans have studied league tables for decades.

Rank is often all that matters

English First Division 1949-50 – final table

Rank	Team	Played	Won	Drew	Lost	GF	GA	G Avg*	Points	
1	Portsmouth	42	22	9	11	74	38	1.947	53	Champions
2	Wolverhampton Wanderers	42	20	13	9	76	49	1.551	53	
3	Sunderland	42	21	10	11	83	62	1.339	52	
4	Manchester United	42	18	14	10	69	44	1.568	50	
5	Newcastle United	42	19	12	11	77	55	1.400	50	
6	Arsenal	42	19	11	12	79	55	1.436	49	
7	Blackpool	42	17	15	10	46	35	1.314	49	
8	Liverpool	42	17	14	11	64	54	1.185	48	
9	Middlesbrough	42	20	7	15	59	48	1.229	47	
10	Burnley	42	16	13	13	40	40	1.000	45	
11	Derby County	42	17	10	15	69	61	1.131	44	
12	Aston Villa	42	15	12	15	61	61	1.000	42	
13	Chelsea	42	12	16	14	58	65	0.892	40	
14	West Bromwich Albion	42	14	12	16	47	53	0.887	40	
15	Huddersfield Town	42	14	9	19	52	73	0.712	37	
16	Bolton Wanderers	42	10	14	18	45	59	0.763	34	
17	Fulham	42	10	14	18	41	54	0.759	34	
18	Everton	42	10	14	18	42	66	0.636	34	
19	Stoke City	42	11	12	19	45	75	0.600	34	
20	Charlton Athletic	42	13	6	23	53	65	0.815	32	
21	Manchester City	42	8	13	21	36	68	0.529	29	Relegated
22	Birmingham City	42	7	14	21	31	67	0.463	28	Relegated

While it may be tempting to think of tables as nothing more than lists of numbers, just as with charts, there are principles that can help readability:

- Right-aligning numbers using fixed-width fonts helps with scanning numbers and keeps units (decimals, tens, hundreds, etc.) in horizontal alignment.
- Use the same degree of precision – notice how all the goal average values are displayed to three decimal places, even when the value is simply one.

And, as with our charts, highlighting the rows of interest at the top and bottom of the table focuses attention on the main points of interest (literally, the winners and losers).

The antiquity of this ancient table reinforces the importance of rank. It doesn't matter that the metrics of football have since changed (two points for a win became three points in the 1980s, and goal average has since been replaced by goal difference). For fans of Portsmouth (champions), Manchester City and Birmingham City (relegated), it is the position in the list that matters more than any other number.

10

Charts of deviation

Emphasise variations above or below a fixed reference point. Typically, the reference point is zero, but it can also be a target or a long-term average. These types of charts are also often used to show sentiment (positive/neutral/negative).

In 2014, UNESCO asked me to review graphics published in a series of reports on access to education in the Asia-Pacific region. I spent a pleasant week in Bangkok working with a knowledgeable and talented team whose passion for their work was unquestionable. We spent most of our time discussing why the charts in their reports were uniformly awful.

For example, take the figure below, Figure 7, the memorably titled "Gender Parity Index of the adjusted net intake rate in primary education, 2009" from the report on Universal Primary Education.

Figure 7: Gender Parity Index of the adjusted net intake rate in primary education, 2009

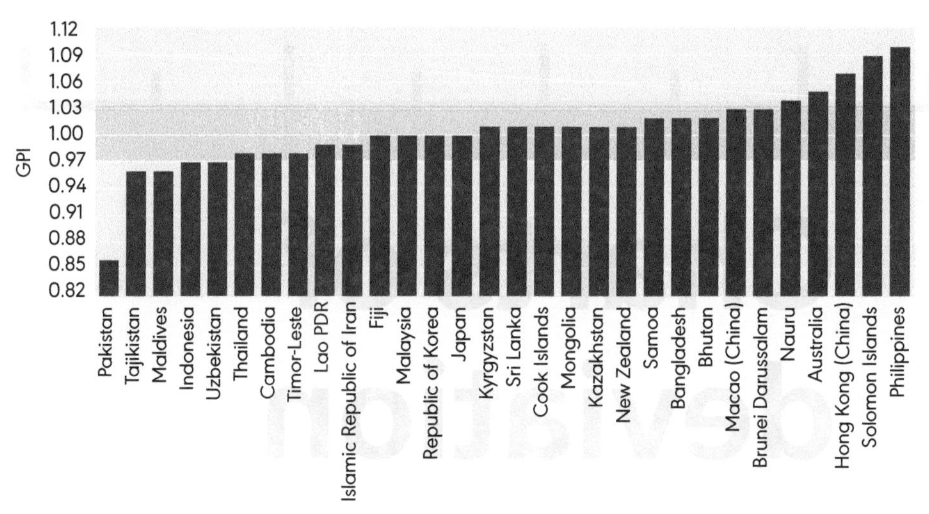

Source: UIS, 2011, Statistical Table 2 appeared in Universal Primary Education. Available at: https://unesdoc.unesco.org/in/documentViewer.xhtml?v=2.1.196&id=p::usmarcdef_0000221200&file=/in/rest/annotationSVC/DownloadWatermarkedAttachment/attach_import_ee89607b-66bc-45d6-a7fd-

This chart breaks one of the first rules of data visualisation. It is not self-sufficient – you need to read the rest of the 73-page report to understand what it is showing. Assuming we even know what the Gender Parity Index (GPI) is, it is not clear what purpose the mysterious grey area in the centre of the chart is serving.

Worse still, this chart might injure you physically. Extended reading requires a chiropractic adjustment, thanks to the rotated labels. The liberal use of bright, saturated red matches the corporate hue of the report's cover but is the equivalent of UPPER-CASE SHOUTING.

How could this data be turned into a useful chart?

As ever, our first thoughts should be about the relationship in the data we are most interested in. With that in mind, let's look at the chart's vertical axis. Why does the GPI start at 0.82 and finish at 1.12? There is, of course, just one reason – it is the default of the software used to create the chart.

The GPI is a measure of gender equality in access to primary education, with a value of one denoting parity between boys and girls. As such, we're not really interested in the size (*magnitude*) of each country's score, but how much it *deviates* from one. Recognising this key point allows us to produce a radical redesign.

Diverging bar chart

To start with, let's anchor the bars on our chart to the GPI value of one and show deviations from this central point by sending higher and lower values in opposing directions.

This allows us to re-orient the chart, making the country labels easier to read. Simple axis labels – and arrows – confirm the shape and direction of the data to the reader.

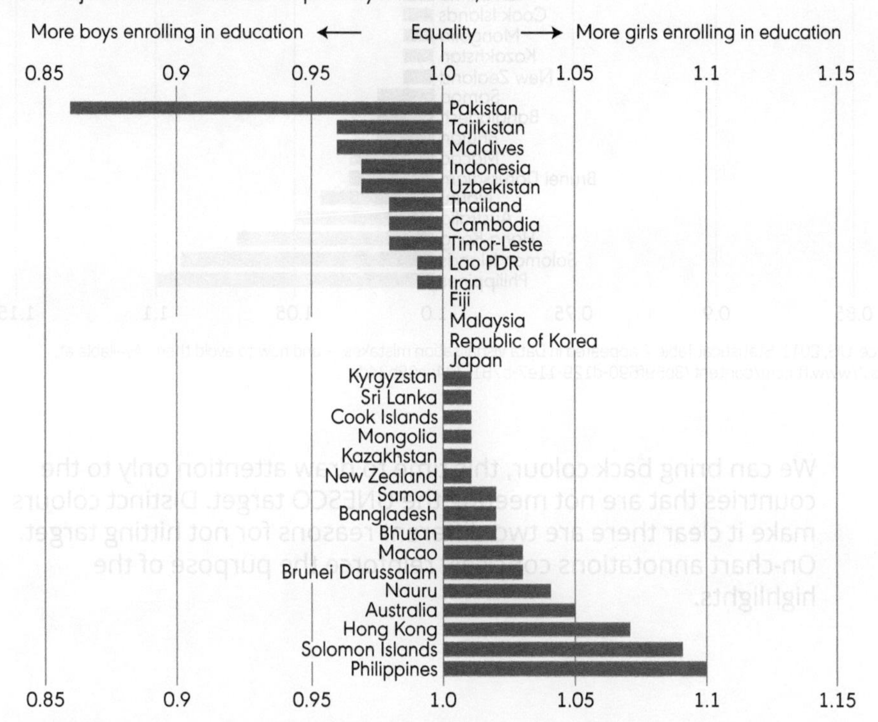

Source: UIS, 2011, Statistical Table 2 appeared in Data visualisation mistakes — and how to avoid them. Available at: https://www.ft.com/content/3b59f690-d129-11e7-b781-794ce08b24dc

Next, we can re-introduce the mysterious grey shaded area. It is UNESCO's performance target. This is essential information because it allows us to place each country's performance in a meaningful context.

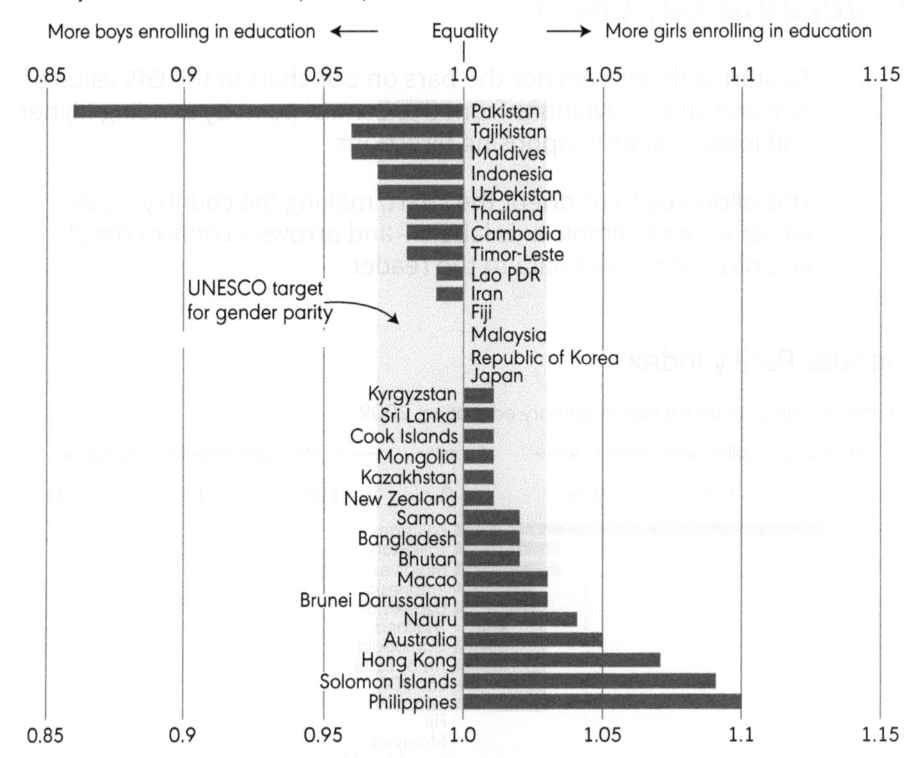

Source: UIS, 2011, Statistical Table 2 appeared in Data visualisation mistakes — and how to avoid them. Available at: https://www.ft.com/content/3b59f690-d129-11e7-b781-794ce08b24dc

We can bring back colour, this time to draw attention only to the countries that are not meeting the UNESCO target. Distinct colours make it clear there are two different reasons for not hitting target. On-chart annotations concisely reinforce the purpose of the highlights.

Gender Parity Index

Of the adjusted net intake rate in primary education, 2009

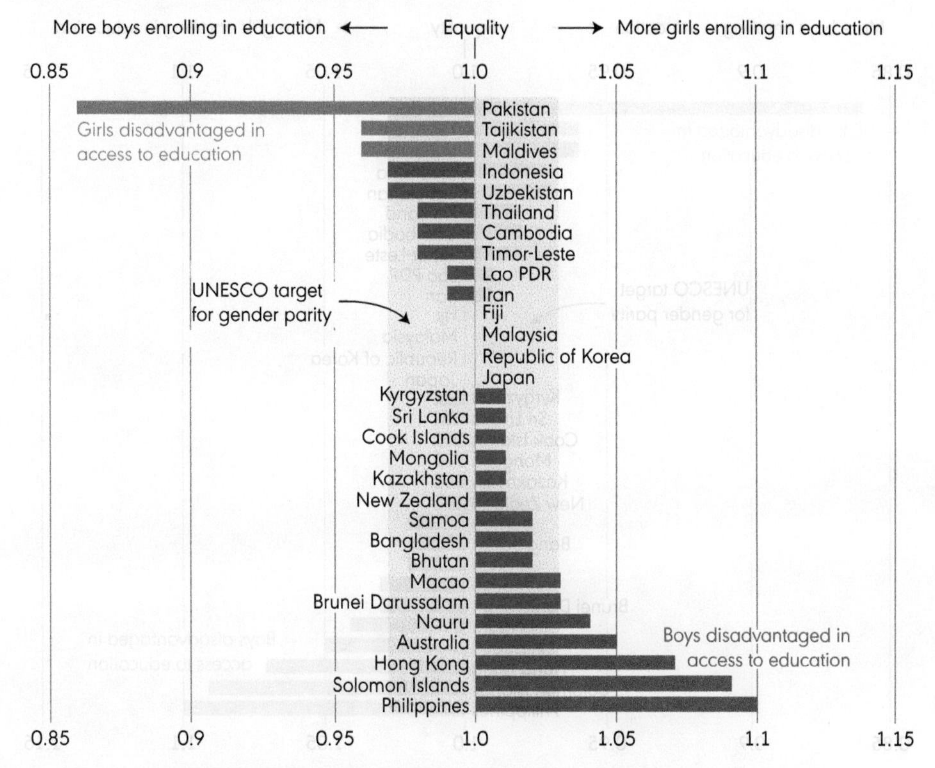

Source: UIS, 2011, Statistical Table 2 appeared in Data visualisation mistakes — and how to avoid them. Available at: https://www.ft.com/content/3b59f690-d129-11e7-b781-794ce08b24dc

Finally, a clear title helps readers tune in to a chart. Technical details can be relegated to the subtitle and footnotes. They contain important information but are not necessarily the first thing the reader should see.

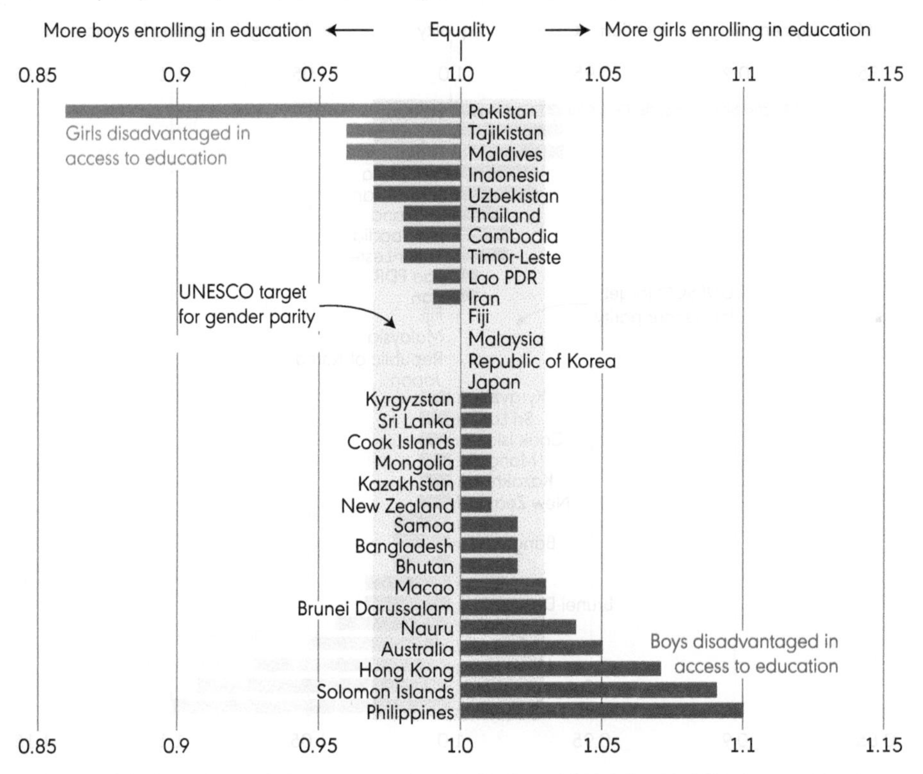

* Of adjusted net intake rate
Source: UIS, 2011, Statistical Table 2 appeared in Data visualisation mistakes — and how to avoid them. Available at: https://www.ft.com/content/3b59f690-d129-11e7-b781-794ce08b24dc

If we compare the original and the reworked version, it seems barely plausible that we can be looking at the same data. Pakistan was previously barely noticeable, now its disadvantaging of girls becomes the standout story.

In fact, it is only by reworking the chart that we can see it is of any use at all. Many charts cannot be transformed in this way, which contributes to an important point: chart makers should adopt a "fewer but better" mantra.

Learning point – Better reports

With well-selected charts taking care of the key questions of "what?" and "how much?", the main text in a report can focus on the important follow-on questions, such as "why?" and "so what?" By conceiving words and graphics simultaneously, reports can be restructured into readable, confident – and shorter – narratives.

The willingness shown by UNESCO staff to critique and improve their own materials is also important. No amount of external consulting will achieve lasting improvements in quality unless the desire to improve is internalised.

When considering *deviation*, we naturally form an association with positive and negative figures, in either absolute (e.g., profit/loss) or relative (sales figures above/below target) terms.

But any number can represent our point of divergence if it represents a contextual anchor. On our GPI chart, we used 1.0 as the point of deviation because it represents an equal ratio of boys and girls entering primary education. Keeping the original metric on the chart – the GPI values – also means we can refer to the underlying figures when describing the patterns on the chart.

On charts where just a relative deviation is shown, we need to be mindful that we lose the ability to see the original figures.

For example, on this chart of European temperature anomalies, notice that the vertical (y) axis does not show the actual temperature recorded, just the *deviation* of the recorded figure from the long-term average. It's impossible on this chart to see what the average temperature in June 2021 was – because the focus is purely on *deviation* not *magnitude*.

Europe reports second warmest June on record

Surface air temperature anomalies for June (C)*

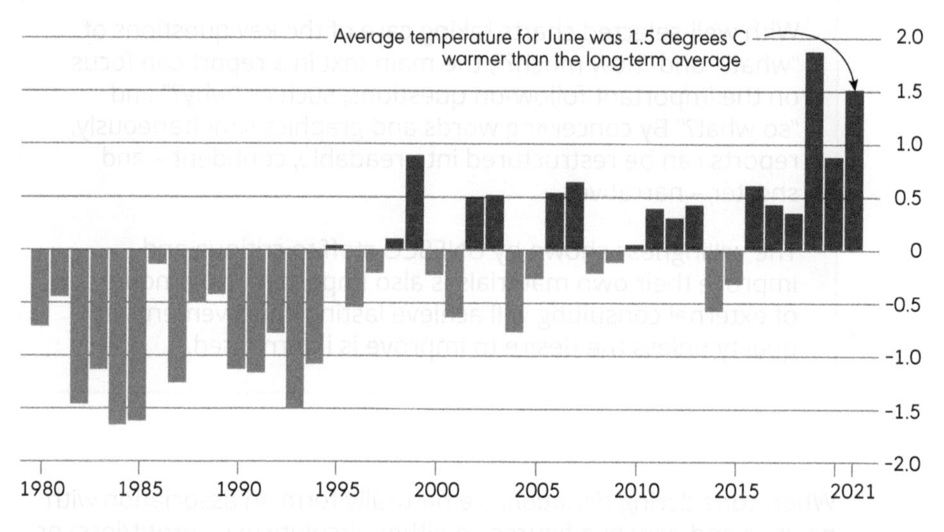

* compared to 1991-2020 average

Graphic: Steven Bernard
Source: Copernicus ECMWF appeared in Leslie Hook and Steven Bernard, Record June heat in North America and Europe linked to climate change, Financial Times, July 9, 2021.Available at:
https://www.ft.com/content/f08156a6-c8ac-4c00-94df-2a955dc56da9

It doesn't prevent this from being a useful chart. And notice how the chart effectively uses colour to highlight the all-important deviations we're interested in, emphasising how the most recent years have seen the warmest June anomalies.

Surplus/deficit filled line

On occasion, our point of deviation might be a moving figure. In such cases, a surplus/deficit filled line chart can neatly track performance above and below. Inspired by William Playfair, we saw in Chapter 5 "Charts of change over time" how useful a technique it can be with economic data, such as imports and exports. But it can also apply to other time-series comparisons where emphasising contrasting fortunes is the primary goal.

Shell underperformed its peers since cutting its payout

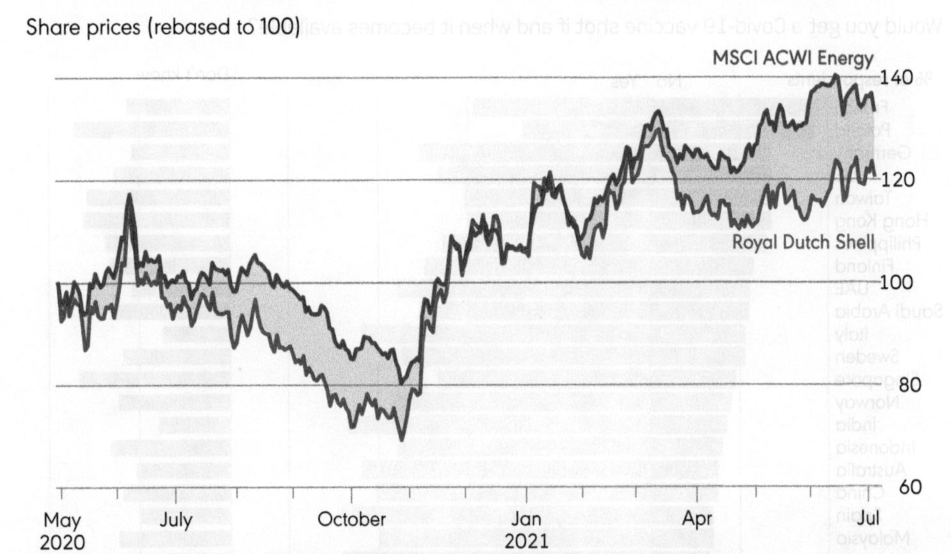

Source: Refinitiv appeared in Shell: dividend dither sends muddled message, July 7, 2021. Available at: https://www.ft.com/content/209b0ec3-28f4-4d44-bcd9-5a79f33a9c40

Spine charts

Spine charts are useful when the data being plotted represent opposing sentiments. This chart of global vaccine scepticism sets the "don't knows" to one side, allowing us to focus our attention on the shifting country-by-country dynamic of those for and against a vaccine.

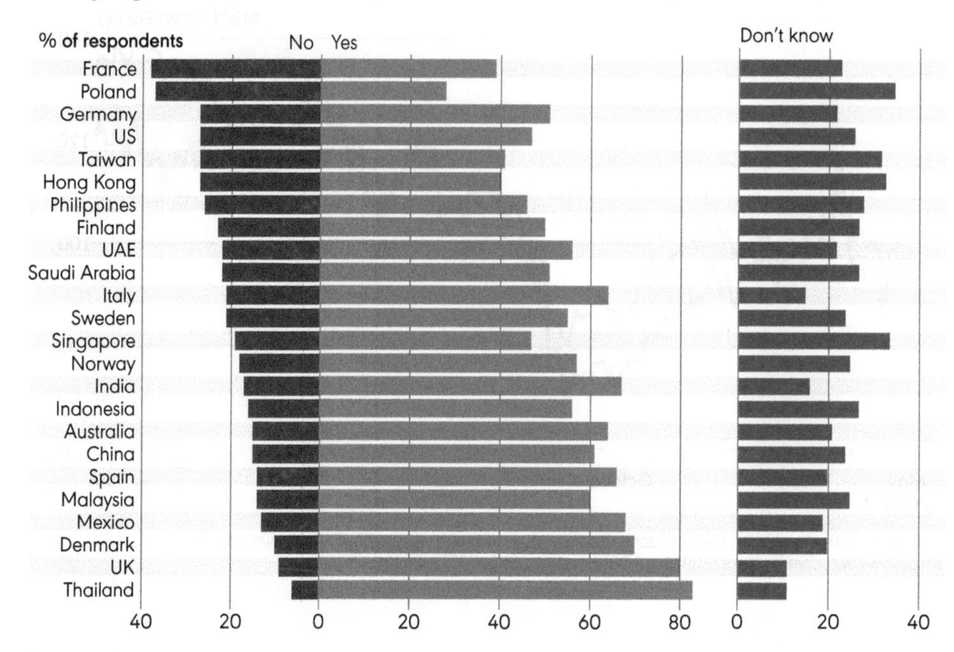

Source: YouGov, Nov 17 2020 -Jan 10 2021 appeared in David Robert Grimes, How to take on Covid conspiracy theories, Financial Times, February 5, 2021. Available at: https://www.ft.com/content/6660cb80-8c11-476a-b107-e0193fa975f9. Used by permission from The Financial Times Private Limited

This type of chart works best when the data are sorted into order (in this case, of those saying "No") – another example where *ranking* can play a complementary role in making a chart primarily displaying another chart relationship readable.

This example uses simple "Yes"/"No"/"Don't Know" responses but is effective with most survey responses that use symmetrical response options (e.g., strongly disagree, disagree, neutral, agree, strongly agree), known as a "Likert" scale.

Compare the same data from our Covid vaccine chart plotted as a regular stacked bar chart, below. The stacked bar chart places much greater emphasis on a *part-to-whole* relationship (that for each country, the No/Yes/Don't Know together comprise 100 per cent). This is useful – but the divergence between No and Yes is, perhaps, a little less emphatic as a result.

Global range of vaccine scepticism

Would you get a Covid-19 vaccine shot if and when it becomes available?

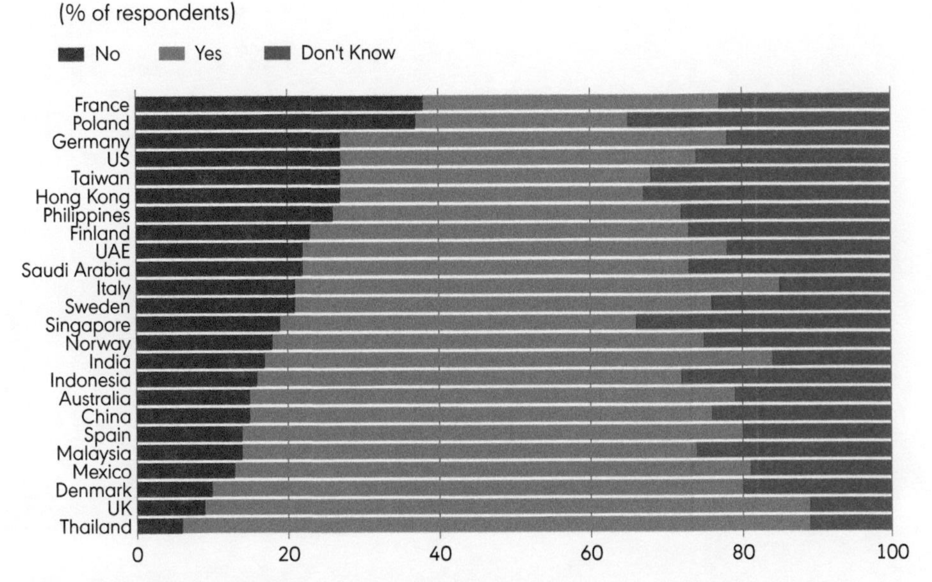

Source: YouGov, Nov 17 2020 -Jan 10 2021 appeared in David Robert Grimes, How to take on Covid conspiracy theories, Financial Times, February 5, 2021. Available at: https://www.ft.com/content/6660cb80-8c11-476a-b107-e0193fa975f9. Used by permission from The Financial Times Private Limited.

Finally, this chart of diplomatic activity shows a clear link between the expulsion of Russian diplomats from countries across the world, and diplomats expelled from Russian soil. The "tit-for-tat" pattern is made clear by using individual dots, each representing a diplomat, in a deviation-style arrangement.

Tit for tat: the 152 diplomatic expulsions announced since April 15

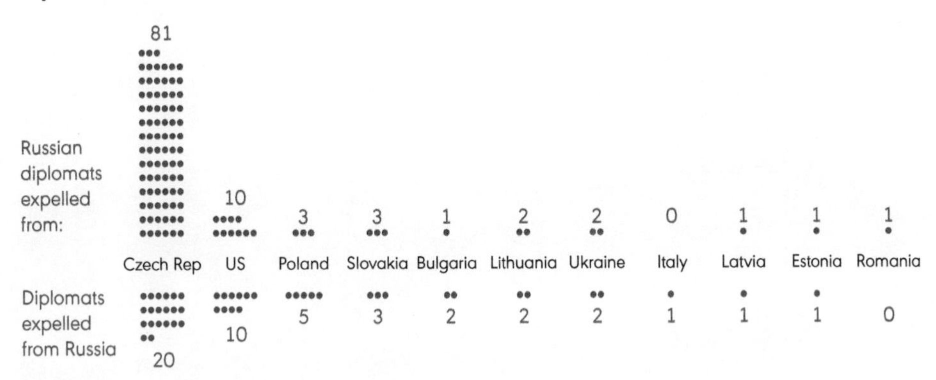

Graphic: Ian Bott
Source: FT research appeared in Diplomatic expulsions diminish Russia's reach in eastern Europe. Available at: https://www.ft.com/content/9476edbf-0ea4-44b9-a27e-0d9bae29cbb7

11

Charts of part to whole

Show how a single entity can be broken down into its component elements. If the reader's interest is solely in the size of the components, consider a magnitude-type chart instead.

Pie chart

The award for most contentious chart type in the world almost certainly belongs to the pie chart. Some data visualisation practitioners view them as the Comic Sans of the chart world. In a similar vein to type aficionados critical of Microsoft's ubiquitous font, they suggest a world without pie charts would be a significant improvement.

Yet, for all their detractors, pie charts remain stubbornly abundant in information ecosystems from the schoolroom to the boardroom. There are few signs of imminent extinction. Rightly or wrongly, pie charts are a ubiquitous part of the general public's chart vocabulary.

Many people are surprised when they see pie charts have a place on the *FT* Visual Vocabulary. They *are* overused – but remain a valid chart within strict limits. Understanding why involves appreciating why William Playfair bothered inventing them at all over two centuries ago.

Pie charts represent a "*part-to-whole*" relationship. That is, they show the relative size of multiple elements which, when combined, represent a total entity of some sort.

Understanding part-to-whole relationships allows us to learn something about the compositional structure of data, be it the colour of students' eyes in the classroom, or a company's earnings by division.

From schoolroom to boardroom: pie charts are a familiar sight

Eye colour of 29 children in class 4F

Share of global revenue (%)

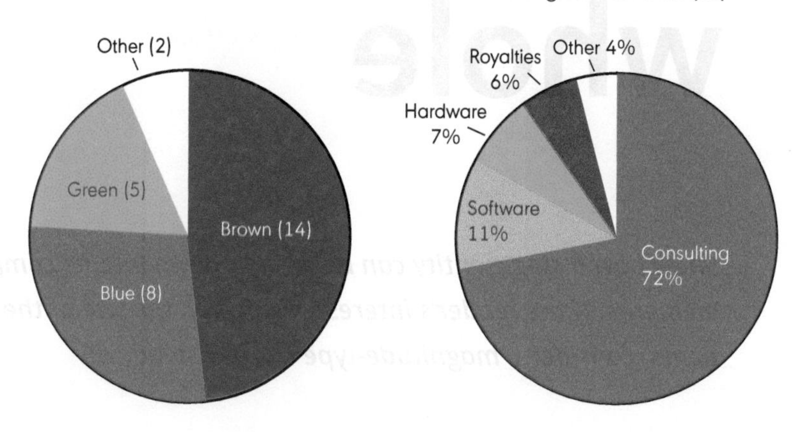

As these two examples demonstrate, pie charts can either show percentage values, or simply *magnitude* values.

Pie charts aren't as effective at showing pure magnitude comparisons of the components as a bar chart (we shall learn why later in Chapter 13 "The science behind good charts") – because readers find it harder to estimate precise values. Indeed, just as in our examples here, pie charts are almost always presented with labelled segments denoting each wedge's value – perhaps a tacit admission of their perceptual shortcoming.

However, what makes pie charts a small but valid part of our chart vocabulary is that, more so than any other chart type, their design emphasises that the individual components collectively represent a meaningful whole, be it everyone in the class or the annual sales of a multinational company. There are several sources of evidence to show how strong this visual cue is.

For one, the pie chart is known by different names across the world, but almost always using a term that evokes its *part-to-whole* structure: in France, they are known as Camembert charts, while in Portuguese they are Gráficos de Pizza. As you can see, gastronomic connotations run deep with these charts too.

It perhaps also helps that most people become acquainted with pie charts early in life – typically at primary school. There may be no such thing as an "intuitive" chart type but learning a chart so early in life might be the next best thing.

Finally, to reinforce our collective understanding of how pie charts work, when they *don't* work, it can become headline news.

In November 2009, a Fox News pie chart of GOP presidential candidates for 2012 went viral on social media. The chart's three segments: "Back Palin" (70 per cent), "Back Huckabee" (63 per cent), and "Back Romney" (60 per cent) added up to 193 per cent. Cue universal outrage – because surely, as everyone learnt in primary school, pie charts should sum to 100 per cent.

A clear abuse of the pie chart form, but it's worth pedantically pointing out that not all pie chart labels will sum *exactly* to 100 per cent, simply due to rounding of the figures used: So, 99.9 per cent – or 100.1 per cent might be acceptable. But not 193 per cent.

A 2016 study by Drew Skau and Robert Kosara (https://kosara.net/papers/2016/Skau-EuroVis-2016.pdf) added considerably to our understanding of how people read pie charts. The wedges of a pie chart encode information in multiple ways, using combinations of angle, arc length and area.

Visual encodings in a pie chart

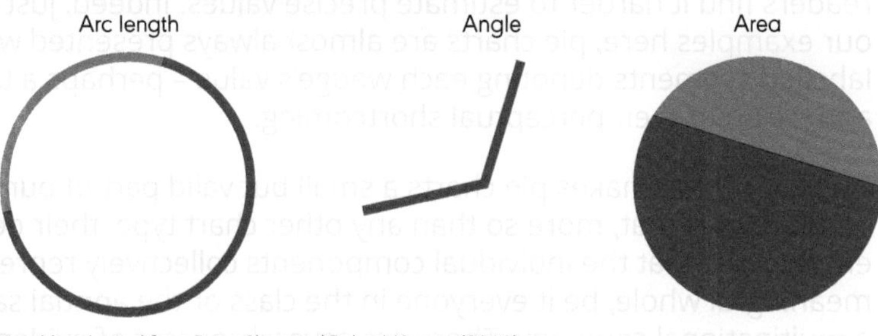

Graphic adapted from Drew Skau and Robert Kosara (2016)

They found, perhaps surprisingly, that angle is the *least* important encoding to pie chart readers, while arc length (the outer line of each pie chart segment) could well be the most important.

Donut chart

A close cousin of the pie is the donut chart. A convenient function of these variants is being able to describe a total value, or some other aggregate information, in the chart's central "hole". This helps emphasise the "universe" of data being presented, which can sometimes be very specific.

Al Alam's clients don't know who Al Alam is

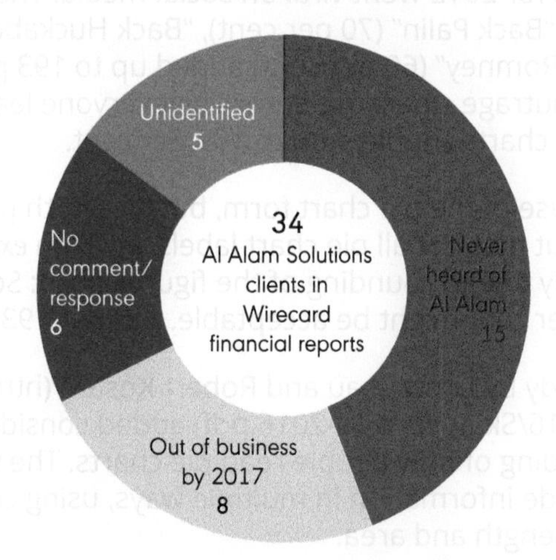

Source: FT research appeared in Dan McCrum, Wirecard's suspect accounting practices revealed, Financial Times, October 15, 2019. Available at: https://www.ft.com/content/19c6be2a-ee67-11e9-bfa4-b25f11f42901

Interestingly, Skau and Kosara found that people read donut charts just as accurately as pie charts, perhaps because arc length is consistent between the two forms.

Following some simple rules for pies and donuts will help to prevent chart disasters:

- The "100 per cent rule" – pie charts should account for a complete set of data.
- Never use 3-d or exploded segments. This is more than aesthetic disdain – Skau and Kosara observe that exploded pie charts lead to higher reader error (presumably due to their non-contiguous arcs).
- Label segments directly where possible – and don't use too many segments, as readers will likely find it difficult to both see fine differences and read labels.

Most importantly, from the perspective of the Visual Vocabulary, pie and donut charts are not the only way to represent *part-to-whole* relationships. Rather than banning pie charts, the world's surfeit could be reduced by simply using more effective chart types in particular situations.

For example, some part-to-whole datasets contain negative numbers: I have yet to see a pie chart that can effectively represent a segment value of zero, let alone negative figures.

Waterfall chart

An ability to reveal positive and negative components makes *waterfall charts* a staple of *FT* data visualisations on the day of the British chancellor's annual budget.

A chart showing the possible profit earned by the owner of a failed airline is another good example of data that would simply be impossible to represent in pie chart form.

The threats to Hammond's budget headroom

£bn (2020–21)

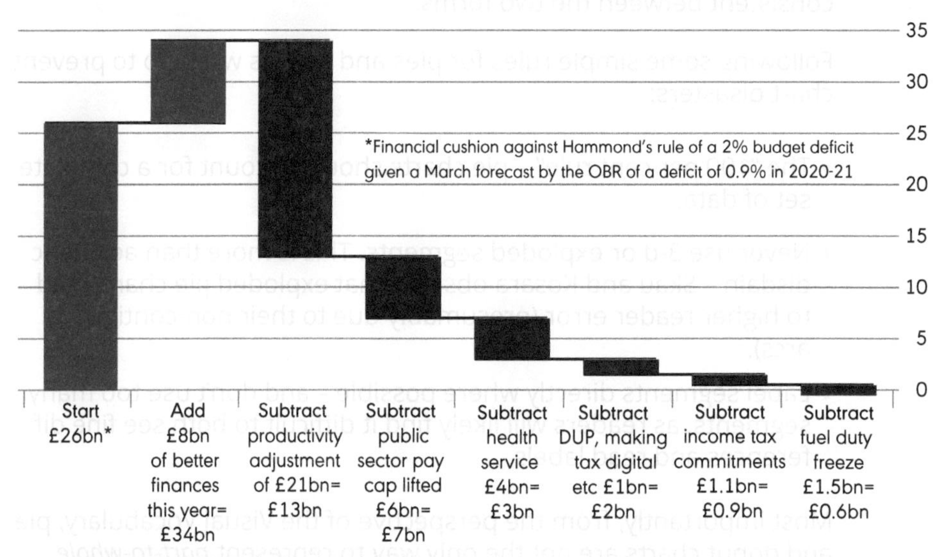

Source: Data from IFS, HSBC, Nuffield Trust, FT research appeared in Brexit and the Budget: Hammond pressed to go 'big and bold' by George Parker and Chris Giles in London, November 14, 2017. Available at: https://www.ft.com/content/66f8e992-c85e-11e7-ab18-7a9fb7d6163e

What Greybull stands to gain from Monarch's collapse

After possible recoveries, the failed airline's owners end up with a £15m profit

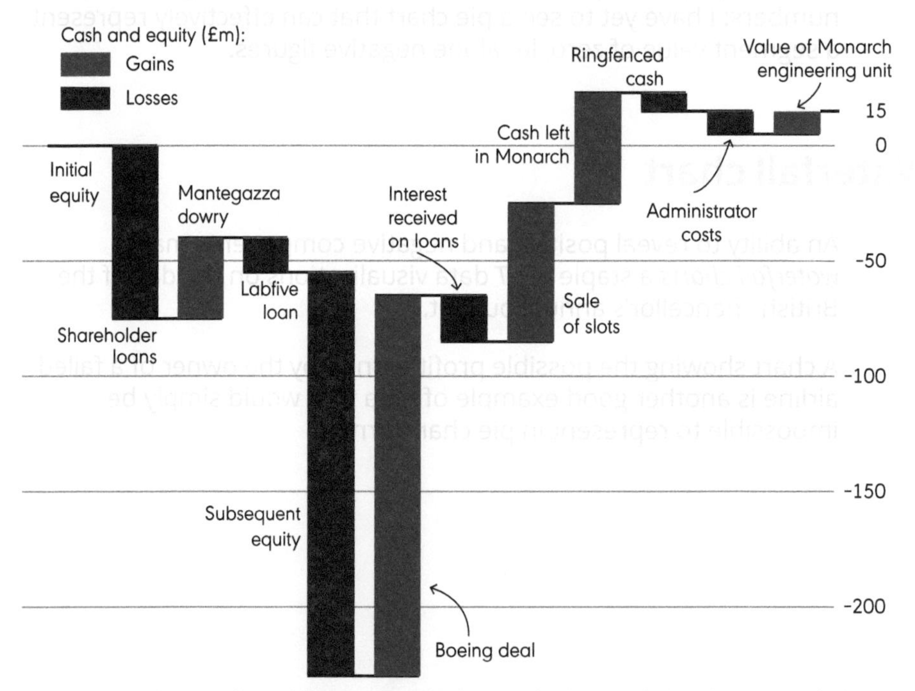

Source: FT research appeared in Greybull stays upbeat despite Monarch collapse. Available at: https://www.ft.com/content/9dbf9aae-a8ea-11e7-93c5-648314d2c72c

Sunburst chart

Pie charts can be adapted to represent multiple levels of hierarchy in our part-to-whole data. This pie chart variant of LSE's revenues – sometimes known as a *sunburst chart* – is an example. With 10 basic wedges organised into three broad categories, the labelling on such charts can sometimes be a challenge, with lots of "leader lines" connecting text to the segments they describe.

LSE's revenues are driven by data services

£m, 2020

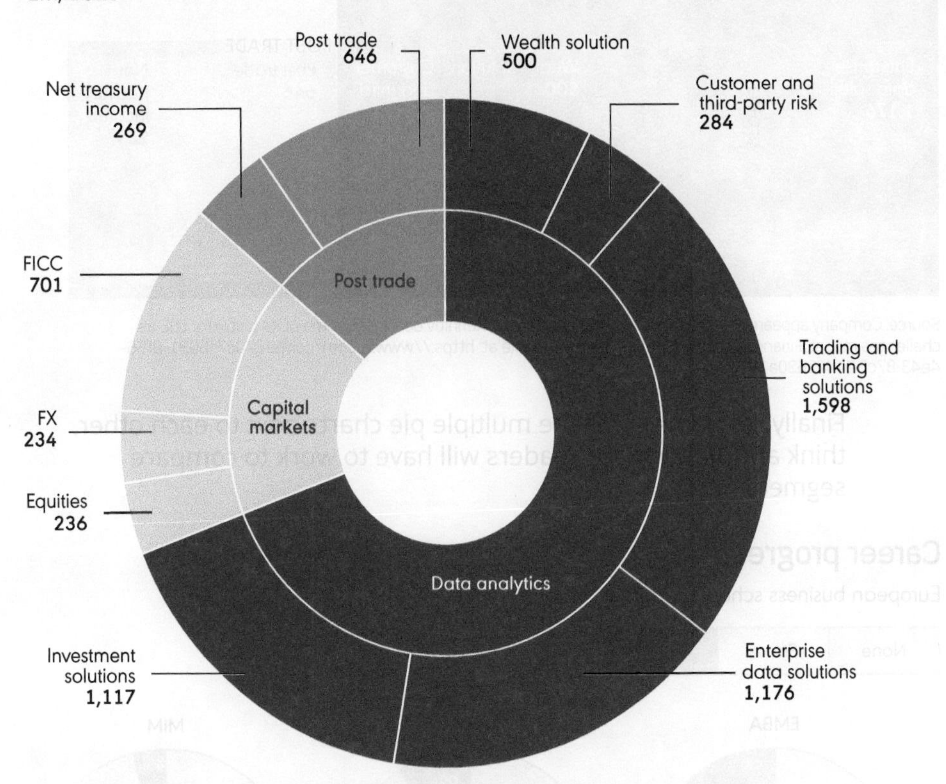

Source: Company appeared in Philip Stafford and Alex Barker, Refinitiv deal loses some of its lustre for LSE as challenges mount, Financial Times, June 30, 2021. Available at: https://www.ft.com/content/0c7c6931-9f56-4e43-87cf-91422630a146

Treemap

Here's another view of the same data presented as a "treemap". These are space-filling algorithms which represent data in hierarchical rectangles. Compared with the sunburst chart, notice that all segments on this chart are directly labelled.

LSE's revenues are driven by data services

£m, 2020

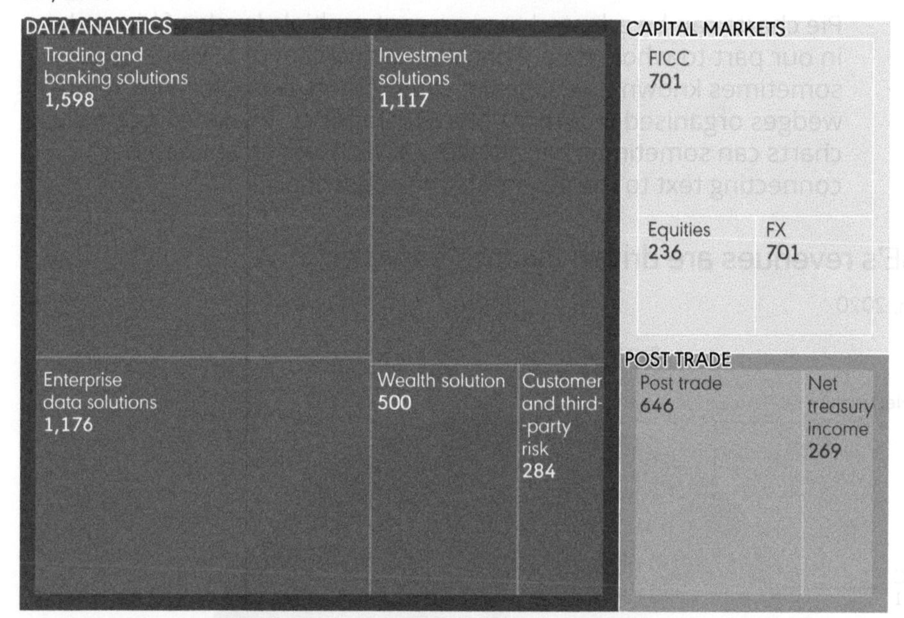

Source: Company appeared in Philip Stafford and Alex Barker, Refinitiv deal loses some of its lustre for LSE as challenges mount, Financial Times, June 30, 2021. Available at: https://www.ft.com/content/0c7c6931-9f56-4e43-87cf-91422630a146

Finally, whenever you see multiple pie charts next to each other, think about how hard readers will have to work to compare segments . . .

Career progress

European business school graduates' progression at work*

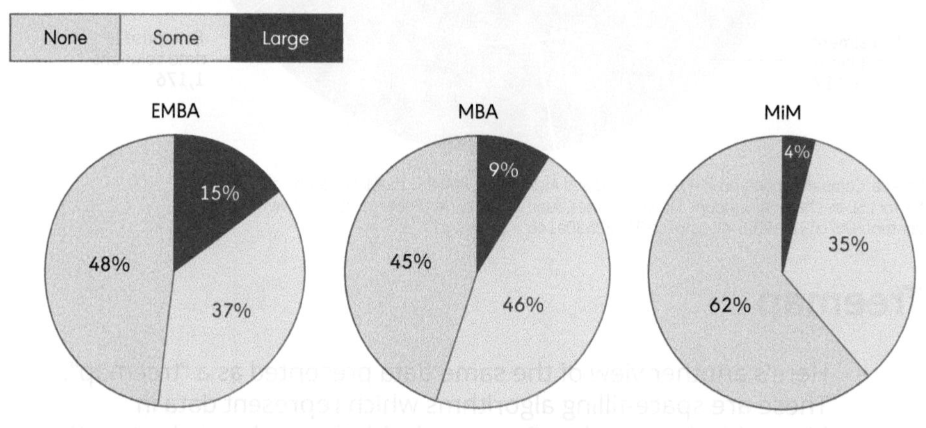

* Alumni surveyed three years after graduation

Source: FT Business Education data appeared in Leo Cremonezi and Sam Stephens, Charting European business school graduates' progress, Financial Times, December 6, 2000. Available at: https://www.ft.com/content/5d834702-daf5-4fcc-b6a7-52afe043e716

This sort of presentation requires the reader to do a lot of remembering – and this is with just three segments on three pie charts. With more complicated data, the problem would be much worse.

Gridplot

This *gridplot* of the same data by Chris Campbell takes the same nine numbers from the pie charts above and structures the information much more coherently. With each plot formed of tessellating rectangles, notice that it also has the advantage that each percentage point unit is countable.

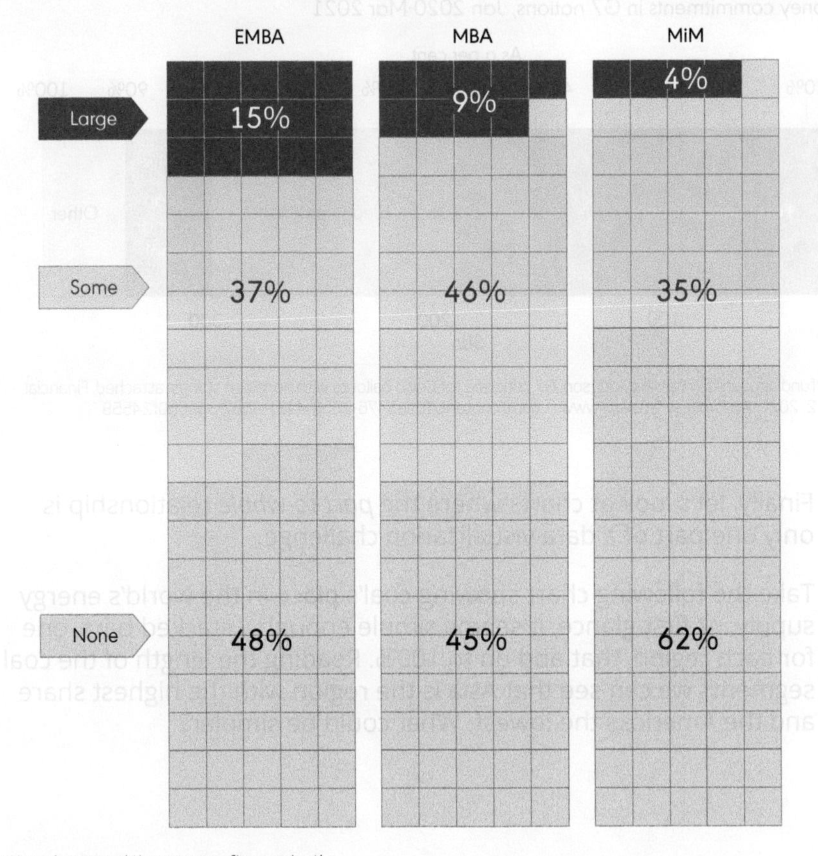

* Alumni surveyed three years after graduation
Graphic: FT Business Education data appeared in Leo Cremonezi and Sam Stephens, Charting European business school graduates' progress, Financial Times, December 6, 2000. Available at: https://www.ft.com/content/5d834702-daf5-4fcc-b6a7-52afe043e716

A gridplot's structure can be flexible too, accommodating a range of layout options as needed (e.g., 10 x 10, 5 x 20). It's a very useful option for multiple *part-to-whole* comparisons.

Stacked bar chart

Stacked bar charts are another effective alternative to pie charts, in either singular or multiple configurations. The use of a conventional chart axis means we don't necessarily have to label each individual value as we do on pie charts. Labelling can also often be cleaner.

During the pandemic, fossil fuels received more than half of the total support for energy-intensive sectors

Public money commitments in G7 nations, Jan 2020-Mar 2021

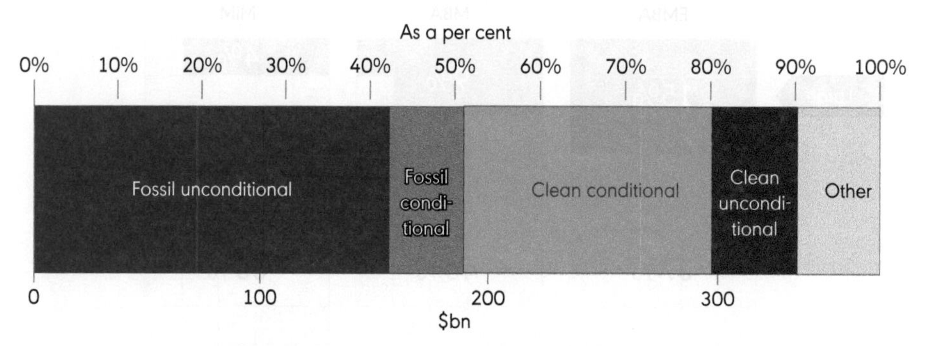

Source: Tearfund appeared in Camilla Hodgson, G7 criticised for Covid bailouts with no 'green strings' attached, Financial Times, June 2, 2021. Available at: https://www.ft.com/content/fdae5476-28b8-4a81-96b7-55a660f24558

Finally, let's look at charts where the *part-to-whole* relationship is only one part of a data visualisation challenge.

Take the following chart showing coal's place in the world's energy supply. At first glance, it seems simple enough – stacked bars, one for each region, that add up to 100%. Reading the length of the coal segments we can see that Asia is the region with the highest share and the Americas the lowest. What could be simpler?

Coal's role in global energy supply

Composition of energy supply, by region, 2019 (%)

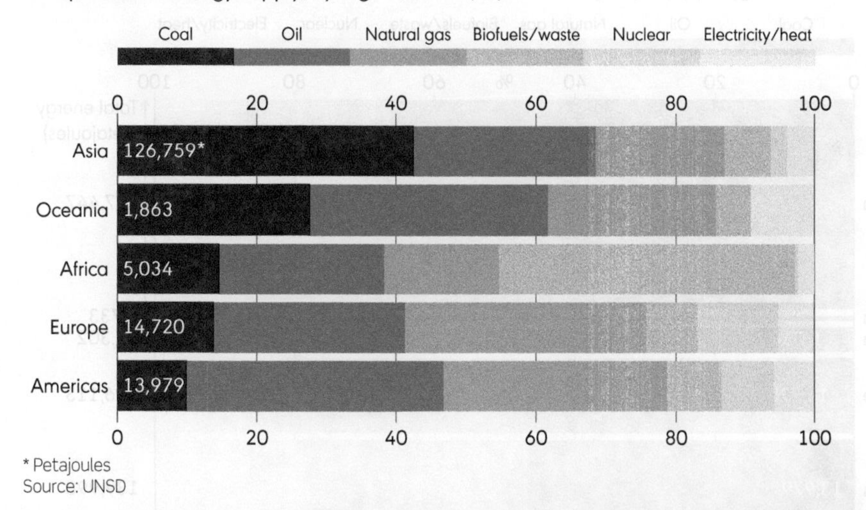

* Petajoules
Source: UNSD

But wait – notice the labels for each coal segment. Sometimes there is nothing more sinister on a chart than an asterisk! The label for Asian coal — the first row of data — points us to a footnote that tells us that the figures themselves are in petajoules. This is at odds with the chart itself, which shows % values. We can see this conflict of units by looking closer at the coal segments - how can Oceania's long bar possibly represent only 1,863 petajoules, while the much shorter bars for Europe and the Americas represent 14,720 and 13,979 petajoules respectively?

The designer of this chart has fallen victim to one of the most vexing and repeating challenges in data visualisation: how to show multiple totals and their components in a single image. This is a veritable data visualisation graveyard, littered with asterisks and freakishly mismatched pie charts.

So, how should we approach this problem?

Using the language of the Visual Vocabulary, we want to show both the *magnitude* (size comparison of energy supply) and *part-to-whole* relationship (share of energy source for each region) simultaneously. There is only one chart type that features in both relationships on the Visual Vocabulary. Welcome to the wonderful world of Marimekko charts.

Marimekko chart

There is something wonderfully evocative about the name — the eponymous Finnish furnishing and textile company's bright repeating patterns defined Jacqueline Kennedy's look during the 1960 US presidential election campaign.

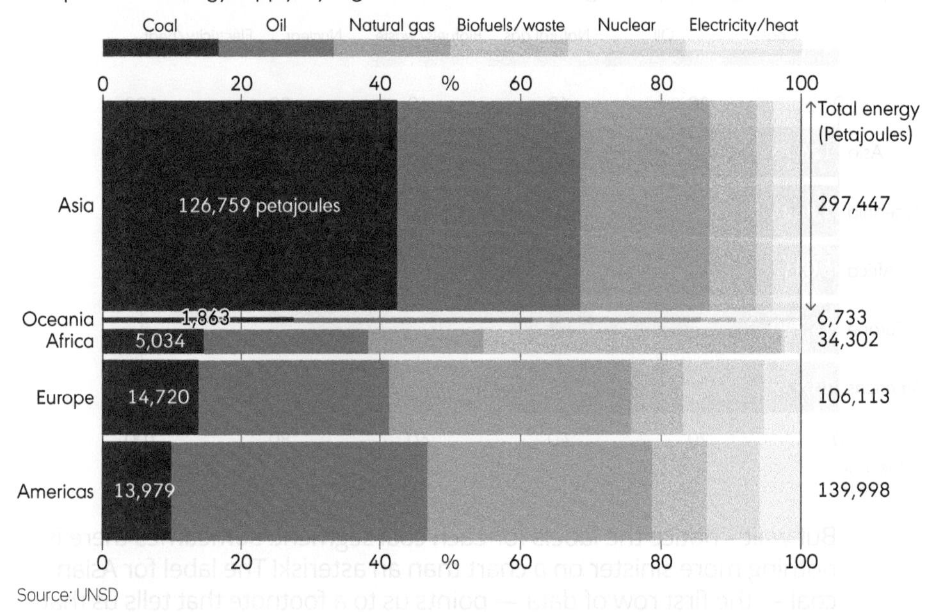

Marimekko charts (also known as mosaic charts and proportional stacked bar charts) can be thought of as a regular stacked chart with an additional axis. This allows us to create charts that feature both a per cent axis and a total axis, using area to represent the overall energy supply. It allows us to see compare totals and their components.

The reworked chart allows us to see the sheer dominance of Asian coal — larger than all the other regions put together. While Oceania's share of coal is second highest, we can see that its overall energy supply is by far the smallest. As for Africa and Europe, while they may both have a similar overall share of coal in their energy supply, we can see that Europe's is a much bigger overall amount.

Any chart that attempts to show more than one relationship in a data set will involve compromise – and that is certainly true of Marimekko charts. Stephen Few, a business intelligence and information design expert, is right when he points out that their use of area to encode value can be problematic. Our perceptual systems are more effective at seeing differences in one dimension (length, or position on an axis) than in two (area).

Few also argues that Marimekko charts "suffer from a problem that plagues any stacked bar graph: it is difficult to accurately make comparisons of the width or height of boxes that are not arranged next to one another along a common baseline". These are both valid points that mean seeing precise differences in the components of Marimekko charts is difficult. The problem escalates with larger data sets.

Few proposes a redesign that involves breaking a Marimekko into separate, more conventional charts, each focusing on a different relationship in the data. Functionally, this does makes sense. But, for me, there is an aspect to Marimekko charts that means they remain a valid part of the toolbox – they allow us to see the *part-to-whole* nature of an entire data set in a single, memorable image. Sometimes, this is more important than being able to see fine differences.

I turned to a Marimekko chart when visualising the size of the banking bailouts for the global financial crisis. The x axis shows the size of each country's bailout as a *proportion* of its gross domestic product, while the vertical axis shows the size of each country's economy.

To allow the reader to see the vast differences between the bailouts of Cyprus (20 per cent of $23bn) and the US (4.3 per cent of $17.4tn), the chart is stretched tall – as shown here, the graphic might be too tall for the pages of this book but was perfect for vertical scrolling online! This depth created a canvas for incorporating quotes on the chart, which helped add context to the numbers. Another design touch – using a repeating pattern to emphasise the zoomed-in focus on the US's bailout recovery – obliquely references the Marimekko's textile origins.

Marimekko charts are like a lot of charts in our Visual Vocabulary toolbox: not likely to end up being a default solution for everything, but an occasionally useful way of keeping important proportions in context.

The banking bailout: big, but not as big as you might think

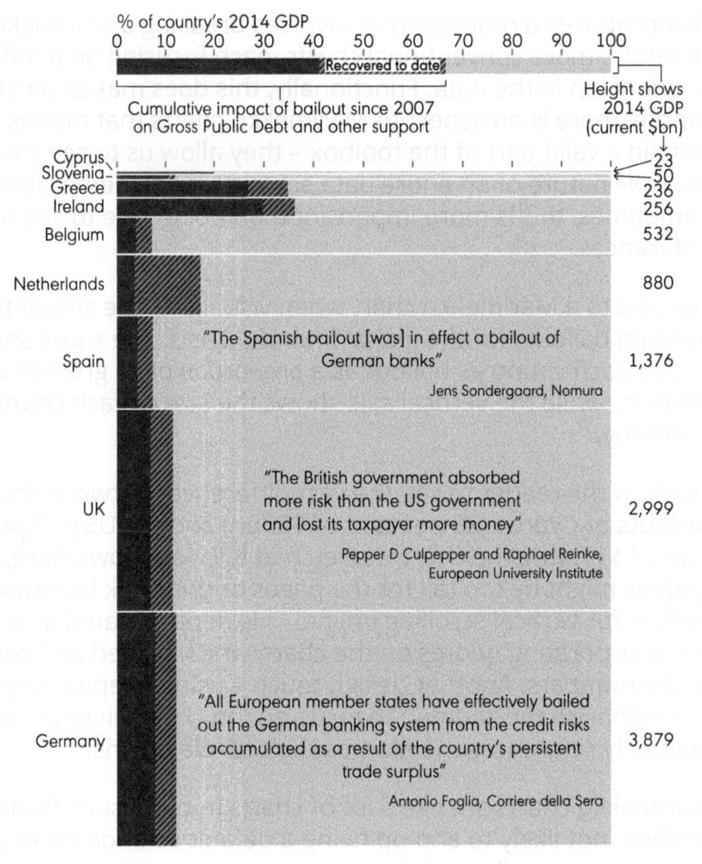
How to read this chart:
% of country's 2014 GDP
0
10
20
30
40
50
60
70
80
90
100
Recovered to date
Cumulative impact of bailout since 2007 on Gross Public Debt and other support
Height shows 2014 GDP (current $bn)
Cyprus
Slovenia
Greece
Ireland
Belgium
Netherlands
Spain
UK
Germany
23
50
236
256
532
880
1,376
2,999
3,879
"The Spanish bailout [was] in effect a bailout of German banks"
Jens Sondergaard, Nomura
"The British government absorbed more risk than the US government and lost its taxpayer more money"
Pepper D Culpepper and Raphael Reinke, European University Institute
"All European member states have effectively bailed out the German banking system from the credit risks accumulated as a result of the country's persistent trade surplus"
Antonio Foglia, Corriere della Sera

This chart continues on the following page.

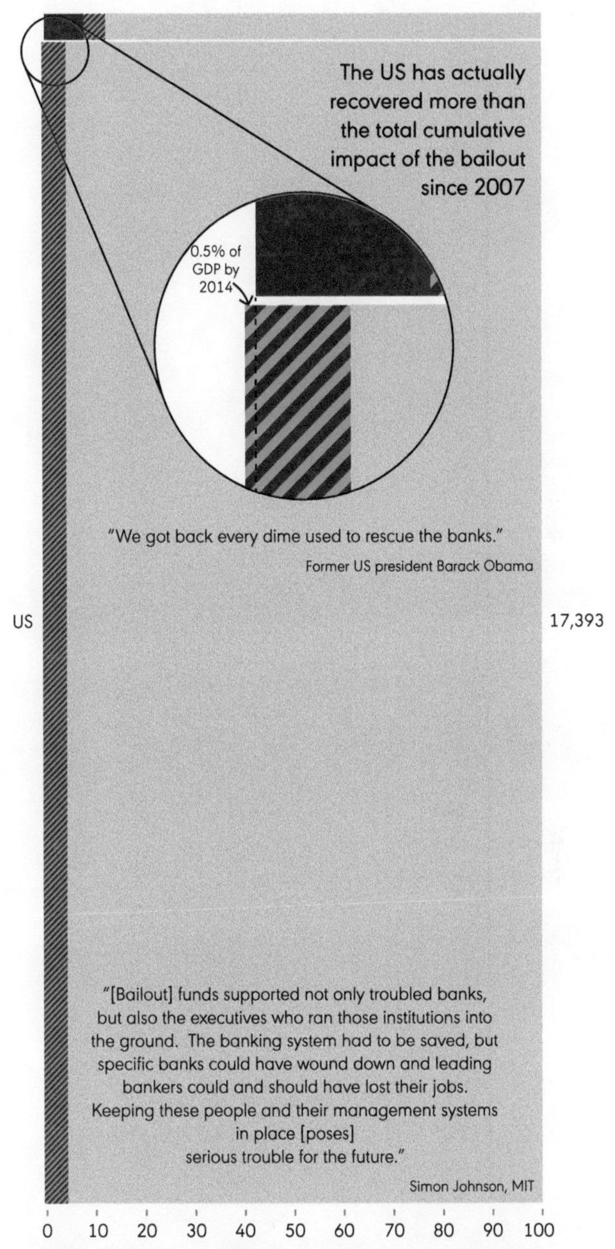

The US has actually
recovered more than
the total cumulative
impact of the bailout
since 2007
0.5% of
GDP by
2014
"We got back every dime used to rescue the banks."
Former US president Barack Obama
US
17,393
"[Bailout] funds supported not only troubled banks,
but also the executives who ran those institutions into
the ground. The banking system had to be saved, but
specific banks could have wound down and leading
bankers could and should have lost their jobs.
Keeping these people and their management systems
in place [poses]
serious trouble for the future."
Simon Johnson, MIT
0 10 20 30 40 50 60 70 80 90 100

Graphic: Alan Smith, Stephen Foley appeared in Bailout costs will be a burden for years, Financial Times, August 8, 2017. Available at https://www.ft.com/content/b823371a-76e6-11e7-90c0-90a9d1bc9691

12

Spatial is special

When precise locations or geographical patterns in data are more important to the reader than anything else.

Maps were my entry point into the world of data visualisation. As a geography student, I soaked up the work of cartographers like Jacques Bertin. Bertin's *Semiologie Graphique*, published in 1967, was a ground-breaking work, not just for aspiring mapmakers like me, but for the field of information visualisation in general.

Bertin introduced the world to a concept of "visual variables" – a taxonomy of geometry, colour and patterns – that still underpins much of today's data visualisation toolkit, including the Visual Vocabulary.

At the *FT*, I continue to be inspired. Our master cartographer Steven Bernard regularly produces maps of such compelling beauty that you can't help but be drawn to them. Steve's work exemplifies the power of maps – their ability to attract and inform, using a schematic of the real world as a canvas.

As this stunning map of lucrative new real estate in Manhattan demonstrates, maps can innately contextualise information like no other form of data presentation.

High-end property reshapes Manhattan's skyline

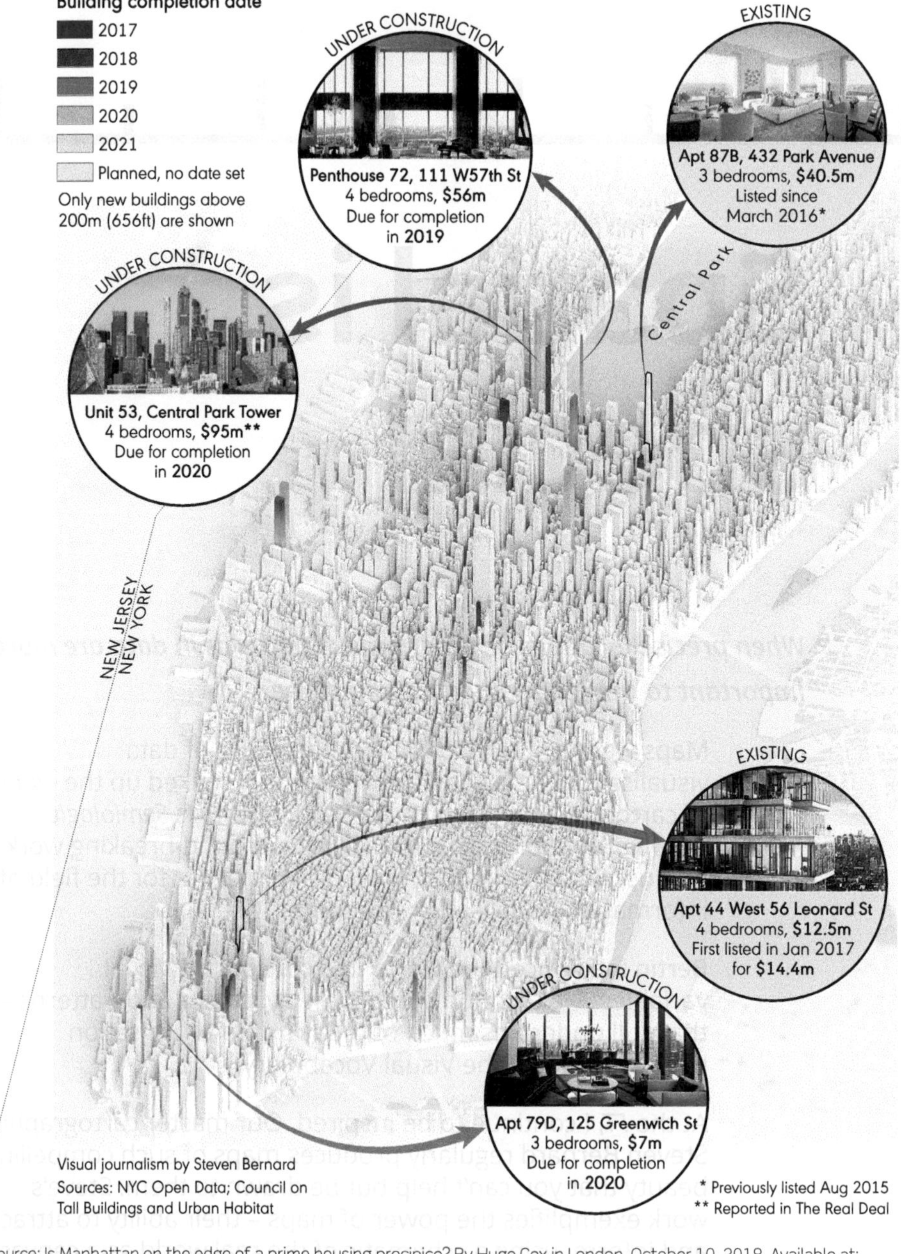

Source: Is Manhattan on the edge of a prime housing precipice? By Hugo Cox in London, October 10, 2018. Available at: https://www.ft.com/content/db675edc-c7f2-11e8-86e6-19f5b7134d1c. Used by permission from The Financial Times limited.

Steven has worked at the *Financial Times* for decades and can remember the newsroom's production workflow shift from manual cartography – tracing by hand from paper atlases – to GIS (geographic information system) software. This innovation proved an efficiency boon for the production of all forms of cartography, but particularly those involving statistics: suddenly, there was a quick way to turn spreadsheets into "thematic maps".

Of course, with great power comes great responsibility – and the speed with which these maps can be produced means that map design principles are more important than ever.

Learning point – The wonderful world of cartography

Cartography is an enormous discipline, with plenty of excellent literature available to guide you. The rest of this chapter doesn't attempt to take on the entire field but discusses thematic maps as part of the Visual Vocabulary. For an in-depth guide to mapping statistics, try the excellent *Thematic Mapping: 101 Inspiring Ways to Visualise Empirical Data* by Kenneth Field.

Choropleth map

Probably the most well-known type of thematic map is the *choropleth*. This type of map sub-divides an area of interest into a mosaic of smaller areas, each of which are then symbolised (usually using different tints of colour) according to an associated statistical value.

This map of opioid prescriptions in the US is typical of the genre. It shows the number of prescriptions per 100 people at the county level (there are just over 3,100 counties in the 50 states and Washington DC). The deeper the colour, the higher the prescription rate, which, in 2015, peaked at a whopping 505 per 100 in Norton, Virginia.

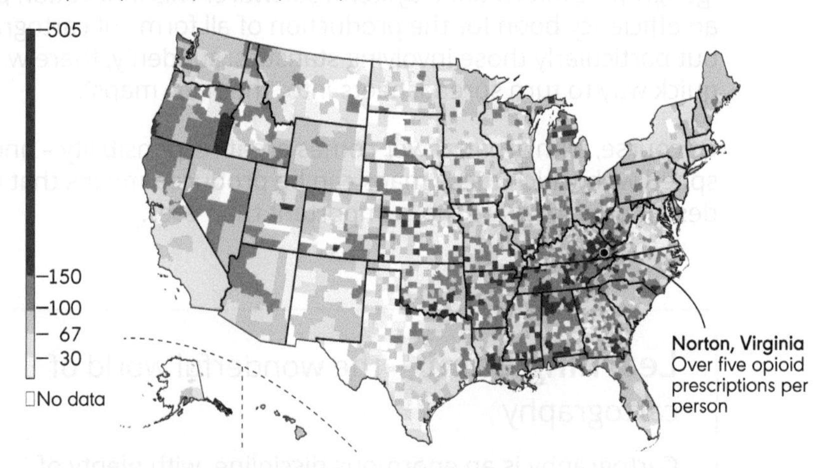

Graphic: Alan Smith and Federica Cocco, Source: Centers for Disease Control and Prevention appeared in Siona Jenkins, Mercedes Ruehl and Neil Munshi, Daily briefing: tough sanctions for North Korea, SoFi head steps down, US grapples with opioid addiction, Financial Times, September 12 2017. Available at https://www.ft.com/content/c787a6a4-96fe-11e7-a652-cde3f882dd7b

The map uses colour to show five "classes" (categories) of data. In counties in the top two classes (100–150 and 150–505 prescriptions per 100), there were more opioid prescriptions than people.

Choropleth maps are at their most powerful when they reveal important, or surprising, spatial patterns in data.

This map of Birkenhead shows one of the steepest gradients in income deprivation in the whole of England. Neighbourhoods from opposite ends of the national income spectrum live "cheek by jowl".

Cheek by jowl: spatial inequality in Birkenhead

National rank of income deprivation, 2019

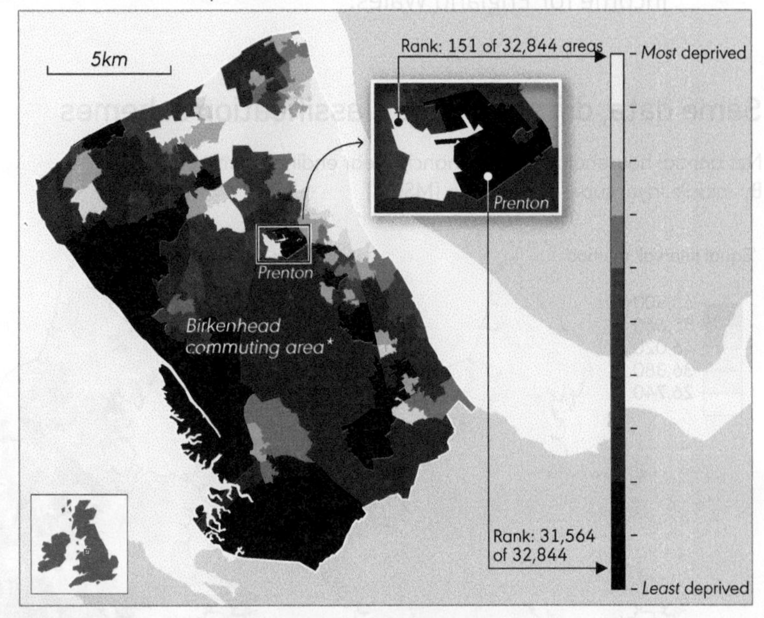

*Travel-to-work area
Source: Ministry of Housing, Communities & Local Government apppeared in William Wallis, England in 2019: Split by wealth but united by Brexit, Financial Times, November 30, 2019. Available at: https://www.ft.com/content/b398d284-11dc-11ea-a225-db2f231cfeae

Unlike our opioid map, which visualised a rate (*something* per *something*), this map shows ordinal data, with colour denoting each small area's *ranking* in the national deprivation index.

So far, so informative – but we should be careful when reading choropleth maps. There are two "banana skins" to watch out for.

First, it is important to recognise that the classes on a choropleth map function rather like the "bins" in a histogram (see Chapter 7 "Charts of distribution" for a refresher). Just as with histograms, the width and number of bins can make a huge difference to the message given by our final visualisation.

A plethora of classification approaches are available. Understanding the impact of different methods is an important development in map literacy. To kick-off, let's look at two of the most well-known and well-used methods.

- **Equal interval** – ensures evenly spaced gaps between the class breaks.
- **Equal count ("quantile") method** – ensures the same number of map areas are allocated to each class.

To illustrate the radical difference that these classification methods can have on a choropleth map, let's map some data of household income for England Wales.

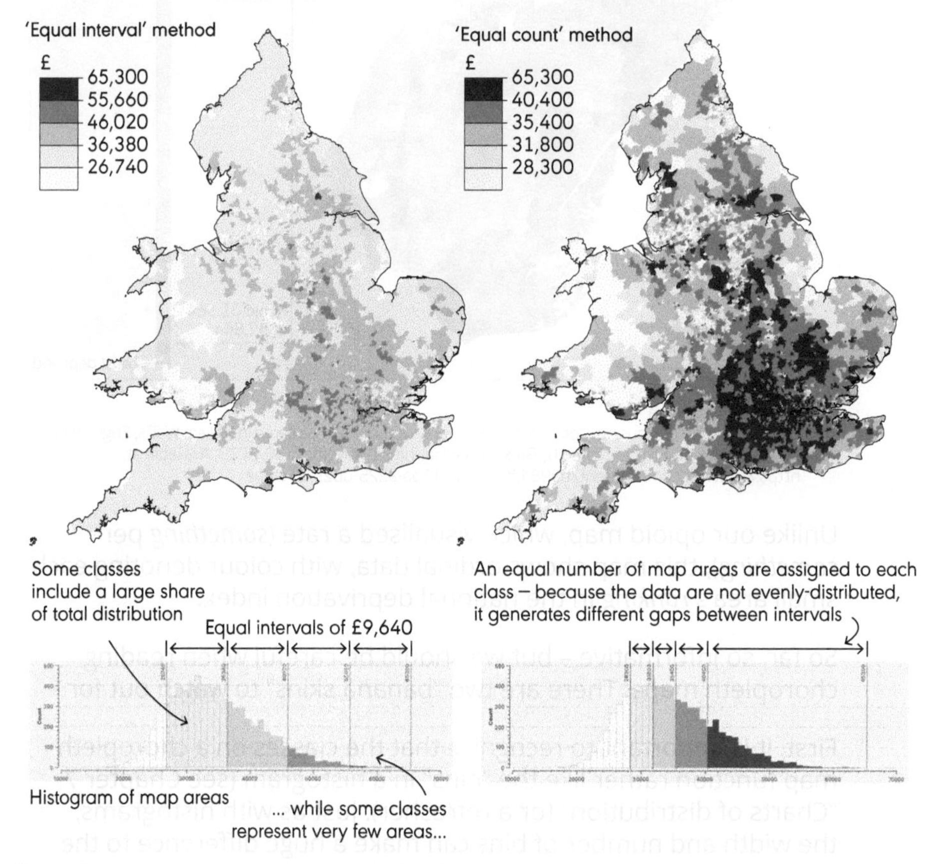
Same data, different map classification schemes
Net annual household income, financial year ending March 2018 (£)
By middle layer super output area (MSOA)
'Equal interval' method
£
65,300
55,660
46,020
36,380
26,740
'Equal count' method
£
65,300
40,400
35,400
31,800
28,300
Some classes include a large share of total distribution
Equal intervals of £9,640
An equal number of map areas are assigned to each class – because the data are not evenly-distributed, it generates different gaps between intervals
Histogram of map areas
... while some classes represent very few areas...
Source: ONS

Looking at the map using the "equal interval" method, it's interesting to see how much insight is hidden – the map is dominated by areas coloured with either the second or third tint. There are very few map areas in the other classes, particularly the highest class. In fact, at the national scale of the map, it's difficult to even see that there are any areas coloured with the darkest tint at all.

Now look at the map on the right, which uses the equal count method. We can see much more spatial variation in the income data because the map areas are evenly distributed across the map's classes. More gradation is apparent at the higher income levels, and we can see differences in income across England and Wales that are not apparent in the first map.

All of this might lead you to think that the equal count method is a more effective technique than equal interval. On this occasion, it is – but have a look at our next map, which shows the share of Wales's population that can speak Welsh.

Same data, different map classification schemes (part 2)

Proportion of population aged 3+ who can speak Welsh, 2011 (%)

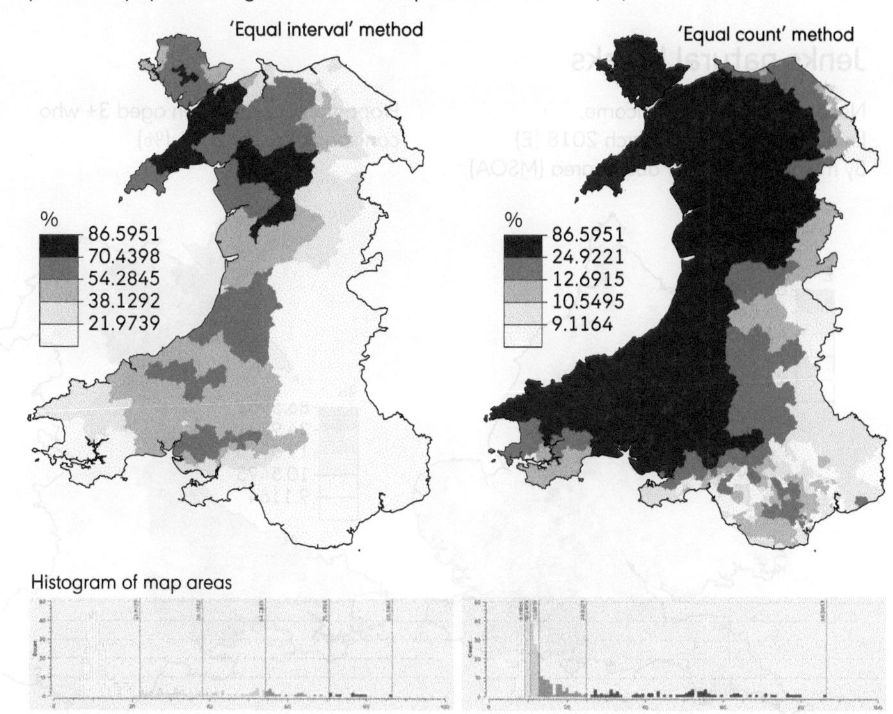

Source: ONS

The histogram reveals that, because there is such a "long tail" to the distribution of values, the top category using the equal count method covers an enormous range from around 25 per cent to over 85 per cent. The map gives the impression that most of Wales is full of Welsh speakers, which isn't the case.

On this occasion, the equal interval method does a better job of revealing the key spatial relationship in the data – that the areas with the highest proportions of Welsh speakers are in the north.

Having seen the spatial havoc that we can wreak with inappropriate classes, wouldn't it be good to have a method that can be relied upon to avoid such obfuscation by design?

Jenks natural breaks method

Devised by statistical cartographer George Jenks, this method optimises class breaks based on patterns or clusters of values in the data. Let's have a look at it in action on the two maps we've just explored.

Jenks natural breaks

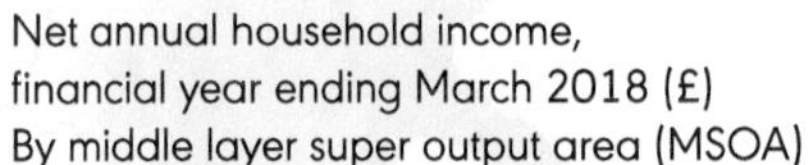

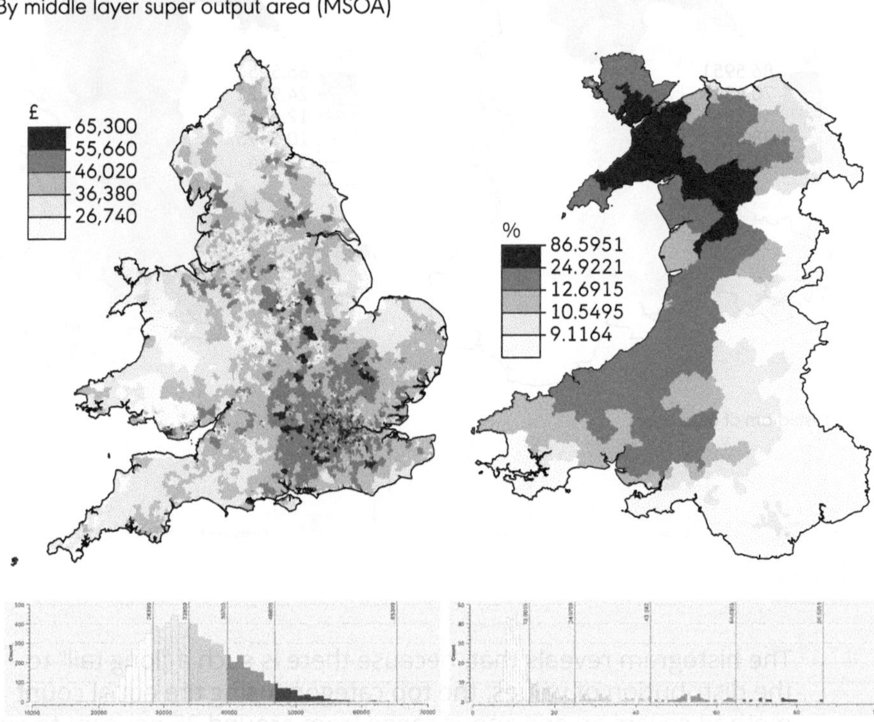

Source: ONS

As you can see, it does a pretty good job in both instances. Importantly, it is less likely than other methods to mislead the reader by hiding clusters or patterns, since it was designed to do just the reverse.

Importantly, because Jenks is optimised around identifying *clusters* of values, it is particularly effective with the bimodal and multimodal *distributions* we encountered earlier in the book.

Jenks is a great "safety-first" starting point, but GIS software makes it quick to audition different classification methods: a little experimentation can go a long way to delivering a better map.

Importantly, whichever initial classification method is used, sometimes it will make sense to manually adjust ranges to improve readability and/or interpretation. The US opioid map we looked at earlier was originally designed with a Jenks method but was adjusted to ensure that one of the range breaks appears at precisely 100 prescriptions per 100 people – an important tipping point in the data.

It's also a good idea to give the reader a visual clue about how the class breaks are distributed across the range of values. On the legend for the opioid map, for example, the uneven gaps between the class breaks delivered by the Jenks method are emphasised by segments of varying length.

Another approach worth considering is to include the histogram as part of the legend, to denote how many areas on the map are allocated to each class. This was a technique I first used in 2010 while creating demographic visualisations at the Office for National Statistics.

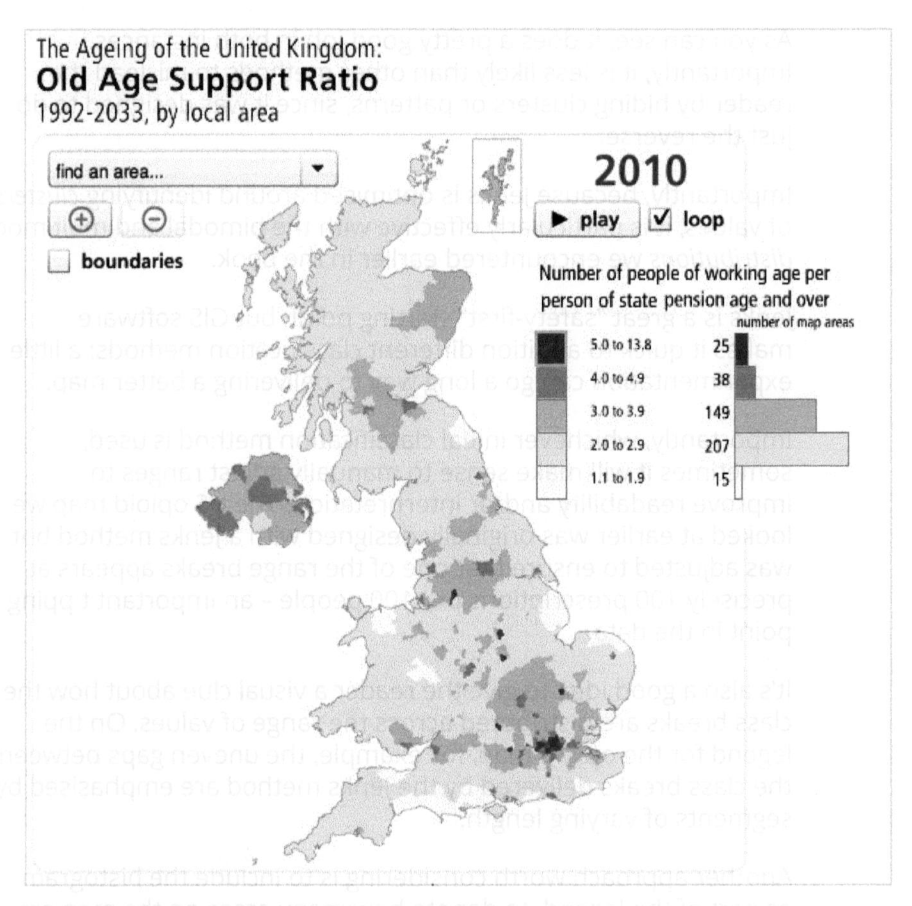

Source: Office for National Statistics

One final issue with choropleth maps to be aware of is that, very often, the largest areas on the map are those with the lowest density of data, meaning our eyes can be attracted to places that offer potentially the least insight.

As an illustration of this, consider the following map of the same income deprivation data we saw for Birkenhead, this time for the area around Portsmouth on England's south coast.

Income inequality in Portsmouth

National rank of income deprivation, 2019

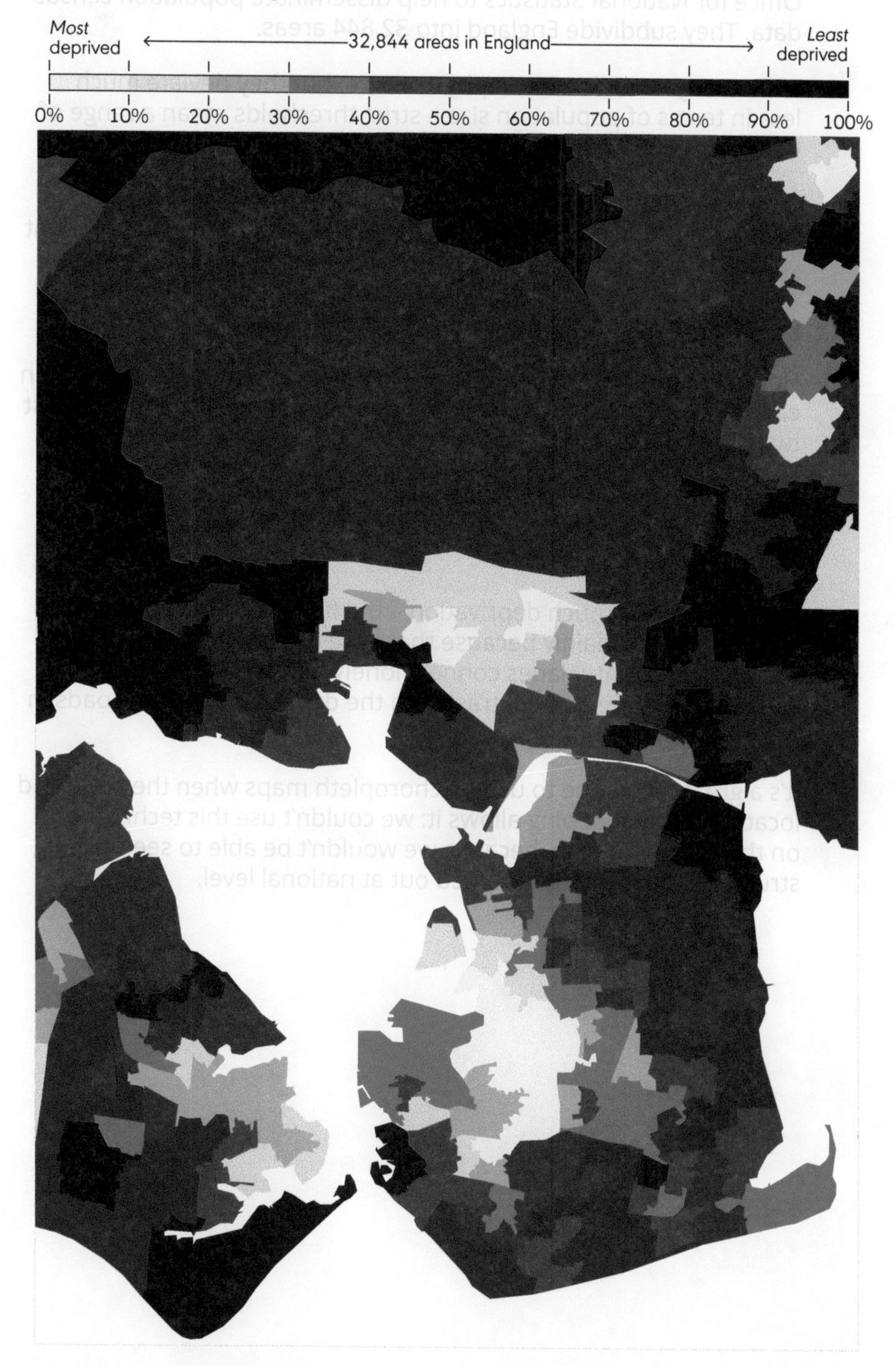

Source: Ministry of Housing, Communities and Local Government

The individual boundaries on this map represent "Lower Layer Super Output" areas (or LSOAs), a statistical unit designed by the Office for National Statistics to help disseminate population census data. They subdivide England into 32,844 areas.

LSOAs vary considerably in physical size, but they deviate much less in terms of population size – strict thresholds mean a range of between 1,000 and 3,000 people in each area.

Two areas dominate the Portsmouth map – the smaller areas of nationally-significant income deprivation near the city centre (bright yellow and orange towards the bottom of the map) and the larger, darker areas on the top half of the map, indicating areas with generally much lower levels of income deprivation.

However, let's filter the map and only colour the built-up area within each LSOA, rather than the contiguous boundaries used for the first map. The map suddenly looks very different.

In the north, we can see the sparseness of rural areas, whose expansive darker shades previously dominated the top half of the map.

Here, there isn't much deprivation – the first map didn't lie in that respect. But it's mainly because there are not that many people there at all. Country lanes connect lonely hamlets and isolated villages. Compare and contrast with the densely populated roads in the city itself.

It's a great technique to use on choropleth maps when the scale and location of the mapping allows it: we couldn't use this technique on the US opioid map, because we wouldn't be able to see building structures clearly while zoomed out at national level.

Inequality in Portsmouth

National rank of income deprivation, 2019

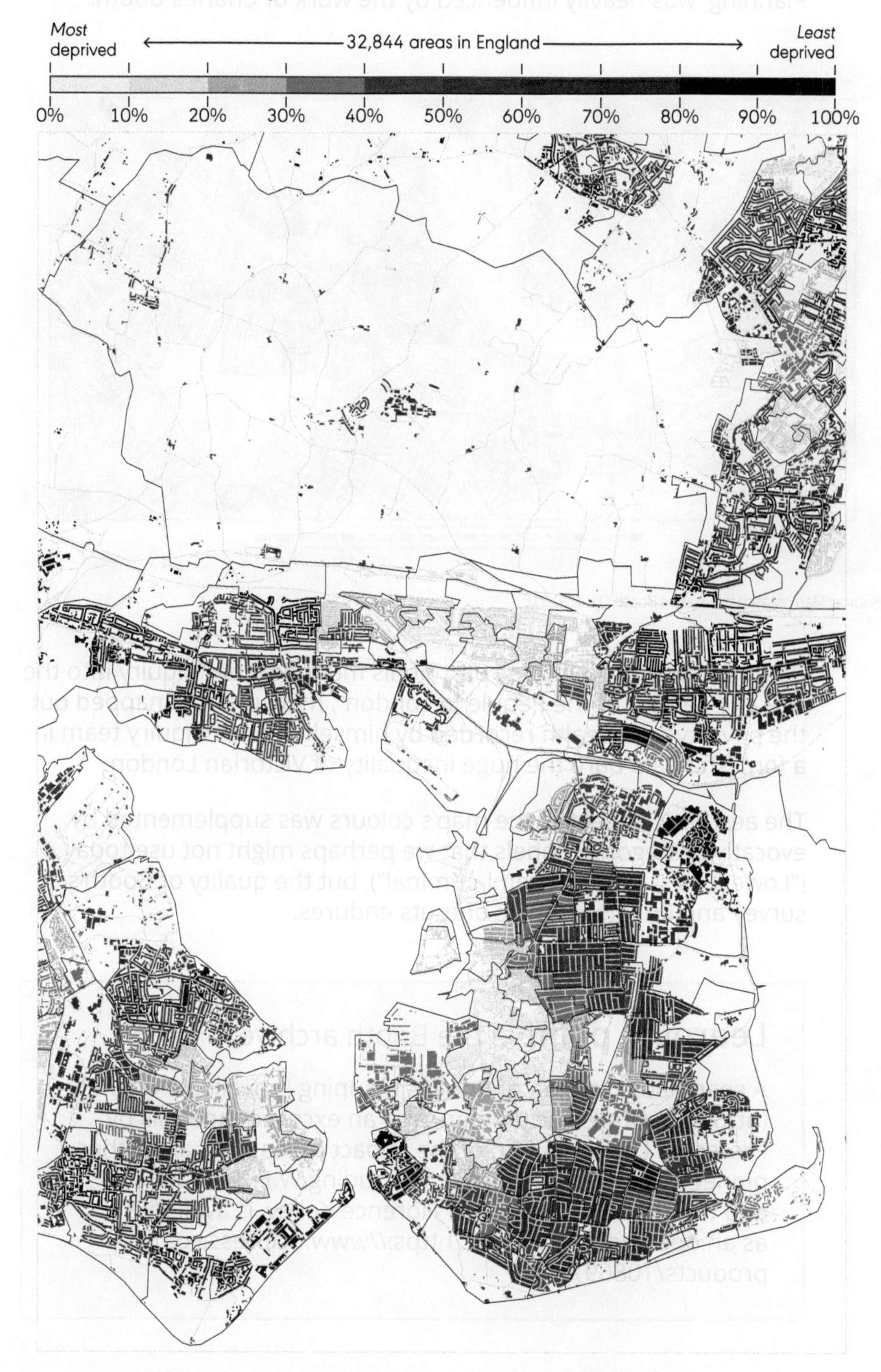

Source: Ministry of Housing, Communities & Local Government

The map, produced as part of a collaboration with Alasdair Rae, a spatial analysis expert and former Professor of Urban Studies and Planning, was heavily influenced by the work of Charles Booth.

Source: Map created by Charles Booth (1840–1916)

Booth's maps, produced as part of his multi-decade "Inquiry into the Life and Labour of the People in London", meticulously mapped out the poverty and wealth recorded by himself and his Inquiry team in a form that laid bare the huge inequality of Victorian London.

The aesthetic impact of the map's colours was supplemented by evocative categorical labels that we perhaps might not use today ("Lowest class. Vicious, semi-criminal"), but the quality of Booth's survey and its cartographic outputs endures.

Learning point – The Booth archive

A searchable version of Booth's mapping is available online (https://booth.lse.ac.uk/map) and an excellent analysis by Professor Laura Vaughn of the impact of his work and other pioneers of social cartography including W.E.B. Du Bois and the Hull House maps of Florence Kelley, is available as an open access book at: https://www.uclpress.co.uk/products/108697.

Choropleth maps are flexible – we've already seen examples that present rates and ordinal (*ranking*) data. However, choropleth maps are generally not suited to mapping *magnitude* data. Let's explore why.

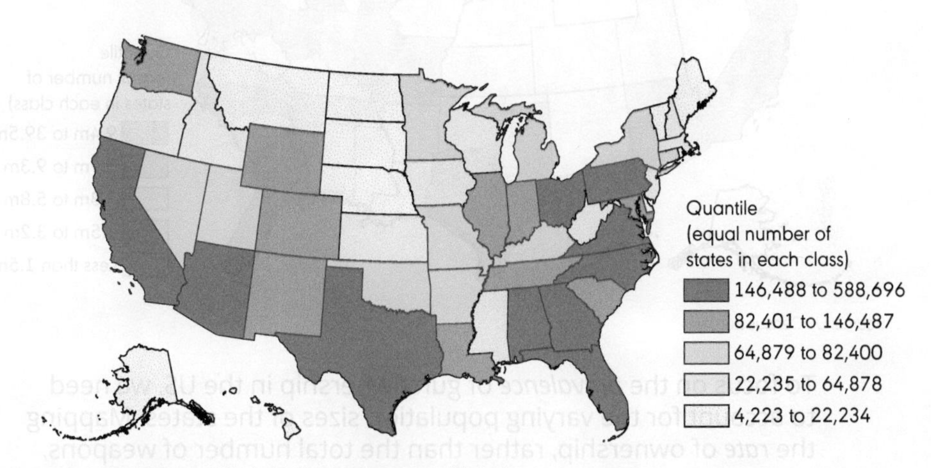

This map of gun ownership in the US seems an open and shut case – mapping the number of guns per state, using the quantile method to allocate an equal number of states (10) to each of the 5 classes, we can clearly see that the states with the highest number of registered weapons include California, Texas and Florida.

But wait a moment – those three states are also the most populous in the US. What we're really seeing in this map is not so much a map of guns, but a population map of the country. This is a recurring problem when mapping data related to human activity: mapping magnitudes gives us pretty much the same map time and time again.

US population

By state, 2020

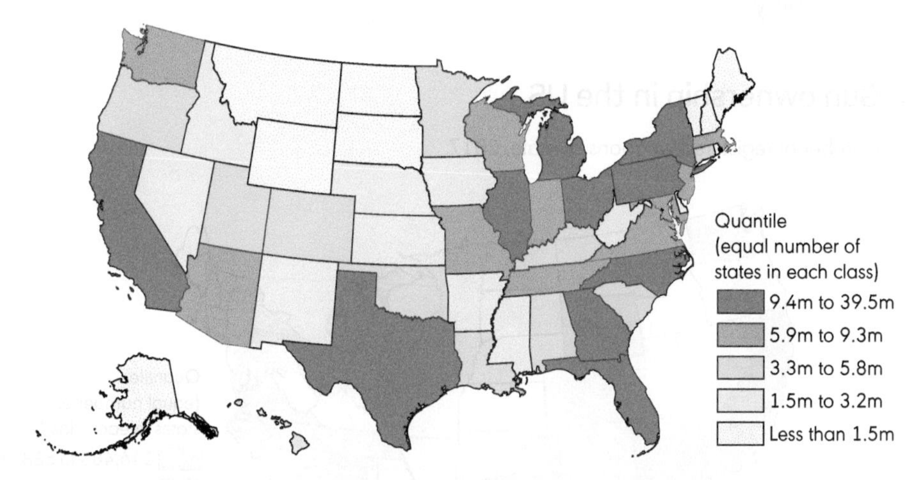

Source: US Census Bureau

To focus on the *prevalence* of gun ownership in the US, we need to account for the varying population sizes of the states. Mapping the *rate* of ownership, rather than the total number of weapons, produces a completely different impression of gun ownership in the US. It's a map that far better reflects the characteristics of the population in each state, regardless of its overall population.

Gun ownership in the US

Estimates of the average household firearm ownership rate*, 1980–2016 (%)

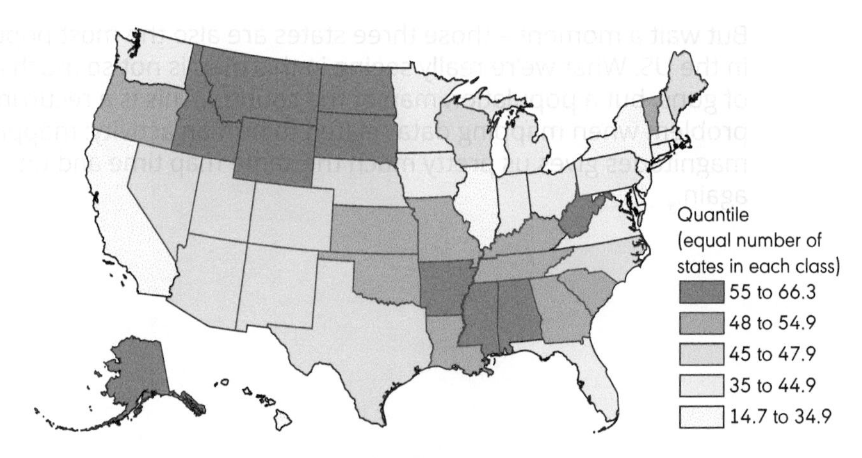

* Proportion of US adults who live in a household with a firearm

Source: Rand Corporation

Among the drastic changes, the most populous state, California, moves from the top category to the bottom. Although it has many registered weapons, the rate of ownership is low relative to other states, once you take its population of nearly 40 million people into account.

The highest rates of ownership are in a cluster of less populous states – Montana, the Dakotas, Idaho and Wyoming – most of which were shaded with the lightest colour on the first map.

At the *FT*, we are far more likely to map raw magnitude data when reporting on natural disasters, such as earthquakes.

Proportional symbol map

We covered the use of *proportional symbols* in Chapter 4 "Charts of magnitude" – and this is a technique that generally translates well into the cartographic world.

This *proportional symbol map* of wildfires in the Mediterranean during the heatwave of 2021 conveys a sense of the scale of the fires that devastated parts of Turkey in late July.

Mediterranean wildfires: Turkey and Italy suffer as heatwave takes toll

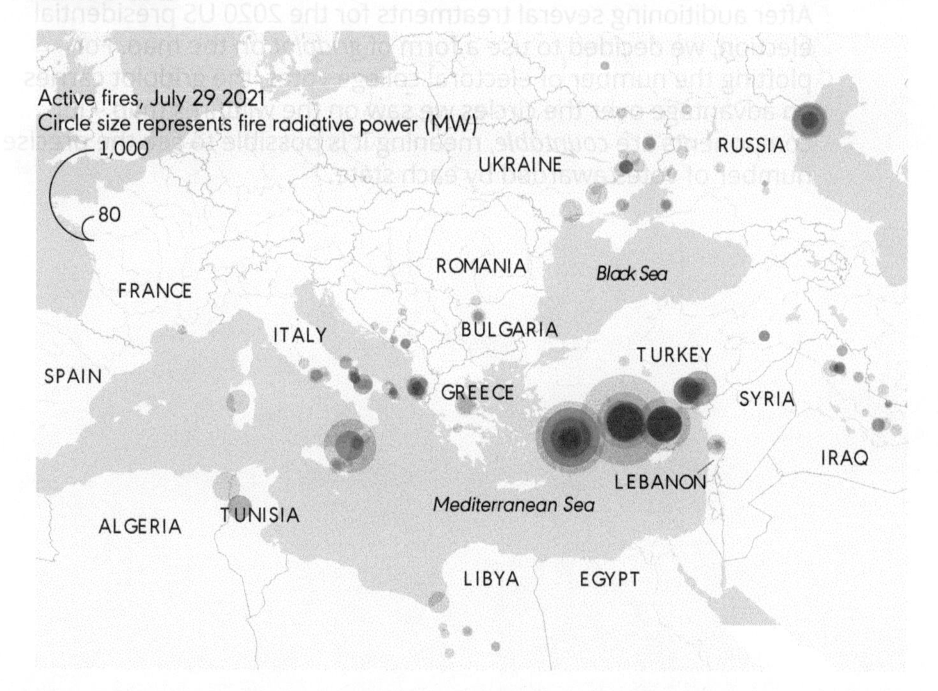

Source: EU Copernicus programme appeared in Alan Smith, Wildfires surge during searing Mediterranean heat, Financial Times, August 9, 2021. Available at -https://www.ft.com/content/e31113e1-41ed-4be0-9667-445249a487c4

Proportional symbol maps serve a useful function; there needs to be a spatial pattern worth articulating. That's certainly the case with the wildfires map, its cluster of red circles along the Mediterranean's northern shores clearly telling the story. But the truth is that they are subject to overuse.

For example, during the early stages of the Covid-19 pandemic, we created plenty of proportional symbol maps to show where localised clusters of coronavirus cases had appeared. However, once the virus had spread to most parts of the world, the value of plotting large circles all over the globe was much diminished and we moved on to other forms of visualisation that helped us visualise how the pandemic was changing (notably, log scale charts which we'll look at shortly).

Election mapping

Another example of magnitude data on a map is provided every four years by the US presidential election. The race for the White House is ultimately determined by the accumulation of electoral college votes – a candidate needs to achieve 270 to win, with the number available in each state determined largely by its population.

After auditioning several treatments for the 2020 US presidential election, we decided to use a form of *gridplot* on the map. For plotting the number of electoral college votes, the gridplot carries an advantage over the circles we saw on the wildfires map – its components are *countable*, meaning it is possible to see the precise number of votes awarded by each state.

Results of the US 2020 presidential election

Each square represents an electoral college vote

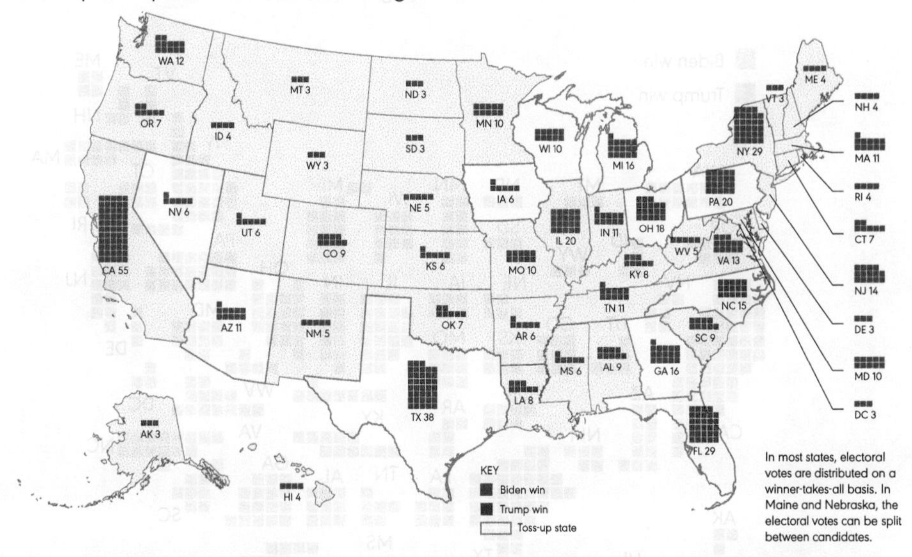

Graphic: Caroline Nevitt, Max Harlow
Source: Data from Associated Press appeared in Biden vs Trump: live results 2020, US presidential election 2020, Financial Times. Available at: https://ig.ft.com/us-election-2020. Used by permission from The Financial Times Limited.

However, for mobile-screen sizes, the use of the orthodox map behind the gridplot map posed a real problem. Even on the larger, regular version, you can see that the east coast looks busy, with "leader lines" connecting the electoral college vote gridplots with their physically small (but often populous) states. Shrinking the map further would make the map virtually unreadable on small screens.

The solution for presenting the results on smaller screens was to use a *cartogram*. Cartograms convert each area on a map to a regular, often equally sized shape, allowing mapmakers to eliminate the physical variations of the real world while preserving most of the geographical relationships.

For our election cartogram, Bob Haslett skilfully used the electoral college units from the gridplots to form a recognisable US shape, keeping most of the benefits of the larger map, while preserving the information on how many electoral college votes were associated with each state.

Results of the US 2020 presidential election

Each square represents an electoral college vote

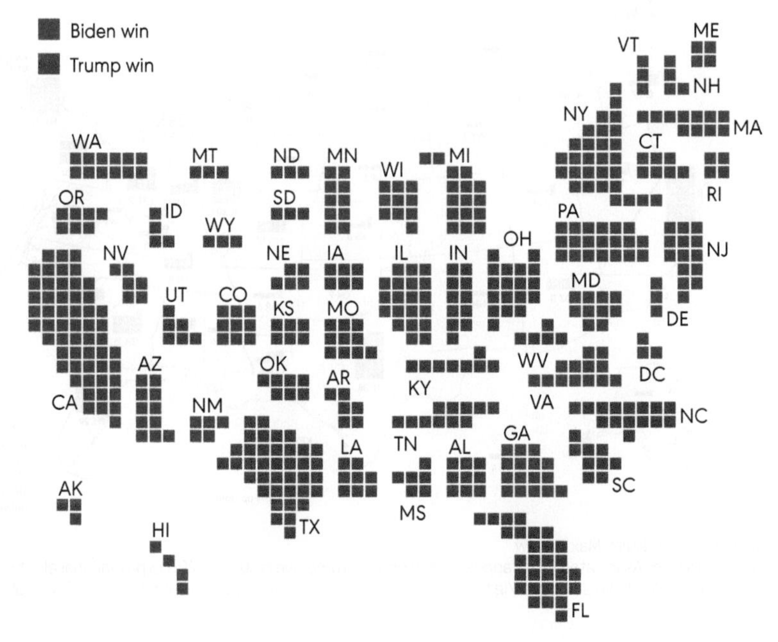

Graphic: Bob Haslett
Source: Associated Press appeared in Demetri Sevastopulo, Courtney Weaver and Lauren Fedor, Tight US election reveals Trump's resilience and flaws in Biden campaign, November 4, 2020. Available at: https://www.ft.com/content/1c950b37-7318-467b-9a70-4078e0028fda

It's a compromise – the geographical distortion means the two-character state codes are essential for decoding which state is represented by each set of blocks – but one we feel readers glancing at results on their phones while standing at the bus stop would appreciate.

One thing worth pointing out is that both versions of the results map are good at showing which candidate won each state – but not who won overall. Of course, we could ask readers to count the total number of blue and red squares, but that's perhaps asking them to work a little too hard . . .

The truth is that the map was designed to show who won *where*, not who won *overall*. That's why the map was always accompanied by a simple stacked bar chart showing the total number of electoral college votes won by each candidate. At a glance, the margin of Joe Biden's victory is clear in a way that is difficult to see using the map alone.

Source: FT Research appeared in Biden vs Trump: live results 2020, US presidential election 2020, Financial Times. Available at: https://ig.ft.com/us-election-2020. Used by permission from The Financial Times Limited.

This observation is a neat lead-in to a key point about maps – they are not the only option for visualising data with a spatial component.

How maps can leave you feeling lost

In 2016, painstaking research by my colleague Laura Noonan, then the *FT*'s investment banking correspondent, produced a dataset of top banking firms' presence in eight cities across Europe lining up to take London's role as the EU's banking centre following the British vote to lead the bloc.

Laura compiled information on nearly 5,000 banking entities from which the highest level of presence for each banking firm in each of the cities was calculated.

When it came to visualising this information, early discussions revolved around a map. This seemed natural enough – after all, the data contained geographical information (level of banking presence in a variety of cities).

As we considered the specific patterns in the data, we wanted readers to be able to see on the map, two key aspects stood out:

1. The relative strength of each city in terms of its banking presence *and*
2. The relative strength of each banking firm across all cities

Let's use a draft map to answer those questions.

The Brexit banking matrix: The contenders lining up for London's crown

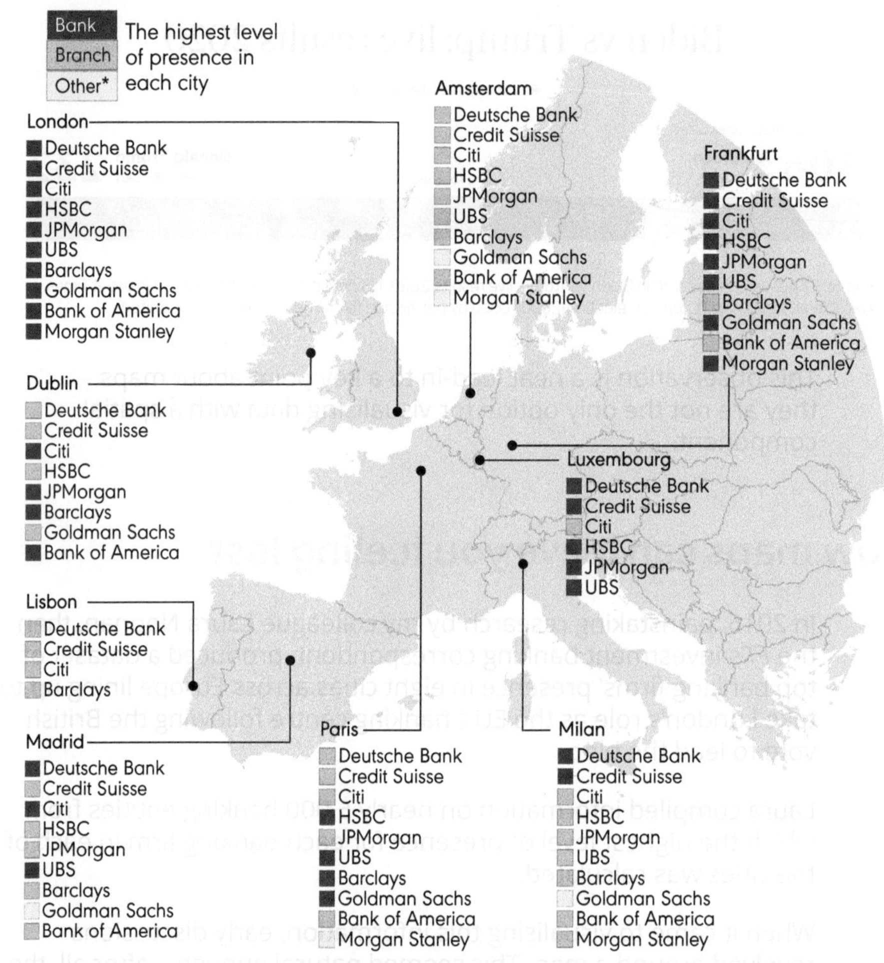

* Broker dealer branches are included for Morgan Stanley and Goldman Sachs as they are a significant part of their European network
Deutsche Bank has a London subsidiary but its main entity is a branch
Source: FT research appeared in Alan Smith, A love of maps should mean using fewer to illustrate data better, Financial Times, October 20, 2016. Available at: https://www.ft.com/content/de3ef722-9514-11e6-a1dc-bdf38d484582

First up, let's consider the cities. The map works well in this respect, allowing us to see, for example, that Frankfurt is strong (lots of red rectangles) and Lisbon is weak (fewer, all orange). So far so good.

But next, try and use the map to see how well federated HSBC is across Europe. And compare it with Goldman Sachs to see which has the strongest overall presence . . . suddenly, things are a lot trickier. Why?

Maps emphasise spatial relationships and locations. So, presenting the banking information on a map might be useful if our primary objective was to show readers the locations of Madrid, Paris or Amsterdam.

Alternatively, a map would also be useful if the *distance* between the cities was of any importance to the story – but it wasn't.

When the key relationship being visualised is not spatial, maps can leave readers with too much information to scan and memorise.

To redesign the visualisation, I shifted from the *spatial* to the *correlation* section of the Visual Vocabulary. A simple *XY heatmap* design was drafted to contrast the relationships between banks and cities.

The new graphic still shows the same information as the map – the highest level of presence for each bank in each city. But structuring the data into a grid and sorting the data into ranks – by the highest level of presence in both rows and columns – transforms the readability of the data.

The Brexit banking matrix: The contenders lining up for London's crown

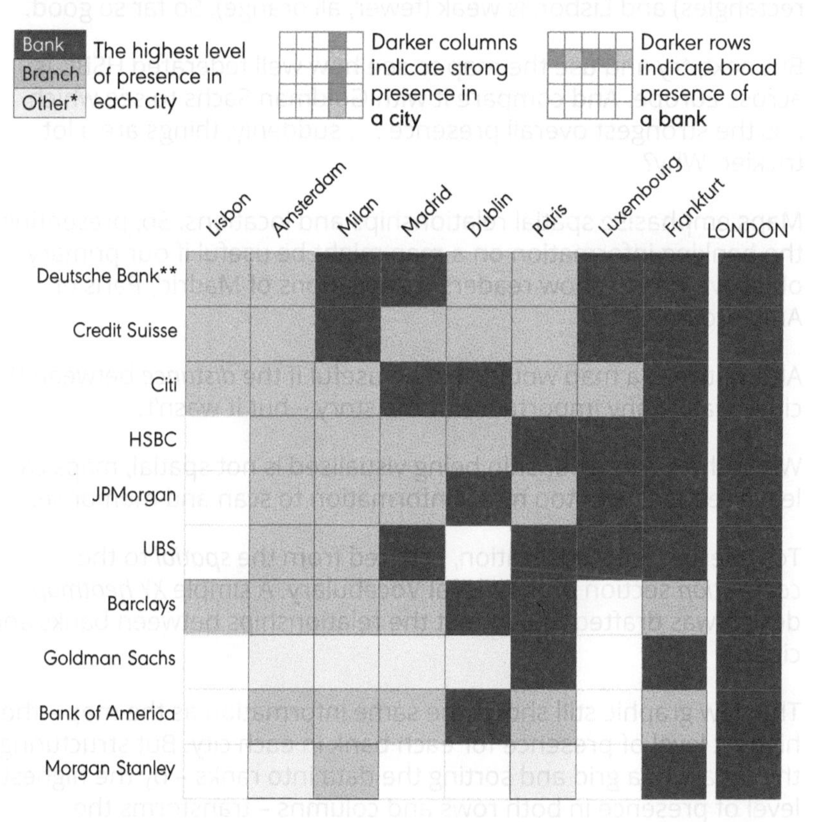

* Broker dealer branches are included for Morgan Stanley and Goldman Sachs as they are a significant part of their European network

** Deutsche Bank has a London subsidiary but its main entity is a branch

Graphic: Alan Smith, Laura Noonan

Source: FT research appeared in Alan Smith, A love of maps should mean using fewer to illustrate data better, Financial Times, October 20, 2016. Available at: https://www.ft.com/content/de3ef722-9514-11e6-a1dc-bdf38d484582

Just as with the map, we can still see that Frankfurt is stronger than Lisbon. But look how much easier it is to see that HSBC is stronger than Goldman Sachs.

I showed the reworked graphic to some colleagues – getting feedback on experimental graphics is valuable because you quickly lose the ability to see your own graphic with neutral eyes.

Overall, feedback was very positive on the new format, but I did receive some incredibly useful suggestions, including adding the detail on how to interpret the chart (columns relate to cities; rows relate to banks).

Similar information on insurers was compiled by our insurance correspondent, which allowed me to reuse the grid design with that data too. Having learnt how to read the first chart, we felt readers would find the second one even easier to digest.

So, as beautiful and flexible as they are, maps are not the solution to every visualisation problem involving geographical data. The Visual Vocabulary emphasises that *spatial* is just one of many possible relationships in data and so they should be used "only when specific locations or geographical patterns in data are more important to the reader than anything else". Ignore this advice and maps may end up leaving readers lost.

Part 2

Putting charts to work

13

The science behind good charts

It's difficult to imagine a world of business communication without charts – but just how effective are we at reading them?

Charts use a variety of visual encoding methods – for example, position, length, area, angle and colour – to translate the data being presented into the ink, or pixels, on a page. But these encoding methods are not necessarily equally effective in allowing a reader to spot important variations in numbers.

In 2019, together with my colleagues Cale Tilford and Caroline Nevitt, I decided to run a little online experiment with readers of the *Financial Times*.

Many *FT* readers are immersed in the world of business and finance, and so will be no strangers to charts. With such a chart-literate audience, we were intrigued to see how much their ability to read information from charts would be influenced by the visual forms in which they are presented.

The experiment was arranged into three sections. First, we tested readers' abilities to compare values when the information was visually encoded in different ways.

Part 1 – do the pies have it?

Many of us learn how to read pie charts in primary education and they are everywhere in the business world. But just how good are they at allowing us to spot the (potentially crucial) differences in data?

We presented readers with a series of five pie charts – for each of them, we asked our readers the same simple question: which segment is the *third* biggest?

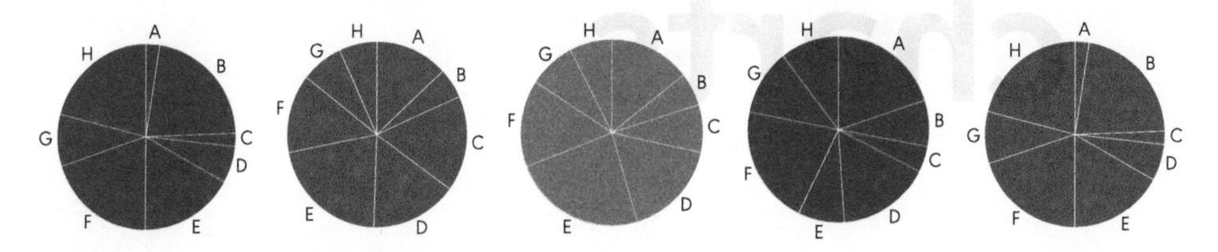

Source: Financial Times appeared in The science behind good charts By Cale Tilford, Alan Smith, Caroline Nevitt, January 22, 2019. Available at: https://ig.ft.com/science-of-charts/

Next, we asked readers to perform the same task – to identify the third largest element – but this time with a series of column charts.

We didn't tell our readers (so they approached each task independently), but the five pie charts contained *the same* data as the column charts.

As an interactive experiment, we were able to collect the answers submitted by readers in response to these challenges, which allowed us to analyse over 12,000 results. It was not good news for pie charts.

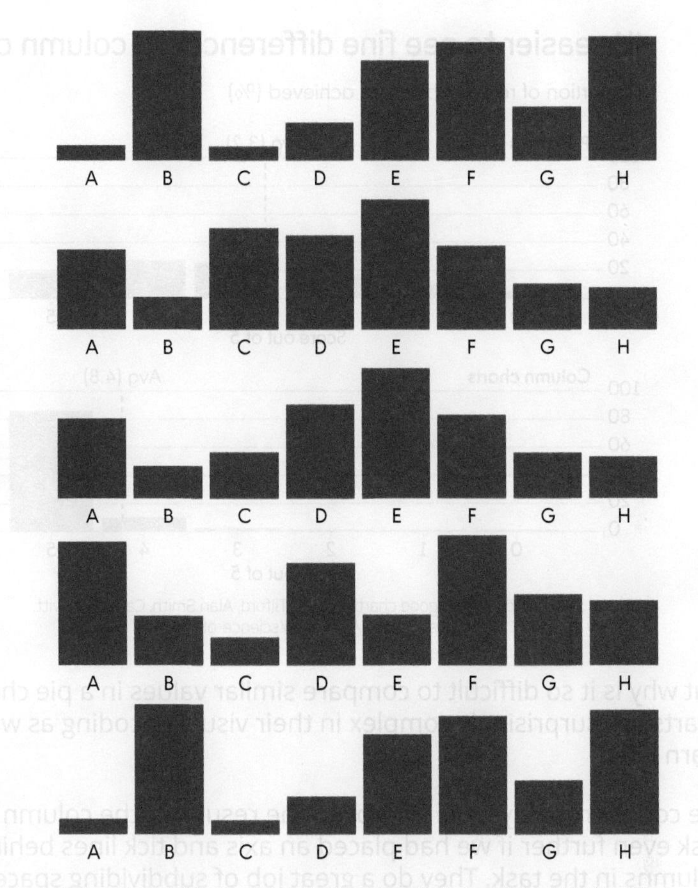

Source: Financial Times appeared in The science behind good charts By Cale Tilford, Alan Smith, Caroline Nevitt, January 22, 2019. Available at: https://ig.ft.com/science-of-charts/

Fewer than one in five readers correctly identified the third largest segment in all five pie charts. However, more than 4 in 5 readers were able to identify all the segments correctly when presented with the same data in column chart form.

For comparing the size of individual values – a magnitude comparison – columns or bars on a uniform baseline, are generally more effective than pie charts, particularly when there are small variations in the values of each element.

In fact, I think many people are intuitively aware that estimating the value of pie chart segments is difficult – which is why most pie charts you see in the real world have the actual values clearly stated as numbers. This is fine, but perhaps detracts from the point of using a chart, as opposed to a table of figures, in the first place.

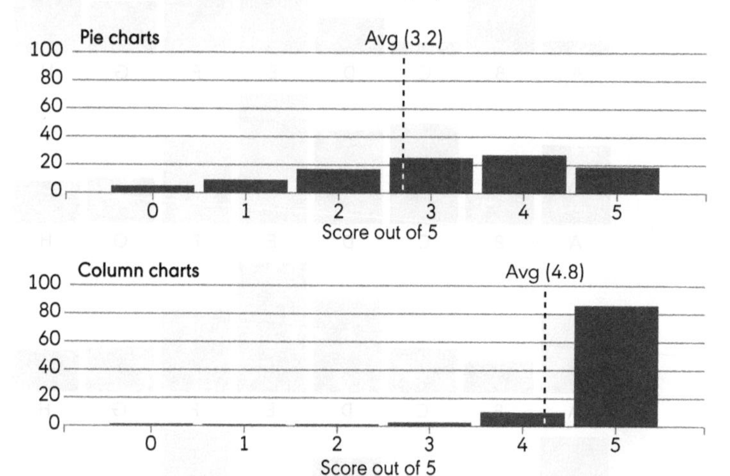

Source: The science behind good charts by Cale Tilford, Alan Smith, Caroline Nevitt, January 22, 2019. Available at: https://ig.ft.com/science-of-charts/

But why is it so difficult to compare similar values in a pie chart? Pie charts are surprisingly complex in their visual encoding as we will learn later.

We could probably have improved the results of the column chart task even further if we had placed an axis and tick lines behind the columns in the task. They do a great job of subdividing space, aiding precise comparisons of the displayed values.

Part 2 – Lost in space

Our first test, between pies and columns, just asked readers to establish the relative rank of the segments to find the third biggest. But it's not always enough to know just which is bigger, we often want to know by *how much*?

In this next test, we asked our readers to compare two shapes and tell us *how many times bigger* shape A was than shape B.

First, we presented a column chart that uses height as the comparative measure (for a one-dimensional comparison). Then we used circles that use area (width and height gives two dimensions) and, finally, a sphere (a three-dimensional object represented on a two-dimensional surface, meaning readers had to compare volumes).

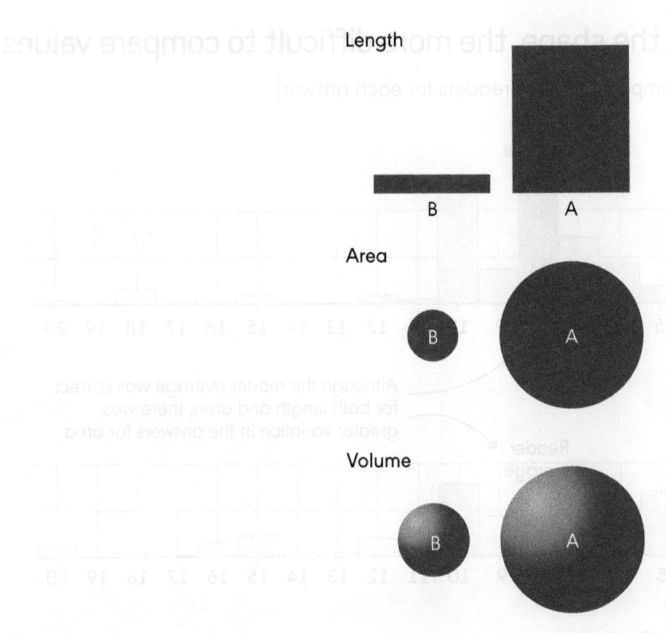

Source: Financial Times appeared in The science behind good charts By Cale Tilford, Alan Smith, Caroline Nevitt, January 22, 2019. Available at: https://ig.ft.com/science-of-charts/

Again, we didn't prime readers with this information, but, in all the above examples, the ratio between shape A and shape B is the same: A is always eight times bigger than B.

The combined results from our 12,000+ results were striking.

The *average* (mean) answer was pretty accurate for length and area, while the average of around 6x for volume meant that readers underestimated the size differential somewhat. But, as is so often the case, the averages conceal more than they show.

Look at the *distribution* of the values for "length" and compare them with "area" – you can see that there was more variation in the answers for area. If you look to the left of the "correct" answer, more readers said that the area difference was much smaller than it really was – over 15 per cent of them said the area of circle A was only 3 or 4 times as big as circle B. Hardly any readers made the same mistake with the lengths of columns A and B.

Readers struggled most with "volume", which produced the greatest scope for ambiguous interpretation. Again, look at the *distribution*. Nearly 1 in 10 readers thought that sphere A was 20 times bigger than sphere B – a similar amount to those who thought it was only 3 times as big.

The more complex the shape, the more difficult to compare values

Readers estimates of size comparison (% of readers for each answer)

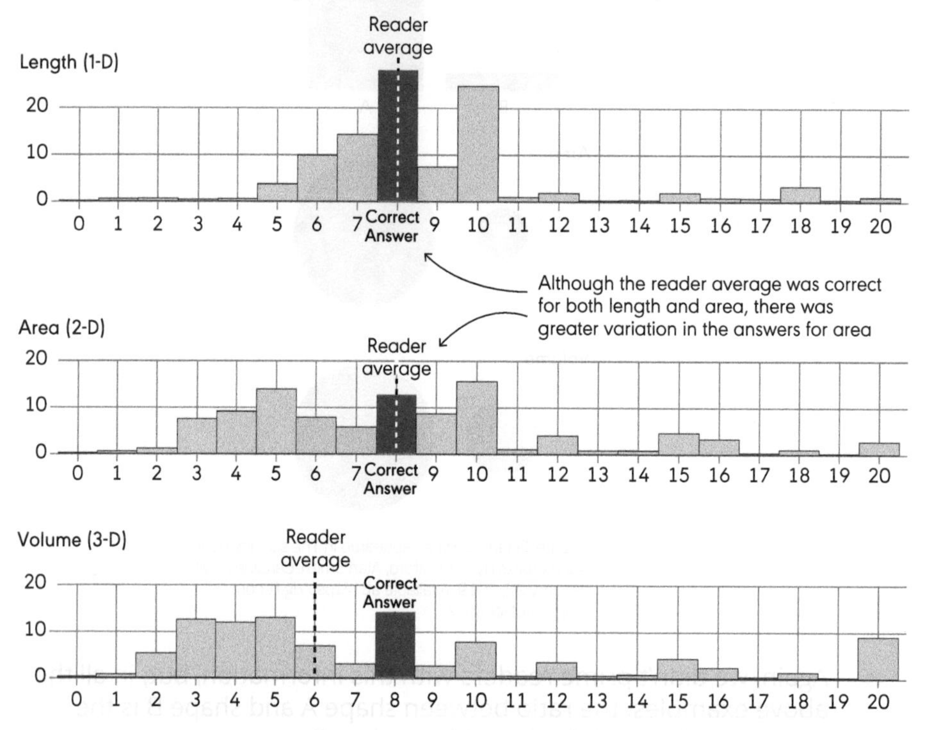

Source: FT analysis of 12,500 reader scores from 2019–20 appeared in The science behind good charts By Cale Tilford, Alan Smith, Caroline Nevitt, January 22, 2019. Available at: https://ig.ft.com/science-of-charts/

Among other things, these results suggest that, although more complex shapes may offer prettier aesthetics – most people would probably consider a sphere more attractive than a rectangle – in a data visualisation context, they can present problems.

It is no bad thing to want a visualisation to look beautiful. In fact, there are likely significant benefits in doing so, because our eyes are generally drawn to beautiful and interesting things. But doing so by introducing greater visual complexity than needed to represent data (most typically, unnecessary 3D treatments) can obfuscate the information being communicated. The journey towards infographic hell always begins by valuing style over meaningful communication.

Conversely, it doesn't mean that we should ban all uses of circles and spheres from business communication. For example, sometimes, we might only want to see if something is bigger or smaller that something else, in which case our circles would be just fine.

Part 3 – Seeing is believing

We gave our readers one final perceptual challenge.

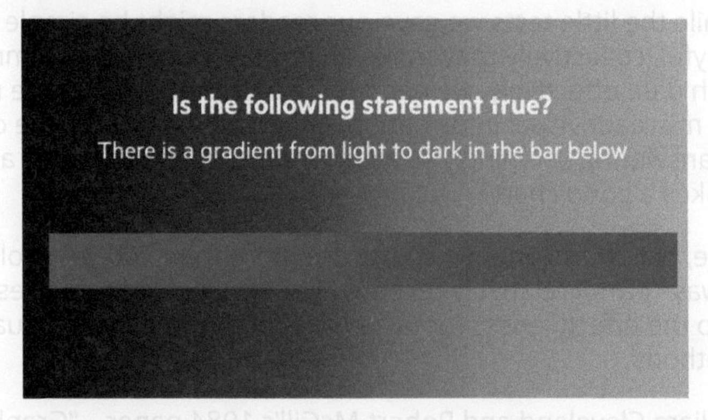

Is the following statement true?
There is a gradient from light to dark in the bar below

Source: Financial Times appeared in The science behind good charts By Cale Tilford, Alan Smith, Caroline Nevitt, January 22, 2019. Available at: https://ig.ft.com/science-of-charts/

Four in ten *FT* readers who took this challenge thought the statement to be true. To these people, the correct answer – that there is absolutely no gradient in the inner bar – must have been barely believable. I certainly received feedback to that end!

What does this tell us? Our visual perception is *context-dependent*; we are not good at seeing things in isolation. There appears to be a gradient in the inner rectangle, because there's a gradient running in the opposite direction in the outer box.

Our propensity to be influenced by context applies to a range of visual properties, not just colour. The famous Müller-Lyer illusion is another example of contextual effects, this time arrowheads influencing our perception of the length of the lines they are attached to.

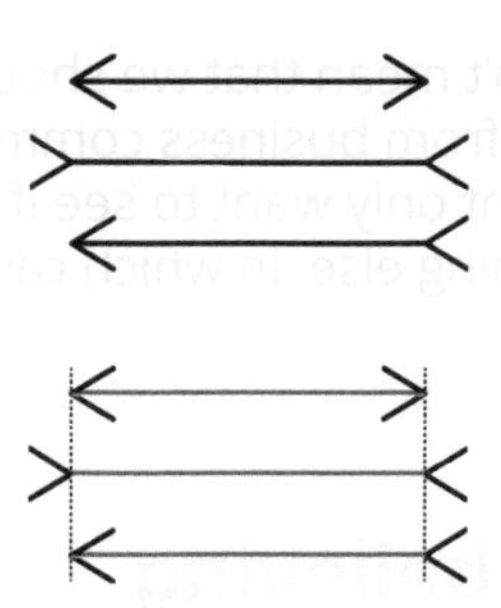

Putting it all together

While the little tests we gave our readers might be simple and playful, collectively they make an important point: to communicate with data effectively, we need to be aware of how people read (or misread) visual information. Otherwise, we have little chance of answering seemingly straightforward questions, such as what makes a good chart?

Line, bar charts and pie charts are more than 200 years old, but it wasn't until relatively recently that we saw dedicated research into the effectiveness (or otherwise) of different data visualisation methods.

William Cleveland and Robert McGill's 1984 paper – "Graphical Perception: Theory, Experimentation and Application to the Development of Graphical Methods" – represented, perhaps, the first significant look at common perceptual tasks and how they relate to data visualisation. Appearing shortly after the influential, but largely essay-based "The Visual Display of Quantitative Information" by Edward Tufte, Cleveland and McGill offered an evidence-based theory of data visualisation that remains hugely influential.

It represented the start of what is now a rich and useful body of academic work – and finding it is now easier than ever.

Robert Kosara, senior research scientist with data visualisation software company Tableau Software, believes that increasing people's awareness of the science behind data visualisation is key to increasing fluency in graphical communication.

"Visualisation research is surprisingly difficult to access, so many people seem to think that nothing has happened since the 1980s. But there is an active research community that is doing a lot of exciting new work," he says.

Kosara, working with Jessica Hullman of Northwestern University, Danielle Szafir of the University of Colorado and Enrico Bertini of New York University, has established a blog to highlight new data visualisation research. "With Multiple Views, we're hoping to make that work visible and easier to access for people who are curious," Kosara explains (see: https://medium.com/)[6].

Learning point – "The Science of Visual Data Communication: What works"

Another fantastic resource is this review of guidelines for creating clear data visualisations – and the research that backs it up. Compiled by Steve Franconeri, Lace Padilla, Priti Shah, Jeff Zacks and Jessica Hullman, this open-access paper is a must read for those wishing to dig deeper into the science behind effective data visualisation[7].

[6] https://medium.com/multiple-views-visualization-research-explained.

[7] Available at: https://www.psychologicalscience.org/publications/visual-data-communication.html.

14

Scales of justice; axes of evil

How big is small?

Type "Tom Cruise" into Google and the search engine's predictive autocomplete algorithm suggests that the famous actor's height is as feverishly searched as his box-office hits.

A quick trip to the Internet Movie Database confirms that Tom is 1.7m tall (about 5 feet and 7 inches) – but just how tall (or short) is that? Let's find out the heights of other famous actors and see how Tom compares.

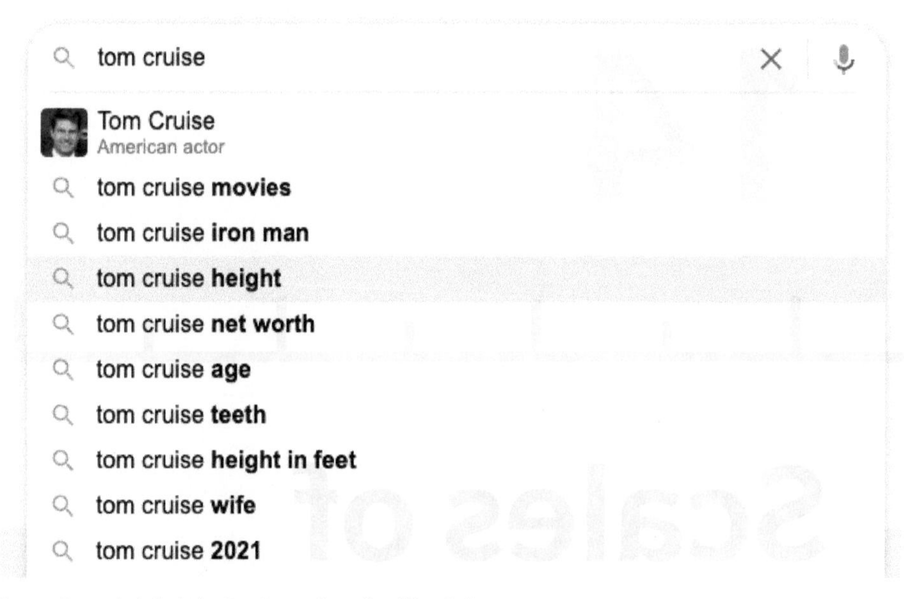

Source: Screenshot displaying Google search results of Tom Cruise

How famous actors' heights compare with Tom Cruise

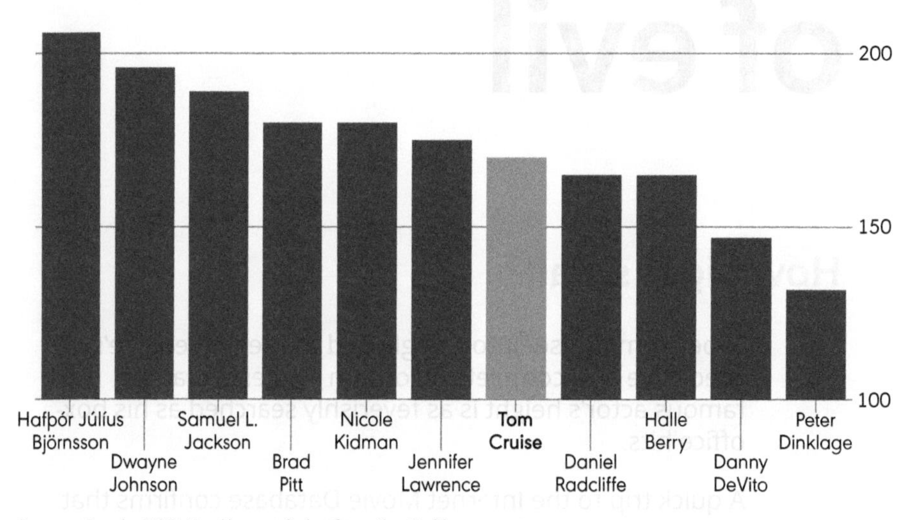

Sources: Google, IMDB. Used by permission from Alan Smith.

Our actors are positioned on a column chart in descending order of height, bookended by two *Games of Thrones* actors who represent extremes of adult height: Hafþór Júlíus Björnsson (a former World's Strongest Man) and Peter Dinklage.

Actors taller than Tom – including his former wife, Nicole Kidman – are lined up to the left. Meanwhile, to the right, we see that, perhaps to some people's surprise, *Harry Potter* actor Daniel Radcliffe is actually a little shorter than our diminutive *Mission: Impossible* star.

All seems well on the chart – but there's a big problem lurking for the unsuspecting chart reader . . .

The premise of this chart is to visually address the question "How do the heights of famous actors compare?" Using the language of the Visual Vocabulary, it is showing a *magnitude* relationship, which we can think of as "How big are these things compared to each other?" In this respect, the chart is lying.

Compare the heights of the two bars representing our *Game of Thrones* actors – Dinklage's bar is only 30 per cent as tall as his co-star's. Björnsson's real-world height of 2.06m means he was well suited to playing the role of Gregor "The Mountain" Clegane in the hit HBO series – but, if the proportions of our column heights were carried over into reality, Dinklage would be just 61cm tall. He's short – but not that short. Dinklage's real height is over twice that (1.32m), but our chart conceals most of it. Why?

The false impression is created by the vertical (y) axis of the chart – if you look closely at the axis (and you can't assume that most people who read charts do), you'll see it starts at 100cm. This means the height of each column on the chart is not sized proportionately because 1 metre of each actors' height is being obscured from us. To give the proper impression of relative height, we must extend the bars to the point at which we begin measuring – the ground (0cm).

Scaling a chart like this to start at zero fixes the ratios – but reveals a fresh problem. It now looks just a little dull, with much finer differences between the heights of the actors.

But, often, the absolute size of something (its magnitude) is not the thing we're most interested in. We're frequently more interested in the difference, or – in Visual Vocabulary language – the *deviation* of things from a known point. So, perhaps we could frame our question slightly differently: "How much taller, or shorter, than Tom Cruise are other actors?"

By changing the relationship we're charting, we're no longer looking at the absolute height of the actors, but the relative differences between them.

With the deviation of each actor from Cruise's height calculated, our chart's axis now has a range a little over the 74cm that separates the tallest and shortest actor. Visually, we've zoomed in – and a central spine, representing zero (Tom's height) is now the focus.

How famous actors' heights compare with Tom Cruise

Height (cm)

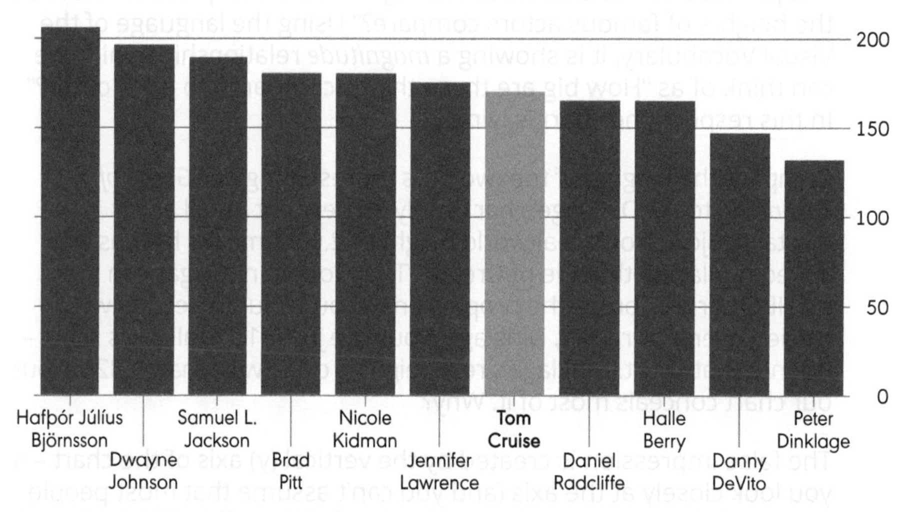

Sources: Google, IMDB. Used by permission from Alan Smith.

How famous actors' heights compare with Tom Cruise

Amount taller/shorter than Cruise (cm)

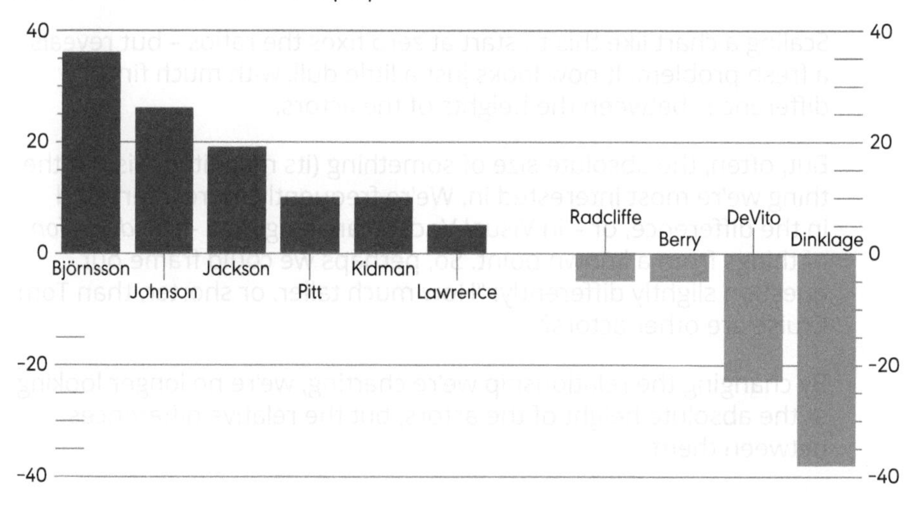

Sources: Google, IMDB. Used by permission from Alan Smith.

A bonus of the new chart is that the bars of those actors who are shorter than Cruise head in a different direction (downwards, because they are negative numbers) from those that are taller, making it even easier to identify those two groups.

This example may seem a little pedantic – after all, what's the problem with distorting the heights of Hollywood actors a little? But what if this chart instead represented a different dataset set to inform a major decision, with units that represent millions of dollars, or thousands of people? The perceptual distortions introduced by not starting the axis at zero become incredibly important.

The main takeaway of this cautionary tale of celebrity heights? Charts that represent a "magnitude" comparison should generally start at zero . . . but, as we are about to see, the rule only belongs to that relationship in the Visual Vocabulary, it doesn't apply to *all* charts.

From zero to hero

Vaccination has been an important topic in global health for decades, but the global coronavirus pandemic brought it even further into the spotlight.

In England, data on vaccinations that protect against a variety of diseases has been routinely published for decades by Public Health England, which means we can easily produce charts to show how vaccination rates have *changed over time*. For example, here is a simple line chart of the rate for the combined measles, mumps and rubella vaccination known as MMR.

Glancing at this chart might give the impression that there's no story here at all – rates have been high and have stayed high in recent decades, with only minor fluctuations. But let's think for a moment about key aspects of the vaccination data we're plotting.

- High vaccination rates are required for populations to achieve the herd immunity that helps contain outbreaks. In the case of measles, the World Health Organisation recommends vaccination rates of 95 per cent.
- In a developed country like England, we would expect vaccination rates to be relatively high – and certainly not below 50 per cent.

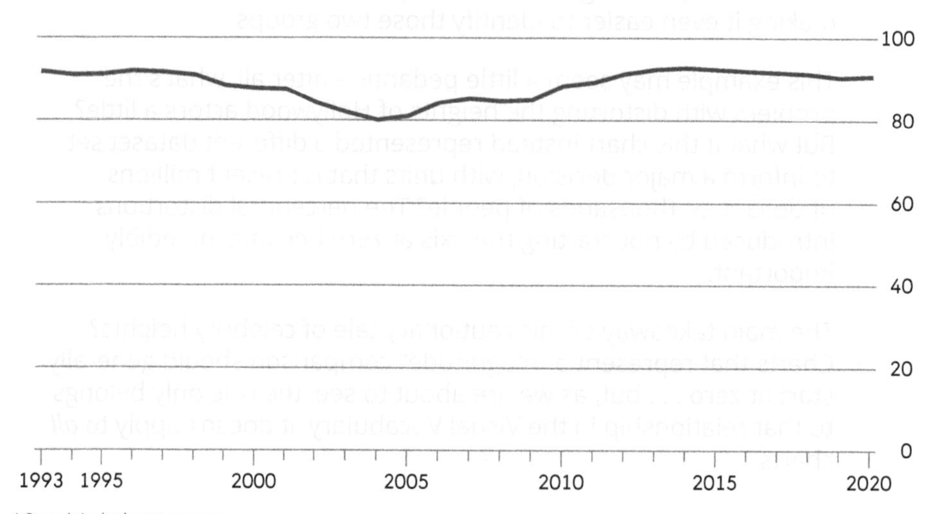

* Completed primary courses
Sources: COVER; Public Health England appeared in Crafting charts that can withstand the data deluge by Alan Smith, January 25, 2016. Available at: https://www.ft.com/content/3f195d40-b851-11e5-b151-8e15c9a029fb

Both points mean that our chart above is concealing information by having its vertical axis anchored to zero, with much of the area of the chart being given to what's not important and where there is unlikely to ever be any data on display.

Let's try adjusting the axis to zoom in a little, so that, instead of showing values between 0 and 100, it now shows a range between 80 and 100. Remember, this is the same data as shown in the first chart – the only difference is the axis scale and the addition of information on vaccination targets. In this new version of the chart, we are now visually declaring that 80 should be considered a *low* number – because, in this context, it is.

So different is this chart from the first version that it's difficult to believe we are looking at the same data. We can now see that there was a significant and rapid fall in the vaccination rate from the late 1990s until the middle of the next decade, which took it well below the level required for herd immunity. An increase in the rate then followed, producing a clear "V-shaped" recovery. The story of this V-shape is associated with a now-discredited paper, published in *The Lancet* in 1998 and retracted in 2010, which had suggested a link between the MMR vaccine and autism.

Measles vaccination rates have been high for decades?

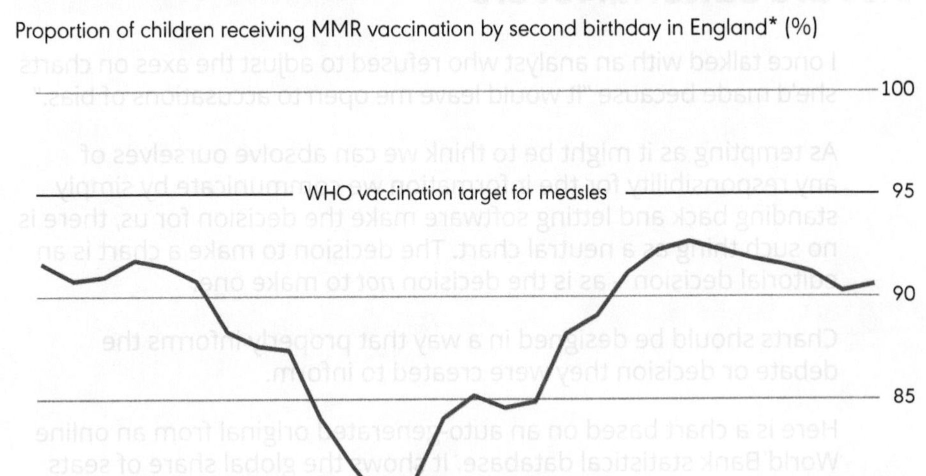

* Completed primary courses
Sources: COVER; Public Health England appeared in Crafting charts that can withstand the data deluge by Alan Smith, January 25, 2016. Available at: https://www.ft.com/content/3f195d40-b851-11e5-b151-8e15c9a029fb

So, what is the fundamental difference that allows us to truncate this chart axis in a way that we couldn't with a chart depicting magnitude?

Most importantly, the units being charted are not a simple *count* (height of actor, number of people, thousands of dollars, barrels of oil) – it's not a *magnitude* relationship that we're showing.

Instead, we are looking at how a *rate* (vaccinations *per* 100 children) is *changing over time*. In this context, it is perfectly reasonable to scale a chart to show the normal, expected or "target" range of data, using the axis as a lens to zoom in.

Of course, it would be perfectly feasible for both charts to be used in a report or presentation, with the first chart showing the overview ("Overall, rates appear to be quite high . . . ") and the second chart the details (". . . however, if we zoom in, we can see the problem"). But, if you had to use just one chart to make an important decision, it would be the latter.

Axes are editorial levers

I once talked with an analyst who refused to adjust the axes on charts she'd made because "It would leave me open to accusations of bias."

As tempting as it might be to think we can absolve ourselves of any responsibility for the information we communicate by simply standing back and letting software make the decision for us, there is no such thing as a neutral chart. The decision to make a chart is an editorial decision – as is the decision *not* to make one.

Charts should be designed in a way that properly informs the debate or decision they were created to inform.

Here is a chart based on an auto-generated original from an online World Bank statistical database. It shows the global share of seats held by women in parliaments across the world.

Great progress in representation of women in parliament!

Proportion of seats held by women in national parliaments across the world (%)

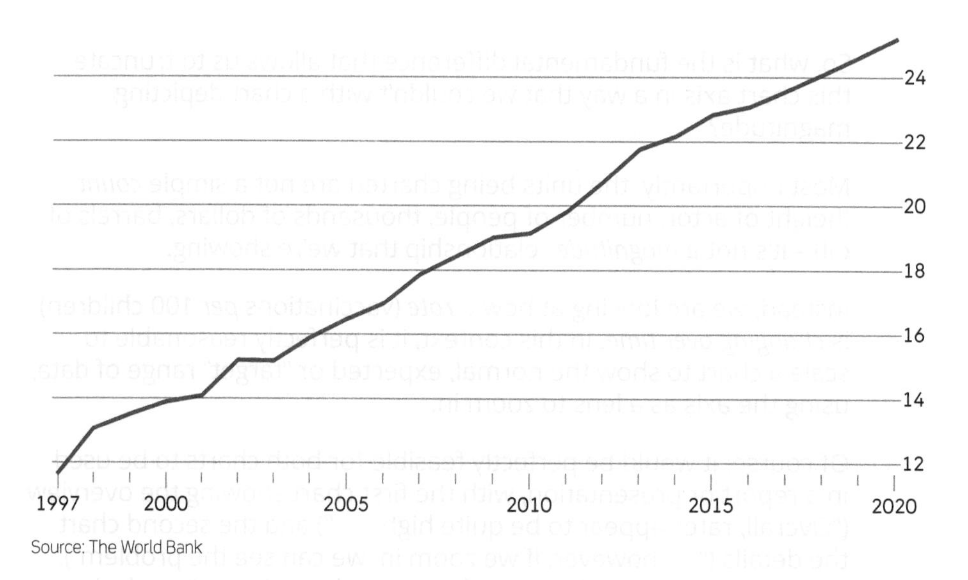

Source: The World Bank

The chart shows how the proportion of women in the chamber has *changed over time* and it reveals a rising trend from nearly 12 per cent in 1997 to around 25 per cent by 2020. Again, ignore the axes values (because some of this chart's audience will) – visually, it looks like the world has solved the problem of gender representation because the data has managed to make it all the way to the top right-hand corner of the chart.

When people use computer software to make charts, software wizards will usually make an "informed guess" about how to scale the axis of a chart (this is particularly true of auto-generated charts like this one). The software typically does this by looking at the minimum value (in this case, a little under 12 per cent) and maximum value (25.2 per cent) of the data being plotted, perhaps rounding the values a little to make things a little neater.

One thing the software does not know much about is *what* the information it is showing represents or why we're making the chart. Accepting the software defaults has resulted in a misleading chart. Let's fix it.

Why would we be making this chart in the first place? To measure the progress towards gender equality in parliament. What does that equality look like? Well, perhaps women would take approximately half (50 per cent) of the seats in parliament.

If we scale the vertical (y) axis to this level, we get a very different chart – the story is now in the blank space on the chart, highlighting

It will take decades for women to achieve equality in political representation

Proportion of seats held by women in national parliaments across the world (%)

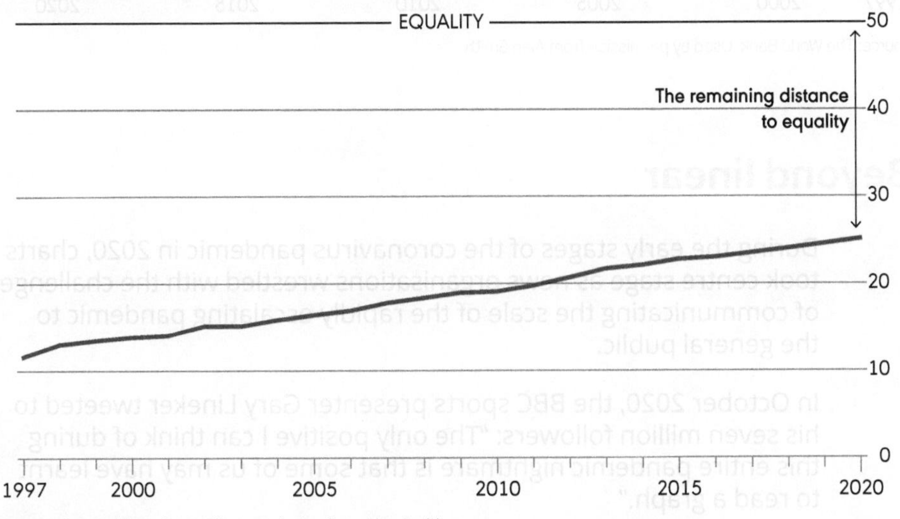

Source: The World Bank. Used by permission from Alan Smith.

the lack of real progress. Again, just as with our measles vaccination example, it is difficult to believe that we are looking at the same data. Notice how the new scale allows us to write a radically different title – at the (slow but constant) rate of progress, it will take decades for the blue line to reach the 50 per cent mark.

Of course, it might be that gender equality is not your policy consideration. If so, scale the axis until it matches the point you are trying to make . . .

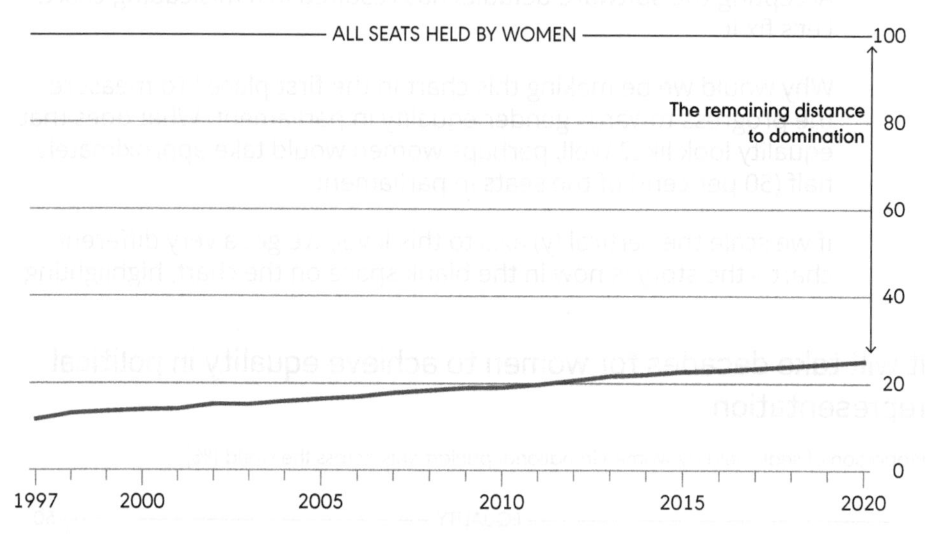

Source: The World Bank. Used by permission from Alan Smith.

Beyond linear

During the early stages of the coronavirus pandemic in 2020, charts took centre stage as news organisations wrestled with the challenge of communicating the scale of the rapidly escalating pandemic to the general public.

In October 2020, the BBC sports presenter Gary Lineker tweeted to his seven million followers: "The only positive I can think of during this entire pandemic nightmare is that some of us may have learnt to read a graph."

One chart, popularised by my colleague at the *Financial Times*, John Burn-Murdoch, quickly acquired darkly iconic status (one reader tweeted that he found John on the internet by googling "*FT* death chart guy").

John designed his coronavirus trajectory chart with the goal of allowing readers to understand how quickly the pandemic was spreading in different parts of the world. For the chart's vertical axis, he chose a "log(arithmic) scale" to denote the number of coronavirus cases.

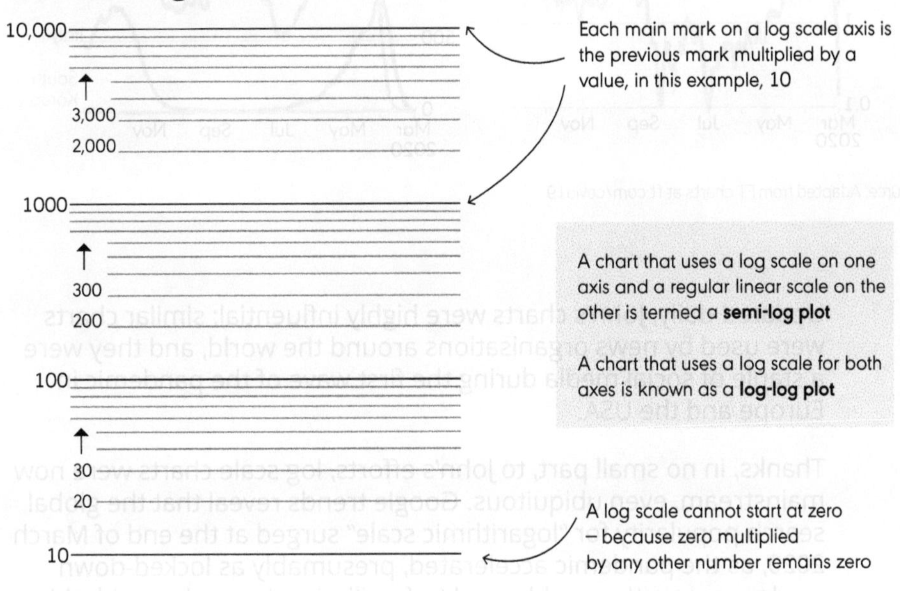
What is a log scale?
10,000
3,000
2,000
1000
300
200
100
30
20
10
Each main mark on a log scale axis is the previous mark multiplied by a value, in this example, 10
A chart that uses a log scale on one axis and a regular linear scale on the other is termed a **semi-log plot**
A chart that uses a log scale for both axes is known as a **log-log plot**
A log scale cannot start at zero – because zero multiplied by any other number remains zero

We can see the enormous visual impact of that decision by comparing two charts of the same data taken from the pandemic – one, a regular plot with a familiar linear vertical (y) axis (i.e., with numbers increasing sequentially); the other uses a log scale axis.

The log scale chart does a far better job of showing the rapid increase in cases early in a Covid wave. On the log scale chart, we can see that Italy and South Korea were briefly on similar trajectories, before their outbreaks diverged. On the linear scale chart, it's difficult to see that South Korea had an outbreak at all.

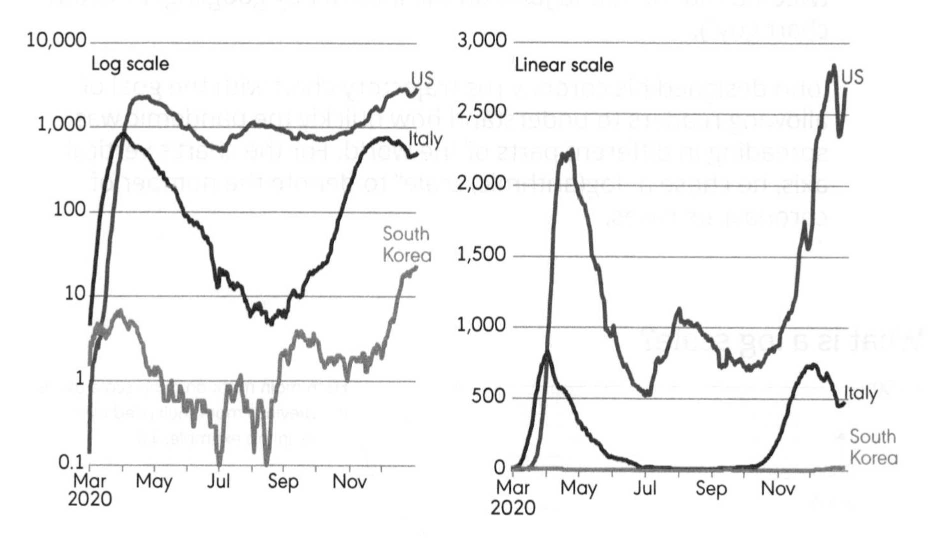

Source: Adapted from FT charts at ft.com/covid19

Updated daily, John's charts were highly influential; similar charts were used by news organisations around the world, and they were a staple of social media during the first wave of the pandemic in Europe and the USA.

Thanks, in no small part, to John's efforts, log scale charts were now mainstream, even ubiquitous. Google trends reveal that the global search popularity for "logarithmic scale" surged at the end of March 2020, as the pandemic accelerated, presumably as locked-down readers across the world raced to familiarise themselves with this previously unknown axis type.

This raises an important question – did people who saw the log scale charts understand them? Researchers from the London School of Economics (LSE) investigated and suggested that they did not.

More worryingly, the researchers found that the log scale charts affected people's attitudes to the pandemic, suggesting that readers "found the curve on the logarithmic scale [to look] flatter and reassuring" in comparison to the traditional linear chart. The LSE researchers finished by recommending that "mass media and policymakers should always describe the evolution of the pandemic

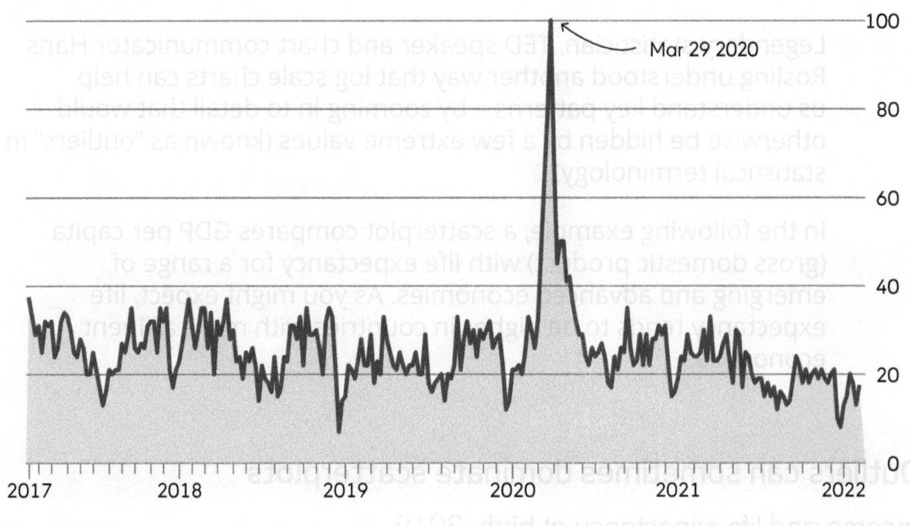

using a graph on a linear scale, or at least they should show both scales" (see LSE log scale research at: https://blogs.lse.ac.uk/covid19/2020/05/19/the-public-doesnt-understand-logarithmic-graphs-often-used-to-portray-covid-19/).

Research of this kind is, of course, always welcome, as we continuously develop our understanding of how people read charts. But it could be that the focus of the research also misjudged the value of the log scale. For example, one part of the research asked participants "whether there were more deaths in one week or another" – this is a task that is clearly better suited to a linear scale, which focuses on levels.

Moreover, the research didn't surprise many data visualisation professionals who have regularly had to explain log scales to confused readers in the past – it would be easy to take this experience, along with the new research and conclude we should never use log scales.

But experience shows us that there are times when a log scale axis can reveal critical insight hidden by its mild-mannered linear cousin, and it pays to develop your chart-reading skills to know how to interpret them. Let's conclude this section on scales by looking at two examples.

Prevent extreme values on a chart obscuring important differences

Legendary statistician, TED speaker and chart communicator Hans Rosling understood another way that log scale charts can help us understand key patterns – by zooming in to detail that would otherwise be hidden by a few extreme values (known as "outliers" in statistical terminology).

In the following example, a scatterplot compares GDP per capita (gross domestic product) with life expectancy for a range of emerging and advanced economies. As you might expect, life expectancy tends to be higher in countries with more affluent economies.

Outliers can sometimes dominate scatterplots

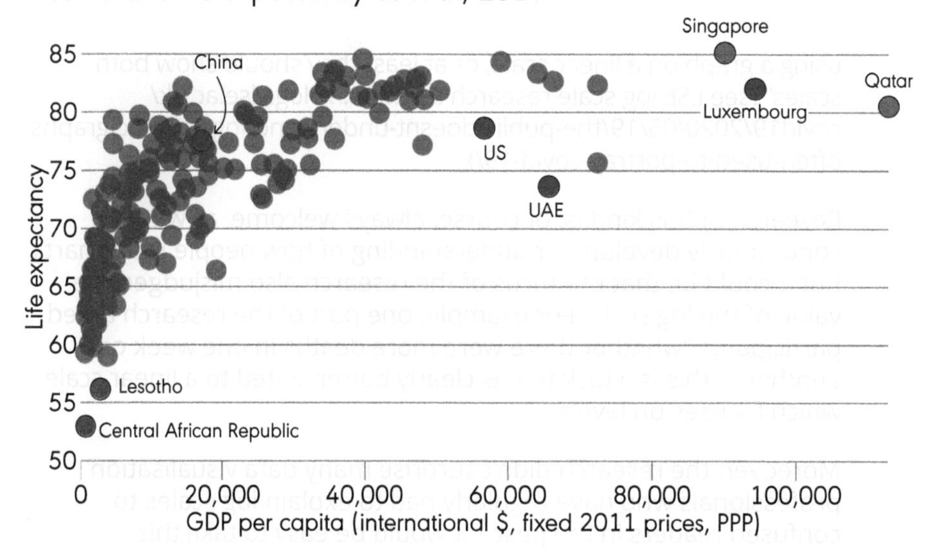

Source: Gapminder (includes data based on World Bank, Maddison Lindgren, IMF and others). Used by permission from Alan Smith.

But understanding the differences between incomes in developing countries is important: there is a big practical difference in the $900 between $100 and $1,000 – more so than the same gap between $39,100 and $40,000. But, here, we once again find issues with the linear scale – low-income countries are cramped into the left-hand side of the chart, because the scale needs to stretch far enough to include affluent nations like Luxembourg.

The logarithmic scale once again comes to our aid – we can clearly see the detailed differences in lower-income countries like Congo and Lesotho. And, indeed, the general pattern of the relationship between GDP and life expectancy becomes clearer too.

A log scale helps us see differences across all the data

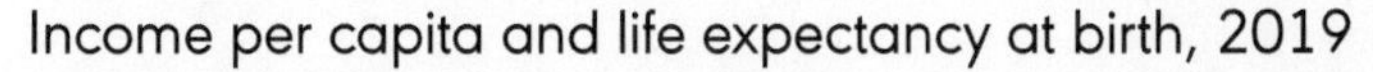

Income per capita and life expectancy at birth, 2019

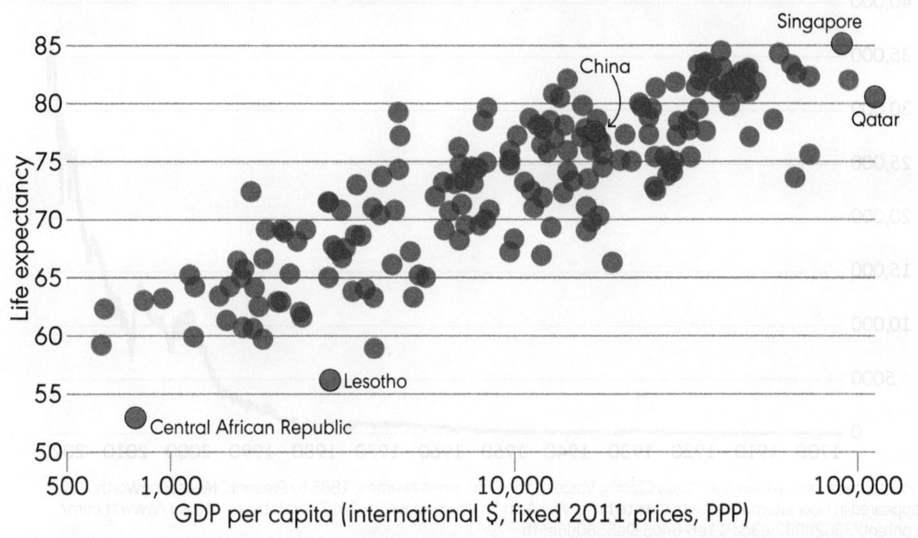

Source: Gapminder (includes data based on World Bank, Maddison Lindgren, IMF and others). Used by permission from Alan Smith.

So, despite the difficulties, it clearly pays to be able to recognise log scale axes and understand how to interpret them. In doing so, we should also recognise that many other people will be unfamiliar with them, which is why careful explanation is needed to contextualise the information presented.

To show rates of exponential growth

The Dow Jones Industrial Average is one of the world's longest-running financial indices. First appearing in 1896, it tracks the stock market performance of 30 large companies listed on US stock exchanges. These days, it is, perhaps, less revered by analysts who rely on alternative indices that are more representative of the overall stock market, but its longevity ensures continuing public interest.

Here is the entire time series plotted on a simple line chart, using a standard linear scale.

What great depression?

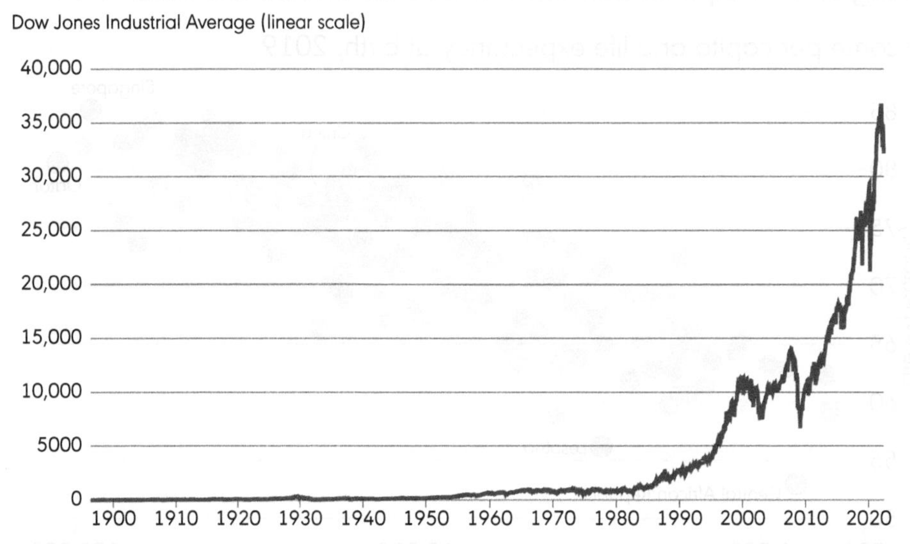

Source: Samuel H. Wllliamson, "Dally Closing Value of the Dow Jones Average, 1885 to Present," MeasuringWorth, 2022 appeared in How alternative facts rewrite history by Alan Smith, January 31, 2017. Available at: https://www.ft.com/content/3062d082-e3da-11e6-8405-9e5580d6e5fb

What is so wrong with this chart? Well, for a start, it effectively hides the impact on the index of the deepest and longest-lasting economic downturn in history. The Dow Jones took 25 years to recover from the damage of the Wall Street crash in 1929, but using a linear scale allows us to hide a quarter-century of turmoil almost entirely. Let's now look at the same data using a log scale.

Peaks of bubbles and troughs of crashes now come into focus throughout the lifetime of the index. On the linear scale chart, only recent events are noticeable – and you can now see that they are overemphasised.

The Dow Jones took 25 years to recover from the Wall Street crash

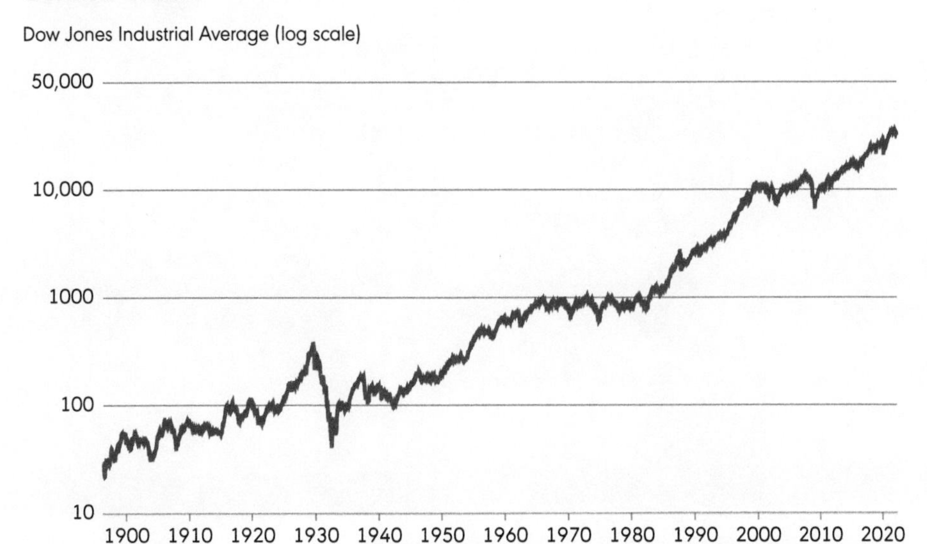

Source: Samuel H. Wlllamson, "Dally Closing Value of the Dow Jones Average, 1885 to Present," MeasuringWorth, 2022 appeared in How alternative facts rewrite history by Alan Smith, January 31, 2017. Available at: https://www.ft.com/content/3062d082-e3da-11e6-8405-9e5580d6e5fb

In this example, the log scale chart is unquestionably more effective because our interest in the index is measured in *relative* terms: our real interest in the difference between 100 and 200 is the same as between 1,000 and 2,000 – they both represent a doubling. This is much like the early stages of a pandemic, helping to explain why we felt log scales were effective during acceleration and deceleration phases.

And what of the famous *FT* log scale coronavirus charts? We responded to research and feedback from our own readers by creating an interactive version[8] that allowed readers to switch between linear and log scales, as well as set other aspects of the chart's appearance.

We felt that allowing the reader to explore the difference that the various settings make to a chart's appearance makes them a valuable educational tool.

[8] https://ig.ft.com/coronavirus-chart.

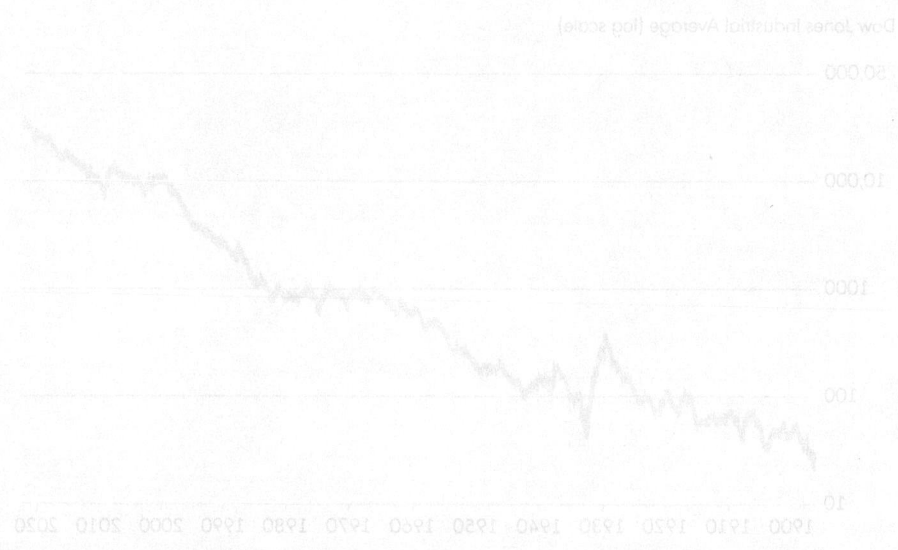

15

The best charts are well written

Words are an essential component of data graphics. As a minimum, we need them to describe and quantify the data we plot. Without this text, charts are little more than abstract geometry.

However, it's probably fair to say that not many people consider writing skills to be at the top of the list when it comes to the attributes needed to be a top chart maker. Academic research suggests that this may be flawed thinking.

In 2015, a team of researchers led by Michelle Borkin from the University of British Columbia and Zoya Bylinskii from the Massachusetts Institute of Technology investigated how data visualisations are recognised and recalled. Notable in the team's findings was an emphatic statement on the importance of words:

> *"Titles and text attract people's attention, are dwelled upon during encoding, and correspondingly contribute to recognition and recall. People spend the most amount of time looking at the text in a visualisation, and more specifically, the title."*

So, text – particularly *narrative* text – is what transforms the role of charts from "*Here are some numbers*" (which you likely won't remember) to "*Here's a story*" (that you probably will). It doesn't take many words to transform a chart from one to the other.

Take the following share price chart of the British bakery chain Greggs prepared by my *FT* colleague Myles McCormick. It's a simple plot created using the *FT*'s own charting tool for reporters, FastCharts.

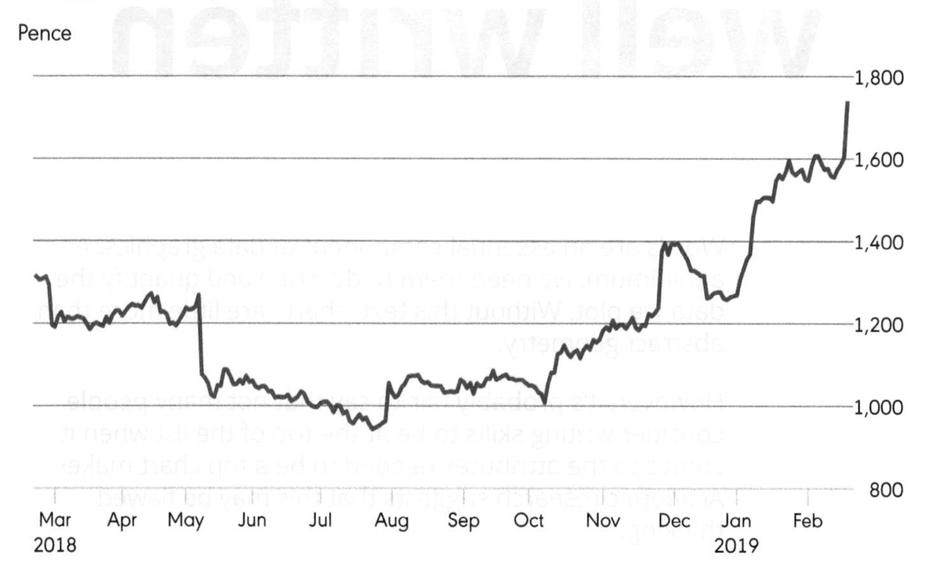

Source: Refinitiv (formerly Thomson Reuters) appeared in Greggs raises annual forecast despite supply pressures, Financial Times, October 5, 2021. Available at: https://www.ft.com/content/47b4f6ee-d008-489d-b621-a4791674dbc1

Now consider the impact when Myles adds detail to the title and succinct annotation pointing to a key moment – the launch of the firm's vegan sausage roll.

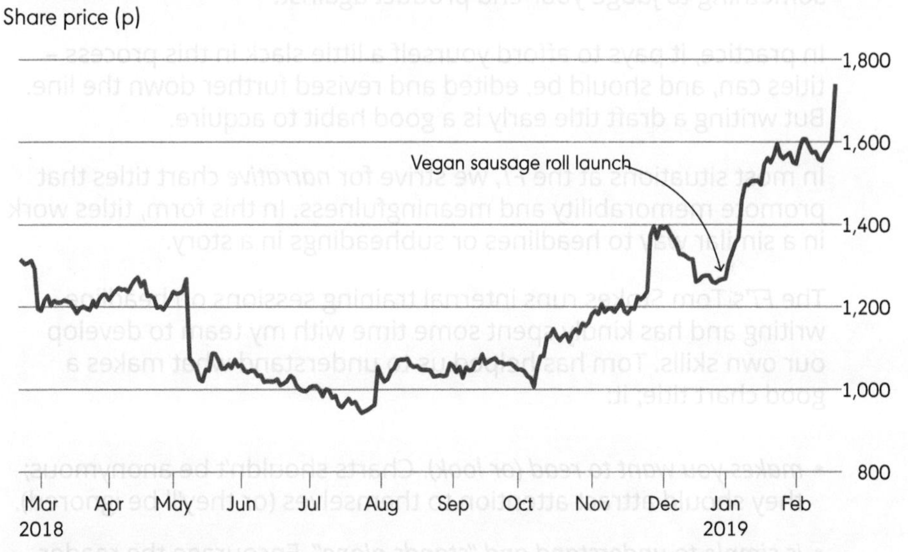

Refinitiv (formerly Thomson Reuters) appeared in Greggs raises annual forecast despite supply pressures, Financial Times, October 5, 2021. Available at: https://www.ft.com/content/47b4f6ee-d008-489d-b621-a4791674dbc1

There's little doubt which version of the chart is going to deliver the more rewarding reading experience. Those 15 extra words in the title and on-chart annotation make all the difference. Myles has turned his chart into a "microstory": meaningful, succinct and memorable.

It's also self-sufficient, which is important. A chart that requires no other external context to understand its basic message is capable of thriving beyond the shores of its parent article, report or slide deck – handy if you want to use charts as part of your social media strategy, for example.

The FT recipe for text on a chart

Borkin and Bylinskii's research did not entirely surprise my colleagues in the *FT* Visual and Data journalism team. We had already developed our own appreciation of the importance of text on charts based on many years of newsroom experience. Practice *definitely* helps – and working with some of the best sub-editors in the business has also kept my team on its toes.

Titles

There's a solid argument that the title should be the first element you create in the chart-making process. After all, if you start by writing down what the chart is supposed to show, then you have something to judge your end product against.

In practice, it pays to afford yourself a little slack in this process – titles can, and should be, edited and revised further down the line. But writing a draft title early is a good habit to acquire.

In most situations at the *FT*, we strive for *narrative* chart titles that promote memorability and meaningfulness. In this form, titles work in a similar way to headlines or subheadings in a story.

The *FT*'s Tom Stokes runs internal training sessions on headline writing and has kindly spent some time with my team to develop our own skills. Tom has helped us to understand what makes a good chart title; it:

- *makes you want to read (or look).* Charts shouldn't be anonymous; they should attract attention to themselves (or they'll be ignored).
- *is simple to understand and "stands alone".* Encourage the reader to go on and learn more about the topic away from the graphic – but make it a follow-on activity, not a pre-requisite to understand what you have put in front of them.
- *includes keywords.* Readers scan text and keywords help them tune in to the content. Online, keywords in a chart title can also help readers find your chart in the first place through search engines and social media.
- *is accurate and truthful.* In an era of "fake news", nothing is more important than making your chart able to stand up to scrutiny.
- *makes a promise that the graphic delivers on.* Given that readers are likely to read the title first, we want the chart's content to offer the evidence that reinforces and justifies the title. The delightfully intricate content of this graphic by Chris Campbell and Patrick Mathurin may contrast with the simple language of the title – but both title and graphic are in complete agreement on what the data shows.

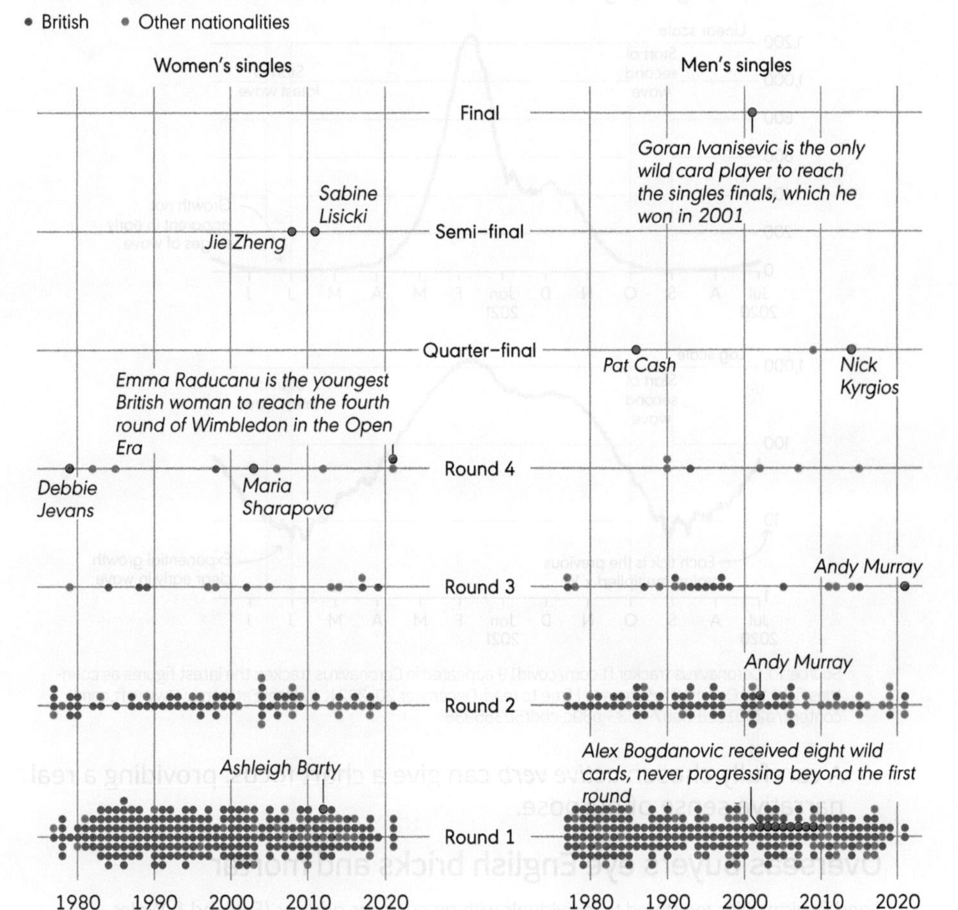

Graphic: Chris Campbell, Patrick Mathurin

Source: Data from Wimbledon appeared in Samuel Agini, Patrick Mathurin and Chris Campbell, Wimbledon wild card success does not disguise financial challenge, Financial Times, July 10, 2021. Available at: https://www.ft.com/content/860b0619-a10e-4f13-abee-c9f27d775b99

For graphics that focus on explaining things, consider using *How . . .* or *Why . . .* – this helps set up "the promise". Notice that annotations – with arrows – help the graphic deliver on the promise of the title. The text on this explanatory graphic helps reinforce what we learnt about log scales in the previous chapter.

How a log scale can reveal exponential growth

Seven-day rolling average of UK Covid deaths

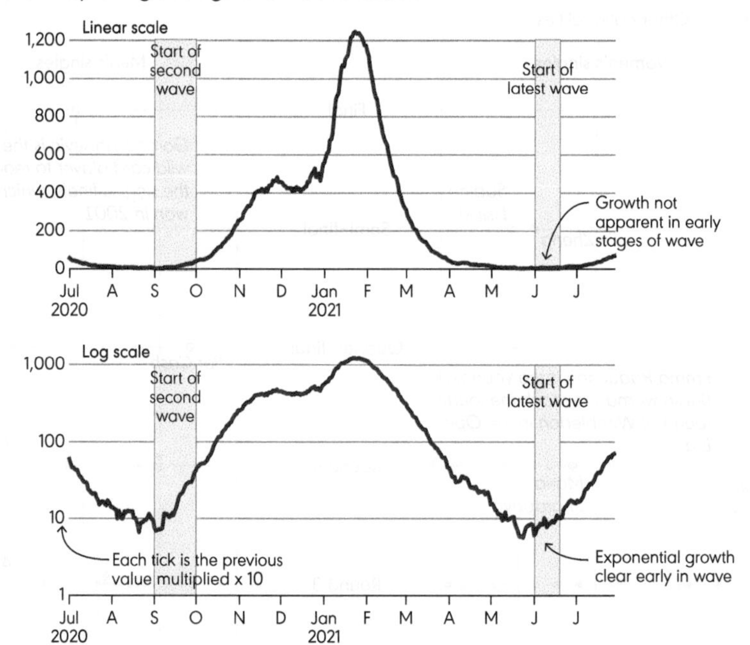

Source: FT Coronavirus tracker ft.com/covid19 appeared in Coronavirus tracker: the latest figures as countries fight the Covid-19 resurgence | Free to read, December 20, 2021. Available at: https://www.ft.com/content/a2901ce8-5eb7-4633-b89c-cbdf5b386938

A carefully chosen *active verb* can give a chart focus, providing a real narrative sense of purpose.

Overseas buyers eye English bricks and mortar

Land Registry titles registered to individuals with an overseas address (England & Wales, 000s)

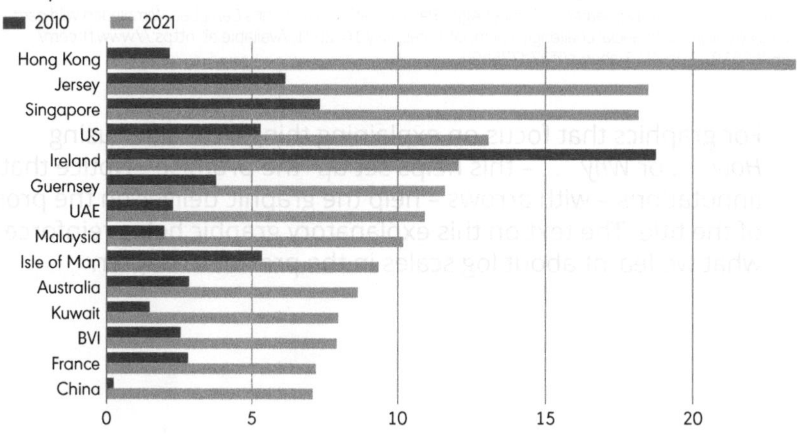

Source: Centre for Public Data appeared in George Hammond, Foreign ownership of homes in England and Wales triples, Financial Times, November 12, 2021. Available at: https://www.ft.com/content/e36cec28-7acd-4154-b57d-923b5d1610da

A *passive* version of this title would be "English bricks and mortar are being eyed by overseas buyers" – not technically wrong but it lacks the impact of the active version.

Appropriate verbs can sometimes be identified by considering the Visual Vocabulary relationships involved in the chart. *Surges* could suggest "change over time", for example, while *rises/falls* could mean we're emphasising "ranking".

We can sometimes use a verb taken directly from the Visual Vocabulary. The word "correlated" in the following chart title is a good way of drawing attention to the comparison in the numbers we're interested in – and helps justify the choice of a scatterplot to present the data!

Vaccine hesitancy is highly correlated to politics

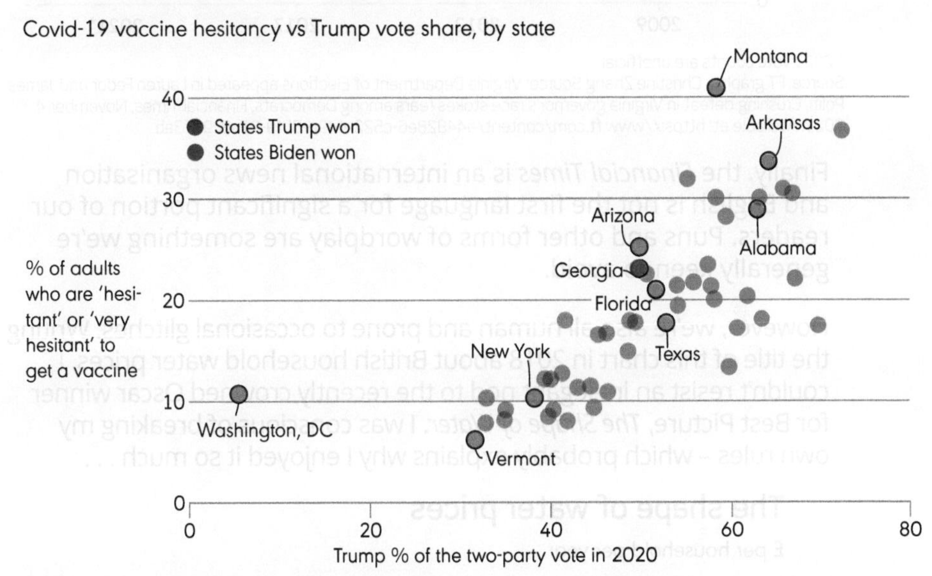

Sources: State-level estimates of vaccine hesitancy from the US Deaprtment of Health and Human Services using federal survey data from May 26 - June 7; Trump vote share by state from Cook Political Report appeared in Nikou Asgari, A form of brainwashing': why Trump voters are refusing to have a vaccine, Financial Times, July 21, 2021. Available at -https://www.ft.com/content/39ff87ce-57b7-4007-9504-7eb2c7bc911f

Titles can be made to work even harder, by using *colour* to highlight key information we should look out for in the chart. The Republican red in the title of this chart from Christine Zhang helps set up the main story of this chart. A legend is also present to formally explain the colours, but the title makes it clear upfront that red is the colour to look out for.

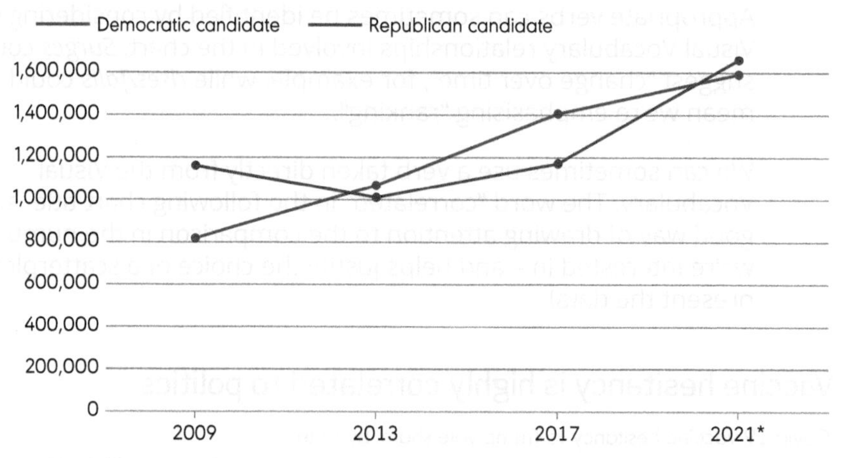

* 2021 vote counts are unofficial

Source: FT graphic: Christine Zhang Source: Virginia Department of Elections appeared in Lauren Fedor and James Politi, Crushing defeat in Virginia governor's race stokes fears among Democrats, Financial Times, November 4, 2021. Available at: https://www.ft.com/content/a44828e6-c522-449e-8f49-91a8c9fff3eb

Finally, the *Financial Times* is an international news organisation and English is not the first language for a significant portion of our readers. Puns and other forms of wordplay are something we're generally keen to avoid.

However, we're also all human and prone to occasional glitches. Writing the title of this chart in 2018 about British household water prices, I couldn't resist an inelegant nod to the recently crowned Oscar winner for Best Picture, *The Shape of Water*. I was conscious of breaking my own rules – which probably explains why I enjoyed it so much . . .

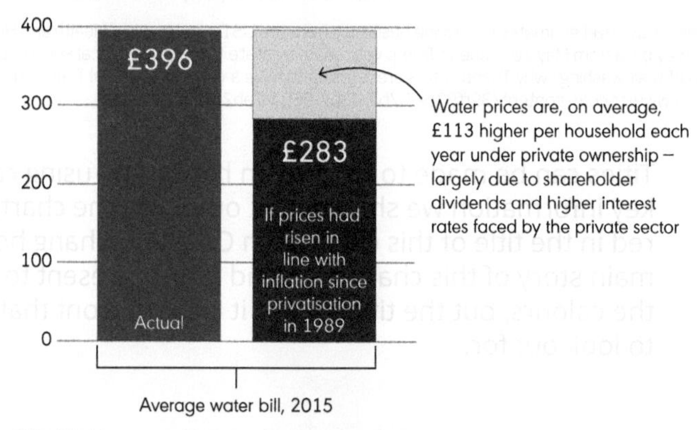

Source: David Hall/NAO appeared in Returning the UK's privatised services to the public. Available at: https://www.ft.com/content/90c0f8e8-17fd-11e8-9e9c-25c814761640

Subtitles

In order to keep our chart self-sufficient, we need to make it completely clear what data is being shown on the graphic – this is the role of the subtitle. We can think of it as a "one-stop shop" for all the chart's metadata. This includes:

- The *data series* – what is being measured? (e.g., Covid vaccination rate/operating profit/armadillo population).
- The *units* to the data (per 100 people/$bn/number of armadillos).
- The *geography* or *universe* of the data (e.g., UK/S&P500/London Zoo).
- If it's not clear from the chart content, the time period being shown (as of 31 December/financial year ending 2019/date of latest zoo census).

For many people, this information will be what they have habitually used as the *title* of a chart. Though important for readers to see, in most cases, it will simply not be memorable enough for us to use as the entry point for a chart. If we want our visuals to speak to readers, use the title and subtitle as a combo to provide a call to look (the title) followed by a show and tell (subtitle and chart).

Source/footnotes

Sometimes, a full description of the data can be too verbose for the subtitle. For example, there may be lengthy definitions that aren't necessary to understand the initial message of the chart but are important to provide for completeness and onward analysis. This is where a footnote can come in useful. As the name suggests, these tend to be placed at the bottom of the chart, so that the title/subtitle retains highest priority in terms of reading order.

Also, at the bottom of the chart, the *source* of the data referenced in the subtitle should be made explicit. This is important for openness and transparency – citing the source makes our chart accountable and potentially reproducible. If that data is available at source online, providing a direct link to it is polite good practice.

The legend

It almost goes without saying that because charts use colour, size, texture etc. to represent information, we should provide a reference to readers to help them decode our encodings – legends provide that function.

However, the best chart designs look to incorporate legends as active parts of the chart where possible. For example, consider the following line chart on the ups and downs of government interventions in the Covid-19 pandemic.

How government pandemic responses' stringency has changed

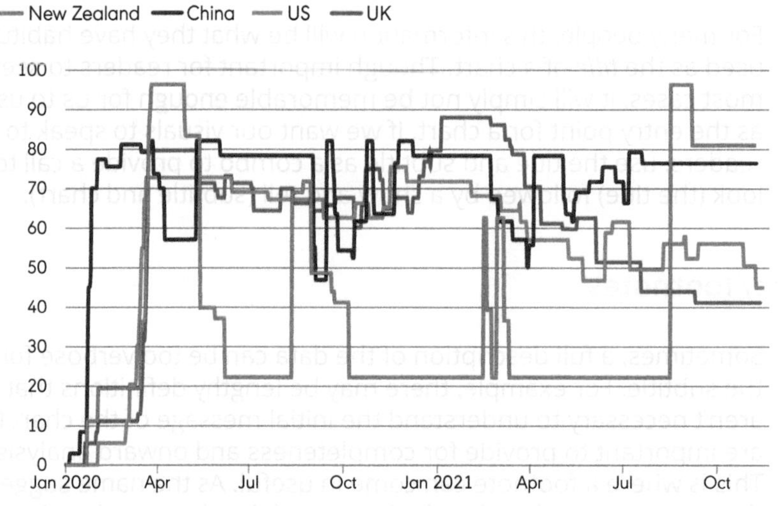

Source: Blavatnik School of Government, University of Oxford appeared in Valentina Romei, Virus restrictions deal European economy lesser blow than in spring, Financial Times, November 11, 2020. Available at: https://www.ft.com/content/7579eaf1-4f12-41bc-a0aa-1f89ac086cc7

A legend is clear and present – but because there are so many lines on the chart, understanding the information requires constant scanning between the chart and the legend. Reading the chart ultimately becomes a memory-intensive task.

Now look at an adjusted version of the chart, this time with the lines directly labelled. We no longer need to look to and fro, we can read each label directly. This approach brings with it another important advantage – we're no longer reliant on colour alone to attach meaning to the lines.

How government pandemic responses' stringency has changed

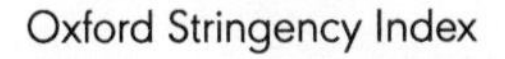

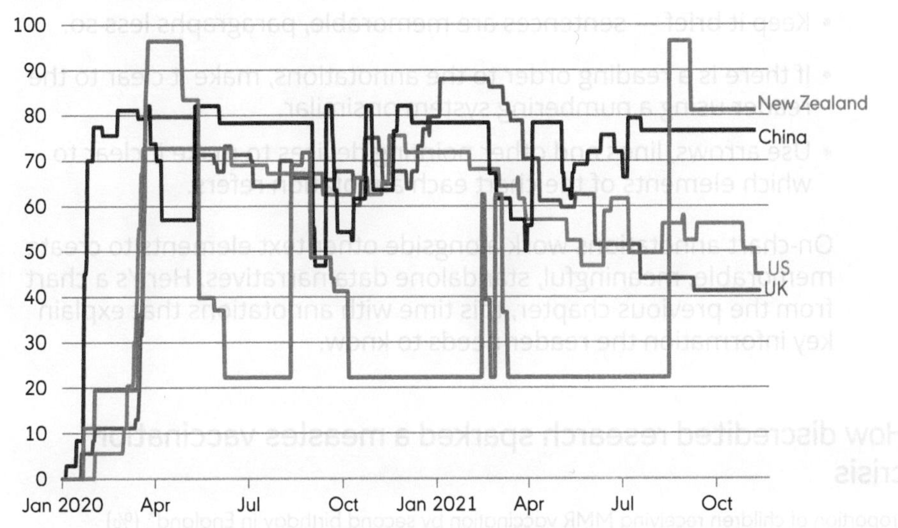

Source: Blavatnik School of Government, University of Oxford appeared in Valentina Romei, Virus restrictions deal European economy lesser blow than in spring, Financial Times, November 11, 2020. Available at: https://www.ft.com/content/7579eaf1-4f12-41bc-a0aa-1f89ac086cc7

Annotations

Many people worry when it comes to writing *on* charts. A research graduate I once worked with told me that they felt as though I was encouraging them to spray graffiti on their wonderfully neutral charts by encouraging them to write "active titles" and embellish them with annotations.

The first thing to dismantle in this argument is the notion that *not* writing on charts somehow makes them neutral. The decision to make a chart is editorial, born of a desire to communicate insights – stopping short of expressing those insights makes them harder to read and suppresses the spread of hard-won knowledge. (By extension, the decision to *not* make a chart – to conceal information and insights – is not necessarily neutral either).

If you don't take my word for it, listen to Amanda Cox, a multi-award-winning data editor and former graphics editor at the *New York Times*: "The annotation layer is the most important thing we do . . . otherwise it's a case of here it is, you go figure it out."

Annotations contextualise data and help readers to understand key information about the patterns on a chart. They can show targets, highlight key moments and emphasise important trends.

In terms writing annotations, there are some general principles of which it pays to be aware:

- Keep it brief — sentences are memorable, paragraphs less so.
- If there is a reading order to the annotations, make it clear to the reader using a numbering system or similar.
- Use arrows, lines and other pointing devices to make it clear to which elements of the chart each annotation refers.

On-chart annotations work alongside other text elements to create memorable, meaningful, standalone data narratives. Here's a chart from the previous chapter, this time with annotations that explain key information the reader needs to know.

How discredited research sparked a measles vaccination crisis

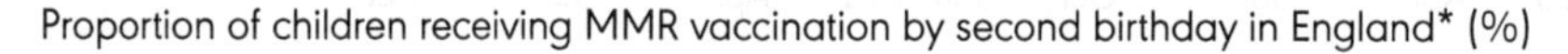

Proportion of children receiving MMR vaccination by second birthday in England* (%)

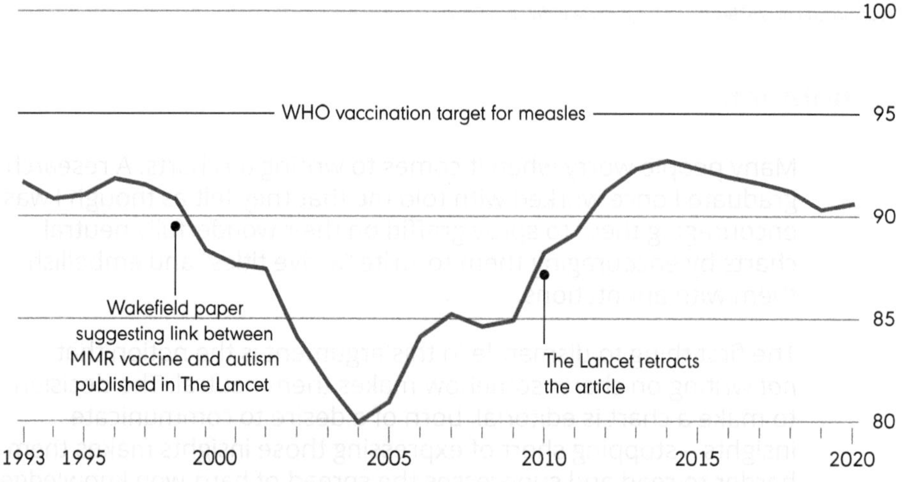

* Completed primary courses

Sources: COVER; Public Health England appeared in David Robert Grimes, How to take on Covid conspiracy theories, Financial Times, February 5, 2021. Available at: https://www.ft.com/content/6660cb80-8c11-476a-b107-e0193fa975f9. Used by Permission from The Financial Times Limited.

16

Designing for charts

In 2010, the BBC's Mark Easton wrote about the local and national challenges Britain was facing in caring for its elderly people. To illustrate these challenges, he used screenshots from an interactive, animated map I had created for the UK Office for National Statistics to accompany "National Older People's Day".

In citing my work, Mark kindly referred to me as "the award-winning designer Alan Smith". This was curious – I had never considered myself "a designer" before. Seeing this on the BBC website, where hundreds of thousands of people likely would read it, made me feel somewhat of an impostor.

Yet, the more I thought about it, the more I realised I had been getting the relationship between design and data visualisation wrong all along.

A designer is simply someone who designs. And charts, as we have seen throughout this book, certainly need designing. So, just as with fashion design, interior design and software design, the design of charts is a field that needs specialised designers. Suddenly, my career started to make a lot more sense. Today, more than a decade on, there are more "chart designers" than ever, a sure sign of a thriving and rapidly evolving field.

This is certainly not a book on general design theory. But, in realising that many people become "chart designers" without having studied other areas of design more widely, there are some core principles that can help enormously with the challenge of creating effective charts.

Colour

For something that is just a trick of visible light, a tiny part of the electromagnetic spectrum, colour is a surprisingly powerful constant in most of our daily lives.

When it comes to charts, colour can make or break our attempts to communicate. That's why it pays to know just a little about what it is and how we can take advantage of it to create better visualisations.

Many people will be familiar with the fact that computer screens display colour using a combination of red, green and blue light. When combined, these three sources can yield any variation that lies within a particular universe, or "gamut", of colour – known as an RGB colourspace. The RGB colour model is the inverse of its print counterpart, CMY(K).

Two colour models compared

RGB
Red, green and blue coloured light is combined to make other colours. When they are all used together at maximum intensity they make white – an *additive* model

CMY(K)
Cyan, magenta and yellow inks are mixed to make other colours. Together, they make a colour approximating black – a *subtractive* model

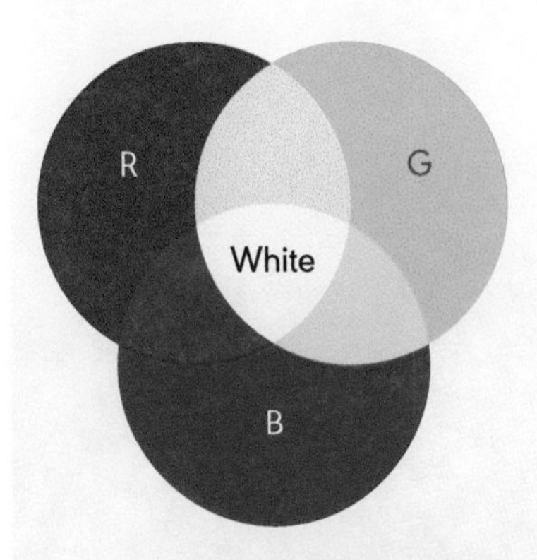

RGB is used in computer displays. It is the colour model of the web

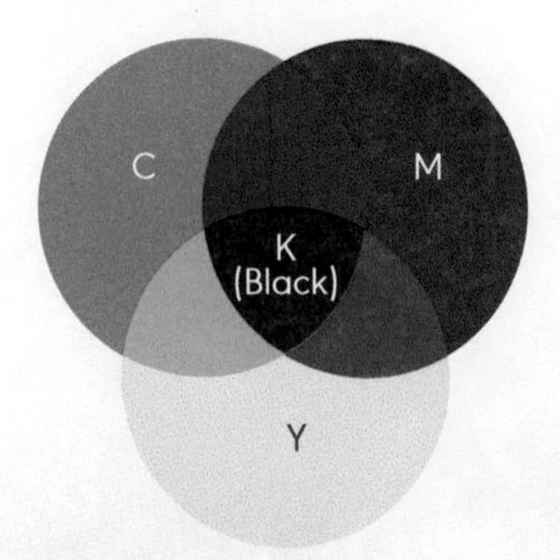

CMYK is used for print. The three main colours (CMY) are usually supplemented by a dedicated true black print plate (K, or 'Key black')

One thing to notice is that the models, as shown above, are simplified. Both can display more than just a few primary or secondary colours – but they achieve it in very different ways. The additive RGB model allows for continuous colour tones through the fine-tuning of RGB light levels . . .

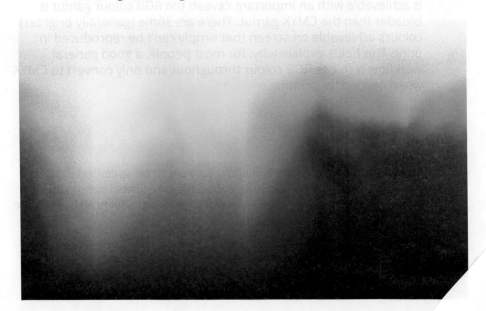

. . . whereas the subtractive CMYK model relies on a print process known as *halftoning*. A halftone image simulates continuous colour by carefully varying the size and placement of dots printed using just the basic colour plates.

A confession – the examples above are entirely fraudulent. For the purposes of printing this book, the RGB colours from my computer screen will have been converted to CMYK, a process that is achievable with an important caveat: the RGB colour gamut is broader than the CMYK gamut. There are some (generally brighter) colours achievable on screen that simply can't be reproduced in print. This helps explain why, for most people, a good general workflow is to use RGB colour throughout and only convert to CMYK when needed for printing.

Creating RGB colour

Most computer software will allow colours to be specified in terms of levels of red, green and blue light. This is nice and simple, but for chart makers, a more helpful view of the RGB model is also available in many software packages: the HSL colour model:

- *Hue* is the "nameable" colour – red, yellow, green, etc. – and is specified as an angle between 0 and 360 degrees.

- *Saturation* is how much of the colour is applied at any given level of lightness. When there is no saturation, there is no colour – all you can see is grey.
- *Lightness* determines how much light is transmitted. When there is no light (0 per cent lightness), the colour appears black. When there is 100 per cent lightness, the colour appears white.

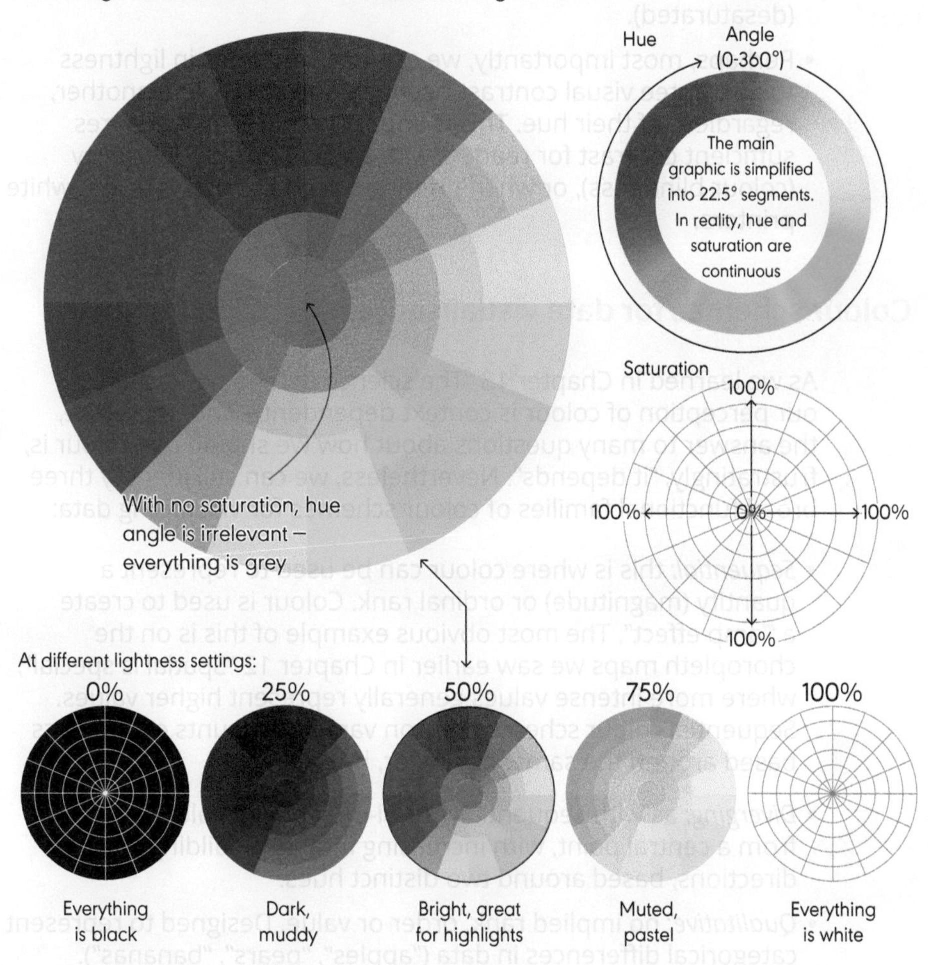

Using an online tool such as HSL Colour Picker (hslpicker.com), it is easy to convert freely in either direction between conventional RGB (where red, green and blue values are each expressed within a range of 0–255) and HSL values (H=0–360, S=0–100, L=0–100). But why is the HSL colour model so useful to work with?

- In HSL, the hue angle (H) is arranged like a standard colour wheel, the sort of thing you might see when choosing a paint scheme or working on interior design. This circular arrangement is extremely useful for creating colour schemes. For example, identifying a "complementary" pair of colours simply involves placing 180 degrees between their hue values – because complementary colours are directly opposite each other on the HSL model.
- Adjusting the level of saturation allows us to emphasise or de-emphasise colours – together with adjustments for lightness, this is great for highlighting (saturated) and lowlighting (desaturated).
- Perhaps, most importantly, we can use variations in lightness to guarantee visual contrast between one colour and another, regardless of their hue. This is important because it ensures sufficient contrast for readers with a colour vision deficiency (colour blindness), or when printing out charts on black and white printers.

Colour schemes for data visualisation

As we learned in Chapter 13 "The science behind good charts", our perception of colour is context dependent – and, therefore, the answer to many questions about how we should use colour is, frustratingly, "it depends". Nevertheless, we can still identify three broad functional families of colour schemes for visualising data:

- *Sequential:* this is where colour can be used to represent a quantity (magnitude) or ordinal rank. Colour is used to create a "'amp effect". The most obvious example of this is on the choropleth maps we saw earlier in Chapter 12 "Spatial is special", where more intense values generally represent higher values. Sequential colour schemes rely on varying amounts of lightness based around the same, or similar, hues.
- *Diverging:* as with sequential, but bi-directional. Values deviate from a central point, with increasing intensity building in both directions, based around two distinct hues.
- *Qualitative:* no implied rank, order or value. Designed to represent categorical differences in data ("apples", "pears", "bananas"). Qualitative colour schemes tend to involve "multi-hue" palettes (i.e., those involving more than one colour).

A good starting point for exploring these colour schemes is the famous Colorbrewer website (https://colorbrewer2.org). Created by cartographer Cynthia Brewer, it's an interactive colour scheme generator, supporting both RGB and CMYK outputs.

Each colour scheme is accompanied by guidance on whether it is colourblind-safe, print friendly, and so on. One learning point to take from Colorbrewer is how multi-hue colour schemes with insufficient lightness contrast are unreadable by colourblind readers, as the example below shows.

Colour schemes for data visualisation

Four-class sequential, diverging and qualitative palettes

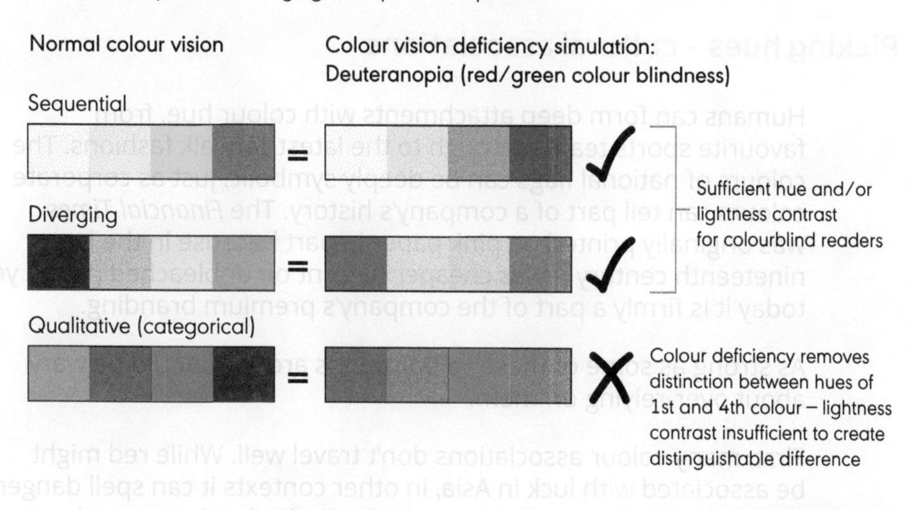
Normal colour vision
Colour vision deficiency simulation:
Deuteranopia (red/green colour blindness)
Sequential
=
Diverging
=
Sufficient hue and/or lightness contrast for colourblind readers
Qualitative (categorical)
=
Colour deficiency removes distinction between hues of 1st and 4th colour – lightness contrast insufficient to create distinguishable difference

Learning point – Hex codes

When you use sites like Colorbrewer, you might find yourself confronted with cryptic-looking colour information – a hash character sign (#) followed by a combination of six letters and/or numbers.

#fff1e5

Don't panic. Known as a "hex code", this is simply RGB values expressed in hexadecimal, a base 16 encoding system. Remember how each value of red, green and blue light can be set between 0–255? Using hexadecimal, this value range becomes 00–FF. So, the six characters in the hex code are three pairs of values, one each for the level of red, green and blue.

Thankfully, you don't need to become an expert on translating between base 16 and base 10 to understand hex colours. Plenty of websites, including hslpicker.com, will translate between RGB, HSL *and* hex code values for you. Type the hex code #fff1e5 above into the site and you'll see translated RGB values of 255, 241, 229, and HSL values of 28,100,95. The salmon pink colour it represents should be familiar to readers of the FT . . .

Picking hues – cultural associations

Humans can form deep attachments with colour hue, from favourite sports teams through to the latest catwalk fashions. The colours of national flags can be deeply symbolic, just as corporate colours can tell part of a company's history. The *Financial Times* was originally printed on pink paper in part because in the late nineteenth century it was cheaper to print on unbleached paper, yet today it is firmly a part of the company's premium branding.

As strong as some of these colour bonds are, we should be wary about over-relying on them.

First, many colour associations don't travel well. While red might be associated with luck in Asia, in other contexts it can spell danger and death. Or just strawberries. In the Netherlands, orange is associated with royalty. Yet, in the UK, purple is the colour that has generally been associated with the monarchy. Except in recent decades, when purple is just as likely to be associated with a particular political party.

A few colour associations *are* near-universal. Green is associated with growth and sustainability to such an extent that environmentally conscious political parties around the world are now named after it. In fact, party political colours are one of the associations we generally stick with in one form or another at the *FT*, as they help readers tune in to data.

Similarly, it would be odd to chart comparative data relating to Manchester United and Manchester City without thinking about using red and sky blue respectively (I would stick to "home kits" only for colour associations that stand the test of time!).

But some colour associations can also reinforce unwanted or anachronistic stereotypes. The notion of pink for girls and blue for boys is a good example of this. Far from being the deep cultural convention that some people assume it to be, it's no more than a twentieth century fashion, already in decline. Before it became popular, there used to be a reverse association (blue for girls, and red or pink for boys), which, in turn, replaced a long-standing tradition of white clothing and accessories for babies all around.

The elephant in the room – corporate colours

It's impossible to talk about cultural associations with colour without mentioning the starting point for many chart makers – strict instructions to slavishly follow the corporate colour palette. There is nothing wrong with incorporating company brand into your chart colour scheme, but I would encourage you to scrutinise the corporate colour palette. Is it functional for sequential, diverging and categorical purposes? Does it allow for highlighting and lowlighting (pulling elements into foreground, or placing into background)? Is it colour-blind friendly? Is it possible that some of these considerations were not taken into account when the branding was established?

Rather than become the corporate rebel and go off piste, try talking with your corporate design and communication teams to explain your functional requirements for colour and identify exceptions or extensions to the corporate scheme. For example, you could use the company's hue angles but add extra tones based on varying amounts of lightness and saturation.

Whatever approach you take, it's always a good idea to define a range of reusable colour palettes so you don't need to face the same colour design problems every time you want to create a chart or map. There will always be exceptions that require a different treatment, but it's good to have a solid default starting point.

Gestalt principles

As I learned about the relationship between design principles and data visualisation, the connection between charts and Gestalt principles of design became increasingly apparent.

The Gestalt school of psychology, which emerged in Germany in the 1920s, argued that humans perceive individual elements as parts of a whole. The German word *gestalt* can be translated as "form" or "shape" – but, in this context, we can think of it specifically describing forms or shapes that are greater than the sum of their individual elements.

Here are six principles of perceptual organisation from the Gestalt school that we can directly relate to the world of charts.

The principle of similarity

In the 10 x 10 grid below, our perceptual systems tell us that one column of dots is very clearly different from the others. This is the principle of similarity in action – objects that share visual characteristics are perceived as more related than items that are dissimilar.

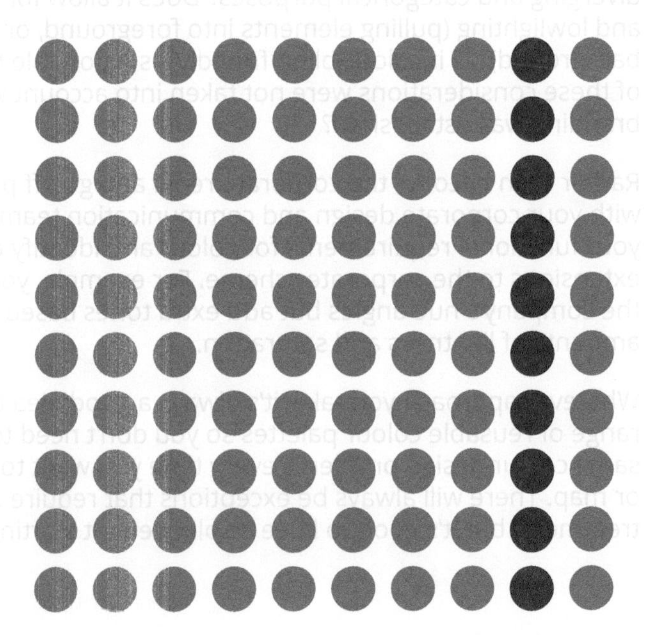

We encountered the work of Otto Neurath, Gerd Arntz and Marie Reidemeister in the chapter on visualising magnitude. The repeating icons used in their Isotype method, developed while the Gestalt school was active, evoke a strong sense of this principle in action. It's a technique still in regular use, as this graphic comparing the navies of the US and China shows.

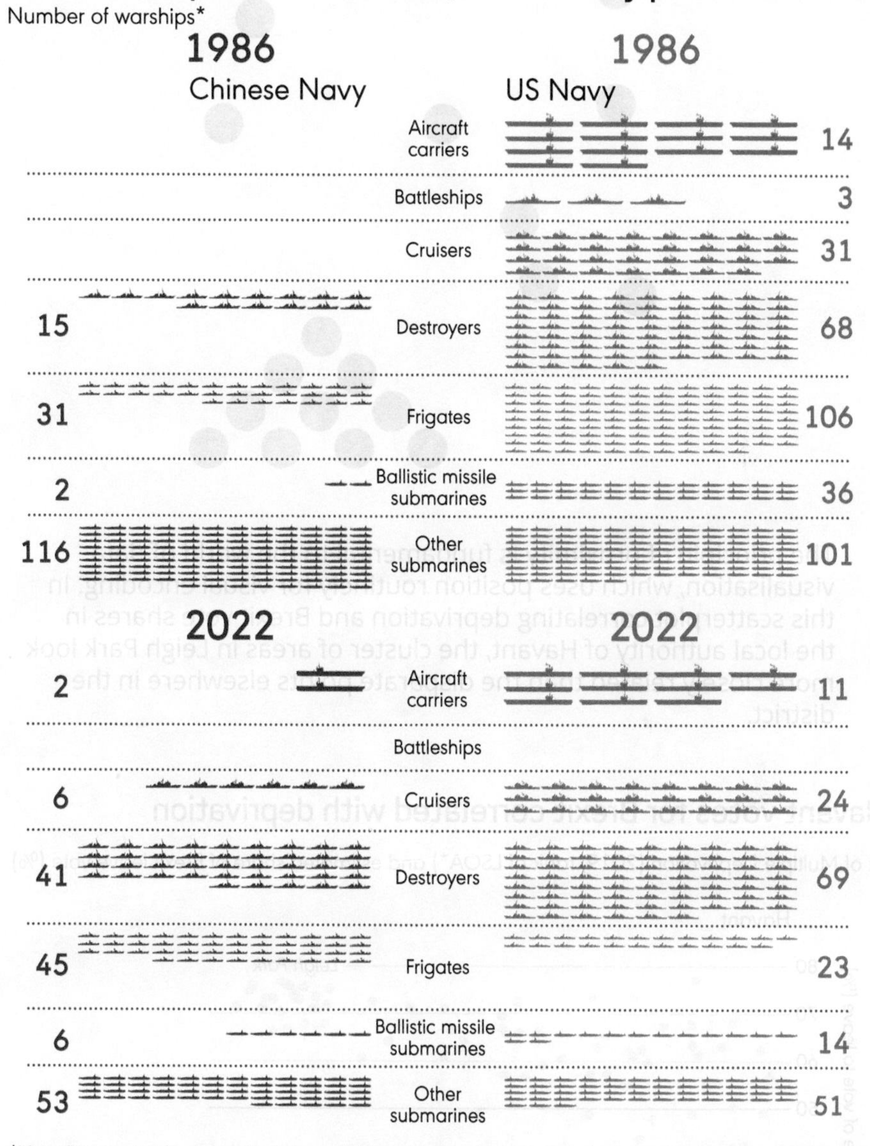

Graphic: Ian Bott

Source: Data from 'Military Balance', International Institute for Strategic Studies appeared in Still Top Gun? What Tom Cruise's new movie tells us about American power by James Crabtree, May 27, 2022. Available at: https://www.ft.com/content/26ebe826-08d7-4966-b104-1a3be1f8ca5c

The principle of proximity

One of the easiest principles to explain: things that are close together appear more related than things that are spaced farther apart. In this image, we can identify two distinct groups. One, forming a triangle at the bottom, is very closely related, the others less so.

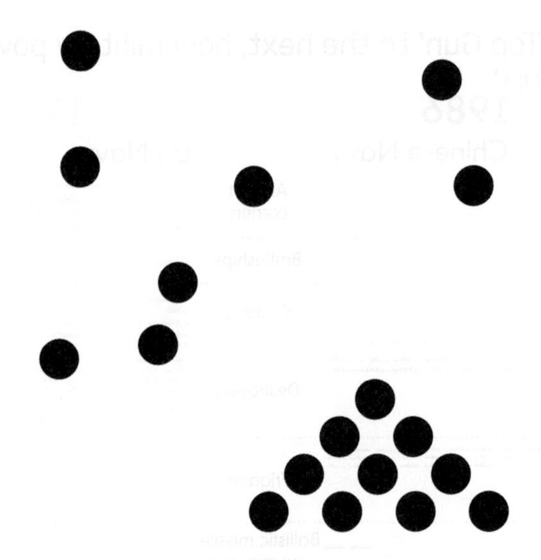

The principle of proximity is fundamental to the world of data visualisation, which uses position routinely for visual encoding. In this scatterplot correlating deprivation and Brexit vote shares in the local authority of Havant, the cluster of areas in Leigh Park look more closely related than the disparate points elsewhere in the district.

In Havant votes for Brexit correlated with deprivation

Index of Multiple Deprivation (2019, rank of LSOA*) and estimated share of Brexit leave vote (%)

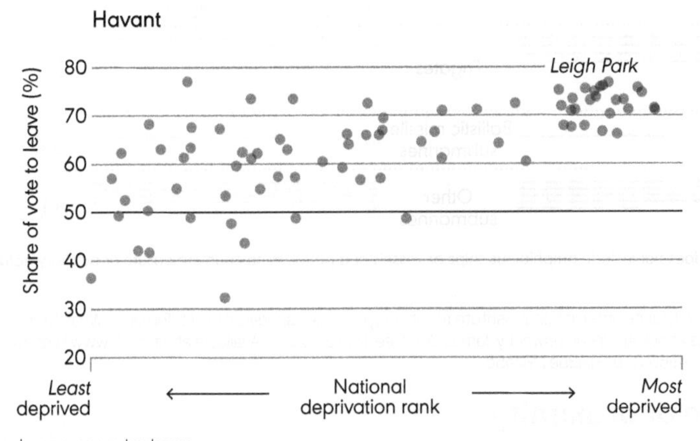

* Lower layer super output area

Sources: Chris Hanretty; Ministry of Housing, Communities & Local Government appeared in William Wallis, England in 2019: Split by wealth but united by Brexit, Financial Times, November 30, 2019. Available at: https://www.ft.com/content/b398d284-11dc-11ea-a225-db2f231cfeae

The principle of good continuation

Consider this image. How many lines do you see? Strictly speaking, there are four lines, but, if you see just two, you can thank the principle of good continuation. This states that figures with smooth edges are more likely to be seen as continuous than edges that are sharp, irregular or interrupted.

Once we realise that our readers will see two lines, it helps explain the effortless grace of Playfair's line chart design. Rather than obfuscate, the points where series overlap (i.e., where one series overtakes another) are what make the graphic interesting, with colour helping to reinforce our understanding of what's happening.

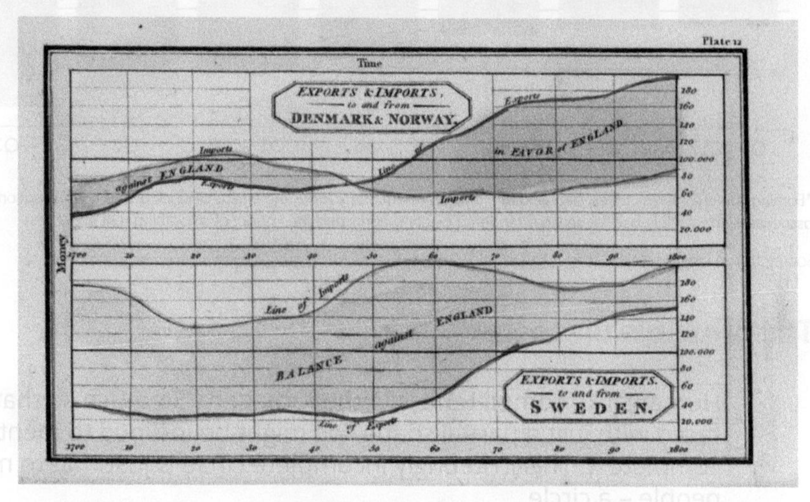

Source: Derivative of File:Playfair TimeSeries.png William Playfair's Time Series of Exports and Imports of Denmark and Norway Published at the Art Direct, May 17th by W. Playfair. Available at: https://en.wikipedia.org/wiki/William_Playfair#/media/File:Playfair_TimeSeries-2.png

The principle of common fate

This principle states that, if we see elements moving together, we tend to perceive them as a unified group.

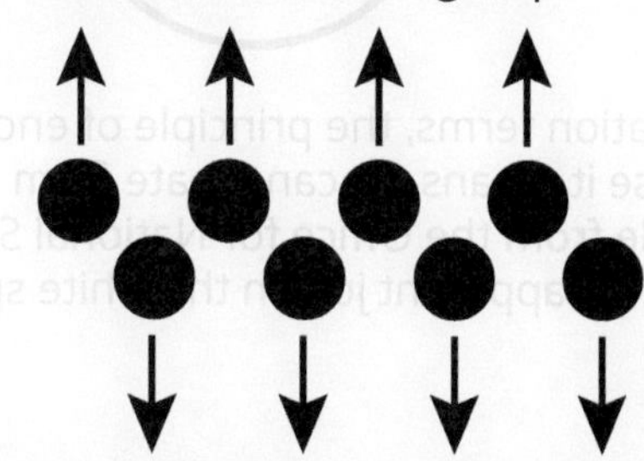

This spine chart of financial data shows how powerful the grouping effect can be. The striking visual contrast between upwards rising sales and downward trending earnings makes writing a descriptive title for the chart remarkably easy.

Losses widen as WeWork expands

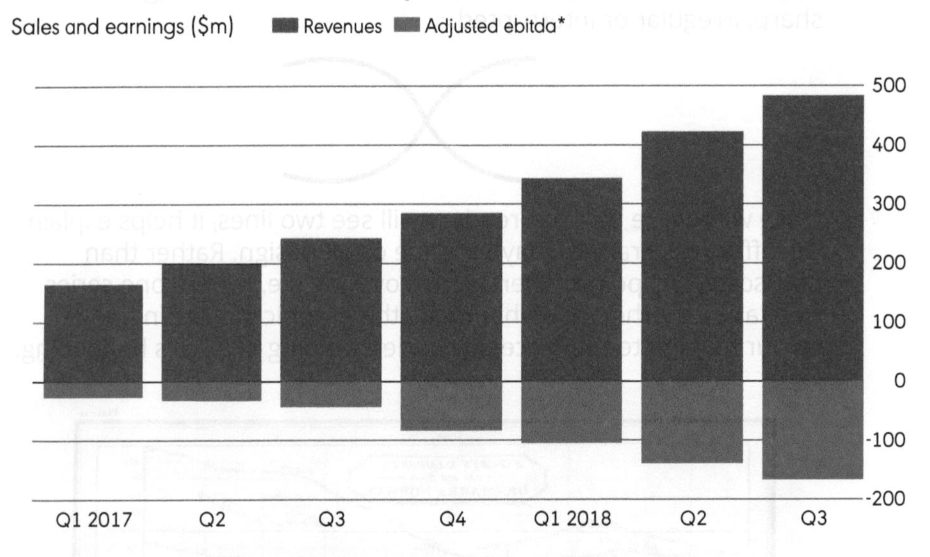

*Earnings before interest, taxes, depreciation, and amortization.Excludes the effects of stock-based compensation, expenses associated with stock issued for services rendered by consultants and the impact of smoothing rent expenses

Source: company

The principle of closure

Humans like completeness in their imagery. So much so that, when faced with just a partial shape, we might be inclined to mentally complete it. This irritatingly incomplete circle is just that to most people – a circle.

In data visualisation terms, the principle of enclosure is useful to know because it means we can create form in negative space. This table from the Office for National Statistics makes rows and columns apparent just in the white space, no gridlines required.

1 UK TRADE IN GOODS AND SERVICES AT CURRENT MARKET PRICES (CP)

Balance of Payments basis

£ million, Seasonally Adjusted

	Trade in goods			Trade in services			Total trade		
	Exports	Imports	Balance	Exports	Imports	Balance	Exports	Imports	Balance
	BOKG	BOKH	BOKI	IKBB	IKBC	IKBD	IKBH	IKBI	IKBJ
Annual									
2015	280 395	406 009	-125 614	245 688	150 006	95 682	526 083	556 015	-29 932
2016	297 909	437 107	-139 198	271 202	165 031	106 171	569 111	602 138	-33 027
2017	337 940	478 418	-140 478	292 161	178 178	113 983	630 101	656 596	-26 495
2018	350 844	493 096	-142 252	312 481	198 527	113 954	663 325	691 623	-28 298
2019	371 955	510 169	-138 214	327 295	209 769	117 526	699 250	719 938	-20 688
2020	308 884	438 326	-129 442	296 458	164 157	132 301	605 342	602 483	2 859
2021	320 474	476 317	-155 843	298 493	171 411	127 082	618 967	647 728	-28 761
Quarterly									
2017 Q1	83 015	117 974	-34 959	72 154	43 731	28 423	155 169	161 705	-6 536
Q2	85 152	120 441	-35 289	72 758	44 624	28 134	157 910	165 065	-7 155
Q3	84 196	120 703	-36 507	74 406	45 047	29 359	158 602	165 750	-7 148
Q4	85 577	119 300	-33 723	72 843	44 776	28 067	158 420	164 076	-5 656
2018 Q1	85 126	119 997	-34 871	76 551	47 968	28 583	161 677	167 965	-6 288
Q2	87 621	122 694	-35 073	76 367	48 788	27 579	163 988	171 482	-7 494
Q3	90 127	123 890	-33 763	77 520	49 155	28 365	167 647	173 045	-5 398
Q4	87 970	126 515	-38 545	82 043	52 616	29 427	170 013	179 131	-9 118
2019 Q1	90 549	142 102	-51 553	78 003	49 602	28 401	168 552	191 704	-23 152
Q2	86 879	123 822	-36 943	80 457	51 915	28 542	167 336	175 737	-8 401
Q3	93 455	125 206	-31 751	83 574	53 575	29 999	177 029	178 781	-1 752
Q4	101 072	119 039	-17 967	85 261	54 677	30 584	186 333	173 716	12 617
2020 Q1	82 353	113 924	-31 571	80 972	48 270	32 702	163 325	162 194	1 131
Q2	72 373	87 875	-15 502	69 821	38 012	31 809	142 194	125 887	16 307
Q3	73 562	107 318	-33 756	70 832	38 374	32 458	144 394	145 692	-1 298
Q4	80 596	129 209	-48 613	74 833	39 501	35 332	155 429	168 710	-13 281
2021 Q1	72 623	111 855	-39 232	73 383	39 901	33 482	146 006	151 756	-5 750
Q2	82 680	116 482	-33 802	75 335	42 219	33 116	158 015	158 701	- 686
Q3	76 301	122 351	-46 050	74 998	44 737	30 261	151 299	167 088	-15 789
Q4	88 870	125 629	-36 759	74 777	44 554	30 223	163 647	170 183	-6 536
Monthly									
2018 Jan	28 819	41 189	-12 370	25 113	15 619	9 494	53 932	56 808	-2 876
2018 Feb	27 791	37 681	-9 890	25 638	16 048	9 590	53 429	53 729	- 300
2018 Mar	28 516	41 127	-12 611	25 800	16 301	9 499	54 316	57 428	-3 112
2018 Apr	28 033	40 644	-12 611	25 670	16 370	9 300	53 703	57 014	-3 311
2018 May	29 190	41 235	-12 045	25 433	16 290	9 143	54 623	57 525	-2 902
2018 Jun	30 398	40 815	-10 417	25 264	16 128	9 136	55 662	56 943	-1 281
2018 Jul	30 424	41 061	-10 637	25 312	16 053	9 259	55 736	57 114	-1 378
2018 Aug	29 603	41 942	-12 339	25 716	16 265	9 451	55 319	58 207	-2 888
2018 Sep	30 100	40 887	-10 787	26 492	16 837	9 655	56 592	57 724	-1 132
2018 Oct	30 044	42 213	-12 169	27 278	17 470	9 808	57 322	59 683	-2 361
2018 Nov	29 605	42 222	-12 617	27 595	17 740	9 855	57 200	59 962	-2 762
2018 Dec	28 321	42 080	-13 759	27 170	17 406	9 764	55 491	59 486	-3 995
2019 Jan	29 272	46 575	-17 303	26 378	16 781	9 597	55 650	63 356	-7 706
2019 Feb	29 682	46 775	-17 093	25 797	16 358	9 439	55 479	63 133	-7 654
2019 Mar	31 595	48 752	-17 157	25 828	16 463	9 365	57 423	65 215	-7 792
2019 Apr	27 656	42 492	-14 836	26 304	16 919	9 385	53 960	59 411	-5 451
2019 May	29 235	41 106	-11 871	26 873	17 383	9 490	56 108	58 489	-2 381
2019 Jun	29 988	40 224	-10 236	27 280	17 613	9 667	57 268	57 837	- 569
2019 Jul	32 117	41 002	-8 885	27 558	17 693	9 865	59 675	58 695	980
2019 Aug	30 659	41 610	-10 951	27 835	17 811	10 024	58 494	59 421	- 927
2019 Sep	30 679	42 594	-11 915	28 181	18 071	10 110	58 860	60 665	-1 805
2019 Oct	32 131	43 277	-11 146	28 476	18 329	10 147	60 607	61 606	- 999
2019 Nov	33 339	38 035	-4 696	28 542	18 361	10 181	61 881	56 396	5 485
2019 Dec	35 602	37 727	-2 125	28 243	17 987	10 256	63 845	55 714	8 131
2020 Jan	30 074	38 290	-8 216	28 141	16 944	11 197	58 215	55 234	2 981
2020 Feb	27 211	39 290	-12 079	27 129	16 533	10 596	54 340	55 823	-1 483
2020 Mar	25 068	36 344	-11 276	25 702	14 793	10 909	50 770	51 137	- 367
2020 Apr	23 432	27 827	-4 395	23 550	13 064	10 486	46 982	40 891	6 091
2020 May	24 293	27 470	-3 177	22 859	12 166	10 693	47 152	39 636	7 516
2020 Jun	24 648	32 578	-7 930	23 412	12 782	10 630	48 060	45 360	2 700
2020 Jul	24 177	34 760	-10 583	23 360	12 681	10 679	47 537	47 441	96
2020 Aug	25 034	34 486	-9 452	23 402	12 830	10 572	48 436	47 316	1 120
2020 Sep	24 351	38 072	-13 721	24 070	12 863	11 207	48 421	50 935	-2 514
2020 Oct	25 953	40 229	-14 276	24 817	13 282	11 535	50 770	53 511	-2 741
2020 Nov	27 032	42 939	-15 907	24 963	13 114	11 849	51 995	56 053	-4 058
2020 Dec	27 611	46 041	-18 430	25 053	13 105	11 948	52 664	59 146	-6 482
2021 Jan	21 337	36 616	-15 279	24 549	13 034	11 515	45 886	49 650	-3 764
2021 Feb	24 535	37 873	-13 338	24 289	13 223	11 066	48 824	51 096	-2 272
2021 Mar	26 751	37 366	-10 615	24 545	13 644	10 901	51 296	51 010	286
2021 Apr	27 630	38 420	-10 790	24 490	13 676	10 814	52 120	52 096	24
2021 May	28 710	38 282	-9 572	25 352	14 177	11 175	54 062	52 459	1 603
2021 Jun	26 340	39 780	-13 440	25 493	14 366	11 127	51 833	54 146	-2 313
2021 Jul	26 112	40 694	-14 582	24 881	14 965	9 916	50 993	55 659	-4 666
2021 Aug	25 140	40 039	-14 899	25 025	14 991	10 034	50 165	55 030	-4 865
2021 Sep	25 049	41 618	-16 569	25 092	14 781	10 311	50 141	56 399	-6 258
2021 Oct	28 730	40 434	-11 704	24 931	14 840	10 091	53 661	55 274	-1 613
2021 Nov	29 605	42 306	-12 701	24 992	14 877	10 115	54 597	57 183	-2 586
2021 Dec	30 535	42 889	-12 354	24 854	14 837	10 017	55 389	57 726	-2 337

The principle of figure and ground

The single most famous image associated with the Gestalt school prompts us to consider what is in the foreground ("figure") and what is in the background ("ground"). It all depends on whether you think the background is pale (you see two facial silhouettes) or dark (you see a vase).

Good contrast enables us to separate foreground from background, content from non-content. This population pyramid might not prompt you to see a vase or two opposing faces, but there's no question where the data is – at the front, ready to be inspected.

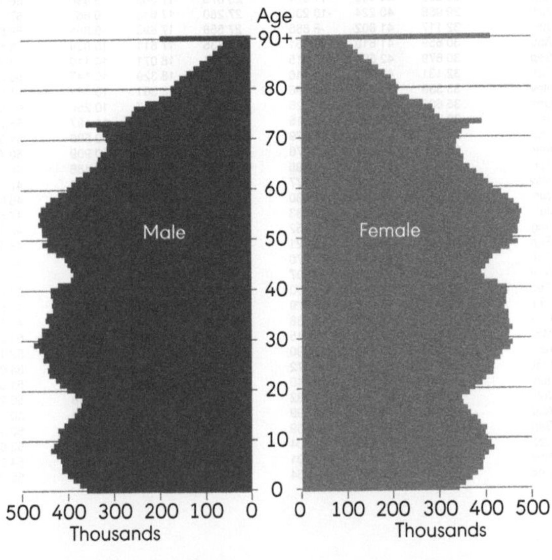

Inclusive design

Charts are an amazing way to communicate patterns in data – to those people that can see them and use them. For people who have visual, motor or cognitive impairments, charts can present enormous challenges, particularly if their needs have not been taken on board as part of the design process.

To make inclusive data visualisations, we need to make its core information as *accessible* as possible.

Not all accessibility needs pull in the same direction. We don't need to cater for just one set of audience needs, but rather to the needs of many different audiences. For example, a visual display might be very helpful to someone with a cognitive impairment, less so to someone who is blind.

Learning point – An accessibility toolkit

Until very recently, guidance on how to make data visualisations accessible has been limited, but things are beginning to change.

Chartability is a toolkit created by Frank Elavsky, a researcher with data visualisation accessibility specialists Fizz Studio. It's a series of testable questions that help identify potential failures in "data experiences".

These failures are organised into seven categories, each of which helps with understanding specific elements of inclusive data design. For example, "perceivable failures" are those where users can't easily identify content using their senses, while "operable failures" cover issues with unusable controls on interactive graphics.

Freely available online (https://chartability.fizz.studio), Chartability is a highly recommended starting point for understanding the issues involved in making charts genuinely accessible.

Whatever software you use to create a chart, there are three steps you can take to instantly improve your chart experience for all readers, while making them available to the widest possible audience:

1. Maximise contrast.
2. Make chart text clear and legible.
3. Include alt text in online charts.

1. Maximise contrast

As we have already seen, ensuring good contrast in lightness can make a huge difference for colour-blind readers. But good contrast helps everyone. And it doesn't just apply to the colours you use for the data on your chart – it applies to the entire visual. Pay particular attention to text.

Contrast is included in the Web Content Accessibility Guidelines (WCAG) published by the Web Accessibility Initiative of the World Wide Web Consortium[9] (the main standards organisation for the internet). You can test your colour schemes for contrast and tell you if they pass WCAG tests for text and graphical elements.

	Background colour	Foreground colour	Contrast ratio	WCAG AAA Pass/fail for normal text
Use light text on a dark background	#1e558c H: 210 S: 65 L: 33	#ffffff H: 0 S: 100 L: 100	7.68:1	Pass
Use dark text on a light background	#fff1e5 H: 28 S: 100 L: 95	#1a1817 H: 20 S: 6 L: 10	15.97:1	Pass
Anything else is a nightmare for readers!	#6e9eec H: 217 S: 77 L: 68	#9a999a H: 300 S: 0 L: 60	1.04:1	Fail

For normal text, WCAG AAA requires a contrast ratio of 7:1 or above

[9] See sites such as https://webaim.org/resources/contrastchecker/.

2. Make chart text clear and legible

We know how important text is to charts, so it's crucial to ensure that it is readable. As well as meeting contrast requirements, as described above, you should ensure your text is large enough to be legible.

Of course, how big any single text element should be depends both on what it is (titles should be bigger than footnotes) and what it is being displayed on (e.g., projector/desktop computer/mobile phone). The most important thing for you to consider in terms of readability is a *minimum* text size. Though there are no strict rules, aiming for 16px (pixels) on an electronic screen meets a consensus.

Even better, if you are publishing in a web environment, instead of specifying size in terms of pixels, consider using a proportional unit such as "em", which adjusts text to the size of the display (1em on a mobile phone screen will be smaller than 1em on a large desktop display).

Another important consideration for text is choice of typeface. Rather like colours, fonts will also be something that many people inherit from their corporate environment. Nevertheless, for chart elements like axis labels, you should generally avoid elaborate serif fonts in favour of cleaner sans-serif variants, which tend to scale better on smaller or lower-resolution screens. Even in print, the difference in legibility can be striking.

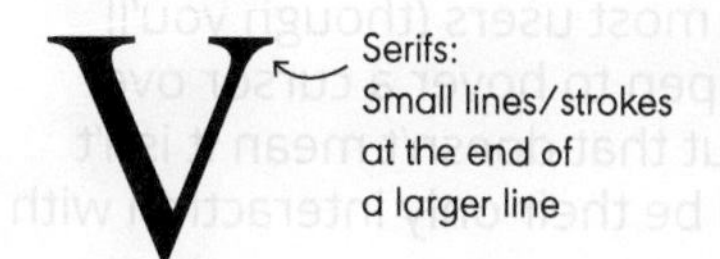

'Sans serif', sometimes
referred to as 'grotesque'
or 'gothic'

40pt Visual vocabulary in Times New Roman

40pt Visual vocabulary in Graphik

14pt Visual vocabulary in Times New Roman

14pt Visual vocabulary in Graphik

Of course, legibility is not the only goal in choosing a typeface. Character and tone are important too, so it's important to arrive at a balanced situation.

Finally, an important principle when displaying numerals is to use "tabular lining" on text. This ensures that each figure takes up the same amount of horizontal space. It is *essential* when displaying figures in tables, and highly desirable elsewhere on a chart, for example in axes labels.

Regular

1,430,000
970,111
10,134
365

Notice how the comma separators are not aligned – because the figures are variable width

Tabular lining

1,430,000
970,111
10,134
365

The clue is in the name – 'tabular' means the layout is designed for tables. Figures have the same width, making reading and scanning much easier

3. Include alt text in online charts

Alt text – an abbreviated form of "alternative text" – is a textual description of an image to accompany online publication. The purpose of this text is to provide a meaningful summary of an image for those people who can't see it. In such cases, screenreader software can be used by visually impaired users, which read the description out loud.

The alt text itself will be invisible to most users (though you'll perhaps glimpse it, should you happen to hover a cursor over an image in your web browser) – but that doesn't mean it isn't important. For some readers, it will be their only interaction with your graphic.

But what method should we use for constructing alt text? As a starting point, we can revisit the *FT* principles for chart titles and annotations we encountered earlier to create a basic recipe:

Alt text = [chart type] of [subtitle] that shows [title]

Let's look at a worked example.

Tax relief has fuelled a filming boom

Expenditure on film and high-end television, UK (£ million)

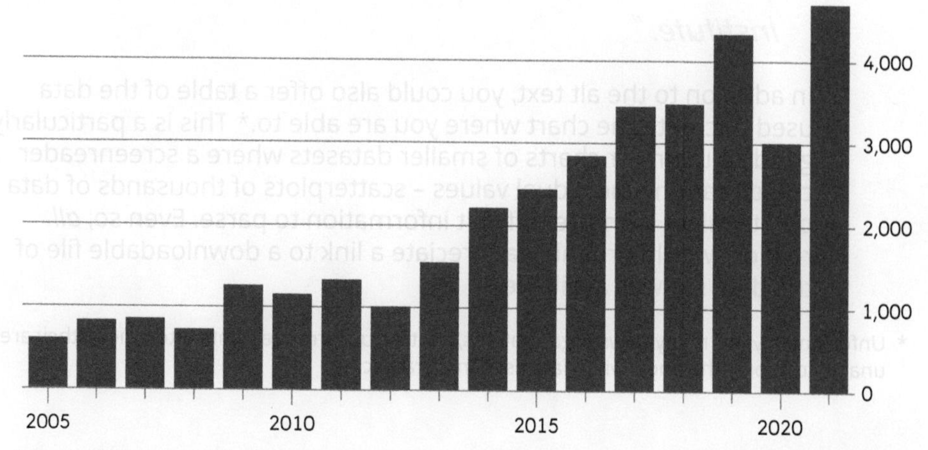

Figure for 2021 covers only first three quarters
Source: British Film Institute appeared in Alistair Gray, Tax rebates fuel UK film and TV boom, Financial Times, December 13, 2021. Available at: https://www.ft.com/content/871aedbf-a982-488a-84d4-38c937da46aa

With the chart's clear title and subtitle using the *FT*'s style for "active titles" – a narrative title, with supporting chart metadata containing descriptions of the data in the subtitle – our corresponding alt text would simply be:

> *"A column chart of expenditure on film and high-end television in the UK (in millions of pounds) that shows tax relief has fuelled a filming boom."*

We could extend this brief description by further describing the trend and adding some figures from the data to give a sense of scale.

> *"There has been a consistent upward trend in expenditure since 2012. In 2021, expenditure reached £4,689 million in the first three quarters alone, compared with a full year figure of around £1,000 million nine years earlier. 2020 was the only occasion in this period where there was a fall from the previous year."*

And, finally, we could add the source:

> *"The source of the data used is the British Film Institute."*

In addition to the alt text, you could also offer a table of the data used to create the chart where you are able to.* This is a particularly good solution for charts of smaller datasets where a screenreader could read the individual values – scatterplots of thousands of data points might be more difficult information to parse. Even so, *all* readers would probably appreciate a link to a downloadable file of the data if it was available.

* Unfortunately, for many news organisations, contractual arrangements often mean they are unable to supply the underlying data used in a graphic.

Image formats

Today, charts are usually published as *electronic images*. But it's important to be aware that this vague term can cover a wide range of formats – and it pays to know the distinctions between them.

The biggest single factor is the distinction between *raster* and *vector* image formats: *raster formats* encode information in a rectangular grid of pixels, the smallest addressable part of a display. Each individual pixel records a single piece of information – its colour. Common raster formats include:

- *Windows bitmap* (commonly known by the *.bmp* file extension)
- *portable network graphics* (*.png*),
- the joint photographic (experts) group, or *jpeg* (*.jpg*)
- graphics interchange format, or *gif* (*.gif*).

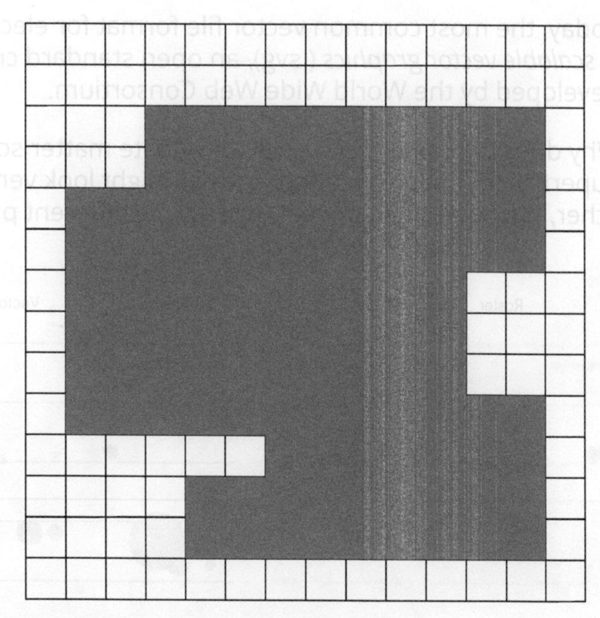

Source: Financial Times

By contrast, *vector formats* encode information on a coordinate system by recording the shape and position of graphical elements using x and y value pairs. Curves between points can even be specified.

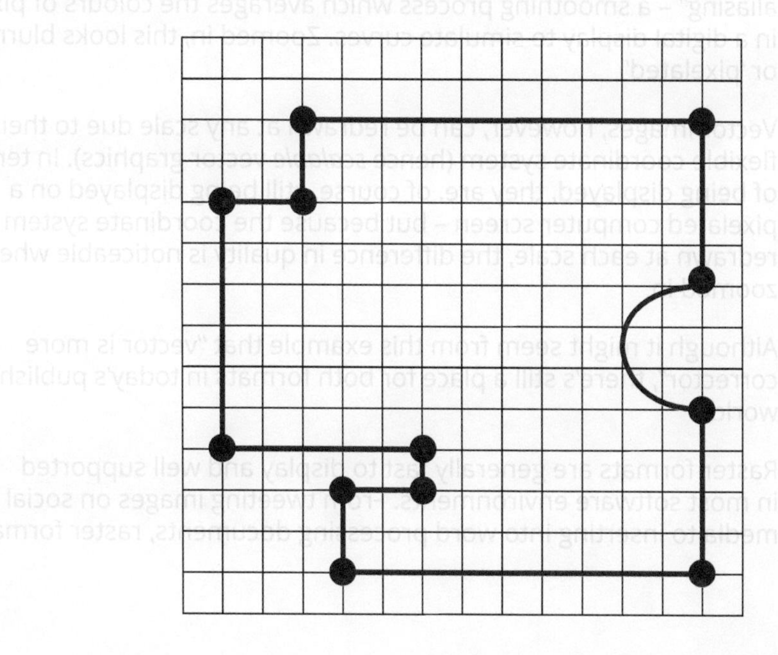

Today, the most common vector file format for electronic images is *scalable vector graphics* (.svg), an open standard created and developed by the World Wide Web Consortium.

Why does the raster versus vector debate matter so much to charts? Superficially, images in either format might look very similar to each other, but zooming in reveals (literally) a different picture . . .

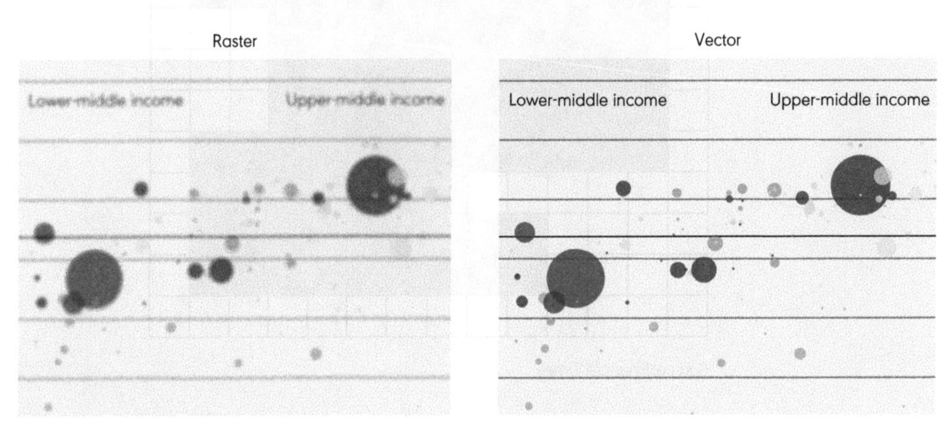

Source: Financial Times

Raster images quickly betray their gridded origins. The illusion of round shapes is only possible thanks to a process known as "anti-aliasing" – a smoothing process which averages the colours of pixels in a digital display to simulate curves. Zoomed in, this looks blurry, or 'pixelated'.

Vector images, however, can be redrawn at any scale due to their flexible coordinate system (hence *scalable* vector graphics). In terms of being displayed, they are, of course, still being displayed on a pixelated computer screen – but because the coordinate system is redrawn at each scale, the difference in quality is noticeable when zoomed in.

Although it might seem from this example that "vector is more corrector", there's still a place for both formats in today's publishing world.

Raster formats are generally fast to display and well supported in most software environments. From tweeting images on social media to inserting into word processing documents, raster formats generally get the job done. Under the raster format umbrella, a general rule of thumb would be to use:

- jpegs for photographs
- pngs for charts and diagrams
- gifs for animated raster images.

Vector formats offer the highest rendering quality on high-resolution screens. Because they also offer lossless resizing, it makes them very useful in print publishing environments.

17

Visualising uncertainty – a case study

Data presented in chart form can seem so authoritative, so seductive, that we might forget to question how much faith we can place in the actual numbers presented. This would be a mistake – understanding the extent to which we can rely on data is an important part of developing our chart literacy.

A key point is realising that data is *never* perfect. Just like humans, data suffers from flaws, sometimes insignificant, sometimes critical.

- *Error*. This can be *systematic* – a measuring device was calibrated incorrectly, or a survey designed with bias so that it's not recording what we think it's recording. Errors can also be *random*, where unpredictable circumstances – a gust of wind – can cause variations in the data we record.

- Error is deeply associated with the concepts of *accuracy* and *precision*. Accuracy is a measure of how close a recorded value is to its real-world value. Precision – a separate concept – dictates the level of detail in our recording. So, while our ideal might be to have highly accurate, precise data, it is possible to have accurate data with low precision and precise data that is inaccurate.
- Another key concept is the *uncertainty* associated with the results of techniques that statisticians use to generate estimates where it is impractical (or impossible) to individually collect every data point. Hans Rosling once memorably summarised a sophisticated technique used to estimate maternal mortality in developing countries as "clever people made a guess".

I am sometimes asked why "uncertainty" is not a relationship on the Visual Vocabulary – surely it deserves its own column?

Uncertainty is so prevalent across all the data that we plot on charts that it's more of a universal concept than a sub-type. Uncertainty in data is unavoidable. The two questions chart producers need to consider are when and how to show it.

The answer to the first part will depend hugely on context. For example, charts in academic papers are generally required to show error and uncertainty because they are important for purposes of reproducibility, a prerequisite when reporting the results of a scientific study.

A common technique used in academic reports to show uncertainty is the *error bar chart* – a conventional column/bar chart where each bar is embellished with a line connecting upper and lower error bounds.

The concept is simple – shorter error bars generally indicate greater faith in the associated column values. Importantly, drawing any meaningful conclusions about chart values where the range of the error lines overlap is difficult – because what might look like clear daylight between two values could just be due to error.

A big drawback with this visualisation technique is that there is no universal convention about what the upper and lower bounds of the error bars show. They could represent one of several statistical measures: *standard deviation*, *standard error*, *confidence intervals* even *minimum* and *maximum* values. That's why it's important to specify what they represent – many charts fail to do this.

In a journalistic context, error bars are not used routinely. But it's essential to embrace uncertainty when it's an important part of the story.

A column chart with error bars

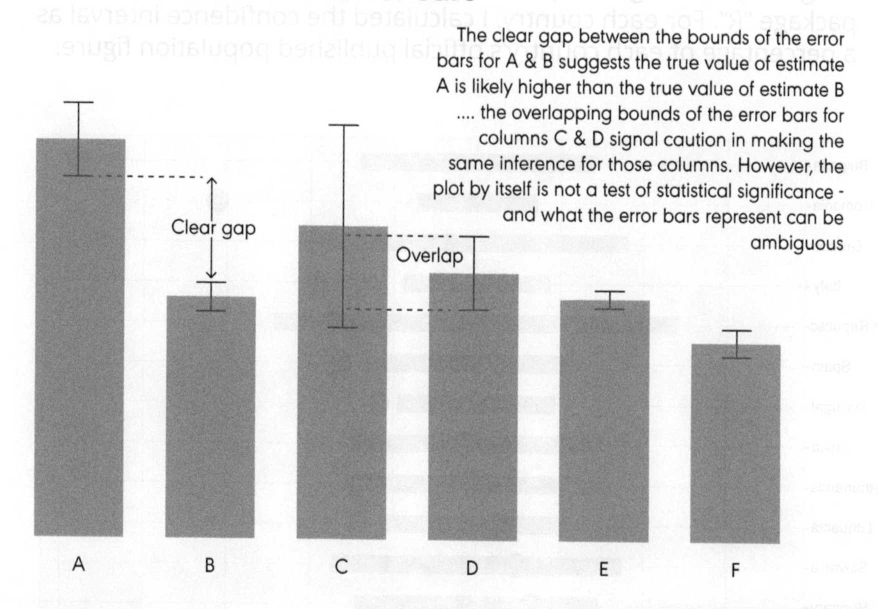

The clear gap between the bounds of the error bars for A & B suggests the true value of estimate A is likely higher than the true value of estimate B .... the overlapping bounds of the error bars for columns C & D signal caution in making the same inference for those columns. However, the plot by itself is not a test of statistical significance - and what the error bars represent can be ambiguous
Clear gap
Overlap
A
B
C
D
E
F

In 2020, figures published by the UK Government revealed that, in many cases, the number of citizens from EU countries who had applied for the right to stay in the UK after Brexit exceeded the official estimates of the number of people from those countries living in the UK.

Not only did they exceed the official estimate, but, in many cases, they surpassed the upper bounds of the published confidence intervals, prompting concerns about the underlying process used for the population estimates.

Learning point – What is a confidence interval?

A confidence interval is a range between a pair of values (the lower and upper bounds) that fall symmetrically either side of a point estimate (a single value). You can think of "confidence" as another word for "probability" – at the 95 per cent confidence level; 95 times out of 100, we would expect the same estimation process to generate a population estimate that would lie somewhere within the interval. Confidence intervals are designed to account for and communicate the variation around a single reported estimate.

I began by creating an exploratory plot using the statistical software package "R". For each country, I calculated the confidence interval as a percentage of each country's official published population figure.

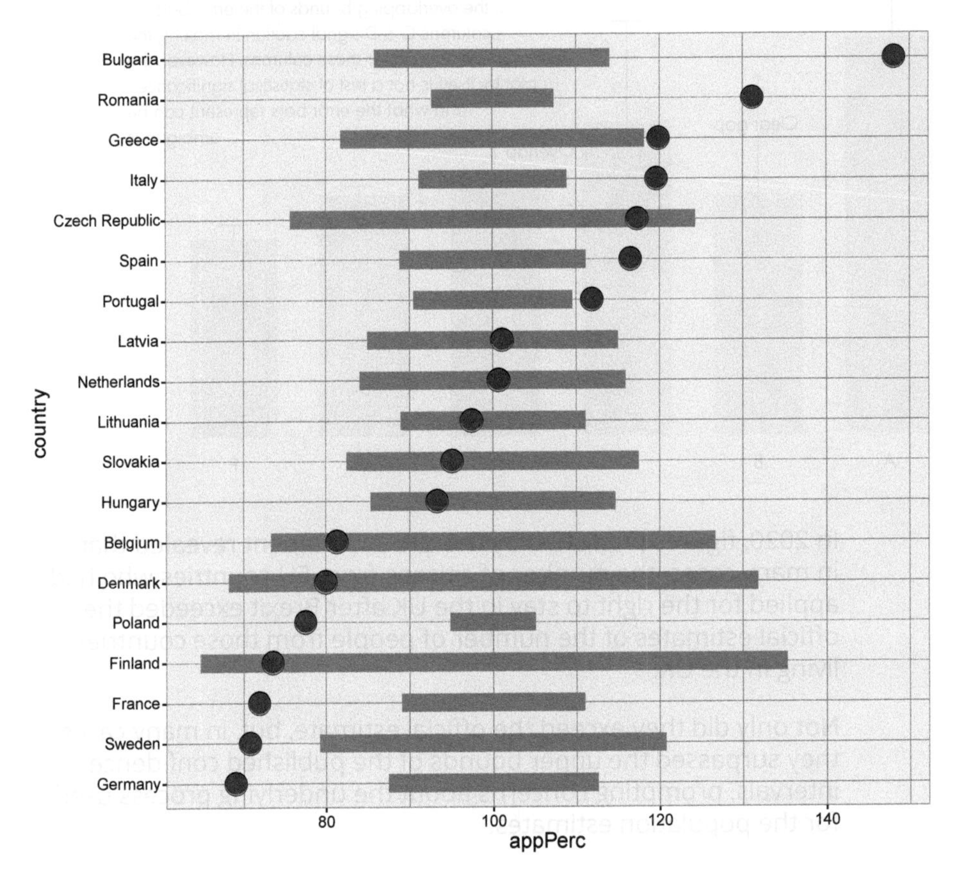

Source: EU settled

Notice that:

- The confidence intervals are always symmetrical – they extend the same amount either side of 100 per cent (the published value).
- The confidence intervals vary in size – because some country estimates are subject to more variation than others.

Turning a draft plot into a finished graphic involved a few key design decisions, the most noticeable of which is gradient treatment on the confidence intervals (or the "smudge of uncertainty", as one reader described it).

On a general level, I think the gradient is more suggestive, visually, of uncertainty than a conventional error bar. Without requiring readers to understand the nuances of statistical estimation techniques, it simply *looks* like we are presenting something that is uncertain.

I think the gradient also shows a "decay from plausibility" the further away you travel from the official estimate. So, in the case of the Czech Republic, the number of applications might not quite exceed the upper bounds, but we can see it's flirting with it.

UK's settled status scheme casts doubt on official population figures

Total applications for EUSS* as a % of official estimate of UK population by nationality**

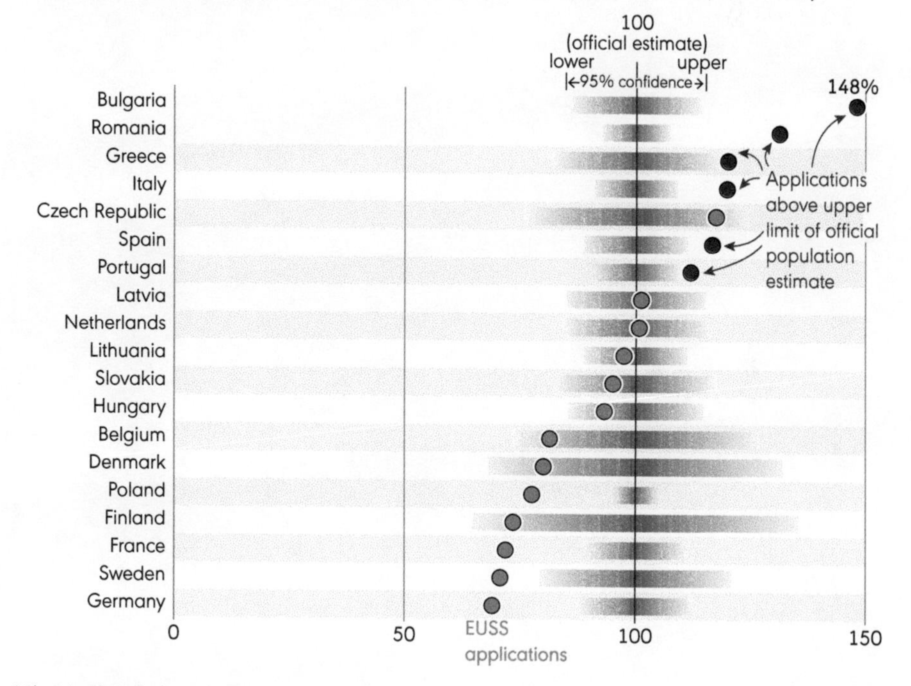

* Since testing of scheme began on 28 August 2018 through to 31 May 2020
** Population estimates are for January 2019 to December 2019
Graphic: Alan Smith
Source: EU settled status applicants exceed official tally by Andy Bounds in Manchester and Bethan Staton in London, July 7, 2020. Available at: https://www.ft.com/content/a611c7ae-8276-4e42-8e63-0b68e3b90f9f

Other design elements of this chart – the active title, a saturated, mid-lightness highlight colour for the countries that exceed the upper bounds, explanatory annotation – should now be familiar, and serve to reinforce many of the design themes we have seen elsewhere in this part of the book.

The finished graphic was a process of evolution from the initial plot. Along the way, I switched software packages (from "R" to Adobe Illustrator) and sought the valued opinion of my colleagues Steve Bernard and John Burn-Murdoch. It's always a good idea to socialise design decisions like this so you can present your final graphic with a little more confidence that what you *think* you can see, readers will be able to see too.

18

Using the *FT* Visual Vocabulary in your own organisation

The *FT* Visual Vocabulary was created to support the needs of journalists analysing data and creating charts at pace.

But its potential use extends well beyond a busy newsroom, which is one of the reasons behind our decision to make it freely downloadable as a pdf file.

The real power of the Visual Vocabulary lies in adapting it to use as a vocabulary for your own work environment. This might involve changing the number and variety of charts on it to your own audience or considering how best to use it as part of your own data strategy.

I spoke with two users of the Visual Vocabulary working in very different work environments to find out more about how it's been useful to them.

The business analyst

Richard Speigal paints a picture that would be familiar to many in the data-driven world of BI (business intelligence): a central team of analysts struggling to cope with the demands of customers from across the business, many of whom are unable to articulate their information needs.

"A huge gap" is how he describes the situation at the Nationwide Building Society (NBS, one of the world's largest cooperative financial institutions), before a concerted effort to move to a "spoke and hub" model aimed at empowering teams across the business from a BI centre of excellence, which he now leads.

Central to the new strategy is the "NBS Visual Vocabulary", an adaptation of the *Financial Times*' original into an interactive workbook using their own corporate business analytics software.

A long-standing fan of the *FT* Visual Vocabulary and its wide range of charts, the NBS version started off as a training challenge for Speigal's team – "How many of these could we build in Qlik?"

As it turned out, the answer was virtually all of them "we surprised ourselves", he freely admits. But the nascent ""BS Visual Vocabulary" soon turned into something more than a training exercise.

A collaboration with the NBS' internal designers – not a traditional partner for the BI team – produced both a corporate look and some extra functionality: "We previously didn't have a categorical colour palette, so they designed one for us, helping us with issues like contrast."

The team started to take the slick new Qlik Sense app with them on their journeys around the business. As a result, it is now in daily use across NBS, by both business users and developers.

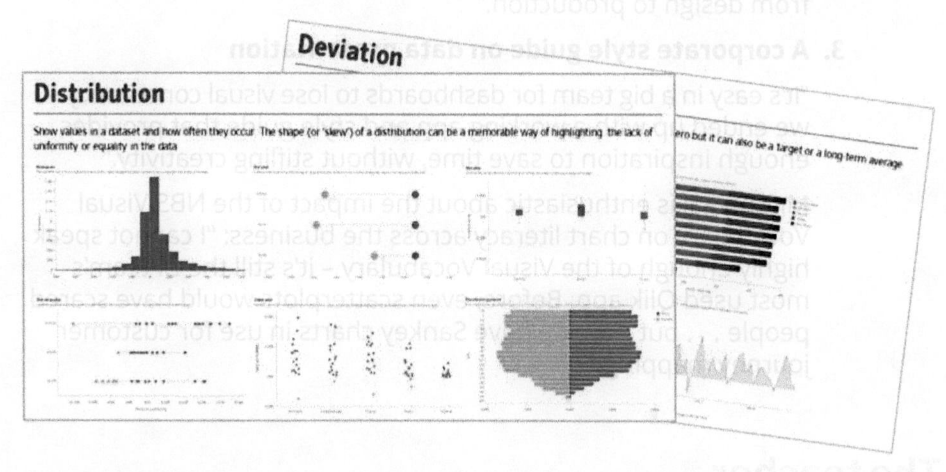

Source: Richard Speigal; Nationwide Building Society. Used by permission from Richard Speigal

Discussing the impact that the NBS Visual Vocabulary has had on his team and the broader business, Speigal identifies three key areas:

1. **Better business conversations**

   "It has completely changed the quality of the conversation of the BI team with the business."

   Working with other teams no longer centres on a formal process of building lengthy statements of requirements. Instead, discussions are social, rapid and iterative, with the NBS Visual Vocabulary at the heart of the conversation.

Analysts and business users regularly meet around the Visual Vocabulary during the design phase, instantly creating an open discussion on the pros and cons of different ways to present data – "I didn't know a dashboard could look like this!" is a frequent comment from business users.

2. **A practical "How to" for developers**

   "The app became a practical learning guide for developers – now, when they see a chart they like, they can quickly look behind the design to see how it was built and implement their own version. It's another simple daily timesaver that helps us move faster from design to production."

3. **A corporate style guide on data presentation**

   "It's easy in a big team for dashboards to lose visual consistency – we ended up with a working app and style guide that provides enough inspiration to save time, without stifling creativity."

   Mr Speigal is enthusiastic about the impact of the NBS Visual Vocabulary on chart literacy across the business: "I cannot speak highly enough of the Visual Vocabulary – it's still the BI team's most used Qlik app. Before, even scatterplots would have scared people . . . but now we have Sankey charts in use for customer journey mapping."

The teacher

Alasdair Monteith is a teacher of geography at Gordonstoun in Moray, Scotland, one of the UK's leading independent schools. For Monteith, the Visual Vocabulary plays a part in developing student data literacy and critical thinking, a topic about which he is passionate.

"The *FT* Visual Vocabulary is great because it shows a greater range of techniques than have been covered in the past. [Geography] textbooks will go to the classic proportional circles, there'll be some spatial data in there, there'll be scatter graphs, there'll be line graphs, but to see the full range of different infographics that can be produced really helps."

As well as an active user of the Visual Vocabulary, he also regularly contributes lesson plans to the *FT for Schools* program, which offers free online subscriptions to students and their teachers in schools around the world.

Based on *FT* stories, the lesson plans cover a wide range of themes, from pollution to migration, political instability to global health. This is in line with Mr Monteith's mission to change the perception of geography from "Oxbow lakes and lists of capital cities" to something more aligned with mathematics in explaining the science behind a rapidly changing world.

But why is using news stories as a source of lesson plans so important? It's all to do with the pace of change: "We use a course textbook that was printed in 2016 – at the end of Obama's final term. Since then, Trump has been and gone and we've had the pandemic."

By way of example, one of Monteith's lesson plans is based on the *FT*'s "Covid-19: the global crisis – in data" story[10], an analysis of the first six months of the global pandemic. Among other tasks, he encourages students to question how different datasets are presented in the story:

> *"What alternative methods of data presentation, apart from the choropleth map, could be used to project the data on Italy's outbreak?"*

Monteith also pushes students to think about quantifying the patterns shown in charts using statistical techniques:

> *"With the scatterplot chart showing places that were hardest hit across Europe in the Spring and Autumn, what statistical test could be carried out to assess the strength of correlation between the spring and summer data?"*

As the questions suggest, Monteith sees "visual-first" stories as a good way of encouraging a broader range of students to improve their analysis and interpretation skills. And he sees definite signs of progress: "Today, I think students are getting better . . . they are presented with far more data and they are more aware of it."

[10] Available at: https://ig.ft.com/coronavirus-global-data/.

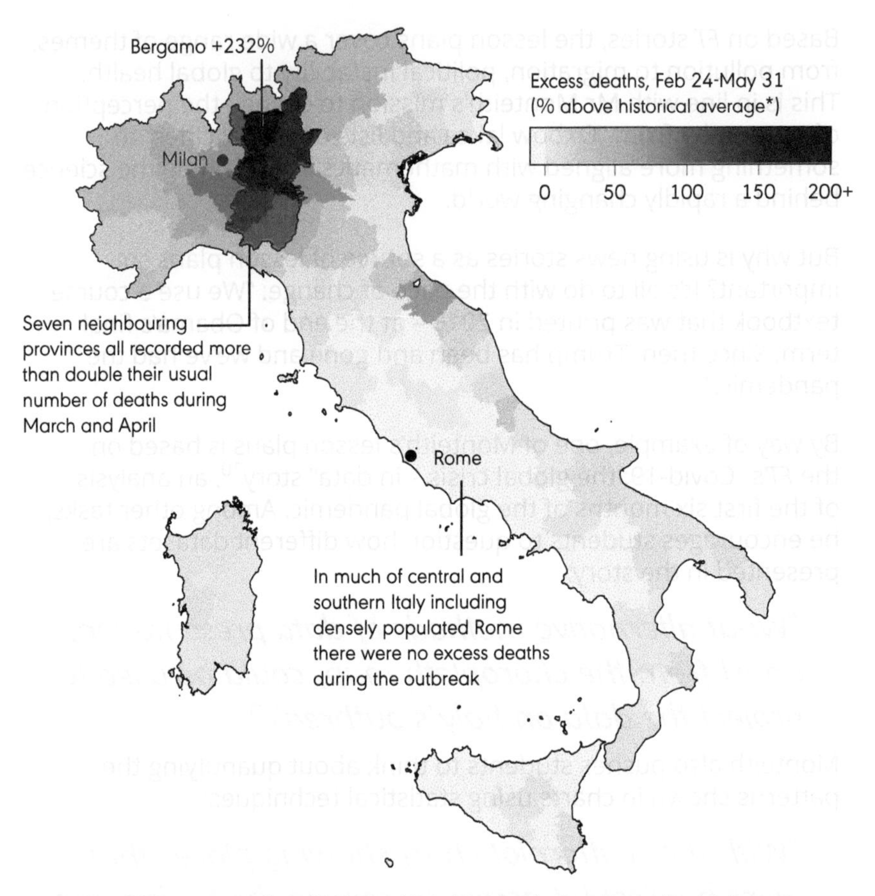
Bergamo +232%
Excess deaths, Feb 24-May 31
(% above historical average*)
0
50
100
150
200+
Milan
Seven neighbouring provinces all recorded more than double their usual number of deaths during March and April
Rome
In much of central and southern Italy including densely populated Rome there were no excess deaths during the outbreak

Source: Financial Times appeared in Covid-19: The global crisis — in data. Available at: https://ig.ft.com/coronavirus-global-data/

However, he warns that increased exposure to data creates a potential overload problem for students: "They need to become better at analysing and interrogating what they see."

He sees resources like the Visual Vocabulary as a useful aid for students to decode the visual language of statistics. And, importantly, it's not just the students that have some learning ahead of them: "As a profession, we still have a long wait to go . . . we've got to get better as teachers in improving our understanding of different ways presenting data."

This is an important goal which the *Financial Times* is happy to support – the FT4Schools project and the Royal Geographical Society have worked together to provide printed copies of the Visual Vocabulary to thousands of UK secondary schools, meaning students and teachers alike can learn and discuss data presentation methods in classrooms across the country.

Software tools

The Visual Vocabulary is a humble analogue device – it's just a poster. This was a very deliberate decision.

I had been making charts long enough to realise that data visualisation enthusiasts are prone to the allure of the latest software tools, rarely questioning whether novelty leads to genuinely better results.

Starting with a particular piece of software involves tacitly accepting its strengths and weaknesses. To put it bluntly, I wasn't happy about starting my organisation's data visualisation strategy from the perspective of "what does the software allow us to do?".

I also felt a poster could help socialise chart design, too often a solitary activity. Free from requiring the know-how of a particular piece of software, people could sit or stand in front of the Visual Vocabulary and simply concentrate on discussing the patterns in data they wanted to show.

That was certainly what generated an initial buzz while using it in the newsroom – the barriers to using it were very low. As an educational tool, it was a great starting point.

There was just one slight problem: as healthy as all this conversation about charts was, we would have to make some.

Making charts in the FT newsroom

Our starting point was not promising. One surprise for me when I arrived in the *FT* newsroom in September 2015 was the discovery that the default software used for creating and publishing charts on the website and in the newspaper was at least 25 years old – the software equivalent of geological eras!

Moreover, the visualisation options in this tool were extremely conservative. The line, bar and pie charts inside the original *FT* underpants graphic featured earlier this book had been created using this software. We needed to move quickly and break the link with the *FT*'s "chartjunk" past.

At the time, off-the-shelf software solutions lacked the flexibility we needed to produce charts from the Visual Vocabulary. Instead, we turned to the open-source data visualisation toolkit "D3".

Created by industry legend Mike Bostock, D3 stands for "Data-Driven Documents". It is a programming library that requires the user to write code (using JavaScript, a ubiquitous programming language of the web). D3 code can generate high-quality, fully customised, animated and interactive graphics from spreadsheet files.

The main advantage of this approach is complete flexibility – there are few constraints placed upon you in terms of what you can and can't produce.

The drawback for widespread adoption across an organisation is D3's high barrier to entry– you need to be able to write code to use it. This represented a problem in our newsroom where only a small portion of our chart makers could code.

Together with colleagues Bob Haslett and Steve Bernard, under the tutelage of senior developer Tom Pearson, we solved the problem by creating a library of D3 *templates*, which required only a little code for others to reuse. Styled for both online and print, these templates closely mirrored the Visual Vocabulary poster, giving us the means to create a much wider range of graphics with little penalty in terms of speed or quality.

Learning point – Use the FT's code!

You can find a working version of our original D3 Visual Vocabulary templates on the code-sharing website GitHub[11].

Each folder in the library represents a different chart type, complete with sample dataset. Running the code creates the graphic; changing chart content (data, titles, annotations) and settings (such as print sizes) is achieved with simple edits to the code.

We soon had a new approach to creating charts, based on the Visual Vocabulary, for both online and print workflows.

The new D3 library represented a major step forward. With just a little training, anyone in the Visual and Data journalism team could now create charts from the Visual Vocabulary. It transformed our ability to create graphics at pace – useful when you need to create

[11] https://github.com/ft-interactive/visual-vocabulary.

Alan Smith
@theboysmithy

A structural shift? Yes, moving to printed pages with visualisations composed entirely in #d3...

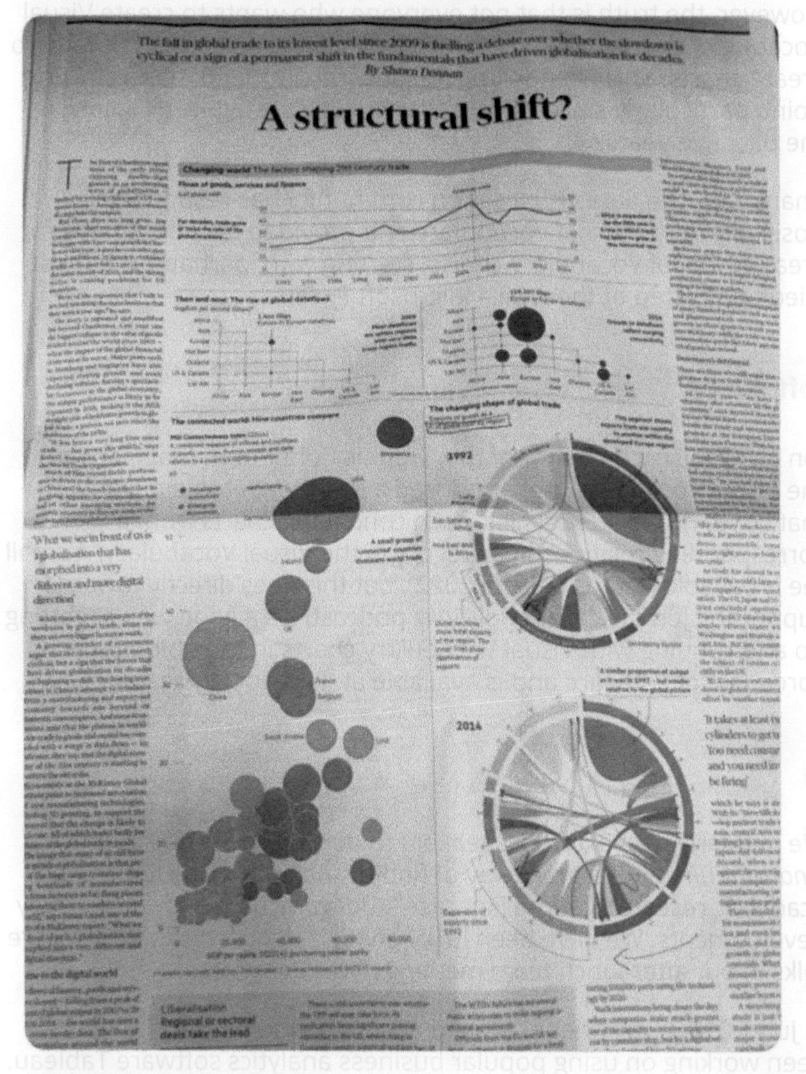

3:59 PM · Mar 3, 2016 · OS X

View Tweet analytics

108 Retweets **1** Quote Tweet **198** Likes

Source: *Financial Times*, https://twitter.com/theboysmithy/status/705422287323975680

100+ custom charts in a few hours after the Chancellor's budget statement!

Our library of D3 code has evolved over the years and it continues to play a role in *FT* data visualisations.

However, the truth is that not everyone who wants to create Visual Vocabulary charts is going to want to write or run computer code to create charts. So, I wouldn't necessarily recommend it as a starting point, particularly since visualisation tools have evolved rapidly in the past five years.

Thankfully, the data visualisation community has responded positively to the Visual Vocabulary and provided *a lot* of options for creating Visual Vocabulary charts, starting with, perhaps, the most tried and tested of them all – Microsoft Excel.

Microsoft Excel

Jon Schwabish, co-creator of the Graphic Continuum that inspired the Visual Vocabulary, has produced a downloadable .zip file that contains eight Excel files, each containing charts from a corresponding relationship category in the Visual Vocabulary. A small fee is payable ($10 as of April 2022), but this goes directly towards supporting Jon's excellent PolicyViz podcast. It's a good way of getting up and running with Visual Vocabulary charts in the ubiquitous spreadsheet software and is available at: www.policyviz.com[12].

Tableau

We regularly host external speakers to our team meeting at the *Financial Times*. It's a great way of finding inspiration, be it the latest academic research, journalism case studies, visual art, or technology developments. We have been lucky enough to host many TED-calibre talks in our after-lunch team meetings over the years.

In July 2018, Andy Kriebel arrived to show us something he had been working on using popular business analytics software Tableau.

Andy is a legend in the Tableau user community – a member of the "Zen Master Hall of Fame", no less. We were intrigued to see what he had been working on. But we still weren't quite

[12] https://policyviz.com/product/visual-vocabulary-in-excel/.

prepared for what Andy showed us that day – a complete working implementation of the Visual Vocabulary in Tableau!

He explained to us that his original goal in undertaking the challenge was to use Tableau to produce chart types he had never attempted before – these included violin plots, Sankey diagrams and circle timelines.

Andy has generously made his Tableau version public, with the intention for others to learn in the same way that he did while making it. You can see Andy explain more about this project on YouTube[13].

If you are a Tableau user, it's your gateway to the Visual Vocabulary. And, inspired by Andy's work, users of other software packages have produced their own versions of the Visual Vocabulary in other software packages[14].

Power BI

Jason Thomas – aka SqlJason – has produced a version of the Visual Vocabulary for Power BI, Microsoft's visualisation and business intelligence product aimed at fans of data dashboards[15].

Qlik

We've already seen the version of the Visual Vocabulary Richard Speigal developed for the Nationwide Building Society. An alternative version from Qlik's own Patric Nordstrom doesn't use any extensions[16].

Vega

Vega is a lightweight declarative programming language for creating, saving and sharing interactive visualisation designs.

13 https://www.youtube.com/watch?v=5M-0e9t_lRM.

14 Available at: https://www.tableau.com/solutions/gallery/visual-vocabulary.

15 Available at: http://sqljason.com/2018/12/financial-times-visual-vocabularypower-bi-edition.html.

16 Available at: https://community.qlik.com/t5/Qlik-Sense-Documents/FT-Visual-Vocabulary-Qlik-Sense-version/ ta-p/1764785.

Data scientist Pratap Vardhan has created a Visual Vocabulary implementation for Vega with over 70 charts. Pratap is one of many who cites Andy Kriebel's work in Tableau as the inspiration for building his version[17].

The R Project for Statistical Computing

R is a free programming environment for statistical analysis and visualisation, with an enormous worldwide community of users.

The Trafford Data Lab, a team within Trafford Council in Greater Manchester, England, has produced a graphics companion for ggplot2, R's popular data visualisation package, based on "the structure of the *FT* Visual Vocabulary"[18].

Flourish

Flourish is a web-based tool that allows non-coders to produce sophisticated interactive charts. A Flourish support article provides guidance on choosing the right charts to make in Flourish using the Visual Vocabulary's categories as a starting point[19].

One thing we are not short of in the world is chart-making software. There are simply hundreds of different packages to choose from and it really isn't the purpose of this book to help (or force) you to choose one.

And, of course, software will continue to evolve and develop in the years ahead. My sincere hope is that the Visual Vocabulary's independence from content creation tools will ensure its continued relevance, making it a reference resource of lasting value for those creating their own data visualisation strategies.

[17] Available at: https://www.pratapvardhan.com/blog/ft-visual-vocabulary-vega/.

[18] Available at: https://www.trafforddatalab.io/graphics_companion/.

[19] Available at: https://flourish.studio/2018/09/28/choosing-the-right-visualisation/.

Index

Publisher's Acknowledgement

3 National Archives of Ireland: Data from Central Statistics Office/1911 Census; **7 William Playfair:** Quote by William Playfair; **13 and 14 Florence Nightingale:** Quote by Florence Nightingale; **8 Financial Times Limited:** How to view all FT graphics in one place, Available at: https://www.ft.com/content/6e76757e-e1d8-11e8-a6e5-792428919cee; **9 Graphics Press LLC:** Edward Tufte, Envisioning Information Graphics Press, 1990; **10 Financial Times Limited:** Referendum results: Press Association EU trade research: John Springford, Philip McCann, Bart Los and Mark Thissen. Graphic by John Burn-Murdoch/@jburnmurdoch appeared in https://twitter.com/ft/status/746275255354818561. Used by permission from The Financial Times Limited; **12 Financial Times Limited:** Referendum results: Press Association; EU trade research done by John Springford, Philip McCann, Bart Los and Mark Thissen. Graphic by John Burn-Murdoch / @jburnmurdoch appeared in "Regions with the biggest votes for Leave are also the most economically dependent on the EU". Available at: https://www.ft.com/content/1ce1a720-ce94-3c32-a689-8d2356388a1f. Used by permission from The Financial Times Limited; **13 John Simon:** Quote by John Simon; **13 Walter de Gruyter GmbH:** William Playfair, Introduction to the Commercial and Political Atlas, 1801; **22-23 Financial Times Limited:** Chris Campbell; Ian Bott; Liz Faunce; Graham Parrish; Billy Ehrenberg-Shannon; Paul McCallum; Martin Stabe Inspired by the Graphic Continumm by Jon Schwabish and Severino Ribecca appeared in "Charts that work: FT visual vocabulary guide", March 8, 2021. Available at: https://www.ft.com/content/c7bb24c9-964d-479f-ba24-03a2b2df6e85. Used by permission from The Financial Times Limited; **26-27 and 28 Jonathan Schwabish:** Used by permissions from Jonathan Schwabish, PolicyViz; **31 and 32 Alan Smith:** Data from Worldatlas.com. Used by permission from Alan

Smith; **32 Financial Times Limited:** No authoritative central database of K2 statistics exists, these figures have been compiled from Eberhard Jurgalski/8000ers.com, Alan Arnette and expedition reports. Graphic: Chris Campbell, Source: Data from Himalayandatabase.com appeared in "Triumph and tragedy on K2". Available at: https://www.ft.com/content/b6340707-25c4-4b01-9747-ad44f0bef50b. Used by permission from The Financial Times Limited; **33 Financial Times Limited:** Goldman Sachs appeared in Aziza Kasumov, "Wall Street braces itself for tax rises from Biden's new stimulus plan", April 5, 2021. Available at: https://www.ft.com/stream/2abbd410-644b-4073-a5ab-dbf9b2ab2c43; **34 Xaquín Veira González:** Xaquín Veira González; **34 Harvard Business School Publishing:** The Power of Visualization's "Aha!" Moments, by Scott Berinato Harvard Business Review. March 19, 2013; **34 Ed Conway:** Quote by Ed Conway; **36, 37 and 41 Alan Smith:** Data from Nimmo et al (2017); Emilio et al (2012); Seidelmann et al (2007); Wikipedia. Used by permission from Alan Smith; **38 Library of Congress:** [The Georgia Negro] City and rural population. 1890. WEB Du Bois (Plate 11); **39 World Publishing Company:** Chart from the British Empire Universities Modern English Dictionary (1912); **40 Financial Times Limited:** Data from State of California Department of Motor Vehicles. Graphic: John Burn-Murdoch appeared in Richard Waters, "Waymo builds big lead in self-driving car testing", February 24, 2019. Available at: https://www.ft.com/content/7c8e1d02-2ff2-11e9-8744-e7016697f225; **43 Financial Times Limited:** Graphic: Liz Faunce, Sources: Data from University of Maryland; CDC; WHO; Johns Hopkins appeared in "From plague to polio: how do pandemics end?" Available at: https://www.ft.com/content/4eabdc7a-f8e1-48d5-9592-05441493f652; **44 Financial Times Limited:** Data from Environmental Research Letters appeared in "Vegans vs vehicles: 50 shades of green", November 16, 2018. Available at: https://www.ft.com/content/31d40402-e998-11e8-a34c-663b3f553b35; **45 Financial Times Limited:** "Capital IQ appeared in Chris Nuttall, Tech prospers in the pandemic", June 19, 2020. Available at: https://www.ft.com/content/a157d303-01ac-4a9b-af2d-d6ffbc3593c2; **46 Financial Times Limited:** FT research, taxhistory.org, figures rounded to nearest 250,000 appeared in Gary Silverman, "Hillary and Bill Clinton: The for-profit partnership", July 21, 2016. Available at: https://www.ft.com/content/83878190-4b64-11e6-88c5-db83e98a590a; **47 Otto Neurath:** "Modern Man in the Making" by Otto Neurath. Available at: https://archive.org/details/ModernManInTheMaking/page/n19/mode/2up; **49 and 50 Financial Times Limited:** "Summer 2020 Global Attitudes Survey appeared in Climate change and disease at forefront of global anxieties" by Alan Smith April 2, 2021. Available at: https://www.ft.com/content/f19afda4-d848-45ae-aebf-6c3e30737c8e; **51 and 52 Financial Times Limited:** Graphic: Paul McCallum, Sources: FT research; Dreamstime appeared in Hugh Carnegy, "Wish I were there: the glory of California's redwoods", October 21, 2020. Available at: https://www.ft.com/content/0cd7146c-374a-4240-8a02-

a5b3fabd98d0; **53 Financial Times Limited:** Graphic: Graham Parrish, Sources: MIT; FT research appeared in Michael Peel, "Lifesaver or false protection: do face masks stop coronavirus?" April 3, 2020. Available at: https://www.ft.com/content/64ac8848-a005-466a-bc93-fb1e38b19182; **56 William Playfair:** William Playfair introduced line charts to the world in The Commercial and Political Atlas (1786); **57 Financial Times Limited:** IFS appeared in Tories seek wriggle room on spending as Hammond sticks to austerity by Gemma Tetlow, Jim Pickard and George Parker, June 21, 2017. Available at: https://www.ft.com/content/5d94202c-55c9-11e7-80b6-9bfa4c1f83d2; **58 Financial Times Limited:** Graphic by Alan Smith, Chris Giles, Source: IMF appeared in Chris Giles, "The UK economy since the Brexit vote — in 6 charts", October 11, 2018. Available at: https://www.ft.com/content/cf51e840-7147-11e7-93ff-99f383b09ff9; **59 Financial Times Limited:** OBR; FT calculations appeared in Chris Giles, "Chancellor navigates fragile UK public finances", March 2, 2021. Available at: https://www.ft.com/content/0e48c8ab-e3b4-404f-8776-d9a42df27ce1; **60 and 61 Alan Smith:** Data from ONS. Used by permission from Alan Smith; **62 Financial Times Limited:** IHS Markit appearead in Adapted from "UK services activity grows at fastest pace in over six years" by Valentina Romei. Available at: https://www.ft.com/content/b254833a-27c9-482c-8492-4b63571e57ee#o-topper; **62 Financial Times Limited:** BofA Global Investment Strategy; Bloomberg appeared in Eva Szalay, "Bitcoin's wild ride leaves traditional money managers queasy", January 13, 2021. Available at: https://www.ft.com/content/0746e3c6-9177-4fcd-91bb-e427aa9f9267; **63 Financial Times Limited:** Vaclav Simil, "Energy Transitions appeared in Bill Gates, Bill Gates: My green manifesto", February 19, 2021. Available at -https://www.ft.com/content/c11bb885-1274-4677-ba05-fcbac67dc808; **64 Financial Times Limited:** OBR; ONS appeared in Gordon Smith, Jennifer Creery and Emily Goldberg, "FirstFT: Today's top stories", November 26, 2020. Available at: https://www.ft.com/content/825c7489-8f9b-4230-b326-97eb6b70f995; **65 Financial Times Limited:** Bank of England appeared in Delphine Strauss, "Why the UK inflation risk after lockdown is hard to assess", March 15, 2021. Available at: https://www.ft.com/content/6925a0bb-f233-4a86-8556-6d03dee23dc0; **66 Financial Times Limited:** EFF; Wikipedia; DeepMind appeared in Tim Harford, "A year in charts: From bitcoin to Trump and chess playing robots", December 18, 2017. Available at: https://www.ft.com/content/7020a6e4-e4e3-11e7-8b99-0191e45377ec; **67 and 68 Financial Times Limited:** US Treasury appeared in Alan Smith, "Sonification: turning the yield curve into music", March 15, 2019. Available at: https://www.ft.com/content/80269930-40c3-11e9-b896-fe36ec32aece; **69 Financial Times Limited:** FT research appeared in Patrick Mathurin, "Premier League shirt sponsorship shifts with the times", August 11, 2018. Available at: https://www.ft.com/content/61f3c8fc-9c86-11e8-9702-5946bae86e6d; **70 Financial Times Limited:** FT Coronavirus tracker ft.com/covid19 appeared in Benjamin Parkin, "Jyotsna Singh and Stephanie Findlay,

India's devastating second wave: 'It is much worse this time'", April 21, 2021. Available at: https://www.ft.com/content/683914a3-134f-40b6-989b-21e0ba1dc403; **71 Alan Smith:** Data from Statistical Annex, UIS, 2011. Used by permission from Alan Smith; **73 Financial Times Limited:** FT visual journalism: Chris Campbell and Patrick Mathurin, Sources: Box Office Mojo; IMDB; FT research appeared in Alex Barker, "The Unhinged bet to jump-start the movie business", June 16, 2020. Available at: https://www.ft.com/content/e68ec86c-cfe8-4d54-996d-da876b4a285c; **74 Financial Times Limited:** Bloomberg appeared in "Apple slides into a correction after iPhone sales disappoint". Available at: https://www.ft.com/content/f1c3e2e0-0853-11e8-9650-9c0ad2d7c5b5; **75 Financial Times Limited:** Wood Mackenzie appeared in "The new North Sea players riding the wake of the retreating majors". Available at: https://www.ft.com/content/93d5f778-833c-4553-ae29-785e3aa3d4d3; **76 Financial Times Limited:** Graphic by Billy Ehrenberg-Shannon, Source: Energy Information Administration, Baker Hughes, a GE Company appeared in "Boom times for US shale oil producers". Available at: https://www.ft.com/content/2c7f6a38-1d37-11e8-956a-43db76e69936; **77 Joseph Priestley:** T.Priestley L.L.D A Chart of Biography (1765), of which a 'specimen' (teaser); **78 Financial Times Limited:** Kinsella and Gist (1995), "US Census Bureau appeared in Emerging countries to account for 80% of world's elderly". Available at: https://www.ft.com/content/19d3879e-1dc9-11e6-b286-cddde55ca122#axzz49U39mTT8; **79 Financial Times Limited:** Kinsella and Gist (1995), "US Census Bureau appeared in Communicating with data – timelines". Available at: https://www.ft.com/content/6f777c84-322b-11e6-ad39-3fee5ffe5b5b. Used by permission from The Financial Times Limited; **79 Joseph Priestley:** Quote by Priestley; **80 Financial Times Limited:** FT research appeared in "Premier League shirt sponsorship shifts with the times". Available at: https://www.ft.com/content/61f3c8fc-9c86-11e8-9702-5946bae86e6d; **80 Financial Times Limited:** Digest of UK Energy Statistics, 2020 appeared in "UK coal mine plan pits local needs against global green ambitions". Available at: https://www.ft.com/content/0e731ce2-1f45-4f50-bcb2-729467156d75; **81 Financial Times Limited:** University of Adelaide Wine Economics Research Centre appeared in "UK wine drinkers face higher prices as Brexit hangover kicks in". Available at: https://www.ft.com/content/2747ddf8-7f6c-4b34-9e40-36d6c4178203; **82 Smith Elder & Co.:** Florence Nightingale's polar area diagrams 1858; **89 and 90 Financial Times Limited:** Federal Returning Officer. Graphic: John Burn-Murdoch / @jburnmurdoch appeared in "Germany's election and the trouble with correlation". Available at: https://www.ft.com/content/94e3acec-a767-11e7-ab55-27219df83c97; **91, 92 and 93 Financial Times Limited:** Gapminder (includes data based on World Bank, Maddison Lindgren, IMF and others) appeared in "The storytelling genius of unveiling truths through charts" by Alan Smith, February 10, 2017. Available at: https://www.ft.com/content/e2eba288-ef83-11e6-930f-061b01e23655; **94 and 95 Financial Times**

Limited: FT graphic: Alan Smith/Laura Noonan, Sources: Companies, FT research appeared in "Women still miss out on management in finance" by Laura Noonan, Alan Smith, David Blood and Martin Stabe April 4, 2017. Used by permission from The Financial Times Limited. Available at: https://ig.ft.com/managements-missing-women-data/; **96 Financial Times Limited:** United Nations Population Division, OECD appeared in "The huge disparities in US life expectancy in five charts". Available at: https://www.ft.com/content/80a76f38-e3be-11e6-8405-9e5580d6e5fb; **97 Financial Times Limited:** Federal Reserve distributional financial accounts. FT graphic: Aleksandra Wisniewska appeared in "The Recessionals: why coronavirus is another cruel setback for millennials". Available at: https://www.ft.com/content/241f0fe4-08f8-4d42-a268-4f0a399a0063; **98 Financial Times Limited:** FT graphic: Chelsea Bruce-Lockhart; Chris Campbell, Source: World Health Organization appeared in "In charts: Healthcare apps target tech-savvy youth". Available at: https://www.ft.com/content/7aba9066-dffe-4829-a1cd-1d557b963a82; **99 Financial Times Limited:** Winton Centre for Risk and Evidence Communication appeared in "Why we shouldn't worry about Covid vaccine blood clots". Available at: https://www.ft.com/content/090f1b3c-95d9-4b10-9a7c-ba3a7f290fee; **100 Financial Times Limited:** Winton Centre for Risk and Evidence Communication appeared in "Experts back UK age limit for rollout of AstraZeneca vaccine". Available at: https://www.ft.com/content/5db4a13f-11b1-4f1e-891b-9f68c639a6f9; **101 Financial Times Limited:** CME Group appeared in "Netscape 2.0: Coinbase stock debut rekindles memories of web breakthrough". Available at: https://www.ft.com/content/cbd46d95-6866-4c32-b7af-51b1772e388d; **101 Hans Rosling:** Quote by Hans Rosling; **103 Bernie Sanders:** Quote by Bernie Sanders; **104, 105, 106 and 107 Financial Times Limited:** Data from Pew Research Center appeared in Sam Fleming and Shawn Donnan, "America's Middle-class Meltdown: Core shrinks to half of US homes", December 10, 2015. Available at: https://www.ft.com/content/98ce14ee-99a6-11e5-95c7-d47aa298f769; **111 Financial Times Limited:** UN appeared in Alan Smith, "Tomorrow's world in charts: Gen Z, climate change, China, Brexit and global trade", December 16, 2020. Available at: https://www.ft.com/content/af4631f3-fed3-476c-b9c0-bd460a930a48; **113 Financial Times Limited:** Jambeck Research Group: Report 'Plastic waste inputs from land into the ocean, (2015)' appeared in "Consumer goods groups join war on plastic" by John Aglionby in Nairobi, Anna Nicolaou in New York and Scheherazade Daneshkhu in London January 22, 2018. Available at: https://www.ft.com/content/61629224-fc9f-11e7-9b32-d7d59aace167; **115 Financial Times Limited:** Graphic: Joanna S Kao, Sources: The Broadway League, FT Research appeared in "Tony winner Oslo set for ticket sales boost". Used by permission from The Financial Times Limited. Available at: https://www.ft.com/content/e864eb26-4e00-11e7-bfb8-997009366969; **115 Financial Times Limited:** Britain Elects appeared in Based on "Boris Johnson's levelling-up agenda takes toll on southern Tories" by George Parker. Available at: https://www.ft.com/content/273c58af-6d3e-4c36-b4a5-4f4e7d941875; **117 Financial Times Limited:** Britain Elects appeared in George Parker, "Boris Johnson's levelling-up agenda takes toll on southern Tories", May 14, 2021. Available at: https://www.ft.com/content/273c58af-6d3e-4c36-b4a5-4f4e7d941875; **118 Financial Times Limited:** Graphic: Steven Bernard, Sources: Plume Labs; Defra; FT research appeared in Leslie Hook, Neil Munshi, "How safe is the air we breathe?" September 5, 2019. Available at: https://www.ft.com/content/7d54cfb8-cea5-11e9-b018-ca4456540ea6; **119 Financial Times Limited:** 'Fashion Transparency Index appeared in How Boohoo came to rule the roost in Leicester's underground textile trade' by Robert Wright in Leicester and Patricia Nilsson in London, July 11, 2020. Available at: https://www.ft.com/content/bbe5dfc5-3b5c-41d2-9637-50e91c58b26b; **120 Financial Times Limited:** Graphic: Liz Faunce, Helena Robertson, Sources: Companies, FT research appeared in 'Executives optimistic on improving gender diversity' by Laura Noonan, Oliver Ralph and Jennifer Thompson, September 10, 2018. Available at: https://www.ft.com/content/80200a46-b27c-11e8-8d14-6f049d06439c; **121 Max Otto Lorenz:** Quote by Max Otto Lorenz; **122 Financial Times Limited:** Medical Expenditure Panel Survey (Nov 2016) appeared in "The huge disparities in US life expectancy in five charts". Available at: https://www.ft.com/content/80a76f38-e3be-11e6-8405-9e5580d6e5fb; **127, 128, 129, 130, 131, 133 and 134 Financial Times Limited:** Refinitiv appeared in Arash Massoudi, "M&A boom set to continue in 2017", December 30, 2016. Available at: https://www.ft.com/content/0e9afdce-cdb6-11e6-b8ce-b9c03770f8b1; **137 Financial Times Limited:** OpinionWay, based on exit polls of 9,010 people conducted in 2017 appeared in Eir Nolsoe and Ella Hollowood, "Emmanuel Macron's election victory over Marine Le Pen in charts", April 25, 2022. Available at: https://www.ft.com/content/f9f5009b-9f67-4d16-920e-22e91449a031; **138 Financial Times Limited:** Department of Health and Social Care. Graphic: Ian Bott appeared in Ian Bott and Clive Cookson, "In graphics: the UK vaccine supply chain", January 30, 2021. Available at: https://www.ft.com/content/8b48a853-5b14-4378-91d4-17026fa15472; **139 Financial Times Limited:** Inspired by a graphic on RCVis.com. Excludes undecided voters, Source: FairVote calculations using WNBC/Telemundo 47/POLITICO/Marist Poll of 876 likely Democratic primary voters. FT Graphic: Christine Zhang / @christinezhang appeared in Gordon Smith, Jennifer Creery and Emily Goldberg, "FirstFT: Today's top stories", June 22, 2021. Available at: https://www.ft.com/content/ebc5fc9d-fa13-4649-bb57-85baf18715c3; **140 Financial Times Limited:** Invisible Institute, George Wood, Daria Roithmayr, Andrew Papachristos appeared in Claire Bushey, "Small share of US police draw third of complaints in big cities", May 28, 2021. Available at: https://www.ft.com/content/141182fc-7727-4af8-a555-5418fa46d09e; **141 Andrew Papachristos:** Quoted by Andrew Papachristos; **144 Financial Times Limited:** Deloitte appeared in Adapted from "Man Utd's financial success belies its on-pitch performance" by Murad Ahmed and Patrick Mathurin January 25, 2019. Available at: https://www.ft.com/content/9d1e5e68-208b-11e9-b126-46fc3ad87c65; **145 Financial Times Limited:** Graphic: Bob Haslett, Patrick Mathurin, Source: Bloomberg appeared in Neil Hume, "How BHP became the UK's biggest listed company", February 13, 2021. Available at: https://www.ft.com/content/2da09da5-3034-4418-9eef-029dbef7fcfe; **148 and 149 Financial Times Limited:** Bank public statements appeared in Joshua Franklin and Imani Moise, "US banks to pay extra $2bn in quarterly dividends", June 29, 2021. Available at: https://www.ft.com/content/1c904432-479c-45b3-84e5-857a06bdadb5; **149 and 150 Financial Times Limited:** University of Oxford appeared in "How to create a durable economic recovery from Covid" by Chris Giles, May 27, 2021. Available at: https://www.ft.com/content/cfb2bd91-6a77-4b5a-8423-b922f6754179; **156 UNESCO:** UIS, 2011, Statistical Table 2 appeared in Universal Primary Education. Available at: https://unesdoc.unesco.org/in/documentViewer.xhtml?v=2.1.196&id=p::usmarcdef_0000221200&file=/in/rest/annotationSVC/DownloadWatermarkedAttachment/attach_import_ee89607b-66bc-45d6-a7fd-; **157, 158, 159 and 160 Financial Times Limited:** UIS, 2011, Statistical Table 2 appeared in 'Data visualisation mistakes — and how to avoid them'. Available at: https://www.ft.com/content/3b59f690-d129-11e7-b781-794ce08b24dc; **162 Financial Times Limited:** Graphic: Steven Bernard, Source: Copernicus ECMWF appeared in Leslie Hook and Steven Bernard, 'Record June heat in North America and Europe linked to climate change", July 9, 2021. Available at: https://www.ft.com/content/f08156a6-c8ac-4c00-94df-2a955dc56da9; **163 Financial Times Limited:** Refinitiv appeared in "Shell: dividend dither sends muddled message", July 7, 2021. Available at: https://www.ft.com/content/209b0ec3-28f4-4d44-bcd9-5a79f33a9c40; **164 and 165 Financial Times Limited:** YouGov, Nov 17, 2020 - Jan 10, 2021 appeared in David Robert Grimes, "How to take on Covid conspiracy theories", February 5, 2021. Used by permission from The Financial Times Limited. Available at: https://www.ft.com/content/6660cb80-8c11-476a-b107-e0193fa975f9; **165 Financial Times Limited:** Graphic: Ian Bott, Source: FT research appeared in "Diplomatic expulsions diminish Russia's reach in Eastern Europe". Available at: https://www.ft.com/content/9476edbf-0ea4-44b9-a27e-0d9bae29cbb7; **168 Alan Smith:** A Year 4 school project; a multi-national corporation. Used by permission from Alan Smith; **170 Financial Times Limited:** FT research appeared in Dan McCrum, "Wirecard's suspect accounting practices revealed", October 15, 2019. Available at: https://www.ft.com/content/19c6be2a-ee67-11e9-bfa4-b25f11f42901; **172 Financial Times Limited:** Data from IFS, HSBC, Nuffield Trust, FT research appeared in "Brexit and the Budget: Hammond pressed to go 'big and bold'" by George Parker and Chris Giles in London November 14, 2017. Available at: https://www.ft.com/content/66f8e992-c85e-11e7-ab18-7a9fb7d6163e; **172 Financial Times Limited:** FT research appeared in

"Greybull stays upbeat despite Monarch collapse". Available at: https://www.ft.com/content/9dbf9aae-a8ea-11e7-93c5-648314d2c72c; **173 and 174 Financial Times Limited:** Company appeared in Philip Stafford and Alex Barker, "Refinitiv deal loses some of its lustre for LSE as challenges mount", June 30, 2021. Available at: https://www.ft.com/content/0c7c6931-9f56-4e43-87cf-91422630a146; **174 and 175 Financial Times Limited:** FT Business Education data appeared in Leo Cremonezi and Sam Stephens, "Charting European business school graduates' progress", December 6, 2000. Available at: https://www.ft.com/content/5d834702-daf5-4fcc-b6a7-52afe043e716; **176 Financial Times Limited:** Tearfund appeared in Camilla Hodgson, "G7 criticised for Covid bailouts with no 'green strings' attached", June 2, 2021. Available at: https://www.ft.com/content/fdae5476-28b8-4a81-96b7-55a660f24558; **178 Financial Times Limited:** How to apply Marimekko to data, https://www.ft.com/content/3ee98782-9149-11e7-a9e6-11d2f0ebb7f0; **179 Financial Times Limited:** Graphic by Alan Smith/ Stephen Foley, Sources: IMF; World Bank appeared in Alan Smith and Stephen Foley, "Bailout costs will be a burden for years", August 8, 2017. Available at: https://www.ft.com/content/b823371a-76e6-11e7-90c0-90a9d1bc9691; **179 Jens Sondergaard:** Quoted by Jens Sondergaard; **179 Sage Publications:** Pepper Culpepper of the European University Institute and Raphael Reinke of the University of Zurich, Structural Power and Bank Bailouts in the United Kingdom and the United States, Sage; **179 Antonio Foglia:** Quoted by Antonio Foglia; **180 Barack Obama:** Former US president Barack Obama; **180 Simon Johnson:** Quoted by Simon Johnson; **184 Financial Times Limited:** Is Manhattan on the edge of a prime housing precipice? By Hugo Cox in London October 10, 2018. Used by permission from The Financial Times Limited. Available at: https://www.ft.com/content/db675edc-c7f2-11e8-86e6-19f5b7134d1; **186 Financial Times Limited:** Federica Cocco, Source: Centers for Disease Control and Prevention appeared in Siona Jenkins, Mercedes Ruehl and Neil Munshi, "Daily briefing: tough sanctions for North Korea, SoFi head steps down, US grapples with opioid addiction", September 12, 2017. Available at https://www.ft.com/content/c787a6a4-96fe-11e7-a652-cde3f882dd7b; **187 Financial Times Limited:** Ministry of Housing, Communities & Local Government appeared in William Wallis, "England in 2019: Split by wealth but united by Brexit", November 30, 2019. Available at: https://www.ft.com/content/b398d284-11dc-11ea-a225-db2f231cfeae; **192 and 266 Office for National Statistics:** Office for National Statistics; **196 Charles Booth:** Map created by Charles Booth (1840-1916); **199 Financial Times Limited:** EU Copernicus programme appeared in Alan Smith, "Wildfires surge during searing Mediterranean heat", August 9, 2021. Available at: https://www.ft.com/content/e31113e1-41ed-4be0-9667-445249a487c4; **201 Financial Times Limited:** Graphic: Caroline Nevitt, Max Harlow, Source: Data from Associated Press appeared in "Biden vs Trump: live results 2020, US presidential election 2020". Used by permission from The Financial Times

Limited. Available at: https://ig.ft.com/us-election-2020; **202 Financial Times Limited:** Graphic: Bob Haslett, Source: Associated Press appeared in Demetri Sevastopulo, Courtney Weaver and Lauren Fedor, "Tight US election reveals Trump's resilience and flaws in Biden campaign", November 4, 2020. Available at: https://www.ft.com/content/1c950b37-7318-467b-9a70-4078e0028fda; **203 Financial Times Limited:** FT Research appeared in "Biden vs Trump: live results 2020, US presidential election 2020". Used by permission from The Financial Times Limited. Available at: https://ig.ft.com/us-election-2020; **204 and 206 Financial Times Limited:** FT research appeared in Alan Smith, "A love of maps should mean using fewer to illustrate data better", October 20, 2016. Available at: https://www.ft.com/content/de3ef722-9514-11e6-a1dc-bdf38d484582; **212, 213, 215 and 217 Financial Times Limited:** The science behind good charts By Cale Tilford, Alan Smith, Caroline Nevitt. January 22, 2019. Available at: https://ig.ft.com/science-of-charts/; **216 Financial Times Limited:** FT analysis of 12,500 reader scores from 2019–20 appeared in "The science behind good charts" By Cale Tilford, Alan Smith, Caroline Nevitt, January 22, 2019. Available at: https://ig.ft.com/science-of-charts/; **219 Robert Kosara:** Quote by Robert Kosara; **222 Google, Inc.:** Screenshot displaying Google search results of Tom Cruise; **222, 223 and 224 Alan Smith:** Google, IMDB. Used by permission from Alan Smith; **226 and 227 Financial Times Limited:** Public Health England appeared in "Crafting charts that can withstand the data deluge" by Alan Smith, January 25, 2016. Available at: https://www.ft.com/content/3f195d40-b851-11e5-b151-8e15c9a029fb; **228 The World Bank Group:** The World Bank appeared in "Data from Proportion of seats held by women in national parliaments (%)", The World Bank. Available at: https://data.worldbank.org/indicator/SG.GEN.PARL.ZS; **229 and 230 Alan Smith:** The World Bank. Used by permission from Alan Smith; **230 Gary Lineker:** Quote by Gary Lineker; **232 Financial Times Limited:** Adapted from FT charts at ft.com/covi19; **233 Alessandro Romano:** LSE log scale research at: https://blogs.lse.ac.uk/covid19/2020/05/19/the-public-doesnt-understand-logarithmic-graphsoften-used-to-portray-covid-19/; **234 and 235 Alan Smith:** Gapminder (includes data based on World Bank, Maddison Lindgren, IMF and others). Used by permission from Alan Smith; **236 and 237 Financial Times Limited:** Samuel H. WIlllamson, "Dally Closing Value of the Dow Jones Average, 1885 to Present," MeasuringWorth, 2022 appeared in "How alternative facts rewrite history" by Alan Smith, January 31, 2017. Available at: https://www.ft.com/content/3062d082-e3da-11e6-8405-9e5580d6e5fb; **240 IEEE: Beyond Memorability:** Visualization Recognition and Recall, IEEE Transactions on Visualization and Computer Graphics, Vol. 22, No. 1, January 2016; **240 and 241 Financial Times Limited:** Refinitiv (formerly Thomson Reuters) appeared in "Greggs raises annual forecast despite supply pressures", October 5, 2021. Available at: https://www.ft.com/content/47b4f6ee-d008-489d-b621-a4791674dbc1; **243 Financial Times Limited:** Graphic: Chris Campbell/Patrick Mathurin, Source: Data from Wimbledon appeared in Samuel Agini, Patrick Mathurin and Chris Campbell, "Wimbledon wild card success does not disguise financial challenge", July 10, 2021. Available at: https://www.ft.com/content/860b0619-a10e-4f13-abee-c9f27d775b99; **244 Financial Times Limited:** FT Coronavirus tracker ft.com/covid19 appeared in "Coronavirus tracker: the latest figures as countries fight the Covid-19 resurgence", December 20, 2021. Available at: https://www.ft.com/content/a2901ce8-5eb7-4633-b89c-cbdf5b386938; **244 Financial Times Limited:** Centre for Public Data appeared in George Hammond, "Foreign ownership of homes in England and Wales triples", November 12, 2021. Available at: https://www.ft.com/content/e36cec28-7acd-4154-b57d-923b5d1610da; **245 Financial Times Limited:** State-level estimates of vaccine hesitancy from the US Deaprtment of Health and Human Services using federal survey data from May 26 - June 7; Trump vote share by state from Cook Political Report appeared in Nikou Asgari, "A form of brainwashing': why Trump voters are refusing to have a vaccine", July 21, 2021. Available at: https://www.ft.com/content/39ff87ce-57b7-4007-9504-7eb2c7bc911f; **246 Financial Times Limited:** FT graphic: Christine Zhang, Source: Virginia Department of Elections appeared in Lauren Fedor and James Politi, "Crushing defeat in Virginia governor's race stokes fears among Democrats", November 4, 2021. Available at: https://www.ft.com/content/a44828e6-c522-449e-8f49-91a8c9fff3eb; **246 Financial Times Limited:** David Hall/NAO appeared in Returning the UK's privatised services to the public. Available at: https://www.ft.com/content/90c0f8e8-17fd-11e8-9e9c-25c814761640; **248 and 249 Financial Times Limited:** Blavatnik School of Government, University of Oxford appeared in Valentina Romei, "Virus restrictions deal European economy lesser blow than in spring", November 11, 2020. Available at: https://www.ft.com/content/7579eaf1-4f12-41bc-a0aa-1f89ac086cc7; **249 Amanda Cox:** Quoted by Amanda Cox, a multi-award-winning Data Editor and former Graphics Editor at the New York Times; **250 Financial Times Limited:** Public Health England appeared in David Robert Grimes, "How to take on Covid conspiracy theories", February 5, 2021. Used by Permission from The Financial Times Limited. Available at: https://www.ft.com/content/6660cb80-8c11-476a-b107-e0193fa975f9; **261 Financial Times Limited:** Data from Otto Neurath appeared in "Still Top Gun? What Tom Cruise's new movie tells us about American power" by James Crabtree, May 27, 2022. Available at: https://www.ft.com/content/26ebe826-08d7-4966-b104-1a3be1f8ca5c; **262 Financial Times Limited:** Chris Hanretty; Ministry of Housing, Communities & Local Government appeared in William Wallis, "England in 2019: Split by wealth but united by Brexit", November 30, 2019. Available at: https://www.ft.com/content/b398d284-11dc-11ea-a225-db2f231cfeae; **263 William Playfair:** William Playfair's Time Series of Exports and Imports of Denmark and Norway Published at the Art Direct, May 17th by W. Playfair. Available at: https://en.wikipedia.org/wiki/William_Playfair#/media/File:Playfair_TimeSeries-2.png; **265 Office for National**

Statistics: Office for National Statistics makes rows and columns apparent just in the white space; **271 Financial Times Limited:** British Film Institute appeared in Alistair Gray, "Tax rebates fuel UK film and TV boom", December 13, 2021. Available at: https://www.ft.com/content/871aedbf-a982-488a-84d4-38c937da46aa; **280 Financial Times Limited:** EU settled status applicants exceed official tally by Andy Bounds in Manchester and Bethan Staton in London, July 7, 2020. Available at: https://www.ft.com/content/a611c7ae-8276-4e42-8e63-0b68e3b90f9f; **281 Financial Times Limited:** Graphic: Alan Smith, Source: FT analysis of ONS and Home Office data appeared in "EU settled status applicants exceed official tally". Available at: https://www.ft.com/content/a611c7ae-8276-4e42-8e63-0b68e3b90f9f; **285 Richard Speigal:** Richard Speigal - Nationwide Building Society. Used by permission from Richard Speigal; **288 Financial Times Limited:** Covid-19: The global crisis — in data. Available at: https://ig.ft.com/coronavirus-global-data/; **286 and 287 Alasdair Monteith:** Quoted by Alasdair Monteith is a teacher of geography at Gordonstoun in Moray, Scotland, one of the UK's leading independent schools; **291 Alan Smith:** Used by permission from Alan Smith.